Y0-EHY-479

NO ROOM IN THE BROTHERHOOD

The Preus-Otten Purge of Missouri

by
Frederick W. Danker

assisted by
Jan Schambach

"Truth is not decided by majority vote."

CLAYTON PUBLISHING HOUSE, INC.
PO Box 9258
St. Louis, Missouri 63117

42656

NO ROOM IN THE BROTHERHOOD, The Preus-Otten Purge of Missouri
Frederick W. Danker
Jacket art by Mr. Ted Smith
Copyright © 1977 Clayton Publishing House, Inc.

Library of Congress Catalog Card No: 77-074386
International Standard Book No. 0-915644-10-X

MANUFACTURED IN THE UNITED STATES OF AMERICA

TABLE OF CONTENTS

FOREWORD

Among the top news stories in the first part of the Seventies was the battle between traditionalists and progressives in the Lutheran Church-Missouri Synod.

The telling of that story is like the writing of death notices, a task to be all the more shirked when the cherished institution is one's own.

Yet the events, actions, and circumstances involved in the tragedy suggest a responsibility to humanity as a whole. For the structure and experiences of the Lutheran Church-Missouri Synod offer students of sociology, psychology, psychiatry, and political science a unique model for understanding the dynamics of institutional self-perpetuation.

Since the very nature of the struggle was such that many of the negotiations and utterances became the immediate property of the world, historical access to the mainsprings for decision in the battle is comparatively easier than for the study of many other moments in the experience of humanity.

Even a partisan in the struggle will therefore find that a stern conscience about the facts is a prerequisite, and the manner in which he interprets them will have many knowledgeable critics.

As a third-generation member of the Lutheran Church-Missouri Synod, I am a partisan. As one who came under fire from my own church body for questioning it on certain issues, I can claim non-partisan objectivity. In addition, more than two thousand former students, who are acquainted with much that has happened, will be quick to note whether I practice the objectivity that I attempted to inculcate. I want to thank them for their questions which helped expand a mind constricted by departures from the Church's mainstream tradition.

Every historian also writes for historians who are to come. Of importance is the question, how are we to convey the past to those who come. Documents and data are cold, but many have their origin in depths of the mind and passion. My presentation and analysis of events and participants endeavors to be faithful to the human spirit that penetrates them. Participants in this conflict felt strongly. Diction, syntax and forms of narration ought to resurrect such dimensions after the obituary has been read.

The reader will have no question in his mind where I stand, but he will not be able to say that he has not "heard the other side." If my colleagues, students, and I were indeed guilty of everything else that we were accused of, one deed we know to the depths of our being was done right—the decision to accept exile from the grounds of Concordia Seminary, St. Louis, Missouri. On February 19, 1974, we, students and faculty, had reached the bottom line of integrity. To have acted otherwise would have been a betrayal of God and humanity. But my heart's desire is that the Missouri Synod may move out of its *Brotherhood* perspective back into the mainstream of the *Church* of the Ages and the Family of God, so as to speak more adequately to the total needs of *all* humanity, brothers *and* sisters of every age, color and station in life.

From 1969 on I knew, as did Thucydides about the Peloponnesian War, that this would be a great and a long war. Experiences during these years fell into place with other experiences in the years that had preceded, especially during my tenure as a parish minister and twenty years at Concordia Seminary. Much of what is contained in this book is the result of personal documentation as the events transpired, with heaviest concentration on the developments from July, 1973 to August, 1974. Speeches and dialogue noted on the spot are naturally reproduced as carefully as possible, but condensation was inevitable. May the speakers forgive me for reducing their claim to oratorical immortality.

Students and colleagues have been liberal with documentation. So liberal, in fact, that I was forced to limit myself to a more narrow compass than I had originally intended. This book, therefore, will be the first part of what will probably become a trilogy.

Without the valued services of Jan Schambach, who organized the massive files and documentation necessary for a work of this type, this book could never have been completed in such a brief compass of time and under the pilgrim-like conditions of our fragile academic community—Seminex. A special word of thanks is due my daughter

Kathleen for editing and other services rendered. As usual, my wife, Lois, has borne the brunt of the battle to make it to the press. She was ably assisted by a number of volunteers to whom we owe special recognition and thanks. All have cooperated in the production of what we hope is a permanent contribution also to the ongoing life and purpose of Seminex. I personally covet any corrections and suggestions, and they will be given careful consideration during the preparation of a succeeding volume, in which the details concerning the establishment of Seminex, the decisions of the English District, and the founding of the Association of Evangelical Lutheran Churches and subsequent developments will be discussed.

Finally, Saint Polycarp's Day ought to remind the Church that its authority is itself under orders and that no one dare claim what belongs to God alone!

Frederick W. Danker
February 23, 1977
Polycarp, Bishop and Martyr

The Synod, and every member of the Synod, accepts without reservation:

1. The Scriptures of the Old and the New Testament as the written Word of God and the only rule and norm of faith and of practice;

2. All the Symbolical Books of the Evangelical Lutheran Church as a true and unadulterated statement and exposition of the Word of God, to wit: the three Ecumenical Creeds (the Apostles' Creed, the Nicene Creed, the Athanasian Creed), the Unaltered Augsburg Confession, the Apology of the Augsburg Confession, the Smalcald Articles, the Large Catechism of Luther, the Small Catechism of Luther, and the Formula of Concord.

Article II Confession
Constitution of the
Lutheran Church—Missouri Synod

"Thou shalt have no other gods before me."

Chapter 1

"TIETJEN MUST GO!"

Among the top news stories of the closing decades of the Twentieth Century was the heresy hunt in an influential American Church, the Lutheran Church—Missouri Synod. At the climax of hostilities in 1974, an editor in New Haven, Missouri, lectured the Synod's administrators in no uncertain terms.

The governing board of Concordia Seminary, St. Louis, Missouri, he ordered, "has its work cut out for them on January 21. Dr. John H. Tietjen, President of the Seminary, must be immediately suspended as the first order of business. . . ." Then, aiming his rhetoric directly at the President of The Lutheran Church—Missouri Synod, "the Rev. Jacob A. O. Preus, Ph.D.," he directed, must "be present at the January meeting of the Board of Control of St. Louis. We do not have his calendar in front of us, but whatever he has scheduled for that day, January 21, he must cancel. . . . no picking up a traveling church dignitary at Lambert Airport, no family matter, no trip to the 'Lake,' is more important than the January meeting at the board. DR. PREUS MUST BE AT THAT MEETING!!! At that meeting, Tietjen must go!"

So screamed a Missouri tabloid, *The Christian News,* on January 14, 1974. The head of a great church had received his orders from the main propaganda headquarters of those who had in effect taken over the management of the Lutheran Church—Missouri Synod.

Accompanying this command performance was a travelogue article featuring dialogue between Jesus and Caiaphas and Pilate. Commenting on Pilate's question, "What is truth?" the writer observed:

> When we were privileged to see the Pavement, the seat of justice, where Christ was tried and Pilate became guilty of the gravest miscarriage of justice, we also recalled that Pilate's name alone is mentioned in the Apostolic Creed. Neither he nor anyone else can wash

1

his hands in innocence. Many a name will be forgotten, but not those of Judas, who betrayed Christ, and Pilate, who sentenced Jesus to be crucified.

Two pages earlier the editor had uttered his own prophecy for a rewriting of the ancient script: "The word is out in the conservative camp that the big day is Monday, January 21."

The blitz was on. The 'hit' to be made. Herman Otten, unofficial journalist of what was once a highly respected church body was, despite a formal repudiation by most of the bishops of the church, titular head of the conservative forces. After Jacob A. O. Preus and his brother, Robert, *de facto* co-regent, the active or supportive management included two vice-presidents of the Synod, Walter A. Maier, Jr., son of the illustrious preacher of Lutheran Hour fame, and Edwin C. Weber; professors Martin Scharlemann, Ralph Bohlmann, Richard Klann and Lorenz Wunderlich; and two bishops, Charles S. Mueller and Arnold G. Kuntz who, in the judgment of moderates, protested too little. Also among their number were Ewald Otto, a minister of Quincy, Illinois, and Chairman of Concordia Seminary's Board of Control, whose hard-line majority had been assured at the Missouri Synod's Convention in New Orleans, Louisiana, in 1973; Charles Burmeister and Eugene Fincke, two of Otto's associates on the Board; and Milton Nauss, minister of a congregation whose suburban core group was composed of refugees from city blight in St. Louis, Missouri.

Although given his instructions by Otten, President Preus was yet determined to prove that he was 'his own man' by holding the beginning of Missouri's Armageddon one day early. Thus it came to pass in the Gateway City that on the evening of January 20, 1974, the bells began their tolling in Luther Tower on the campus of Concordia Seminary. One of them, donated by Charles Burmeister, bore the name "John H. Tietjen."

Had the suspension of Dr. Tietjen taken place as previously scheduled for December 17, 1973, just before vacation break, events could have assumed a different shape and church history might have run other channels. For Dr. Preus had promised members of his church, usually referred to as the LC-MS, that most of their problems would be taken care of through the removal of key personnel by the end of the year. But on December 13, 1973, Arthur Carl Piepkorn, age 66, internationally known theological expert, voluminous writer, and eloquent participant in ecumenical dialogues, strode into a barbershop on Clayton Road, threw his coat partially off, and took a chair to catch his breath. It never came. He had in the days and months before petitioned the Seminary's Board to clear his name of the charges of false doctrine implicitly brought against him in Resolution 3-09 at the New Orleans Convention in July, 1973. The Board failed to honor his request. On December 17 he wore the martyr's color of red in his coffin and was buried with military honors at National Cemetery, Jefferson Barracks, Missouri.

Some would interpret his death as divine intervention, a timely halt to an ecclesiastical juggernaut. Still others, who at first might have found it difficult to square their understanding of the omniscience of God with Piepkorn's apparently unconscionable time of dying, would take refuge in the thought that God had foiled a clever plot to destroy the Synod. Various actions, they said, pointed to an attempt to "polarize the Synod by destroying confidence in President Preus, the Board of Control, the New Orleans Convention and all present leadership of the Missouri Synod." However, rejoiced an informer of *The Christian News:* "The entire plan collapsed when God in His grace and wisdom took one of the principal actors in the whole plan to Himself in heaven. Professor Piepkorn died. The Board out of respect to him and his family postponed their meeting."[1]

These words in effect declared Dr. Piepkorn a saint, despite the Synod's implication in formal resolution at New Orleans in 1973, that he, along with most of his colleagues, espoused doctrines which could not be "tolerated in the church of God."[2]

But only two pages before the statement of canonization, the prime architect of the 'final solution' for heresy at Concordia had carried against Dr. Piepkorn the posthumous charge of "diversionary tactics," and of introducing "totally irrelevant material in order to confuse the issue and conceal his real anti-scriptural position."[3]

That God Himself was put on the spot for welcoming into heaven a professor who was not to be tolerated in the Missouri Synod, apparently never crossed the editor's mind.

President Preus, who on December 17 had left Piepkorn's memorial service before the celebration of the Holy Eucharist, practiced laudable restraint in concealing his satisfaction over the fulfillment on January 20 of a vow made publicly in 1973, "Tietjen must go!" To his supporting circle he gave assurance that the faculty "phalanx," as he had termed their solid coherence, would soon disintegrate. With the "mesmerizing" power of Tietjen gone, faculty consensus was certain to crumble. With a gutsy man at the helm, Concordia Seminary would sail into serene harbor!

Dr. Preus has been much maligned, but history is not well served by indulgence in personal recrimination. The fact is, Dr. Preus was a perceptive administrator of sorts and could make even dreams come true. He was well aware of the dreams Dr. Martin Scharlemann, a member of the faculty with rare pedagogical gifts, was having. Rumors had spread that this man had once counted himself in the running for the presidency of Union Theological Seminary, and it was an open secret that he had hoped to head Concordia, and considered Dr. Tietjen's election to that post in June, 1969, a major disaster for the seminary. Now, as the night sneaked into January 21, 1974, Dr. Jacob Preus' "gutsy" choice found fulfillment of his ambition to run a prestigious theological institution. Elated, he called his father and informed him to this effect: "I was just appointed president of Concordia Seminary."

Classified by associates in the Air Force Chaplaincy as "very military," General Scharlemann had intended that same morning to issue his army of students the orders of the day. But his planned rhetoric might have assumed a different cast had he known that over the weekend students were with prophetic sensitivity busily at work putting the finishing touches on a warhead that was to ensure brevity for his incumbency. Less than five hours after their newly assigned leader had shaved, the students delivered to Concordia's Board of Control a declaration of moratorium on all classes.

The battle was joined, but what the students were not aware of was the continuity of their action with Dr. Scharlemann's own protest against theological developments in his church fifteen years earlier.

4

Chapter 2

CORPORATE EGO

In the early months of 1959, Dr. Martin Scharlemann put the finishing touches on a bomb that was to shatter forever the fragile peace of the Lutheran Church-Missouri Synod. He did not realize at the time that only a decade later he would be allied with the very "fundamentalist" frame of mind he had put under bombardment in April, 1959. The missile was named "The Bible as Record, Witness and Medium." It was read in full on April 3, 1959 to the Missouri Synod's Council on Bible Study and then in part on April 7 and 8 to a District Pastors' Conference in Northern Illinois. This essay, twenty-six pages single-spaced, was not a bit of powder hastily crammed into a casing, but according to his own "Author's Note," "the product of more than six years of investigation and reflection."

The editor of *Christian News* for years insisted that the Missouri Synod's troubles with Concordia began in 1955, but Scharlemann's research moved the beginnings of 'heresy' back to 1953. The General had now 'come out of the bushes,' and his tanks were directed toward the very nerve center of the Missouri Synod—its corporate identity, infallibility.

To understand the character of the battle at this earlier juncture is to appreciate the nature of the charges and countercharges that were to surface over a decade and a half, down to the year 1974. In one of his favorite illustrations, Prof. Scharlemann likened secular culture to a "Mercator map." "It is impossible," he said, "to squeeze a polar map or a globe into its narrow limits. The extra dimension," he pointed out, is "God's act of breaking into the closed circle of our existence for the purpose of making Himself known as the Lord of all life,

5

all history and all nature." But this self-communication of God, His "revelation," is "not primarily a method of transmitting a body of information." Following Professor G. Ernest Wright,[1] of Harvard, Scharlemann emphasized God's activity especially in relation to Israel in His great rescue act, the Exodus. Rather than being "primarily a source book of information, a collection of divine truths," the Bible, he insisted, is "a record of and witness to God's redemptive acts."

Man's ability to think makes it possible for the beneficiary of God's mighty acts to respond "with his whole person to God's disclosure of Himself," for wholeness of person includes the rational faculty. When God relates himself to man he also involves man's reason in the process, and thoughtful response to his revelatory act becomes a "witness to God's redemptive acts." Since the Bible concentrates on a meeting "with God Himself as He is revealed in His Son," the "capacity for absorbing right information" is secondary to understanding oneself in "proper personal relationship to God." "What the sacred writers record and what they give their witness to is God's faithfulness in keeping His promises. They do so, moreover, from within their own personal limitations in terms of historical, geographical, or scientific information."

Once truth or revelation is no longer viewed as having to do "primarily with the inculcation or acquisition of information," one can be liberated from "inappropriately" using the word "inerrancy" in reference to the Scriptures. Since this term is ordinarily "used on the level of observation and factual precision," it tends to obscure "the nature of Biblical revelation." In place of the word inerrancy, Scharlemann suggested "reliability," for the Biblical documents are the witnesses to God's revelation of Himself "as utterly dependable in keeping His promises and carrying out His will." The Scriptures are to be sure, an "infallible rule of faith and practice," but "this is quite different from insisting that every piece of information given in the Bible is factually accurate in our contemporary sense."[2]

The effect of such words on the Missouri Synod was something akin to a pin ball machine lit up on tilt, or like a fifty car collision on a turnpike with police car flashers piercing through the fog. M. H. Scharlemann was headed for crucifixion.

Of course it proved difficult for many Christians to understand how the statement "The Bible contains errors" could possibly disturb a major church body, for most church groups had that campaign behind them. Some light may be gained, however, from a simplified review of the history of the Synod's corporate ego.

6

Saxon Pilgrims

In November, 1838, a group of Saxon pilgrims left Germany in search of religious and civil liberty. Early in 1839 they arrived in St. Louis and some of their number found spiritual refuge in the basement of Christ Episcopal Church. On March 3, 1839, the Right Reverend Jackson Kemper made the following announcement to his parishioners:

> "A body of Lutherans, having been persecuted by the Saxon government because they believed it their duty to adhere to the doctrines inculcated by their great leader and contained in the Augsburg Confession of Faith, have arrived here with the intention of settling in this or one of the neighboring states, and having been deprived of the privilege of public worship for three months, they have earnestly and most respectfully requested the use of our church that they may again unite in all the ordinances of our holy religion. I have, therefore, with the entire approbation of the vestry, granted the use of our church for this day from 2 p.m. until sunset to a denomination whose early members were highly esteemed by the English Reformers, and with whom our glorious martyrs Cranmer, Ridley and others had much earlier intercourse."[3]

Other Saxon immigrants settled farther south in Missouri. There, apparently unmindful that they were dangerously opting for the status of a sect, the pilgrims threw their crowns at the feet of their leader, Martin Stephan, who aimed to impose his will in all religious and business matters on the little community. His alleged immoralities might have been forgiven, but combined with arrogant lust for power they offered his disillusioned followers sufficient cause for dismissal in 1839, approximately five months after he had been declared bishop.[4]

It was an expensive lesson in the hazards of establishing and maintaining corporate ego. Heated debates followed and ominously forecasted the future of a church that would, one hundred and twenty-five years later, run through a similar script with the language changed from German to English.

Ultimately the little band in Missouri linked arms with other Lutherans scattered mostly around the Middle West of the United States, and on April 26, 1847 they formed a cooperative organization known as "The Evangelical Lutheran Synod of Missouri, Ohio, and Other States." Some Lutherans protested that there was no scriptural sanction for the founding of such an institution. Such fundamentalist biblicism was met with the reminder that Christians had the freedom to do things like this, and besides, the Synod was only an advisory body, and member congregations were privileged to reject whatever resolutions they might find contrary to the Bible or unsuitable in their situation. Nothing however, was said as to what might happen if a faculty or even some of the church's bishops (District Presidents) should one day pronounce such negative verdict on a synodical resolution.

From its very founding in 1839, Concordia Seminary served as a facade of academic respectability for these German-speaking Lutherans with their compulsive drive for social coherence. The combination was to prove volatile, for it concealed a latent totalitarianism that could, given appropriate historical growing conditions, produce a crop of evil completely alien to the avowed claims and objectives of the young church.

"Public Doctrine"

As the years went by, even architecture served the interest of uniformity at what some have termed a clearing house for approved and proper doctrine. Dormitories, with all the evils attendant on an all-male atmosphere, ensured uniformity. Most of the synod's ministers who became a part of her clergy down through World War II still recall the smarts on their buttocks from early years spent under the surveillance of sometimes sadistic upper classmen substituting for parental guidance. Along with other conditioning factors, such pattern of dormitory life helped entrench the idea that obedience to authority took priority over the privilege of conscience. Young men training for ministry soon learned to become experts in maintaining a comfortable status-quo; for expression of deviations, not so much from moral rectitude as from the party-line, ensured ostracism or exile from the 'in' group.

Most suspect was a student who studied too much, and disagreement with the ruling group suggested emotional instability. As an instructor at Concordia Seminary in the 1940's dictated in a lecture: "Through the dormitory life abnormal phases in character are removed, either polished off or knocked off... Without making our clergy stereotyped or cut on the same patterns it makes for uniformity in outlook and ideals—the scholastic type." Women were not allowed to interfere with the packaging process. As late as the 1930's, even engagement was tantamount to grounds for expulsion from Concordia Seminary.

To further ensure the uniformity of the product, only instructors in good standing within the synod or its approved affiliates could teach at Concordia Seminary. Receipt of degrees from institutions labeled "unorthodox" by Missourians was reviewed in language appropriate to a description of the hazards of ingesting rat poison. As late as 88 years after the founding of Concordia Seminary and almost 50 years before the heresy hunt of 1973–74, one of the professors received a letter cached in brimstone: ". . . concerning these men" (Professors Paul E. Kretzmann and John Theodore Mueller) "and their ungodly degrees" I have set "forth why I consider these professors no longer useful to the Church. Both should at once resign or, at the very least, return their titles to the heretics who conferred them, and make a public apology."[5]

In another letter the same correspondent trumpeted with the same sound: "The true Missourian will sever his connection with those who occupy the wrong position . . . No, brother, let us get back to simplicity."[6]

Simplicity was assured for twenty years more as Concordia's professors droned out their lectures, with students accepting the dictation. "One generation comes and another goes, but the Word of the Lord endureth forever," said the Psalmist. Yet not even Yahweh thought to achieve such conformity of rhetoric and syntax as did Concordia's professors. One generation went and another came, and it was not necessary to study, for an elder brother had already taken the notes. The examinations varied but little. Students joked that professors could catch up on their sleep while lecturing. The yawn was catching, and students slept with such regularity in the classroom that more than one professor would suggest that the dormitory might be more comfortable for such extra-curricular activity.

To be sure, not all professors had taken the corporate sleeping pill. Dr. Theodore Graebner was the most notable exception. He had once recommended as an emblem for the Missouri Synod "a rooster violently flapping his wings and crowing lustily at the setting sun."[7] Almost singlehandedly he preserved the synod from the throes of organizational *rigor mortis.* With a strong sense of professional responsibility, and enviable command of United States diction, Dr. Graebner pleaded for secretarial help and larger quarters to carry on his research and his vast correspondence with 25% of the active clergy. In his request for two rooms he said, "Now let me speak plainly. As a matter of fact, some of my colleagues would not know what to do with *one* room. They would be very indignant if they should be deprived of their office but as a matter of fact they use it only to deposit books

9

and hats, etc., between lectures. I think you realize—and I am now touching on a delicate subject,—that some of our colleagues do not work so very hard . . ."[8]

Under such conditions, battalions of graduates, uniformed in seventeenth century dogma, marched out into the world with a sense of 'mission' that aimed to set up the image of the Synod's corporate ego on every continent. Supported in their indoctrination program by similarly trained parochial school teachers, they made certain that in all Christendom there would be no church body that could claim to be as correct and orthodox as the Missouri Synod. One wit was heard to exclaim that not even God hewed to the line with such doctrinal uniformity as did the Missouri Synod. Discrepancies and theological diversities in the biblical text, and anything else that might promote lack of consensus, dissolved in the face of the synodical alchemy of pure and unadulterated 'Missourian doctrine.' The magic word was 'public doctrine,' a term that oozed a more captivating mystique in its Latin form, *Publica Doctrina,* that is, the "doctrine that is public, or generally recognized or accepted."

Missouri's public doctrine served somewhat the function of a concrete casing for a coffin. Public doctrine was to the Missouri Synod what the Mishna has been to Jews and what tradition is to many Roman Catholics. But by saying "doctrine" instead of "tradition," Missouri was able to tell itself that its traditions were not like those of "the Jews" and of "erring" church bodies such as Methodists, Baptists, and Roman Catholics, not to speak of maverick Lutherans, especially those of the Lutheran Church in America, with heretical virus constantly germinating at their Mt. Airy Seminary in Philadelphia, Pennsylvania.

Whatever its name, tradition in any special group comprises the collective memory of the corporate ego and outsiders wanting in are expected to acquaint themselves with the content of the collective data-bank. That was not easy in Missouri, for Missouri's public doctrine included more than 618 items, which in July of 1973 would be resolved at an official convention into "etc." It embraced whatever formulations, interpretations, or practices had gained so strong a foothold in the Missouri Synod that to deviate from them would brand one as "un-Missourian," the equivalent of ecclesiastical leprosy.

High on the list of public doctrine, official or unofficial, were standardized interpretations of biblical texts. A number of these had been sponsored by Saint Martin himself, but some of the more informed views of the great reformer had given way to doctrinaire interpretations by far less brilliant and imaginative seventeenth century Lutheran dogmaticians and by fundamentalists in the nineteenth and early twentieth centuries. Historical-critical method was as welcome in such an atmosphere as the two-party system in Soviet Russia. Thus it came to pass that guardians of Missouri's faith made the unitary authorship of Isaiah, the authorship of the first five books of the Bible by Moses (but among the more radical, minus his obituary at the end of Deuteronomy), the literal swallowing of Jonah by a big fish, the creation of the world in six days (usually twenty-four hours each), identification of the Roman Catholic papacy as the ANTICHRIST, etc., prime criteria of doctrinal purity. Suggestions of discrepancies and theological diversities in the Bible were unthinkable, for a God with creative divergence in His utterances would be an embarrassment to Missouri's drive for consensus. It was inconceivable that God would even want to be at odds with the corporate ego of the Missouri Synod, for the Missouri Synod was in existence to ensure the Omniscience of God.

The strong arm of consensus reached down even to the everyday levels of corporate life. For decades scouting was forbidden to Missouri's youth. Dancing was until recently a no-no at a synodical school located in Ann Arbor, Michigan; since some parents, with the words of a Missouri patron saint, C. F. W. Walther, ringing in their ears, might object were it permitted on campus, students discreetly used other premises. As late as 1932, trade unions were denounced by synodical leaders. Insurance was wrong until the Synod discovered that God's lightning did not ignore Missouri's real estate.

The view that conscientious objection to a particular war was doctrinally wrong was so ingrained that it took three conventions of the Synod, climaxing in 1969, to pass a resolution in relief of the consciences of Missourians on that score. To this day there are congregations in the Synod which consider it doctrinally incorrect for women to vote in their church assemblies. Like many other Lutheran groups, the American Lutheran Church authorizes the ordination of women, but not a few Missourians considered such practice grounds for suspending relations with that body.

Other aspects of Missouri's doctrinal tradition were responsible for an unhealthy progeny of racial prejudice. Some in Missouri thought that the curse on Canaan's son, Ham, rests on the black community; and "nigger" is not a rarely heard term. Likewise, Missouri Lutherans must bear some share of collective responsibility for the view that Jews of all time fall under the curse recited in Matthew 27:25, "his

11

blood be on us and on our children."

Representative of such views are interpretive remarks made by the Rev. William Dallmann, one of the Synod's most popular preachers. With respect to Genesis 9:25, 27, he wrote: "The plain meaning of Noah's words is that the descendants of Canaan should be slaves, those of Shem should be a blessing, those of Japhet should rule. Has this prophecy been fulfilled? The Negro is the leading living descendant of Ham and Canaan, and history shows that the Negro has been the slave of the world. Even today the slave-trader of Africa cracks his whip over the quivering flesh of his human victim. . . . Japhet shall enlarge his borders. And is he not doing it? Europe belongs to the Caucasian, North and South America, Australia, the Isles of the sea, almost all Asia, and now he is slicing up the continent of Africa. What shore does not echo to the conquering tread of the lordly white man?"[9]

In a discussion of the conclusion of the Ten Commandments, another clergyman wrote, "As for temporal punishments, it is a truth which not only the Word of God teaches, but which we see illustrated in everyday life, that children must often suffer because of the sins of the fathers. Thus Canaan, the son of Ham, and all his descendants must bear the consequences of Ham's evil deed, Genesis 9:25; and the Jews must to the present day be strangers and be despised and persecuted in all the earth because of the curse which their fathers have provoked, Matthew 27, 25."[10]

Surrounding and embracing 'public doctrine' as it came from the pulpit was the uniform worship of the congregations. One might well have said: "As far as the Missouri Synod was concerned, God could safely rest on the Sabbath, for He could count on the same words in the liturgy Sunday after Sunday." Approved handbooks for the pastor's use in worship guaranteed that the Almighty would not be disturbed with any shocking novelties. Deviants from the standard terms and tones were labeled "high church," something like calling a progressive Republican a Democrat in Communist's clothing. An 11 year old in the Seventies who transferred to a Missouri church with freed-up worship patterns sized history well: "At the other church the pastor didn't understand kids; he just read out of a book."

Matching the uniformity of words was a uniformity of mind-set. Missouri Synod Lutherans did none of their worshiping with Lutherans who were not officially recognized as equally pure in doctrine. Tons of literature and thousands of hours of synodical time were spent on questions relating to "prayer-fellowship," that is, can a Missourian pray with other Christians without denying his allegiance to pure doctrine. One missionary in India, Adolph A. Brux, made the mistake of saying grace with non-Missourian colleagues and brought down on himself the wrath of the synod's corporate ego.[11] To this day it is possible to identify Missourians who attend church with relatives who happen to be members of a non-Missourian church. Hard-line Missourians do not stand when the rest do, and they do not sing with the "heretical" congregation. Dr. Walter A. Maier, famed radio speaker on "The Lutheran Hour," was bombarded with "hate" mail for praying with Presbyterians, Methodists and Baptists, but, as one of his sons later commented, refused to "do battle with brethren of constricted mind."[12] Nor was it considered orthodox practice to serve communion to non-Missourians. During World War II three soldiers went to a middle western church and asked to receive the Sacrament. The pastor asked, "Are you Lutherans? " "No." "Well, then I cannot give you communion."

It is understandable that some suspicion of prejudice should attach to historical description emanating from injured parties in an institutional strife. Some might even call it "caricature." But that the preceding sketch of a diseased corporate ego errs on the debit side of description is clear from a protest presented in 1862 at the Central District of the Missouri Synod, only twenty-three years after the Saxons had built their log cabin seminary. The text is cited according to the publication, Speaking the Truth in Love,[13] described in the succeeding chapter:

Propositions on Unevangelical Practice

1. Evangelical practice consists not in this, that we teach and treat nothing except the evangelical message (the Gospel), but in this, that we treat everything in evangelical fashion.
2. This means that since we expect justification before God, the renewal of the heart, and the fruits of the Spirit only through the Gospel, we in everything that we do have this one thing in mind, to give free course and sway to the Gospel.
3. For this very reason, when we follow evangelical practice, we do not discard the Law or make its edges dull through bringing in the Gospel, but we rather preach it with all the more seriousness in its full severity, however in evangelical fashion.
4. The Law is used in an evangelical way if it is employed solely for the purpose of preparing the soil for the evangelical message (the Gospel) and of submitting a divine norm for the manifestations of the new life

13

which spontaneously arises through the evangelical message.

5. It is not evangelical practice to cast the pearls before the swine, but much less is it evangelical practice to keep them in one's own pocket.

6. Evangelical practice drops not one iota of the things which God demands, but it demands nothing else and no more than faith and love.

7. Evangelical practice demands manifestation of faith and love if we desire to be saved, but it does not issue commands about their various manifestations as far as aim, amount, and mode are concerned.

8. Evangelical practice demands fulfillment of even the smallest letter of the Law, but it does not make the state of grace dependent on the keeping of the Law.

9. Evangelical practice endeavors indeed to prepare the way for the operations of the Gospel by the Law; but it does not endeavor to aid the Gospel in its real functions by the Law; and since it expects the fruits of the Spirit to be produced solely by the Gospel, it is willing to wait for them, too.

10. Evangelical practice considers nothing an essential gain that does not come through the Gospel, that is, through faith; therefore it rather bears with all manner of defects, imperfections, and sins than to remove them merely in an external manner.

11. Evangelical practice limits pastoral care *(Seelsorge)* to specific applications of the Law and the Gospel; the scrutiny and judging of the hearts it leaves to God, the Searcher of hearts.

12. Evangelical practice insists on good human order, but still more does it insist on Christian liberty, and for that reason it lets *adiaphora* remain real *adiaphora,* that is, it leaves the decision concerning them to the conscience of the individual.

13. Evangelical practice is faithful in little things; yet it considers matters in their larger aspects and totality more important than individual details.

14. To be wise as serpents, to redeem the time, not to let Satan gain an advantage over us, to become all things to all men in order that by all means some might be saved, are likewise elements of evangelical practice.

15. Evangelical practice is equally far removed from Antinomian and from legalistic practice.

16. Evangelical knowledge and disposition should issue in evangelical practice, but do so rather seldom and slowly.

17. Usually we do not advance beyond legalism, or we fall into Antinomian laxity; to such an extent the Gospel is foreign to our nature.

18. There is danger in both directions. For us at present the greater danger is still in the direction of legalism.

19. Apart from the natural tendency of the old Adam and our origin in pietistic circles, etc., our present situation and the necessary reaction against the prevailing moral laxity in principles and in life are responsible for this state of affairs.

20. Or how many are there not who secretly fear more to give the blessings

of the Gospel to an unworthy person than to deny them to a poor sinner or to curtail them? Whose conscience is not hindering him to follow the example of Paul and to become all things to all men? But where this is the case, one surely still finds legalistic practice.

21. Legalistic practice does not consist in this, that one does not treat anything except the Law, but in this, that one treats everything in a legalistic manner, that is, in such a way that one's main aim is to see to it that the Law gets its due and that one tries to accomplish through the Law or even through laws what only the Gospel can accomplish.

22. In addition, the more (as is often the case where the inner motive power really still is the Law) fiery zeal asserts itself which not even permits love to be the queen of all commandments, which spurns Christian wisdom as its counselor, and which even when it appears merely to teach, to reprove or to admonish, in reality applies coercion, and at that the worst kind of it, namely, moral coercion—all the more unevangelical our practice gets to be.

23. Unevangelical, legalistic practice is found not only in churches and congregations, but likewise in schools and in the homes, and besides in our fraternal intercourse.

24. The instances of unevangelical practice which are still most frequent with us in the realm of ministerial work, the cure of souls, and congregational government are perhaps the following:

   a. In sermons:

   overabundant castigation *(durchgeisseln)* of individual sins, unwholesome conditions or perhaps even of matters of personal dislike—the portraying of well-known sins of well-known persons, instead of laying bare the bitter roots out of which all evil fruits grow—mere so-called testifying without real instruction and admonition—unnecessary or premature or unedifying polemics—urging that repentance and faith be manifested, instead of preaching that which produces repentance and faith—a pietistic classification of the hearers—attaching conditions to the Gospel promises *(Verklausulierung des Evangelii)*—preaching faith preponderatingly as to its sanctifying power—presentation of the grace of God only to build demands on such presentation;

   b. With respect to Confession and the Lord's Supper:

   To demand more for admission than is absolutely required for its salutary use—schoolroom catechizing and inquisitorial searching of the heart of those announcing—postponing reproof till announcement for Communion or Confession—to use refusal of Holy Communion as a coercive, terrifying or disciplinary means—to refuse even when a state of unrepentance cannot be proved;

   c. With respect to Baptism:

   To be either entirely unwilling to baptize children of heretics or unbelieving people who, however, are in contact with the Word *(die unter dem Schall des Wortes leben),* even if there is no intrusion in somebody else's domain *(in ein fremd Amt greifen)* or only after various human guarantees have been given—to put the acceptance of sponsors on a level with admission to Holy Communion;

d. At marriages:

To refuse to perform marriages of people who are outside the congregation even if they are not manifestly wicked—a meticulous insistence on a certain form of parental consent and of engagement;

e. At funerals:

Absolute refusal of burial in the case of all who did not somehow belong to the congregation or at least requested the visit of the pastor —adherence to the principle that at every funeral the salvation or damnation of the deceased must be asserted publicly, that sins have to be castigated and the occasion must be used to take a fling *(anzustechen)* at the sins and failings of the survivors;

f. In the care of souls:

Constant trimming and pressing *(hobeln und feilen)* on everybody till all wrinkles have been removed—acceptance of every kind of gossip *(Zuträgereien)*—mixing into house, family, and matrimonial matters even if no public offense has been given—to judge of one's attitude of heart on the basis of a few words and works—the application of moral coercion through exaggeration, etc.;

g. In congregational government and church discipline:

Exaggerated demands at the reception of new members—a denial of, or peremptory fixing of time limits for, participation in the spiritual treasures of the Church as a guest, especially for attendance at the Lord's Table—mandatory imposition of dues on church members, requiring the same amount from all—or coercive taxing of the individuals—use of church discipline as a measure against matters which are not evident, mortal sins, or even against self-provoked sins—to consider a person as convicted in his own mind or as opposing maliciously because he is not able to reply to the arguments and charges uttered against him, or even assents—to lay more weight on the correct form of the proceedings than on the achieving of the purpose of the discipline—to demand the same form and the same degree of publicity for all confessions of sins which may have to be made—the endeavor to make the chasm between those who are in and those who are outside the congregation really large, instead of building bridges for the opponents and for those who are on the outside.

25. Legalistic practice in itself makes the Gospel law, the Law a taskmaster (but not unto Christ); it makes confession a torture, the cure of souls hypocritical fawning; the Sacrament a testimony and seal that one is acceptable (to the pastor); it makes Christian liberty a mere pretense, church discipline an oppression of consciences, the people painfully meticulous, self-righteously pharisaical, and the church a police institution.

26. Legalistic practice has the appearance of greater conscientiousness, courage, and quicker success only for the blind. Looked at carefully it

16

lacks true courage to allow God to reign and His Word to work. Its conscientiousness is that of an erring conscience and in itself one of the greatest hindrances of the working of the Law as well as of the Gospel.

27. Legalistic practice behooves no church less than the Evangelical Lutheran.
28. To make the fine customs of old established churches the standard for such as are in process of establishment—is not Lutheran.
29. There are plenty of things in which we cannot avoid giving offense; let us not give it by unnecessary severity in practice.
30. Let us courageously make an end of all unevangelical practice; but let us not forget that there is but one step from legalistic to antinomian practice.
31. Antinomian practice would beware of legalism and would effect everything only by the Gospel. But since it lacks the severity of the Law it also lacks the fervor of the Gospel. Therefore it will result in laxity and undisciplined conduct.
32. If we fall from legalistic into antinomian practice, evil has become worse.

Balance

Here is laid bare, without the hazard of partisan self-interest, a penetrating probe of the malady of unbalanced corporate ego. With only slight deviation, subsequent medical reports on the health of the Synod agreed with the diagnosis pronounced from various quarters of the Synod in the early 1860's—hardening of institutional arteries.

But if the institution was so clogged with sluggish blood, how did it manage to survive so many decades? The fact is that part of the mystique of the Missouri Synod in the years before 1969 was its ability to maintain in balance a lust for corporate consensus with a dedication to the interests of the gospel of Jesus Christ. However, nothing is so powerful as misdirected religion to coax tyranny out of the human race, for fear and anxiety and a longing for social coherence reach out most eagerly for the balm of religion. Finding the right moment, these elemental concerns can become instruments of rapacious lust for power. Such power, given the reality of the Fall of Adam and Eve, will naturally slumber beneath a cover of concern for truth.

St. Paul candidly exposed this cancerous threat to the religious life when he confessed that according to his institutional standards he was blameless and had in fact persecuted Jesus Christ and the church out of concern for the truth. But, as Missourians have always insisted,

17

NO ROOM IN THE BROTHERHOOD

sincerity is no guarantee of truth. Paul himself, after his conversion, saw that his past had been a terrible self-delusion. Determined, therefore, under God not to let it happen again, he said of himself in his new situation as a captive of Jesus Christ: "Forgetting what lies behind me, I forge on ahead, with only the goal in mind, and all for the prize of God's upward call in Christ Jesus." (Philippians 3:13–14) The same strong passion with which he forged chains for humankind before his conversion now exposed any attempt to use Christian religion as a front for individual and corporate ego seeking to justify existence in history at the expense of the creative purposes of God for people. Of course, Paul did not condemn institutions *per se,* for corporate strength can wield the clout of justice in behalf of those exploited by self-interested power. Institutions become diseased, however, when the philanthropic rationale for maintaining social cohesion gives way to institutional perpetuation, in the course of which people become expendable.

It took all the skill of a water skier attempting to keep his balance on threatening waves with one foot in the air, but the Missouri Synod did manage through the extraordinary dedication of her pastors and teachers to keep institutional self-interest from developing into a totally debilitating cancer. On the frontiers they and their families suffered appalling hardships. For decades they worked at pitifully low salaries. Even Dr. Walter A. Maier, who did more to advertise the name of the Missouri Synod than any other man in its history, earned little more than $200.00 per month plus rent in the lush 1940's.[14] Missourians are especially sensitive to curiosity of the media, and when the financial data concerning Dr. Maier appeared in a feature article in the Saturday Evening Post, the President of the Synod, Dr. J. W. Behnken, expressed dissatisfaction over the embarrassing disclosure.

Like the Roman public officials in the outpost provinces of the Roman Empire, these pastors and teachers loved their synod, but individually gave priority to Jesus Christ and labored faithfully to spread the gospel. Their concern for pure doctrine undeniably came out of a profound sense of loyalty to that mission. Faced with the hazard of confusing the voice of God with the institutional formulation of that voice, these dedicated servants of the Lord for the most part listened to the admonitions of the gospel, as reflected in such presentations as "Propositions on Unevangelical Practice." In ancient Israel and in the early Christian church, the prophetic voice supplied the critical function that is so necessary for maintaining on their course institutions which are dedicated to high truth. With similar periodic exposure to

18

the Spirit's critique, the Missouri Synod managed to maintain its corporate mental health and eventually to articulate the gospel of Jesus Christ to the world.

This is not to say that it had bought tickets on an express train to the future. With what some in good synodical humor called "teeter-totter" resolutions, the Synod managed in its regular conventions to satisfy both progressives and traditionalists. This was the politics of balanced corporate ego. As in the dormitories where the Synod's workers were trained, no responses too critical of the corporate body or of its segments received institutional sanction in the synodical resolutions, but dissenting views were recognized in cautionary clauses. Yet when the last gavel had sounded, the Synod went out after each convention to the four corners of the earth, firmly convinced that nothing had changed, that the doctrine remained inviolate, and the consensus uncracked. Even a casual observer could readily conclude that this church was not hospitable to questions, for ultimately, conviction that is forged by truth in spoon-fed scholastic form likes answers endowed by the past with the mystical power that can only emanate from specious simplicity.

Such, then, was Missouri's corporate ego, a balance of hardline tradition and commitment to far-flung outreach with the gospel of Jesus Christ. It was a combination that spelled a precarious hold on sanity, for there was the constant danger that concern for the tradition would outbalance dedication to the gospel. All bedlam could break loose. Even a slight suggestion that Missouri should consider modification, especially in its approach to the interpretation of the Bible, could trigger a massive hemorrhage.

Dr. Scharlemann, who had been working with Professors Krister Stendahl of Harvard and Otto Piper of Princeton on a project in modes of Biblical interpretation, thought it was high time for the Synod to come abreast of the contemporary scene in biblical studies. Had he made more careful reconnaisance of those whom he appeared to consider his opposition, he might have modified his rhetoric on those fateful days in April, 1959. But gutsy man that he was, having bravely ministered during the war years to GI's under the heaviest enemy fire, he did not flinch from charging head-on into Missouri's tradition, which was guarded by a phalanx of ecclesiastical soldiers dedicated in the subterranean bunkers of their minds to the preservation of corporate infallibility.

Much was at stake here. If Scharlemann was right, they could have been wrong—not once, not twice, but for a whole lifetime! One man's ego against a batallion of egos, against Missouri's public doctrine! Historical criticism and the arrogance of scholarship were on a collision course with infallibility. Against such odds, even the gutsiest was bound to lose.

Chapter 3

THE GATHERING STORM

Fifteen years before Dr. Scharlemann dropped his bomb on Missouri, forty-two pastors and professors and one layman, W. C. Dickmeyer, met on September 6 and 7, 1945, in Chicago, to discuss methods of getting the Missouri Synod into the twentieth century. Forty-four men actually signed the document entitled *A Statement*, which developed out of the meeting. One was Dr. Oswald Hoffmann, successor to Dr. Walter A. Maier on the International Lutheran Hour. Among the other signers were some of Concordia Seminary's most revered professors, including William Arndt (subsequently co-editor of a revision of an internationally recognized lexicon of the Greek New Testament), Paul Bretscher, E. J. Friedrich, Theodore Graebner, and W. G. Polack. Dr. O. P. Kretzmann, long-time head of Valparaiso University, which has enjoyed generous support from the members of the synod, also added his signature. Their affirmation forms part of a publication entitled *Speaking the Truth in Love.* [1]

A STATEMENT
We, the undersigned, as individuals, members of Synod, conscious of our responsibilities and duties before the Lord of the Church, herewith subscribe to the following statement:

ONE

We affirm our unswerving loyalty to the great evangelical heritage of historic Lutheranism. We believe in its message and mission for this crucial hour in the time of man.
We therefore deplore any and every tendency which would limit the power of our heritage, reduce it to narrow legalism, and confine it by man-made traditions.

21

TWO

We affirm our faith in the great Lutheran principle of the inerrancy, certainty, and all-sufficiency of Holy Writ.

We therefore deplore a tendency in our Synod to substitute human judgments, synodical resolutions, or other sources of authority for the supreme authority of Scripture.

THREE

We affirm our conviction that the Gospel must be given free course so that it may be preached in all its truth and power to all the nations of the earth.

We therefore deplore all man-made walls and barriers and all ecclesiastical traditions which would hinder the free course of the Gospel in the world.

FOUR

We believe that the ultimate and basic motive for all our life and work must be love—love of God, love of the Word, love of the brethren, love of souls.
We affirm our conviction that the law of love must also find application to our relationship to other Lutheran bodies.

We therefore deplore a loveless attitude which is manifesting itself within Synod. This unscriptural attitude has been expressed in suspicions of brethren, in the impugning of motives, and in the condemnation of all who have expressed differing opinions concerning some of the problems confronting our Church today.

FIVE

We affirm our conviction that sound exegetical procedure is the basis for sound Lutheran theology.

We therefore deplore the fact that Romans 16:17,18 has been applied to all Christians who differ from us in certain points of doctrine. It is our conviction, based on sound exegetical and hermeneutical principles, that this text does not apply to the present situation in the Lutheran Church of America.

We furthermore deplore the misuse of First Thessalonians 5:22 in the translation "avoid every appearance of evil." This text should be used only in its true meaning, "avoid evil in every form."

SIX

We affirm the historic Lutheran position concerning the central importance of the *una sancta* and the local congregation. We believe that there should be a re-emphasis of the privileges and responsibilities of the local congregation also in the matter of determining questions of fellowship.

We therefore deplore the new and improper emphasis on the synodical organization as basic in our consideration of the problems of the Church. We believe that no organizational loyalty can take the place of loyalty to Christ and His Church.

SEVEN

We affirm our abiding faith in the historic Lutheran position concerning the centrality of the Atonement and the Gospel as the revelation of God's redeeming love in Christ.

We therefore deplore any tendency which reduces the warmth and power of the Gospel to a set of intellectual propositions which are to be grasped solely by the mind of man.

EIGHT

We affirm our conviction that any two or more Christians may pray together to the Triune God in the name of Jesus Christ if the purpose for which they meet and pray is right according to the Word of God. This obviously includes meetings of groups called for the purpose of discussing doctrinal differences.

We therefore deplore the tendency to decide the question of prayer fellowship on any other basis beyond the clear words of Scripture.

NINE

We believe that the term "unionism" should be applied only to acts in which a clear and unmistakable denial of Scriptural truth or approval of error is involved.

We therefore deplore the tendency to apply this non-Biblical term to any and every contact between Christians of different denominations.

TEN

We affirm the historic Lutheran position that no Christian has a right to take offense at anything which God has commanded in His Holy Word. The plea of offense must not be made a cover for the irresponsible expression of prejudices, traditions, customs, and usages.

ELEVEN

We affirm our conviction that in keeping with the historic Lutheran tradition and in harmony with the Synodical resolution adopted in 1938 regarding Church fellowship, such fellowship is possible without complete agreement in details of doctrine and practice which have never been considered divisive in the Lutheran Church.

TWELVE

We affirm our conviction that our Lord has richly, singularly, and undeservedly blessed our beloved Synod during the first century of its existence in America. We pledge the efforts of our hearts and hands to the building of Synod as the second century opens and new opportunities are given us by the Lord of the Church.

✠ SOLI DEO GLORIA ✠

In Witness Whereof, we, the undersigned, affix our signatures this seventh day of September in the year of our Lord 1945, at Chicago, Illinois.

Acker, Lawrence	Hemmeter, H. B.
Amling, C. M.	Hillmer, Wm. H.
Arndt, W.	Hoffmann, Oswald
Bartels, H.	Kretzmann, A. R.
Bauer, W. E.	Kretzmann, Karl
Behnke, C. A.	Kretzmann, O. P.
Bernthal, Aug. F.	Kuechle, Geo.
Bobzin, Aug. F.	Kuntz, Werner
Bretscher, Paul	Kurth, Erwin
Bruening, Wm. F.	Kumnick, H. H.
Brustat, A. W.	Lindemann, Fred H.
Caemmerer, Rich. R.	Lindemann, Herbert
Coates, Thomas	Loose, F. W.
Deffner, L. H.	Meyer, Adolf. F.
Engelbrecht, H. H.	Miller, Paul F.
Friedrich, E. J.	Polack, W. G.
Geiseman, O. A.	Sauer, O. A.
Gieseler, C. A.	Schroedel, Theo. H.
Glabe, E. B.	Theiss, O. H.
Graebner, Theo.	Weber, Edmund W.
Hanser, Arthur R.	Wenchel, J. Frederic
Hemmeter, Bernard H.	Wind, H. F.

Words of Judgment and Prophecy

Supporting this prophetic protest against the octopus-like stranglehold of legalistic tradition were a number of essays that called for repentance. In confession of his own guilt, one of the signers, Theodore Graebner, apologized for his share "in that legalism which these long years has perverted our testimony, which has had a noxious influence on our practice and which now threatens to close the doors of expansion and service to our Church in a period which should make her the light of the world. Fear, suspicions, tyrannized consciences, perversions of Scripture, the binding of souls through human interpretations, —how can a Church so afflicted with the manifestations of legalism do her work in a manner befitting her opportunities in a world stricken as never before in all the record of our race?"[2]

"We are apt," he went on to say, "to call in for the fight on the seven demons of liberalism, the Beelzebub of separatism and legalism."[3]

"When we have made the Church the interpreter of Scripture," he warned, "then we have popery, full blown, then we have the mother of all modernism and radicalism in the Church, an unscriptural, schismatic, loveless separatism."[4]

"Anything," he continued, "seems fair against the man who makes a gesture contrary to the traditions received among us. I despair of ever making clear to this type of Missourian the Bible concept of unionism or that of separation of Church and State. They have suffered a hardening of brain fibre on these spots."[5]

Speaking of attitudes toward a brother with whom one finds himself in disagreement, he said: "We denounce him to the President of Synod. Not only that, but when those publicly attacked plead to be given the opportunity to settle the matter in private conference, they have been turned down with a curt, 'I will not meet you'—for which we have much documentary evidence. Certainly loveless legalism can go no further in its wounding of the body of Christ to the utter confusion of the laity . . . There is need of repentance here and of a complete change of attitude."[6]

Diagnoses of traces of corporate insanity brought on by theological pollution receive corroboration from a verdict such as this: "These offenses are merely symptomatic of a disease so wide spread that quite generally the atmosphere has so long been contaminated with these effluvia that they are mistaken for a mark of orthodoxy."[7]

For a church just emerging out of German this was creditable Anglo-Saxon prose, but the essayist went on to climb further rhetorical heights: "Even our plea for a return to evangelical habits is denounced as liberalism."[8] Moving in on the evil fruits of legalism, the essayist thundered: "And what intolerable arrogance to express the thought recently set down in cold type, that there 'might be as many true Christians in the world outside the Missouri Synod as in it!' Does not this make of us an orthodox Jehovah's Witness sect?"[9]

There "is a notable increase," he continued, "and a very general one, in bad manners toward any brother with whom we differ. Insinuation is no longer a vice, as it is among business men, scientists and even politicians. It causes no revulsion to see the sincerity of a teacher publicly attacked and his name dragged in the gutter. Grossly insinuating language is regarded as an over-wrought expression of an attitude rather to be commended—a high regard for the truth. It is rare to hear such offenses reproved as violations of the law of love and as expressions of legalistic arrogance. We should do public penance for the spirit which has during the past thirty years invaded our discussions. We have not had theological controversies but caricatures of such." [10]

In a strong call for resistance "against every form of legalism," he went on to predict: "Legalism and a loveless zeal for orthodoxy is going to breed radicalism, liberalism, strife and division."[11] Of Carl Ferdinand Wilhelm Walther, Wilhelm Sihler, Friedrich Conrad Dietrich Wyneken—Missouri's Abraham, Issac, and Jacob—he lamented that they "could hardly be able to retain their Synodical membership in some of our conferences."[12] And, as though he were writing a verse for the Bible, he underlined part of his concluding prophecies: *"Nothing so certainly leads to a liberal and unionistic reaction as an undue stressing of uniformity in externals."* Repeat: *"the reaction will be certain."* [13]

"Finally," he said, "one of the most pernicious effects of a legalistic judging of brethren is the premium which it places on theological illiteracy. The thorough student is bound to get himself into trouble. My correspondence shows that this is a Synod-wide condition. There is a discount on research and scholarship, especially in the field of exegesis. This places a handicap on our future as an orthodox body since only Biblical scholarship will preserve unto us a conservative confessionalism."[14]

Supported with such scalpel-wielding skill, the Statement of the Forty-Four, the cream of Missouri's ministerium, endeavored to lay bare for healing the malady of a corporate ego that was closing its vision to avowed objectives out of twisted concern for conformity to spirit-stifling tradition.

But the patient did not lie still for the operation. Howls of protest against the action of the Forty-Four went up and down Missouri from St. Paul to Dallas. In ominous prelude to the events of 1969–1974, twenty-eight ministers, torch-headed by Dr. Paul E. Kretzmann (who had been bypassed for the presidency of Concordia Seminary), demanded in memorials to the Synod's Convention held in 1950, an investigation of the faculty of Concordia Seminary. Included in the protesting language of another memorial was a rebuke to the faculty for stating on May 24, 1949, "that betrothal or engagement must not be regarded as tantamount to marriage."[15] The faculty, without realizing it, had begun the march to Armageddon.

With its customary institutional serenity, the Synod in Convention in 1950 heard 'both sides,' assured itself that pure doctrine remained unimperiled, and recommended matters for continued study by the members of the Synod. Out of it all came an uneasy armistice. The more creative and progressive teachers, ministers, and laypeople in the Synod welcomed the anti-legalistic bombardment, for they were beginning to ride the post-war boom on full crest, and their own contributions to the policy-making committees quieted the fears of Missouri's mainstream swimmers. New steeples were ascending everywhere with the name of Missouri emblazoned on the bulletin boards below. "The Church of the Lutheran Hour," read the subtitle. This was no time to rock the boat. Mainstreamers, for the most part voting straight policy-making committee tickets, and wary of extremists on either side, were relieved that pure doctrine, and with it the church's mission, could be maintained without the embarrassment of legalistic restriction.

Exposing the Nerve Center

Missouri's nerve center, however, remained untouched by the Forty-Four. Their plea for sobriety was not seen as a request for academic freedom at Concordia Seminary, but as an encouragement to maintain momentum in the current evangelism boom with Lutheran emphases. Any other sort of deviation from synodical tradition whether towards legalism or liberalism could, however, therefore expect to encounter strong resistance from the same type of balance-keeping committees that calmed the waters in 1950. For the basic issue posed by the Forty-Four, Missouri's tradition of always being right, had not been faced.

In support of that conviction was Missouri's doctrine of biblical inerrancy. The syllogism ran:

1. Major premise: The Bible is inerrant.
2. Minor premise: Missouri teaches according to the Bible.
3. Conclusion: Missouri is always right.

So it came to pass that in April, 1959, half-way to Armageddon, Dr. Scharlemann, 'gutsiest' man in the Synod, did what no man in Missouri had ever done: expose the main nerve center controlling Missouri's corporate identity. He should not have been surprised to see himself facing not one battalion from Missouri but almost its entire army.

With his essays he had upset a precarious balance. He had introduced reason as a formative element in theological expression. But his most heinous crime, equivalent to flourishing a 'joint' in front of a judge after being arrested on charges of possession was to ask questions in a church that was in the habit of parading itself as having all the answers. Once permit questions to be asked, and one fence after the other would collapse. Where would it all stop? Besides, fences were helpful in keeping other people at a distance. Ask questions about what really separated Missouri from other Lutheran bodies, not to speak of other Christian groups, and one might discover that the fences were not really legitimate according to the Bible and the Reformation Confessions. Once permit inerrancy of the Bible to be questioned and the whistle would blow on all attempts to proof-text inherited and parochial practice. As one delegate at the Synod's convention in 1959 put it: "What's the point in maintaining the Missouri Synod, if we are going to adopt the same positions as other Lutherans?"

Scharlemann, the epitome of indiscretion for even attempting to assault the church's infallibility, had felt the full weight of the church's dormitory tradition. Soldier that he was, he should have known the penalty for pulling rank by thinking differently from the rest of the army. But to put such thought into words—that was the supreme arrogance, for every man with his mind fixed on the tradition as it was dictated to him in the classroom five, ten, fifteen, twenty, forty and fifty years before, felt himself suggested into imbecility by the scholarship of Scharlemann. One could in the course of ministry be in error once in 1920, twice in 1925 and occasionally in 1940, but not completely wrong for fifty years nonstop. To paraphrase Festus, Scharlemann had studied too much!

At the point of personal defence, then, precariously balanced corporate ego fought back, and on June 27, 1962, in Cleveland, Ohio, Martin Scharlemann surrendered at general headquarters. His statement, reported the very next day in the Convention Bulletin read in part:

> I deeply regret and am heartily sorry over the part I played in contributing to the present unrest within Synod. . . . By the grace of God, I am—as I have been in the past—fully committed to the doctrine of

28

the verbal inspiration of the Sacred Scriptures. I hold these Scriptures to be the Word of God in their totality and in all their parts and to be utterly truthful, infallible, and completely without error. . . .
Herewith then I withdraw the following papers in their entirety:

1. The Bible as Record, Witness and Medium of Revelation;
2. Revelation and Inspiration;
3. The Inerrancy of Scripture; and
4. God is One.

During discussion that followed his apology several delegates, who must have thought they had come for a crucifixion, asked whether Dr. Scharlemann had withdrawn the doctrinal errors in his teaching to which objection had been made. The committee in charge of this portion of the Convention's business said in part: "We have been assured by those who have the responsibility for supervision that charges of false doctrine made against Dr. Scharlemann have not been sustained to date." This reply was more than polite rejoinder. Translated out of Missouri dialect into United Statesese, these tribal code words said: "Missouri always bows to authority. There is no higher authority in the synod as a visible body than the president of the synod and the synod's appointed channels for determining the orthodoxy of its members. Authority has spoken, therefore let all the members of the Synod keep silence."

Since synodical authority itself had spoken, and since the Missouri Synod speaking in Convention could not possibly err in matters of doctrine, and since dramatic resistance at a convention was as yet unthinkable for a Missourian, Dr. Scharlemann was not a false teacher. And because he played according to the rules of the game, he survived the battle of Cleveland. Surrounded by what must have seemed irrationality in the face of his most reasoned pleas for understanding of God's modes of revelation, Scharlemann, who was not prepared for the role of Savonarola, did the most rational thing—he apologized.

To a Missourian, affirmation of the authority of the Synod is tantamount to orthodoxy. Since consensus is paradise for Missourians, apology for causing unrest in the Synod is tantamount to reconversion to the truth, without the necessity of confession of false doctrine. One can practice the American way of life, racism, and almost any other great heterodoxy or shameful syncretism and remain a member in good standing in the Synod, so long as one does not make propaganda for the aberration. One can especially dispense with love, if the polemics against false doctrine sound hateful enough.

To be denied the opportunity to attack the false teacher is one of the most terrible fates for a committed member of the Missouri brotherhood. Wallace H. MacLaughlin, a convert from what was once called the United Lutheran Church in America, described his agony in these terms: "The tyranny of a unionistic principle which *forbade* doctrinal discipline became with each new instance of its power a more crushing load and a more exquisite torture to a conscience which *demanded* it."[15a]

In view of such and similar attitudes a theologian might well conclude that a large percentage of Missourians in effect think they can get to heaven, despite St. Paul's and Luther's strictures to the contrary, on the basis of their good works of orthodoxy.

Faced with such realities, Scharlemann, to all intents and purposes admitted that he, on his part, might have committed procedural or rhetorical blunders and lacked tact or patience. At the same time, with his phrase, "as I have been in the past," he disavowed the legitimacy of any charge of false doctrine. With this stance, Scharlemann was more in tune with Alfred Loisy than with Clovis. The latter surrendered to the words of St. Remy: "Adore what you once burned, and burn what you once adored." Alfred Loisy's response to the Sacred Congregation, after having five books placed on the Index of Prohibited Books in 1903, reserved some space for conscience:

> I receive with respect the judgment of the Sacred Congregations, and myself condemn in my own writings whatever in them is reprehensible. . . . I must nevertheless add that any adherence to the sentence of the Sacred Congregations is purely disciplinary in character; I reserve the right of my conscience, and do not wish to be understood, in bowing before the judgment rendered by the Sacred Congregation of the Holy Office, as abandoning or retracting the opinions put forth in my quality as historian or as critical interpreter.[16]

For blunders in procedure any Missourian ought to apologize, and there is no place in all the world so forgiving as Missouri when the prodigal acknowledges the Synod's authority. By a vote of 650 to 17 on the evening of June 27, 1962, Dr. Scharlemann received forgiveness, not for challenging God, but for discomfiting the corporate ego.

There were still some who thought that Scharlemann was doing a double-take, but when he said, in apparent contradiction to his own earlier thesis, that the Bible does not contain errors, he was really mentally translating into the dialect of Missouri. As he said in a special meeting held on September 26–27, 1961, in St. Louis, at which Dr. John W. Behnken, President of the Synod, was present:

> I have never denied what the church meant by the doctrine of inerrancy. As I stated once before (Lutheran Witness, April 4, 1961, p.

164), my concern with the term inerrancy was in no way intended to be either an attack on the doctrine of inerrancy or an assault against the Scripture itself. Whatever references were made to the Scriptures in this connection were selected to support the view that the use of this term (inerrancy) led some people to misunderstanding. I sincerely regret that I, at one time or another, gave a different impression.[17]

To the Missouri Synod, inerrancy of the Bible ultimately means "I can count on my Bible from beginning to end. It's a true book, and God means what he says. If the pastor tells me that in this book and in this book alone I can find the way to heaven, I believe it, for this book cannot possibly make a mistake." Dr. Scharlemann still remained convinced that the word 'inerrancy' did not really help much in the explanation of what God was up to when he inspired the Bible, and in a publication bearing the date of 1972, he praised the Roman Catholics for dispensing with the term. But in 1962, why battle over words?

Scharlemann had discovered two truths, which every thinker at some time or other in the church has learned: the first, that biblical writers may think one thing, the official church another; the second, that mediocrity is the foundation of authority. And so on that June day, Scharlemann did not stonewall it, nor did he say, "Here I stand," but under his breath he might have uttered some theological equivalent of Galileo's "Il muovo": Theology moves for all that!

The Cleveland convention was not yet a decisive battle. Collective ego had indeed met a great test, but the rocked boat on which it was traveling managed to right itself. A scholar of the church, despite exploration of the truth, had apologized and thus legitimatized Missouri's *public doctrine,* and he did it in approved diction! Not a word had been cancelled, but withdrawal of the documents had cleared aches from administrative heads—for the moment.

Retimed Bomb

The bomb was in fact being retimed, and with a short fuse at that. Scharlemann had withdrawn essays, but he never withdrew his basic conceptions. Even during the first week that he served as Acting President at Concordia Seminary, when asked about these essays, he was quick to inform students that "there was no false doctrine in them," thus in effect rehabilitating them for discussion. And that he spoke truth is supported by the fact that in an essay published in 1972,[18] a year after he had filed charges with the president of the

31

synod against his own colleagues, he repeated much of the methodology and some of the major conclusions expressed in the essays he had formally withdrawn at Cleveland.

Even though Scharlemann's engagement with the collective ego of Missouri was not decisive, there did emerge, after the dust of the battle had dissipated, a clearer division of combatants. The Forty-Four were a mixed group, representing many disciplines. But Scharlemann, a member of Concordia Seminary's exegetical department and head of its graduate school, symbolized in his person a strain of independence in Biblical interpretation that posed as great a threat to consensus in the Missouri Synod as Baal did to Mosaic tradition in the 9th century B.C. The Forty-Four fought on many different fronts. Scharlemann, as Hans Küng was to do in another sector,[19] directed his missile at one point—infallibility. The patrol on guard at that front was composed of the systematicians, who did double duty as the academic quartermasters of orthodoxy.

Traditionally in the Missouri Synod professors of systematics have handed down to their students the approved doctrinal tradition in scholastic form. Since the founding of the synod, the systematicians had a tacit agreement with the exegetes that the latter were to come up with nothing that contradicted the systematicians. In practice, this meant that biblical interpretation could not move appreciably beyond the 17th century. Therefore, historical criticism, which was of 18th and 19th century vintage and which might lead to a challenge of 17th century dogma, was out of bounds to Concordia Seminary's biblical staff.

Scharlemann, to say it again, spoke the truth when he told the synod that he affirmed biblical inerrancy, for what he was really attacking in his essays was the bondage of contemporary exegesis to outmoded systematics. To be Lutheran, in his judgment and that of his colleagues, means to this day that the church's doctrinal formulations are always to be subject to the scrutiny of the Scriptures, and not the other way around. To accord the Scriptures such high position is another way of affirming their inerrancy. That is the position taken by the Lutheran Confessional writings, and if a Missourian is serious about remaining truly Lutheran, he must follow the same route. But when a church has become accustomed to interpreting every tradition or formulation as doctrine, the exegete who insists that a favorite interpretation in support of a tradition may have a different meaning will find himself suspected of being an enemy or a termite in the house of faith.

After 1962, the battle lines were to be drawn ever more sharply in terms of exegesis and systematics, for most of Missouri's biblical interpreters and their students had tasted the exhilarating new wine of the freshly uncorked biblical texts and would never go back to a brew diluted by rationalistic presuppositions. But who in all this cloud-cuckooland of ecclesiastical polemics would ever have suspected that the very same man who before June, 1962, had taken on the Lutheran dogmaticians of the 17th century, would after June, 1969, join cause with their chief spokesmen at Concordia Seminary?

As late as November, 1967, Dr. Scharlemann, still smarting from the various pressures that led to his apology, warned an assemblage of District Presidents and Faculty members from the seminaries in Springfield, Illinois and St. Louis, Missouri:

> If our church body is to survive as a strong force in Christendom, it cannot afford to practice anything less than integrity. Quite frankly, it will not be false doctrine that destroys us. There is none now and there has been none during our lifetime. What may well fragmentize us, however, to put it bluntly, is the practice of shabby ethics both within the Synodical Institution itself and its relationship to others.

Apparently he was making reference here to the fact that the Missouri Synod was always doing what some in more frivolous moods described as a raising of the stakes in Missouri's poker game with the Lutheran World Federation. For Missouri, dedicated to union with fellow-Christians, but always on the basis of doctrinal harmony (Concordia), was anxious to "avoid any appearance of evil." Hence Missouri played harder to get than the chastest virgin.

Martin Scharlemann was now helping others peek down the pike. Like that of the Forty-Four, his was prophetic vision. But a brand of ethics he had never dreamed of was waiting to mesh with his more traditional concepts. Preus' Radical Integrity was to blend with what Scharlemann liked to term his own Radical Orthodoxy. The prospect of the resulting mixture might well have caused one to anticipate the apocalyptic battle of forces strangely allied which was looming over the horizon. Many in Missouri were to regret that they had voted delay for the day of judgment, which according to First Peter begins at the house of God. Martin Scharlemann had spoken wisdom, but Missouri's ears were as deaf as its eyes were blind.

Chapter 4

DRILL FOR CONSENSUS

After Dr. Scharlemann had come 'out of the bushes,' Concordia Seminary rushed into the twentieth century. Faculty members had begun in 1955 to undergird biblical interpretation with instruction in basic methodology. This was a revolutionary development in a church so long accustomed to paint-by-number theology.

Instead of being programmed with what approved scholars had said, Concordia's ministerial candidates, in imitation of Luther, began to taste the heady wine of private discovery. Trained to work with the finest tools of the interpreter's craft, and stimulated by the fresh scholarly resources brought to the Seminary through the expertise of librarians Edgar Krentz, James Michael, and Lucille Hager, they found the study of the Bible an exciting enterprise.

For almost two decades preceding this new development, Dr. Richard R. Caemmerer had valiantly succeeded in bridging the scholar's shelf and the pew with courses in preaching that offered the student meaty theological fare not found in some of his other courses. Now under the impact of fresh enlightenment through the biblical text itself, the quality of biblically-oriented preaching in the Missouri Synod moved on to further excellence. But besides being exposed to a broader spectrum of ideas also in other courses, Concordia's students enjoyed practical field-work experience, which helped prepare them for professional competence in a world vastly different from the days of Missouri's infancy.

In ministerial circuits dominated by senior pastors accustomed to preserve and transmit unsullied the public doctrine of Missouri, such 'over-educated' theological neophytes would be welcomed with the warmth accorded a rookie promoted to Fire Marshall. At stake was the individual and corporate ego that had drummed tradition with

34

loyal beat into the ears of Missouri. Who would rescue the Synod from this iniquitous plague of 'liberal theology' that was crippling the Synod's posture of infallibility? Who would weed out the culprits of Concordia Seminary's 'hot bed' of rationalism and 'higher criticism'? When no one in a seat of power seemed in their eyes to care, the tabloid published in New Haven, Missouri, programmed their plaintive plea.

No propaganda minister ever did his job better, and from the beginning the editor, Herman Otten, was destined to succeed. He possessed an unerring instinct for the basic weakness of his principal reading public—the egos that were threatened with the loss of consensus in the group. They were convinced that he was sent in a crisis to save truth and faith for the church.

Now one of the best ways to bolster sagging ego is to feed it with the assurance that truth is accessible without effort, knowledge without pain, and all available on the same terms both to the learned and the unlearned. Otten implied that the answers given in the classrooms thirty or forty years earlier were definitive and needed no further discussion in the second half of the 20th century. Older men gained a new lease on life as the tabloid week after week thundered against the "heretics" at Concordia Seminary. Like a refrain ran the request for answers to a set of questions that varied with the rapidity of a snail coaxed into a race by a turtle:

Should LC-MS professors be allowed to teach, hold, or maintain (the terminology varied) that:

1. the Bible contains errors and contradictions;
2. the first five books of the Bible came from various sources designated as J, E, D, and P by Bible critics who do not believe Jesus was correct when he said that Moses wrote these books;
3. man does not have an immortal soul;
4. man evolved from an ape-like creature;
5. Isaiah did not write chapters 40–66 of Isaiah;
6. the story of Jonah is a parable rather than historic fact;
7. some of the words attributed to Jesus in the New Testament were not actually said by Jesus but were dubbed in by the early church;
8. women should have the right to murder their unborn infants;
9. women should be ordained to the Holy Ministry;
10. the Hebrew *almah* in Isaiah 7:14 should be translated with "young woman" rather than "virgin" as Matthew says in Matthew 1:23.

The ordnance corps was tireless, and the artillery barrage unceasing. Week after week Otten's true-false test examined Missouri's constituents, and a steadily rising percentage of Missourians were scoring the required passing grade of 100% for zero per cent "yes" answers.

So enamored was the editor of the word inerrancy, that in almost every issue he challenged his readers to show where he himself was in error. And occasional corrections mercifully indicated that he was sensitive to mortality.

Outsiders have expressed amazement that any editor could make such low estimate of his readers' intelligence and powers of discernment and get away with it. The fact is that a variety of letters protesting Otten's editorial methods offered some reassurance that the Missouri Synod had not yet completely lost its collective theological marbles. But too many 'evangelical' Missourians thought that such 'insanity' would through the sheer weight of its radicality turn right-thinking people off. Some sneaked a look at the paper as though they were handling a flagrant issue of *Playboy* or *Playgirl*. Others said, "I throw it in my circular file without reading it." Still others said, "At least it has more news and facts than the official papers of our synod."

Unfortunately, further consideration would have revealed that Otten's attitude and rhetoric were not really a new phenomenon in Missouri but part of a continuing polemical trajectory that could on landing explode with disastrous force. At the beginning of the Twenties, a minister proposed at a meeting of the Synod that its official proceedings be printed in English. A colleague confessed that for a time he considered the brother pastor a radical for proposing this assault on the Synod's German,[1] which to the mind of many was a linguistic shrine for orthodoxy. In 1922, Theodore Graebner himself described the Synod's continuing peril: "So it was in the early years, so it was through the decades that followed, so it is today. Then, the raids of fanatical sects, penetrating the very wilderness, encompassing heaven and earth to make proselytes, a revivalism gone mad ravaging the churches of the land; today the hosts of evil that march under the banners of New Theology, Higher Criticism, and Evolutionism, of Indifferentism and Unionism, assailing the Christian Church both from within and from without."[2]

What Graebner had seen mobilized outside Missouri's gates, Otten viewed as a Trojan horse filled with saboteurs of Missouri's traditional position. He knew that there were many in Missouri who did not like change any more than did ministers who had been brought up in the German language. He also knew that he could count on support from fundamentalist non-Missourians, who similarly reacted negatively to change or a threat to cherished ways and institutions.

Had all, therefore, who dismissed the paper as a "scandal sheet" scarcely worth appraisal made more careful examination of the contents, they would have seen as through a prism a broad public that included underpaid readers, underloved readers, soured-on-life readers, vocationally-dead-ended readers, fellow-travellers-of-the Ku-Klux-Klan readers, ambitious readers, anti-Black readers, anti-Semitic readers, racists-of-any stripe readers, real-doctrinally-concerned readers, and would-be-potential-leader readers. All found either renewed vitality for flagging energies or encouragement for self-serving crusades in the theological soap opera that Otten staged each week. Nothing complicated. The simple gospel of Otten. The same cynical drill in hunting down the heretics. Missouri's version of the CIA. Week after week, month after month, year after year—line on line—always the predictable arousal to hate—but equally always under the rubric of "love your brother." THE CASUALTIES OF SUCH LOVE WERE TO BE MANY.

A dominant cause of Otten's constant barrage against Concordia Seminary, with diversionary sorties against a miscellaneous host of enemies, was his own conflict with the collective ego of the Missouri Synod. As a student he had challenged the orthodoxy of some of his professors, and Dr. Scharlemann for a long time was his principal target. During this 'McCarthy era' in the Missouri Synod, any professor who deviated an inch from the traditional could expect sentences to be taken out of lecture-context and transmitted to synodical authorities, including even the President of venerable memory, Dr. John W. Behnken. Even private dialogues between a professor and student were no longer considered private, for a student previously coached might have an interview with a professor while a student outside his door took notes.

Instead of following academic 'due process,' whereby any real doctrinal deviation could have been disciplined, Otten shared his concerns with pastors and officials of the synod. Such procedure was considered 'unpastoral' by the faculty and the administration of Concordia Seminary, and in the face of Otten's refusal to acknowledge his error in pastoral approach, the seminary denied Otten certification for a pastorate in the Missouri Synod. That the faculty was not erroneous in its judgment appeared partially confirmed by the fact that those in power at the seminary after Dr. Tietjen's dismissal did not forthwith initiate certification of Otten.

Like Judas, Otten could make contributions to power, but power in turn found Otten an uncomfortable liability, as is attested by the further fact that Dr. Jacob Preus himself in 1969 disavowed the editor's journal as "divisive." Ultimately, therefore, history will be forced to assess not Otten's lack of pastoral sensitivity, but power's exploitation of Otten's ego-weakness. And the verdict may well read: "Otten was more sinned against than sinning."

In the Fifties, though, Otten's thoughts were uninterrupted by any suggestion of the ingratitude that was to follow on his efforts. The Mayor of Casterbridge once "took an aweful oath," with dire consequences. Similarly, Otten, committed with ever-renewed ardor to the eradication of heresy at Concordia Seminary, belched out of his editorial firing base a constant barrage of incendiary articles, and all under the banner shared by Preus, "Crisis of Faith."

Chapter 5

RADICAL INTEGRITY VS. OPEN INTEGRITY

The ability to assess the primary ingredients that go into the making of history is a prerequisite of the academician. But to be consciously responsible for the mixture is an accomplishment of the totally political person. Such complete dedication, without interference of a delaying conscience, bears so large a mark of wholeness that it might well be termed *radical integrity*. Dr. Jacob Preus was a man of such complete dedication to the political task. And in the New Haven paper, with editor dominated by a monolithic view of truth, he ran into a rare opportunity to implement his distinctive virtue.

Without an understanding of radical integrity, the chance observer would be completely perplexed by Dr. Preus' words and actions. He might even be tempted to brand him a scoundrel, who not merely transformed lying into a moral category, but raised it up as a pillar of ecclesiastical stability. Yet that is precisely the superficial mistake many observers have made in their evaluation of conditions in the Missouri Synod under his presidency.

The fact is that Dr. Preus was master of what is called in the political world 'inoperative' statement. He possessed exceptional ability to transmute into pure and chaste word and performance any thought, word or action—something only radical integrity, the prime virtue of the supremely ambitious politician, can do.

Radical integrity, the ego at its apex, performs semantic miracles. Words cease to have their normal meanings and evoke whatever definition the speaker requires when history catches up with the utterer. Radical integrity thus controls history, and actions of the past can be made to fit into whatever mold the future may fashion. Opponents are diseased with paranoia. Opposition forces who refuse to be led into the apocalyptic paradise of radical integrity are divisive. A Spiro

39

Agnew clears himself in his own eyes of any guilt. A Richard Nixon insists that he is hounded by a hostile press. And a Dan Walker retains his patronage appointees and claims that his opponents misunderstood him when he said that he would, as governor, cleanse Illinois of the spoils system. The sponsor of radical integrity can do no wrong, for he communicates to the masses the facts as they *ought* to be. He transcends responsibility for conformity to more pedestrian views of truth, justice, and fair play, and he excuses himself from general accountability. Charming and likeable, with a disarming manner calculated to win friends easily, he moves in a highly rarified atmosphere where the words addressed to Adam require fresh exploration: "You shall be as gods knowing good and evil."

One obstacle, however, stood in the way of Dr. Preus' move to power. Missouri was historically opposed to political activity—and for a simple reason. It could ruin coveted consensus. Besides, a man was sought by the office, not the office by the man. Yet, in Dr. Preus' favor was the generally unrecognized fact that throughout its existence the Synod had been operating with two poles of thought, which in the day of accounting would make the Synod fat for plucking. On the one side was collective ego interested in social cohesion maintained by conformity to tradition symbolized in the office of the president; on the other side was the evangelical thrust of commitment to high purpose in the proclamation of the gospel of Jesus Christ.

Past administrations of the Synod had managed to encourage the supremacy of the latter and kept Missouri from veering off into a sectarian cast of thought. To be sure, along this route Missourians remained institutional-theological schizophrenics, but they did find balance in the corporate task. They knew they were Missourians, and, except for a few who had spun off, would rather fight than switch. But the fighting was done through channels of 'due process.' And after the Synod had spoken with approved passwords in convention, with whereases balanced equally on the two ends of a committee's proposal, and with resolutions stating that there was no need to depart from practices the Synod had previously found so helpful in carrying out its work, Missourians drank beer together, embraced one another in Gemütlichkeit, and returned to their parishes to raise more money for the "programs of Synod." Such was Missouri's counterpart to the Masonic Order, and all in the brotherhood wore the lambskin apron of pure doctrine.

Everyone loved to talk about this "old Missouri." Actually it never existed, any more than did the Wild West of the flicks, or "the good

40

old days" of The Stanley Steamer. But nostalgia was so strong that reality faced discount in the presence of the glittering dream.

Now into this paradise of corporate harmony had slithered the ugly serpent of doctrinal confusion. With his essays, Dr. Scharlemann had upset the balanced pattern of Missouri's schizophrenia, and the fresh freedom of biblical inquiry at Concordia Seminary had filled the minds of many pastors with anxiety concerning their identity, for identity was to be had chiefly in the corporate ego. But corporate ego was dependent on uniformity of doctrine, and purity of doctrine meant agreement with tradition! In effect, the two poles that spelled Missouri had steadily moved farther and farther apart, and Missourians found themselves labeling one another as *conservative* and *liberal.* In other words, the old "evangelical" politics was no longer working, and Missouri was in fact going through the birth-pangs of a two-party system.

Dr. Preus, convinced that his unique talents were tailored for Missouri's situation, did not discourage the mandate issued by the New Haven editor for his election at the convention of the synod held in Denver, July, 1969. And so it came to pass that the Synod perpetrated the first of a long series of unbelievable actions. In unparalleled rejection of tradition, the Synod during its meeting in Denver ousted its incumbent president who was of German extraction, Dr. Oliver Harms; elevated a descendant of Norwegians, Dr. Jacob Preus, to the position of chief pastor in the Missouri Synod; and voted to establish relations with another church body, The American Lutheran Church, a move bitterly contested by many of Dr. Preus' most vocal supporters.

"Good guys," still thinking they were in the "Old Missouri," thus voted a balancing act. To keep the corporate ego from becoming unglued, both "liberals" and "conservatives" had to pay proportionate political fees. Bring Preus in and satisfy the concerns of conservatives for a harder administrative line at Concordia Seminary, but endorse Harms' campaign for establishment of relations with The American Lutheran Church. Thus spoke the amateur politicians. The teeter-totter still seemed to operate, but Jacob Preus, the pro, knew how loose the bolts really were.

Disclaimer

Dr. Preus lost no time in coping with administrative challenges. Having done his homework carefully, he knew that his main base of support was the lay membership of Missouri's congregations, especially

41

those in the Middle West. Many of the clergy in that area were also in his pocket, but in view of the fact that his election had meant the displacement of Dr. Harms, a churchman highly respected throughout the Synod, he would have some fence-mending to do, especially among members of the clergy who might suspect him of going on a head-hunting expedition. To disarm them with one shot and at the same time run the Synod through its first drill in consensus under his regime, he, together with the bishops, or presidents, of all Missouri's districts, signed a disclaimer of the very New Haven newspaper that had catapulted him into office.[1]

With this one blow, he hoped to unite the authority structure of the Missouri Synod. Bishops inclined to be suspicious of Preus were quick to support this unexpected attack on the editor who had programmed the unseating of Dr. Harms. On the other hand, District Presidents to whom Dr. Preus' pleas for traditional Missourian doctrine were sweet music could hardly disagree with their new leader, and there was the added advantage of enjoying the fruits of Otten's labors without the continuing embarrassment of association with Otten's tactics. To top it off, Dr. Preus was saying very clearly to his opposition that he would follow a hard line against any questioning of his authority through "liberal" publications within the synod. He was also saying to Otten and to the world, "I am my own man."

It was a bold stroke and portended the lengths to which Preus would go to secure consensus in Missouri. If he could do this to his friends, what would he do to those whom he would construe as political enemies? Of course, Otten would have to understand that it was nothing personal. Radical integrity required objectivity. Besides, the New Haven paper must go on, for there was much work yet to be done before the Synod could be returned to its pristine purity. Dr. Preus knew he could count on Otten to deliver the goods, for Otten still had his bomb sights focused on Concordia Seminary; without Preus' governing machinery, Otten could never expect to balance his books with some of his former teachers.

Game Plan

Yet what would be the game plan? Running strongly in favor of Dr. Preus' aim to control with firm administrative hand was the Synod's respect for authority. But the roots of administrative authority, whether in the parish or in upper synodical levels, were deep in the tradition of fixed doctrinal formulation. When challenged, a pastor could say, "The Bible says it, and that's that". The Bible ordinarily agreed with the pastor, for the synod, being the purest doctrinal church in Christendom, had made the pastor a channel for absolute truth. Thus the individual egos in the synod found support in the collective ego of the synod. So long as the synod spoke with one voice, pastors and lay-persons would continue to recite with absolute assurance the same answers given by their fathers and by their fathers' fathers.

Having grasped the situation, as only radical political integrity can grasp it, Dr. Preus hit on the brilliant strategem of gathering up the collective ego and identifying it with his own person. In short, Preus would represent and say what the Synod had always said, and the Synod would maintain Preus in power so that it might continue to say through him what it had always said. Recognition of authority could fly to no higher heights on the earth, beneath the earth, nor above the earth. It was the ultimate political dream of managerial efficiency.

To realize the dream would require subordination of other wills to the controlling political will. High priority was the elimination from the scene of all who attempted to affirm individuality. From Dr. Preus' vantage point, the sinners in that category were in charge of what was once the chief factory for public doctrine, Concordia Seminary. And Dr. John H. Tietjen, the chief of sinners, stood in the competing shrine of *Open Integrity.*

From the time he took office, Dr. John H. Tietjen aimed to keep his church informed of what Concordia Seminary was thinking and doing. Forthrightness and honesty were to be the marks of his administration. Never was the church to say that Tietjen's faculty was up to something in a corner, or that Tietjen talked out of both sides of his mouth. Therefore, at a Missouri District convention in 1970, he frankly told the delegates that scholars at his seminary used historical-critical methodology in their explanations of the biblical text. He further emphasized that it was necessary to practice such methodology if an interpreter aimed to understand biblical documents in the light of the historical context in which they originally found expression. To older pastors brought up on the old rote method of predigested traditional interpretation, the use of such methodology was tantamount to advocating heresy, and especially so since the word "criticism" suggested an arrogant questioning of the Sacred Scriptures.

Now the last thing radical integrity can endure is the asking of questions, for radical integrity feeds on conformity and submission to the one controlling ego. It is not surprising therefore that Dr. Preus should have recited with variations the theme: "What this church needs is not more questions but more answers." And the church was to discover in a very brief space of time how radically he meant that.

To his role as prophet of this radical integrity, the editor of *Christian News* brought a long record of editorial assassination of well-known scholars throughout the world, but the Scripture men at Concordia Seminary were his chief targets. The only questions editor Otten raised were those in other people's minds concerning the orthodoxy of the men under attack. After Dr. Tietjen's avowed support of his faculty, the editor escalated bombardment of the presidential office at Concordia Seminary. Dr. Preus, who had already diagnosed the opportunity that anxiety about historical-critical method had generated, saw in his confrontation with Dr. Tietjen fresh uses for Otten's tabloid. The axe used by Otten might as well chop at the undergrowth standing between himself and the achievement of consensus. Ultimately, Tietjen must see the light and co-operate in ridding the seminary of its "liberals," or Tietjen himself would have to go. For with the head cut off, the purge of heretical scholars would be no problem.

To rid himself of his main rival would not be easy. But the editor of *Christian News* co-operated by informing his anxiety-ridden public of the roadblocks the "liberals" were putting in Dr. Preus' path. Dr. Preus kept piling up a huge munitions bill with Otten, but the New Haven editor did not mind extending credit, for his monopoly on the inside story of the take-over in Missouri meant he could call in his notes at any time dictated by editorial necessity.

Dr. Preus, who liked to consider himself his "own man," could not have been unaware of the hazard posed by the fact that his administrative performance more and more coincided with the editorial pattern at New Haven. But blinded by the brilliance of his own strategem of disclaiming association with Otten's tabloid, Dr. Preus continued to accept support from the notorious propaganda arm, which at the time seemed to cost nothing but moral erosion.

While the editorial volcano at New Haven kept belching lava on St. Louis' Sodom and Gomorrah, Dr. Preus refined the tactics of his move against the faculty. Adept in his favorite political tactic, division-making, he welcomed exposure of lack of consensus at Concordia. That would offer him the constitutional excuse he needed to introduce himself as arbiter of pure doctrine. Strangely coincidental with this logistical necessity was a minor theological skirmish between Dr. Scharlemann and some of his colleagues in the biblical (exegetical)

44

department. Of their number, Dr. Everett Kalin was especially vulnerable, for he appeared to his adversaries to suggest that the Holy Spirit's inspiration extended beyond the boundary of the traditional sixty-six books of Sacred Scripture.

Understandably, Missourians have always been wary of the Holy Spirit. God the Father is at least predictable, for he spoke clearly through the Ten Commandments of Moses; and God the Son tells all in the gospels. Nothing there to interrupt consensus or public doctrine, if only exegetes would stop asking questions. But give rein to the Holy Spirit, and a church lets itself in for all kinds of surprises, a commodity in no demand among administrators and certainly not in a church that preferred its doctrine without verbal deviation. Had not Lutheran dogmaticians once and for all brought the prophets, evangelists and apostles into scholastic harmony, that is, *Concordia?*

The fact that Prof. Kalin's views and conclusions were within the mainstream of sane Lutheranism was lost on those who heard only one thing—another Professor at Concordia Seminary was upsetting Missouri's tradition. And to those who stood on the sidelines of the heresy court, lofty theological concern would seem to be the prime mover of any disciplinary act against Kalin. But historians are not put off so easily. Over 2300 years ago, Thucydides, historian in ancient Greece, observed that the words spoken by personalities involved in a conflict do not necessarily reflect the real reasons for their action.

Similarly the truth of church history is not discernible without awareness of that extra Mercator-map-like dimension, in which personality conflict is often the trigger for theological warfare. The truth is that Dr. Kalin posed a direct threat to his colleague Brigadier General Martin H. Scharlemann, but not because of his views on the history of the biblical canon. At issue, rather, was the question of the morality of involvement in the Viet Nam War. Kalin voted against the country's engagement, and General Scharlemann was not pleased. So far as he was concerned, Kalin was part of the 'sinister forces' that were undermining the American way of life, and John Tietjen was doing nothing about it! But it would be difficult to clear such accusations through Missouri's disciplinary channels. Much more effective in a synod accustomed to judge in terms of adherence to pure doctrine would be some kind of process whereby Kalin's lack of synodical orthodoxy could be exposed, and then Tietjen would be forced to show his hand.

The Key

After some attempts to discuss the question of inspiration in the biblical (exegetical) department, it was apparent to Scharlemann's colleagues that there was an ecclesiastical-political agenda. Finding answers to questions was apparently not the real objective. What was to be an academic conversation bore all the marks of a fishing expedition designed to secure evidence that answers were not always being given in the precise form anticipated by a church accustomed to lock-step theology. What the colleagues did not know was the close linkage of Scharlemann's personal agenda and Preus' political aims.

Subsequent developments very clearly suggest that near the end of March, perhaps even Easter Day, 1970, Professor Robert Preus, who had been in on the discussions between the biblical interpreters (exegetes) and the systematicians, must have had conversations with his brother Jacob concerning procedures for investigation of doctrine at Concordia Seminary. Such conversation must have included the question of advisability of President Preus' immediate personal involvement in the contemplated investigation process, the role to be played by Dr. Scharlemann in getting the drama under way, and the preparation of some kind of doctrinal statement to be used as a yardstick for determining orthodoxy in the Synod.

As the case may be, on April 9, 1970, Dr. Jacob Preus conveniently had in his hand the key he needed to open administrative doors. It was a letter from Dr. Scharlemann requesting the President of Synod to appoint a committee on inquiry to investigate the doctrine of Scharlemann's colleagues at Concordia. From this development it was apparent that the run-in with Dr. Kalin was but an episode, a diversionary tactic, covering up the fact that there were bigger fish to fry. General Scharlemann's unprecedented direct communication with Missouri's Chief of Staff sent out a message that needed no decoding: Dr. Tietjen was himself ultimately to be court martialed. Professor Arthur Carl Piepkorn, Scharlemann's colleague in the chaplaincy, was so shocked by what he considered, according to his closest associates, Scharlemann's violation of officers' protocol that he wept openly in a faculty meeting later in the month. The editor of *Christian News,* offering a different interpretation, primed his cohorts for the Battle of New Orleans with this version: "Dr. Piepkorn did not have the courage to vote for Scharlemann against President Tietjen. Piepkorn broke down and wept bitterly when he voted. Some felt that Piepkorn knew that he was acting against all principles of justice and conscience and friendship, but Piepkorn caved in to the political brutality of President Tietjen."[2]

With the receipt of Scharlemann's letter, legal initiative fell into Dr. Jacob Preus' hands. Moreover, two doctorates were behind Scharlemann's practical indictment of his colleagues. Missouri could not fail to be impressed, for though consensus abhorred thinking, it liked the prestige which appearance of scholarship gave to the Synod; for the degrees, accreditation, and Princeton-Cambridge-style lecture halls and dormitories made the consensus respectable.

Apparently giving no thought to the havoc that might be wreaked in a personality, President Preus moved inexorably nearer to his objectives. There was no question in his mind about the need of an investigation. Only the details had to be worked out.

After much skirmishing between May and October of 1970 with the faculty and the Seminary's Board of Control, Dr. Preus finally unveiled on October 12 his blue ribbon panel of inquisitors. Being a man of total integrity, Dr. Preus made certain that his committee would be totally acceptable to the seminary's adversaries, who also happened to compose the party that had helped him unseat Dr. Harms. As he himself said, they were "made up of people who have the confidence of the Church—particularly those who have the greatest degree of doctrinal concern."[3] Even Solomon could not have devised a fairer way. If there was heresy in Concordia's den of iniquity, this committee could be counted on to smoke it out. And if there was none—well, what had the faculty to lose? Clearance by a stacked committee would permeate them all with the odor of spikenard imported from Eden. Had not Dr. Preus himself expressed in Missouri's official paper the "very sincere hope that the criticism may be shown to be unfounded and then silenced?" In such event the seminary's opposition would lose its bark and in the bargain "get off Jack's back." Public doctrine would survive, and the collective ego would be free to mend its fences.

This apocalyptic dream of ecclesiastical paradise landscaped through the political expertise of Preus was indeed mind-blowing, but few at the time could calculate the eventual brain damage. And some who read Dr. Preus' earlier "Brother to Brother" communication of February 11, 1970, wondered what Brother Jack meant by the sentence: "Let's get on with it and plant Christ's cross in more and more hearts." Later they would feel the pain, and with the pain they would no longer wonder.

Chapter 6

UNDER INVESTIGATION

As I indicated in my preface to the publication of the specific investigation to which I was subjected by Dr. Preus' committee, I did not welcome such an inquisition. It seemed to me a most unpastoral procedure. Colleagues shared the same view, for most of us had been pastors of parishes over a period of years, and we found it repugnant that the chief pastor of our church should do what no pastor would ever think of doing: investigate an elder of his congregation without the elder being able to face either accuser or specific charge. Official acknowledgement of rumor-mongering had no place in law, much less in the church, and the attempt to circumvent the rights of the individual by undertaking a collective fishing expedition was consummate demonstration of what would far and wide be interpreted as arrogant disregard for elementary human rights.

But Public Doctrine included instruction to suffer in the face of injustice, and teachers at Concordia Seminary had to set a good example of obedience to authority. Besides, as Dr. John H. Tietjen pointed out, the Investigation was to show "how Lutheran we really are and what it means to be Lutheran." Dr. Tietjen, contrary to allegations of unwillingness to cooperate with synodical officialdom, took the lead. If anything, he went overboard in zeal to accommodate the wishes and will of Preus.

In a meeting with students, he was asked whether the interviews with the fact-finding committee would be open to the seminary community. "No," said Tietjen, "but you can be assured that we will be talking freely to one another. . . . Public release will come through mine and Dr. Preus' offices. But faculty colleagues will be free to talk about their interviews."

"Do you consider the committee qualified? And do you think, in view of the financial situation, that the huge expenditure is justified?" To this Tietjen replied, "The investigation will be underwritten by non-seminary resources. I am not really in a position to express an opinion. It's Preus' committee and he's entitled to have whom he wishes. The people of the church will have to determine whether these men are the best qualified to do the job."

"I would be upset," commented a student, "if there were a challenge to the adequacy of someone's ordination vow." Tietjen: "The faculty *is* concerned about public profession of faith being called into question. But we are ready to be questioned by anyone at any time."

Once more the question of opening the meetings to the students came up. Tietjen firmly told them, "You don't normally go to a meeting to which you have not been invited."

"What are the presuppositions and what are they going to do with their facts?" someone else asked. Tietjen: "We have complaints on that, and the Board of Control is trying to nail down the criteria."

"What can we do to alleviate the fear that's permeating this place?" Tietjen: "Relax and keep cool. It's my conviction that God has placed before us a problem which is also an opportunity. There will be an inquiry, but let us transform it into a learning experience for ourselves and the church. . . . We have a good many people in the Synod who do not know what it means to be Lutheran. So let them investigate us and let us show how Lutheran we really are."

By their questions, the students showed far more perception of the ultimate realities than did either Tietjen or his faculty. Few among us anticipated that the demonstration of Lutheranism, described in almost euphoric terms by Tietjen, would be made in the rocket's red glare. In our arrogance we thought that all the church required was our individual and collective testimony, and after that basic honesty, integrity, wisdom, love, intelligence, sensitivity, justice and sense of fair play would recognize our innocence. We were not aware at the time how shallow now were the roots of all these virtues that once spelled the 'good old Missouri Synod.' We thought that Jesus Christ was still in charge. He was, but his tourbook included Golgotha, and we were blind to the route.

That we were caught in a dilemma was obvious. Disobedience to Preus' edict would first of all mean disobedience to our immediate superior, President Tietjen. On principle we found Dr. Preus' procedure abhorrent; but Dr. Tietjen's interpretation of the situation was an invitation to restrain triggerhappy morality. For principle is like a single-barreled gun with one bullet. It is sheer waste of critical ammunition to expend it in a lesser moment of history and expose an entire regiment to disaster. Besides, most subtle temptations of life confuse ego with principle and light with fireworks. Therefore, those of us who might have been inclined to resist at this point held our fire. In any case, Dr. Tietjen was scarcely guilty of the malfeasance in office with which he was later charged, for he did not attempt any cover-up of theological expression at Concordia Seminary.

It had been clearly evident what the pattern of the investigation would be. The *facts* were not in fact to be derived from the faculty. The five agents of Dr. Preus were possessors of the facts before they even started on their assignment. The facts were *public doctrine,* that is, the tradition in Missouri, and in many instances couched in specific words and phrases. The investigators' task was to determine to what extent each professor adhered to the traditional view and form of statement. As we were later to learn, wherever there was conformity to tradition, that was a brownie point; wherever there was a divergence, that was a demerit. Dialogue, under such conditions, was bound to be a formality. They were like the operator of a coin shop who was invited by a customer to make a mutually profitable trade. He replied, "It's got to be mutually profitable to me."

Interview

The interviews were held at the headquarters of the Missouri Synod, then at 210 North Broadway in St. Louis. Mine took place on January 23, 1971, from 12:30 to 2:00 P.M.[1] The format included a courteous suggestion to supply some autobiographical information, followed by a series of questions. Asked to say something about myself, in my opening remarks I pointed out that in my earlier years in the ministry I tried as much as possible to follow the party-line and did not discover until later what the Scriptures meant with *joy* and *freedom* in the Gospel. During my student days at the seminary, I was, for all practical purposes, a non-believer; imbedded, I told them, in concrete, and with much of the spirit of the seventeenth century dogmatician Abraham Calov, who prayed daily, "fill me with hatred for the heretics."

I was a non-believer at the time, I said, for instead of relying on Jesus Christ, I put my faith in "what Mother Church believed."

In 1638, I observed, a number of Lutheran divines, including Quenstedt, Hollaz and Calov of the faculty in Wittenberg, Germany, had decreed that it would be blasphemy against the Holy Ghost to charge writers of the New Testament with barbarisms or bad grammar. Calov went even further and claimed that it would be impious and profane to change a single dot in a Hebrew letter of the alphabet. An atmosphere of that sort, I pointed out, does strange things to a person.

Humorless Missouri

One of the things that gradually dawned on me over the years, I further observed, was the comparative joylessness of Missouri's church services. I emphasized this, for Luther, like Jesus, had a great sense of humor, but somehow this was lost to German Lutherans along the way. To laugh in church, even when the preacher told a funny story, was unheard of. Stony-faced piety encouraged consensus. Laughter meant display of emotions, and religion with emotional appeal was dangerous, for the Word of God might easily be lost in spontaneous expression by the individual. And individualism was a threat to the collective ego. Joyful welcome of the newcomer was especially fraught with hazard, for the 'Stranger' threatened the cohesion of the group, and even those who went the route of adult confirmation found it difficult to break into the congregational cliques.

This reluctance to recognize joy, both in its external and internal expression, as a normal ingredient of Christian personhood was evident for years at Concordia Seminary's chapel services. It appeared time to open some windows and one morning I preached on the theme "Laughing with God" and ended with the words "I had fun today! I hope you did, too."

Had I known how heavily popular piety had been underwritten by academic theology and how intimately connected were the Synod's concern for consensus and the cheerless type of worship that maintained in many congregations, I would have been somewhat prepared for the reaction. Most of our chapel services were broadcast over radio station KFUO located on the campus. A few days after the delivery of the sermon, I received a letter from a pastor in southern Missouri to the effect that I had subjected the Word of God to ridicule, for he had heard the students laugh at frequent intervals during the broadcast. But, I told my interrogators, the real tipoff was the exception the pastor and his colleagues in the area took to an expression I had used: "country bumpkins."

In my sermon I had referred to the angels at Bethlehem and the apparent waste of a good message on people who from the perspective of Jerusalem's social set were "country bumpkins." This descriptive phrase, torn by critics out of context, had threatened their collective ego. I answered my correspondents to the effect that no one enters the Kingdom of God until identification is made with people who, like the shepherds, are lowliest in the eyes of the religious elite. I was a country bumpkin myself, I wrote to the pastors. I had been born in rural Michigan, spent part of my boyhood in corn-fed Iowa, and was back on the farm in Michigan for a six-year pastorate. It was time for us country bumpkins to wear our association with pride. Country-boy is beautiful! My whole point, of course, as I explained to the committee, was to show that in front of the manger *all* humanity becomes the object of God's love. All titles, all ensigns of status, all pride and pomp, the fear of lack of recognition—all such arrogance, including paranoid fences of the collective ego—all are stripped off and torn down—and all of us are country bumpkins.

I did not enter with the committee into all the reasons for such failure to understand, but, aside from the inability to laugh at our institutional pomposity, one of the major diseases displayed in the course of Missouri Synod history was an irrational fear of individuality. In the preparatory schools that fed students into the seminary, one of the most heinous crimes was to be found studying more than the rest. Taverns were off limits, but the rules were broken regularly, and the breakers of the rules were the "regular guys," some of whom, the jests ran, would become District Presidents. The use of a phrase like 'country bumpkins' therefore signalled an attempt by one member of the group to raise himself above the rest, and retribution was understandably swift.

Reductionism

I had hoped that excursion into the theme of joy would lighten the load of the Fact-Finders, for my wife had reminded me just before I left for the synodical headquarters: "These men will probably be pretty tired." She was right, they looked very stern and unrelaxed. But there was much more to my autobiography, including especially research on the theological content of sermons in the Lutheran Church-Missouri Synod.

As I moved into this sector, the chairman observed that they were limited in time, but I reminded him that "the clock was made for man and not man for the clock." By this I meant to say that there was no better way to secure a multitude of facts than to give me the green light. Besides, since it was quite evident that they were interested in what we rejected theologically, it was imperative to lay on the table what I considered to be bad theology and what I viewed as essential to theological communication. At the same time, I reminded them that every position I had taught in the classroom was well known in conferences around the country. The President of the Synod and the District Presidents had heard my theological position, I said. But since none of them had ever made a single complaint, I had no reason to think that I was in their judgment running off the Missouri Synod's theological and doctrinal tracks. Therefore, it must be presumed, I said, that my presence at the interview was in the interest of bridging the credibility gap between the administration of the synod, the seminary, the clergy, and laypeople. Since they had assured me there was no selectivity in the investigation and that *all* colleagues were being queried, I felt encouraged to go on and share with them my alarm at untheological developments in the synod.

A researcher in our circles, I went on to observe, had in the course of a sampling discovered the *fact* that "In 43 sermons there was no statement of the atonement beyond a definitely worn-out, hackneyed phrase of the catechism." Since the sampling derived from an official Missouri Synod publication, *The Concordia Pulpit,* it was like quoting the Bible. The *fact* that 55% of the sermons analyzed had absolutely no discussion of sin or need appeared to me theologically catastrophic. Only about half, according to the researcher, proclaimed the cross in relation to the Christian life; yet these sermons came from a church body claiming the inerrancy of Paul's statement: "I am determined to know nothing among you but Jesus Christ and Him crucified." Is it possible, I thought at the time, that if we paid more attention to Jesus than to Jonah we might once more find ourselves as a church useful to God? But I suppressed much of what I wanted to say, for my academic superior, Professor John Damm, was next in line, and it would have been imprudent to encroach on his time. Instead, I went on to observe, only 48 of the sermons announced Christ's death for the forgiveness of sins—and this in the church that proclaimed "Christ to the Nations"!

Some people had heard the slander that the doctrine of the resurrection was imperiled at Concordia. The *fact* is, not one faculty member has ever put the doctrine in doubt and all of us have stressed it, I said, but in this *Concordia Pulpit* with prestigious endorsement of the Synod's own publishing house, there were, I emphasized, 171 out of

206 sermons sampled in which *no* mention was made of the resurrection of Jesus! Only 28 of the sermons, I went on, suggested even a slight connection between the goals of the sermon and the work of the Holy Spirit. Again, this in a church that shot down self-justification with regular Reformation volleys! The Synod was indeed in worse shape than anyone had even imagined, and my own investigation undertaken in the spirit of I Peter 4:17 had antedated theirs!

Since it had been rumored that there were some among us who thought Isaiah was written under God by two penmen, I observed that in 10,000 pages of sermons in the same *Concordia Pulpit* used by a large percentage of our clergy, I could not find a single sermon on the third epistle of John. Yet, I exclaimed, this is one of the most potent epistles ever written on the subject of hospitality. But the theme is opposed to our group consensus, for we are experts in building fences, and we tend, I said, to specialize in keeping other people out of the brotherhood! My point was: What is more detrimental to a proper view of God's word? Attribute two authors to a document (for example, Isaiah) and obey its message, or erase in silence the message of an entire book while paying lipservice to it via a canonical list? Interpret the story of Jonah as a parable and heed the call to the Ninevites of this world, or combine insistence that Jonah was swallowed by a whale with disobedience to the Lord's mission? Who is really "taking our Bible away from us"? I thought to myself.

Nor was the third epistle of John an exception. Who hears sermons out of Leviticus, or Esther? I asked. Who preaches on anything after chapter 4 in the Book of Revelation? And what about Numbers, 2 John, 2 Peter, 2 Thessalonians? All of these drop out of the running, I lamented. Yet the words of the Holy Spirit declare that *all* Scripture is inspired and is profitable for doctrine. (2 Timothy 3:15)

What is a Lutheran?

I did not think it necessary to prolong the plea for more emphasis on biblical instruction in our church and instead went on to point out that the synodical officialdom had axed a commentary I had written on St. Luke (*Jesus and the New Age According to St. Luke: A Commentary on the Third Gospel,* published about a year later, May, 1972, by Clayton Publishing House, Inc.) The editors of the series of which the commentary was to be a part had accepted the manuscript, but a subcommittee of an official board responsible for doctrinal purity of Concordia Publishing House publications complained, among other items, that the work included too many biblical citations, especially to the Book of Wisdom in the Old Testament, as well as references to non-canonical Jewish writings! I did not wish to take up the committee's time in refutation of this and other equally un-Lutheran and tenuous criticisms, for I desired exploration of other publications of mine in order to help clarify the theological picture. Instead the chairman observed that "it would be fair" to me "to get down to some of the essentials here in your theology."

I could not believe my ears had heard what must have sounded to others as a sarcastic insult, for I had been covering a good many items Christians consider "essential" for any meaningful communication of the Gospel. In the exchange that followed, I discovered they had not even read all my publications. Yet they wanted to discover *facts.* But they were not interested in the *facts* I was volunteering out of my own researches and practice as a teacher. Finally the truth dawned on me; they were not eager to know, but only to inquire whether I agreed with what *they knew.*

Patience and obedience to authority, however, are the principal equipment of every Missouri Synod soldier, and I submitted to the direction to tell them what it meant for me "in practical terms" to be loyal to the Confessions of our Church. Not that I relished the assignment, for my commentary on St. Luke had proved embarrassing to the Synod. How many rockets, then, would be fired when I got into the official Lutheran Confessions, for in those radical sixteenth century documents pulsed the heart of true Lutheranism.

It was an invitation to the lion's den, but I had no choice. I began by explaining that the Reformers came out of a situation in which they had experienced the loss of the gospel under a tyrannical regime and had learned what it means to encounter the demonic in human existence. The demonic, I pointed out, manipulates people behind a front of religious piety and endorses such manipulation through encrusted formulations. By contrast, the Reformers put Jesus Christ at the center of God's communication to the world. These Confessors, I said, emphasized above all else that we are made right in God's sight by God's free gift, which is joyously received through faith.

Since the Confessors were so jealous of the Gospel, I continued, they were reluctant to introduce any documents not recognized by the entire body of confessing Christians and thereby jeopardize the unity of the church. I said this in view of the Synod's own repudiation in 1962 of an attempt made in 1959 to elevate a document called "A

Brief Statement" to a position of doctrinal authority. At the time, however, I was not aware that Dr. Jacob Preus already had in preparation a Statement that was to replace the repudiated statement. Within six months he would, in fact, successfully cajole the Synod in convention at Milwaukee (July, 1971) to grease the constitutional wheels for the adoption of his own contemplated *A Statement of Scriptural and Confessional Principles* as a binding document at New Orleans in 1973.

But in what way are the Confessions binding? I was asked. Noting again their concern for the clock, I tried to duck this one, for a number of items leaped into my mind, and it would have taken considerable time to air them. Besides, I thought, did they really want to know? They had their chance to get off the hook, but when they took their own bait I summed as briefly as possible some of the differences among eminent Lutherans on the subject. Naturally I started at the top. I pointed out that in 1522 Luther rejected James as an apostolic writing. (How radical, I thought to myself, can you get in this church?) Melanchthon, however, according to the Apology to the Augsburg Confession, was convinced that James was in complete harmony with the Apostle Paul. But, I observed, there was no conflict, no inquisition was formed; no heresy hunt organized to eliminate people who either disagreed with Melanchthon or agreed with Luther. In fact, I said, Luther commended the Apology, thereby demonstrating that it was not necessary to divide the church over matters of this sort. Thus Luther was himself, I emphasized, in disagreement with the Lutheran Confessions on a point of biblical interpretation!

I went on to show that in 1538 Luther, in his appendix to the Smalcald Articles, disagreed with Melanchthon on the interpretation of Matthew 16:18. Luther would not even use I Peter 3:19 in support of Christ's descent into hell. He thought the passage was 'hopelessly obscure'. What a way, I indicated, to talk about an apostle's writing! Historical critics today are not nearly so radical as Luther on many points. I thought, but bit my tongue: Luther is dead, and sainted radicals are always safe.

Quite evidently it was most pertinent to inquire into the attitudes of the purest Lutherans on questions that concerned the Missouri Synod in the twentieth century. How else could one determine what kind of thinking was Lutheran and what was sub-Lutheran? Why whistle-stop in the seventeenth century when the sixteenth brought one closer to the station of truth? But such exploration of the issues had been all too rare in the Synod's conflict and it was, to my naive surprise, even discouraged by the investigators, and this in the face of Dr. Preus' repeated pleas to get at the issues.

After some parleying as to pertinence, I was asked whether the confessions were in any sense not binding. Since I disagreed with Luther on the question of the obscurity of I Peter 3:19 (my own research had convinced me of its substantial clarity), I found myself in harmony with the Confessions. Apparently the fact-finders were satisfied, for despite an earlier assurance that they were only to find the facts, not to make judgments, they pronounced "fine" on the preceding observations and then asked what my concept of the gospel was.

What Is The Gospel?

Again I suggested that since I had already said a good deal about the gospel in previous remarks, time could be saved by skipping this one. But despite my endeavor to spare them, they insisted I proceed and told me to look on them as a congregation. I had not counted on preaching at the time and on a Saturday at that, but surprises were the normal routine in this conflict, and I lost no time in sketching God's rescue act in Jesus Christ, beginning with His election of Israel and the message of prophecy as recited in the Old Testament. I then moved into St. Luke's gospel, for my own concept of the Gospel had been shaped by the Third Evangelist, and I explained that the mighty are brought down from their perches to make room for the humble. The Kingdom of God, a principal theme of Luke's gospel, is the Establishment of the New Age. This New Age is not to be identified with any systems of this world. That was the error of liberalism.

Far from being a progressive development inside history, the New Age is actually God's movement with His own Son, Jesus Christ, into history. Opposing God's Establishment of the New Age, I said, is the Kingdom of Satan, the Establishment of the Old Age. This means a clash, culminating in the crucifixion. Especially in Mark's gospel this clash of God's purpose with the demonic finds expression, with profound probing of the broader dimensions of demonic objectives. The religious establishment in power, headed by the chief priest, helped arrange the crucifixion of Jesus, I observed. But a gospel like Mark's, I went on, is not in the first instance aimed at outsiders, but is addressed to the church, so that the church may not herself be bad news to the world. I emphasized this point because of the anti-semitic tone of much preaching and biblical interpretation which pillories Jewish Scribes and Pharisees while overlooking contemporary institutional

57

crimes against the teaching of Jesus Christ. In my commentary on Luke I had endeavored to avoid such injustice.[2] After a few minutes more spent in such vein, I was generously thanked, with the assurance that the sermon was very fine. Someone else was complimentary enough to say that he thought it was only the introduction. I said to myself, Dr Preus' committee certainly was comprised of gentlemen! Only later was I to learn that in their report to the Board of Control of the Seminary they would take a different tack.

What is Reconciliation?

We came now to the main theme—Reconciliation. Dr. Preus had for some time been captivated by the word, but under its banner he had in fact supported and encouraged a major device to make reconciliation impossible, as witness the tilted committee on all sides of me at the official headquarters. The committee asked me to state how I would explain to students St. Paul's word about God making Jesus to be sin for us. The text is included in St. Paul's second letter to the Corinthians, in a paragraph extending from 4:14–5:21.

Now it is a primary principle of interpretation to view a text in its context, but I experienced great difficulty trying to convince the committee of this interpretive principle, which most Lutherans, along with other Christians, consider basic. Instead, they kept on asking huge questions, for which they had the answers ready in their own minds, and were not in the least interested in a professor's precise and detailed expositions. Yet the route of detailed answer is normal procedure in the classroom and their direction had been very explicit, that I tell them how I would explain St. Paul's phrase to my students.

Concentrating on Paul's reference to the "Now-Time," I said: If our church had only stressed this now-theology of the apostle Paul, which "identifies us with the continuing action of God in Jesus Christ, who is not dead but lives, we would have the church really moving toward its goal of reaching people with the gospel before the hours of time are out." I then went on to show how the church wastes and fritters away much time in internal debate and how in the face of possibilities for progress it applies the brakes with either deferral of action or referral to sub-committee.

Encouraged to go on with the exposition of verse 21, I pointed out that in the context Paul warns against the power of the "flesh." Flesh has to do with the customary standards of judgment adopted by the world around us. Racism, and the difficulties we have in relating to one another are, I explained, examples of fleshly, or self-centered living. Reconciliation, I said, is God's great aim, and he goes about it through Christ Jesus. But the church insists on getting into battles over words, and Christians separate into warring camps and factions. Instead of being able to bring the world good news they themselves are bad news to the world. The remedy for such default is to be found in the demolition of our legalism at the cross. Law kills! In the name of law, I said, Christ gets crucified. But along that route Jesus Christ took our sins on himself to the limit and thereby rescued humankind from the killing power of the law. My entire destiny, my entire fate, I told them, is tied in with Golgotha and the resurrection of Jesus Christ. "It's a package deal! That's the good news," I concluded.

Yes or No

At this point a member of the committee wanted to know what I thought about the view that the story of the tribute money (Mark 12: 13–17) was an invention of the later church. Having been brought up in a church that was now doing its best to stifle creativity, and knowing from the New Testament how unperceptive even the twelve apostles were before Pentecost, I assured them that if any story could be traced back with certainty to Jesus, it would be this one. For our Lord was pre-eminently the victim of an institutional vendetta. I explained how the established forces were lying in wait for Jesus and tried to trap him with typical yes-or-no questions. This is characteristic, I said, of anyone who is out to destroy the validity of the other person's witness.

As a scholar, I concluded, I do not wish to perpetuate distortion. Therefore I submit myself, I insisted, to the discipline of other scholars. I thought it was necessary to emphasize this point, for some people have the weird notion that biblical scholars are united in some sinister plot to discredit the Bible by twisting the evidence, whereas the fact is that much of our research is spent in trying to correct or modify a colleague's view or to show how better justice might be done to the data at hand. The best antidote against fanatical individualism and *Ichtheologie* (I-theology) is in fact sound scientific method, and, frankly, I was indignant that people in my church should be swindled into thinking that most of their theologians were crooks.

How would the Missouri Synod's bankers respond if theologians suggested that most bankers were probably embezzling funds from their own depositors?

How would Missouri's farmers feel if theologians accused the great majority of them with profiteering while the poor starve?

How would Lutheran used-car salesmen respond if theologians implied that most of them sold shoddy merchandise at a high level of misplaced customers' trust?

How would Missouri's housewives feel if their theologians spread the rumor that most of them were neglecting their families by watching soap operas most of the day?

Yet there were those among Missouri's bankers, farmers, housewives, and other professionals who actually believed we were stealing the Bible from Missouri's constituency. In protest, I said, "Sometimes we scholars are cursed with the burden of infallibility, but at the cross of Jesus Christ we find it possible to drop that burden." In other words, the Bible raises problems, and honest facing up to problems is not a crime. At the same time, pride of ignorance is not a virtue.

A few minutes after this exchange, I was confronted with a summary of a book review I had written. Something about it did not sound right to me, for consistent methodology should have led me to call into question what I was alleged by the committee to have affirmed in the review. Since I did not have the review at hand, I took the tack of discussing my own alleged views in the review from the standpoint of a neutral observer. Later in the day I checked the published review alongside the book in question and found my suspicion confirmed— the committee's summary of the review had been garbled, but my criticism in the review squared with what I told the committee!

The conversation then moved to specific query about "imaginative enlargements" in the Old and the New Testament. I called the committee's attention to the many instances of imaginative expression in the Book of Revelation, and how the early church had the guidance of the Spirit to help them ponder the meaning of Jesus' words. I also observed that Jesus spoke about hell fire. Was this an example of imaginative expression, or is hell a place filled with what one ordinarily calls fire? Evidently the Missouri Synod does not think so, for a Manual on Evangelism published a few days earlier had, along with the 17th century scholastic Calov, demythologized hell. I was convinced that too much attempt was being made within the Missouri Synod to import twentieth century man's interpretation of reality into the Biblical documents. Missourian fundamentalism was, in my judgment, fundamentally rationalistic.

As for the story of Jesus' walking on the water, I myself had no doubt about the Lord's powers. I assured the committee that if they had had a camera on the occasion they would have broken it. That is to say, the reality that Scripture conveys to us transcends our poor powers to understand it all. For the scriptures are like a vast sea, and scholars' work is but a dipping with small vessels. The committee, however, appeared to have no interest in exploring the depth meaning of the biblical accounts, and I heard the Lord in good humor say to me, "I did, but I won't invite *them* to try it."

Despite the fact that they were always complaining about the clock, they consumed more time talking about imaginative enlargements. The subject appeared to be an obsession with them, and I tried to cure them of it by reassuring them that exegetes are the watchdogs of the church and that they could count on the church to be the least likely place for endurance of creativity or imagination. Moreover, I said, no scholar worth his degree would willingly endorse assumption of "imaginative elements" in a biblical narrative when careful study of the text revealed that there was no evidence in support of such assumption.

In conclusion of the interview I said: "I tell my students: One of the first things you have to recognize—I am sorry to disappoint you—but I do not have all the answers!" That was a mistake, for this committee shared a point of view that did not major in humility. In a church that was arrogantly accustomed to have all the answers, I should, in their judgment, have possessed less awe of the divine mysteries and instead practiced more institutional infallibility.

Alas, in their case they were permitting the world to set the agenda for theology. I was convinced on January 23, 1971, that the Holy Spirit did not have a ghost of a chance in Missouri.

Chapter 7

DOUBLE JEOPARDY

Despite some negative feelings concerning Preus' interview process, our faculty on the whole reacted positively to it. Colleague Carl S. Meyer, who died in December, 1972, consoled us with a variation of the theme: "If you're going to be sold down the river, you might as well enjoy the ride." I was determined to enjoy it, and, as my transcript reveals, endeavored to share as much of my thinking as possible between questions, so that the church might know where I stood on a number of issues.

I had hoped that by sharing the Good News with the committee they might be able to loosen up a bit. Between their questions and my own theological emphases, the interview had followed a five-fold structure around the general theme: WELCOME TO THE GREAT PARTY. I viewed my answers as homiletical presentations and found support in the committee's own suggestion at one point, that I look on them as a congregation.

Since the seminary community looked a little glum, I thought they might welcome something in a lighter vein along with the 'heavy words' when it came my turn a few weeks later to conduct the chapel service. We needed to do some laughing together—and *with* the church. Briefly summarizing my experiences with the committee, I outlined the five main parts as follows:

1. "Mortification of the Ego." Romans 7.
2. "A Flying Trip through the Confessions." Romans 3:28.
3. "Mark's Gospel."
4. "You Can't Stop Change," or, "Don't Flag God Down." 2 Corinthians 5:21.
5. "How to Flush Out Heretics in Three Either/Or Questions." Luke 20:20–26.

"I have no worries any longer about the Lutheran Church-Missouri Synod." I went on to say, "and I want our radio audience to know that, despite all the apparently adverse publicity, what has happened merely shows the great power of God. The Missouri Synod is bound to survive. Any group of men who can listen to me for an hour and a half, five sermons running, and still come out and say 'we would like to hear you again'—I would say that shows we have great stamina and resources for survival and to speak the gospel."

After such introduction, I continued with an exposition of Matthew 14:22–33, the story that was of such concern to the Fact-Finding Committee. The address is presented here in condensed form:

Walking On Water

Matthew's Word about Peter trying to walk on the water, is a very important Word for us to consider precisely in these times. There is just too much water-walking going on without people really having the ability to do it, and always the Lord has to reach out His hand to rescue us.

The gospel tells us: "Forthwith He ordered the disciples to embark and go on ahead of Him to the other side until He dismissed the crowds. After He had dismissed them, He went up a mountain by Himself to pray. When it was evening He was there alone, and the boat was now quite far from shore, and there was a strong wind blowing up. So in the fourth watch of the night He came to them walking on the lake, and the disciples saw Him as He was walking on the lake and they were filled with consternation, saying, 'It is a ghost,' and they cried out for fear. Immediately Jesus said to them, 'Courage! I am here; no need to fear.' And Peter said to Him, 'Lord, if you are here, then order me to come to you on the water.' And He said, 'Come.' So Peter got down out of the boat and stepped on the water and came to Jesus. But when he heard the wind he was afraid and began to sink, crying out, 'Lord, save me!' Forthwith Jesus reached out his hand, took hold of him and said, 'Little-faither, why did you hesitate?' When they got into the boat the wind stopped. Then those in the boat knelt down before Him saying, 'You really ARE God's Son.' "

Note what happens according to this passage. Peter tries to walk on the water, but he doesn't get too far, and the Scriptures suggest reasons for that failure. The epistle lesson, 2 Timothy 4:1–5, spoke of myths. Now, there are a number of myths that make it impossible for *us* really to walk on the water. One of those is the myth of *Reductionism.* To phrase it another way, the church is often led to believe that its success is in direct ratio to its ability to reduce Jesus Christ to the level of its own thinking and specific interests.

Of interest is the Christological conjugation that takes place here in Matthew 14. It is a striking demonstration of the reductionism we are talking about. The first, second and third person singular forms of the Greek verb, *einai,* "to be," are: *eimi* (I am), *ei* (you are), *estin* (he is). Notice that in the text Jesus says, *Ego Eimi* (I am). We are reminded of the great I AM. Peter recites the second person *su ei* (you are), which means, "If you are the I AM." If you are namely what you say, then order me to walk on the water. But, as the sequel shows, he was really governed by the statement in the third person, *phantasma estin,* "It is a ghost." So there you have it: I am, you are, it is. That is the way the church very often conjugates and declines Jesus Christ. Since Peter's time the myth, for example, has gained credence that the church is not really visible but invisible, despite the fact that St. Paul told the saints to "kiss one another," but we have managed to show that the saints aren't really kissable. Indeed we could pass though all kinds of illustrations of the declination that takes place, but the Holy Spirit throws out to you right now this challenge, to examine your own pet propositions, your own procedures, how you conjugate the great *ego eimi,* the great I AM, into fantastic reductions of the person of Jesus Christ as well as of your own personal responsibility.

The next myth has to do with the matter of *Image Preservation.* Peter is mentioned quite often in the New Testament. In Jerusalem he ate at the *Steak 'n Shake;* in Antioch at the *Swine and Dine.* He hoped to maintain an image in both places. And Paul rubbed in his name, "Old Rocky," with a Palestinian accent, *Kephas:* "You can't say and do one thing in Jerusalem and another in Antioch, just to keep the folks happy. The image of Christ is more important than your own public image, and it may take some ego-swallowing." Some of you people are trying to build up false images, but unless you hear this gospel, and unless you come to the PARTY, you are going to be a source of trouble for the church. What you are to be concerned about is the image of Christ that is being formed in you. You don't have to be uptight. All you have to do is come to the GREAT PARTY and realize that God isn't interested in your old image; he wants to give you a new self.

Associated with the myth of image preservation is the *Don't-rock-the-boat-motif.* Now this is something I could never understand. The church's symbol is the nave. The members of the church ought to be able to brave the storm and not be like the disciples who blubbered in fear as soon as the wind got high. But the fact is, sometimes the church gets hung up on reefs or sandbars. Anyone who has done any fishing knows that at such times you have to rock the boat to get it back on course. So for goodness' sake, when you find the church hung up on a reef, don't worry! Just get it off. But first of all get the signals of the Spirit to make sure you are getting it on the right course. Whatever you do, don't just rock the boat to say, "My, doesn't this rock nice."

Out *there,* in the world, people get worried about their images and try to have gag rules on the news. At Jefferson City, Missouri, recently certain members of government departments were reminded that it is not "healthy to talk to reporters." But Matthew, Mark, Luke and John, St. Paul and all the rest of the reporters in the New Testament reveal a community that was not afraid of being accountable to the world. Of course, there were exceptions, like Ananias and Sapphira. And you may find yourself embarrassed in some of your actions. Our seminary may find itself embarrassed in some of *its* actions, but the world must know that we can take it and that we are not too proud to admit where errors or sins are committed. In fact, the world will say, "There *is* something to what they claim; they do believe that they can't walk on the water without the help of Jesus Christ." What a relief! That's GOOD NEWS, that we don't have to walk on the water by ourselves.

Prejudicial Summaries

President Preus was later to complain that people taped some of his conversations without his knowledge and with a view to trapping him. To his own Fact-Finders, however, he offered no reproof when they submitted my chapel address to the Board of Control as part of a summary of my interview with them.

The preparation of such summaries of each faculty member's transcript of his interview was an act of mercy toward the members of the Seminary's Board of Control, who had to be spared ploughing through hundreds of pages of dreary theological non-syntax. The manner in which the Fact-Finders carried out this portion of their assignment, at least with respect to my interview, indicates that Preus' vaunted claim of interest in objective gathering of facts concerning professors' theological positions and views was another handful of dust in the eyes of the jury.

In their preface to the "Summary of Interview," the Fact-Finders went far beyond their assigned task by making negative judgments about the length and formal aspects of my statements during the interview. This was a flagrant violation of President Preus' own assurance as announced in *The Lutheran Witness Reporter*[1]: "The Committee is merely to ascertain facts . . . and has no legislative, judicial, or executive power." They also criticized me for not being willing to extend the time of the interview, citing correctly a statement I had made in termination of the interview: "My wife is waiting for me outside in the front of the building. She has to go around the block, and I told her I would be done at 2 o'clock." "The fact is," they wrote, "that the corner nearest to the Lutheran Building has three large parking areas." It was, of course, easy for them to make this objection, for they were all males. The hazards confronting a woman seated alone in an automobile on a parking lot on a Saturday afternoon in the heart of a big city apparently never crossed their minds, not to speak of the *fact* that it would have been ungallant to keep such a charming chauffeur waiting!

Most of the summary itself had to do with what they termed "Imaginative Enlargement." After making the judgmental assertion that their questions suffered the "fate of evasive comment," the summary went on: "Danker seems to be extending the point that 'many of the phenomena... of God are not completely susceptible to our understanding . . . to mean that the facticity of, e.g., Peter's walking on the water, is not a proper and profitable question." They went on to quote a further observation of mine: "It isn't important whether I think it happened, but the important thing is that I understand what the Lord was doing when He was walking on the water, and what the text is saying that He was trying to tell me through that event." To this day, I cannot understand why this was a problem for them. Who in the Synod cared what *I* thought. The church was paying me to help the students discover what the writer of the text thought. To approach recitals of miracle with an assumption that the miracles do not take place is to force a biblical text into a philosophical presupposition. I was not in the philosophy department, but in Biblical interpretation. I thought I had stated both the miracle as fact and the meaning of the miracle in very succinct language: "what the Lord was *doing when he was walking on the water,* and what the text is saying that he was trying to tell me *through that event."*

In their concluding paragraph, entitled "Observation," the committee complained that even though I denounced "the thesis that the early church was not so imaginative as is often affirmed, Danker did not specifically answer the question whether he disagreed with modern scholarship's theory of 'imaginative elements in the Gospels.' His answer: "I'd have to look at the texts and see what these modern scholars (have to say), what texts they adduce."

What else could I say? The term 'modern scholarship' covers a broad territory. Therefore the expression "modern scholarship's theory" was meaningless to me. There is no substitute for looking at all reference to my Gospel-oriented outreach that wished to in-specific texts and the specific remarks of specific scholars. But the committee had, to my recollection, cited no specific scholars' books. Jesus himself possessed a very lively imagination. The Gospels contain much imagery, and the scholar is obligated to identify it when it occurs. As for recitals of miracle, if anyone should care what I *think*, I state my position here clearly and unequivocally: I do not think that the canonical evangelists invent miracles. However, the ability to walk on water does not make Jesus the Son of God. Similar claims have been made for fakirs, and there is no reason to deny their "facticity" any more than in the case of Jesus. I have seen dervishes come unscathed through unbelievably hot temperatures, but this does not make them instruments of salvation. Revelatory event, as Dr. Scharlemann tried to tell his church, requires revelatory word. The Gospels offer that nexus and only the Holy Spirit can create faith. In my student days at Seminary, as I had told the Committee, I had been a non-believer. Now I was a believer, and I confronted the Fact-Finders in that capacity.

Although I had emphasized the conjunction of event and its interpretation, the committee insisted on summarizing in pejorative tone that my "emphasis here on the purpose of the text would appear to make it possible to say that the thing that happened is not important, but the important thing is what is the theological message of the text."

Beyond debate, the most important question is the message God aims to convey through a recorded event. John 6:14–15 makes this very point. But in no way had I indicated that the event being interpreted was unimportant. I merely wanted to avoid denuding faith of its chief defenses against unfaithfulness.

Even more exasperating was the committee's continuation of their line of thought: "The question may be asked whether or not this same hermeneutical principle may not then be used with reference to the vital historical accounts of Scripture and specifically our Lord's resurrection?"

Since I had throughout my interview repeatedly emphasized the resurrection of Jesus and His living presence, this was a low blow. My hermeneutical principles quite evidently did not lead to a denial, but to affirmation of the Lord's resurrection. The committee's judgment was irrelevant, immaterial, and completely void of substance.

The committee's concluding paragraph of their summary again took up the theme of "invented" story. They noted with fairness my stricture against approaching biblical texts with presuppositions that might be prejudicial to the data. They also included the following question addressed to me along these lines during the interview: "Suppose I come up with an interpretation that, for example, cancels the deity of Christ. Would I not say this is a wrong conclusion. . . ?" The last sentence of their summary went on to read: "The answer of Danker to this question is that he then must submit himself to the discipline of other scholars, and he adds that we have to say with the apostle that we see some things darkly, but he gives no other controls."

Their example was, of course, not well chosen. The deity of Jesus Christ is beyond question affirmed in the New Testament. Scholars do not eliminate data nor do they destroy evidence. Likewise, the resurrection of Jesus Christ is taken for granted from the beginning of Matthew to the end of the Book of Revelation. A scholar may choose not to believe in it, but he cannot negate it. In my reply I tried, therefore, to rescue the question from absurdity and put the church at ease by observing that if I were to come up in my studies with an interpretation that disagreed with hitherto assured results of biblical interpretation, I would most certainly subject my findings to the critical scrutiny of other scholars. Without such humility a scholar turns into an ideologist or a jackass. Such seemed to me the pertinence of I Corinthians 13:12. When the truth of God at any time is no larger than my present apprehension of it, I am indeed a noisy gong. On the other hand, the best antidote to any denomination's fear of erosion of biblical truth is exposure to the larger world of scholarship. "Great Planet Earth" theology, the impossible script of "Passover Plot," variations of "The Jesus Myth," alleged "Homosexuality of Jesus" gossip and other eccentricities must dissolve under the bright glare of sober scholarship. The committee's lament that I gave "no other controls" also seemed odd after their complaints that I had been too lengthy in my remarks. A discussion of contemporary interpretive method would have required several hours at a minimum.

It was evidently impossible to satisfy this committee and I so informed the Board of Control in my "Response" to the Committee's Report.[2]

> TO THE BOARD OF CONTROL:
> I am horrified by the amount of time spent and energy consumed by colleagues, secretaries and administrators; I am appalled by the questioning of one's Christianity and theological integrity; I am distressed by the sometimes slurring publicity and general humiliation and harassment suffered by families, friends and LCMS supporters because of the Investigation. Perhaps hundreds of thousands of dol-

lars, in time and money, have been wasted while we professors are distracted from our compelling task of preparing men for today's ministry. All smoke! I appreciate your invitation to respond.

A charge of being uncooperative with a President's Committee is grave indeed. To spare the Board further intrusion on its own valuable time I state that according to the committee's summary, when I do not expand I am "obscure" or "evasive," and when I submit facts in detailed elaboration of what I believe, teach and confess, I am demeaned as "long," "rambling," and "discursive." The committee did in fact ask me to speak as one would address a congregation and at another point to display how I would explain matters to students. Elaboration of presentation will differ greatly from congregation to seminary student to peer within the profession.

I met the committee's requirement of time for the interview, and yet they lament that my schedule did not permit an extension of interview time on that date.

After celebrating the 26th year of my ordination, I all the more reject their charge of uncooperativeness and observe that the transcript reveals that I submitted as many relevant theological facts as possible to assist the President in reassuring the church of my fidelity to the Scriptures and to the Confessions and to the purposes and objectives for which our Synod exists. It appears, therefore, that I was examined with a predetermined need to find fault. The charge on which their judgment is made is one of evaluation of rhetorical ability and is therefore irrelevant. And even this evaluation is gross distortion of fact. Moreover, the summary is based on a totally inadequate transcript. My own transcript underlying the attached copy was completed within one day of the interview by a most competent transcriber.

Where, then are the substantive charges? By whom made? How can I respond to smoke? I love to teach, but deplore this harrassment of which the summary is a sample. Our church acts as though it has all the time and resources in the world. With you and all others who love the Lord, I share the view that we must get back to our business of learning to speak the love of Jesus in a way that God would have us speak it in today's world.

Included in my supporting evidence were the following remarks:

1. The summary but faintly reflects my theological concern that we remember that God investigates us, not we God.
2. St. Paul expressly forbids engagement in *logomachies* or battles over words (2 Timothy 2:14). Convinced that we were tempted by Satan to that point, I had gently warned the committee near the end of the interview. Certainly obedience to the apostolic admonition takes priority over personal inclinations. However, the summary omits any mention of my concern in this respect as well as

all reference to my Gospel-oriented outreach that wished to include all in the Great Banquet of the Lord.

3. A chapel sermon copyrighted by me shows clearly my desire to share with the family of God at Concordia. The community had been greatly disturbed by the investigation and I wanted to cheer them up. That's what the Gospel is for. Perhaps we in LC-MS tend to take ourselves too seriously. Actually the joke was on me, for I showed the students how I had undertaken to answer in a few minutes questions dealing with matters that I take through with them over an entire quarter. My love for LC-MS is evident in the remarks concerning stamina. This sermon was in fact a real invitation to win back some of the sense of humor that we need in order to laugh at ourselves and with God.

Chapter 8

"A STATEMENT"

On March 3, 1972 President Preus sent a four-page letter to the members of the Lutheran Church-Missouri Synod, including congregations, pastors, and teachers. In the letter he affirmed his desire to conform to the instructions given him by the Synod's Milwaukee Convention Resolution 2-28. Under this resolution, he was to report within one year on "the progress made by the Board of Control of Concordia Seminary, relative to the Report of the Fact Finding Committee." However, he said, "developments relative to the teaching status of Prof. Arlis Ehlen made an interim progress report necessary."

According to Preus, the four-year contract of Ehlen, assistant professor in Old Testament, came up for renewal at the Board of Control meeting on December 13, 1971. "Extension of the contract on a four-year basis would have involved the granting of permanent tenure." At the meeting, the Board spent "considerable time," Preus wrote, on Ehlen's position "regarding the doctrine of angels and a personal devil." It also tabled a motion to reconsider its action not to renew Dr. Ehlen's contract. On December 20, the Board held a special meeting and heard Dr. Ehlen report that "he, through personal study and counsel from his brother faculty members, had become convinced of the existence of angels and a personal devil." But in further discussion at the same meeting, with President Preus participating, "another problem arose relative to the doctrinal stance of Dr. Ehlen," Preus wrote. Ehlen "was very frank to state that, although he believed the Exodus account to be the Word of God and to be inspired, he did not believe certain miraculous events recorded in scripture in connection with the Exodus had actually taken place. There was not then and there is not now any question as to Dr. Ehlen's personal honesty, integrity, or sincerity in the positions he adopts relating to such doctrinal stances. After a long discussion in this meeting the Board of Control again decided not to renew his contract." In January the Board took no positive action, Preus continued, but in February, "in a reportedly close vote the Board resolved to renew Dr. Ehlen's contract for one year."

Preus went on to say that if he had been a member of the Board, he "would not have voted for the renewal of Dr. Ehlen's contract because of the fact that he was unable to state that he believed in the historical facticity of certain of the miraculous elements surrounding the Exodus of the people of Israel from the Egyptian captivity. . . ."

In the balance of his letter Preus emphasized the theme of "responsibility to see to it that the teaching at our schools is in keeping with the Word of God *as we have been taught it, understand it, and have applied it heretofore* (italics ours)." He fleshed this out by calling attention to his enclosure of a set of "guidelines" entitled:

A STATEMENT OF SCRIPTURAL AND CONFESSIONAL PRINCIPLES

"The purpose of these guidelines," he said, "is not to serve as a new standard of orthodoxy, but rather to assist the board of control in identifying areas which need further attention in terms of the Synod's doctrinal position. The board of control may well request the faculty members of the St. Louis seminary to indicate their stance toward these guidelines."

After a plea for prayers, he continued: "It is quite obvious to me that some things must be changed. I am convinced that there has been teaching which is at variance with the way in which our Synod understands the Word of God and its confessional position."

Citing Dr. John W. Behnken's warning in 1959: "European theology is infiltrating the American churches, also Lutheran churches," Preus stated that Behnken's list of topics contained "the same topics that trouble us now . . . verbal or plenary inspiration, infallibility and inerrancy of Holy Writ, the historicity of Scriptural accounts, the parabolic interpretation of Genesis 1–11, Messianic prophecies, and a proper regard for the facticity of the miracle accounts." Both Behnken and Dr. Oliver Harms, observed Preus, "were deeply concerned over doctrinal purity and unity in the Synod. Thus your President today is attempting to follow a noble example. The difference, if any, from previous generations is that the historic scene today demands an immediate resolution of the doctrinal issues that sprouted in earlier years and that are in full bloom today. Our church faces a great crisis. It is a *crisis of faith and confession."* (Italics ours).

Then, with a climactic reapplication of what is known in theological circles as the "domino-theory," Preus warned:

> Few, if any, among us would deny the possibility of miracles on principle. However, the use of a technique of Biblical interpretation which leads in practice to the denial of the miraculous events in the Scriptures reminds us that it is only a short step from a denial of the miraculous elements surrounding the greatest redemptive act of the Old Testament (the Exodus) to a denial of the miraculous elements in the greatest redemptive act of all—the deliverance from sin, death, and hell. I am thinking in particular of the incarnation of our Lord Jesus Christ and of his resurrection from the dead.

Concluding with an appeal to meditate on the great deliverance signalled by the Lenten season, Preus urged repentance and admitted, without specifics, "I want to be the first to confess that I need God's grace in my weakness."

> "We have the richest of all treasures in the Gospel of the crucified and risen Savior. May we gather this Lenten season in the shadow of His cross, hear His Word, and in this our 125th year as a Synod go forth renewed in faith and life. Let our hearts burn within us as did the hearts of the Emmaus disciples on Easter evening. Together we go forth into the world with the saving message of the risen Christ!"

In His name

(signed)

J. A. O. Preus
President

This letter was a masterpiece of consistency to the constituency. The long introduction with details about Ehlen dovetailed into the concluding paragraph concerning the dependence of the truth of Jesus' resurrection on maintenance of the historicity and facticity of the details surrounding Old Testament recitals of Exodus.

The average recipient of the letter was of course not expected to worry about the perils of this rationalistic approach. What, for example, would the average reader of Preus' letter say when he discovered that a biblical writer spoke of mountains skipping like rams, and hills like lambs, when Israel came out of Egypt; and that the Jordan ran backward (Psalm 114), instead of standing still, as Joshua 3:14ff states.

Concordia Seminary's Board of Control could not deny the evidence submitted by Ehlen, but Preus could bridge all exegetical complexities simply by asserting that it was his responsibility to see to it that professors taught the Word of God "as we have been taught it, understand it, and have applied it heretofore." This sentence was the real clue to the presidential program for the Lutheran Church-Missouri Synod. It did not matter what a scholar found the Bible actually saying, he could only repeat what had been said in the past in approved fashion within the Synod. Professor Martin Sommer of Concordia Seminary typified the attitude when in the Thirties he said in respect to a question of liberalizing the Synod's attitude toward prayer with non-Missourians: "I am not open to instruction in this matter. I ceased to be open to instruction from the day I took office in the ministry."[1]

Scharlemann's Buried Plea

Unknown to Preus, his self-assigned task as custodian for preservation of Missouri's doctrinal environment clashed with an answer given a decade earlier by another professor who would within two years become Acting President of Concordia Seminary. In a discussion held Sept. 26–27, 1961, professor Scharlemann was asked: *"What do you mean by statements you have made that the Synod must be brought up to date? Answer:* I do not mean that the doctrine of our church is out of date. Rather these statements were made to emphasize the responsibility of studying theology as an ongoing task of the church. New problems demand new application of old truths. The truths of Scripture must be applied to present-day problems."[2] *New applications of old truths!* This was the Scharlemann whose fine intellect and vigorous anticipation of the challenging future could not be completely obscured by mindless proceedings a decade and more later. Here he breathed the oxygen of pure Lutheranism. This is to be emphasized, for a person whose lesser moments must face the light of history ought in all fairness to be remembered also for his finer hours.

Supporting Scharlemann in 1961 were some of the very administrators mentioned by Preus in his communique to the Synod. Dr. John W. Behnken, one of the Synod's most revered presidents, found nothing wrong with Scharlemann's liberal view of the theologians' and the church's task. Nor did Oliver R. Harms, who was to succeed Behnken. Nor did Roland P. Wiederaenders and Gerhardt E. Nitz, other champions of tradition in the Missouri Synod. But Preus' political maneuvering had now buried Scharlemann's brilliant plea for openness in theology. Now with even the *application* of a biblical text officially fixed by the Synod's tradition and under the total authority of Preus, who was echoing the editor of *Christian News,* any deviation therefrom could put any professor, pastor, or other teacher into ecclesiastical jeopardy.

How was this different from what Pope Leo X told Luther? Did Preus have such a low view of Lutheran commitment in the Missouri Synod that he actually believed what he wrote in this letter? But there was no mistaking his administrative aim—*immediate resolution.* This meant that Preus had conceived in his mind a plan to overcome procedural roadblocks. If Preus could tell the Board of Control and Concordia Seminary's president what Ehlen could or could not teach, no classroom would be immune to Preus' thought control.

The letter clearly indicated that Preus would brook no challenge of his authority. "I have written to the president of the seminary," Dr. Preus assured his constituents, "that Dr. Ehlen not be permitted to teach courses 'in which he would have opportunity to advocate his higher critical views concerning Biblical interpretation' until it has been satisfactorily determined that his doctrinal position is in complete accord with the Bible and the confessional position of our church as we have been taught it. (This in no way nullifies the board's extension of Dr. Ehlen's contract.)"

This paragraph of the letter was in effect an ultimatum. If Tietjen obeyed the directive, he would not only jeopardize the seminary's bid for full accreditation but in effect abdicate his responsibility as president of an academic institution. If he failed to carry out the order, Preus could inform the church that Tietjen was uncooperative and in contempt of synodical authority.

Through his guidelines, A STATEMENT OF SCRIPTURAL AND CONFESSIONAL PRINCIPLES, Preus had, in the last analysis, equated his own will with the Synod's collective will. Anyone who challenged his Statement would in effect be challenging the Synod. This was managerial efficiency with a vengeance. It was the ultimate in ecclesiastical politics, outbidding Roman Catholic administrative competence. For here a man spoke *ex cathedra* in five closely printed pages without the intrusion of a series of church councils, and the case against Ehlen supplied the practical interpretation.

A STATEMENT OF SCRIPTURAL AND
CONFESSIONAL PRINCIPLES

I. CHRIST AS SAVIOR AND LORD

We believe, teach, and confess that Jesus Christ is our Savior and Lord, and that through faith in Him we receive forgiveness of sins, eternal life, and salvation. We confess that "our works cannot reconcile God or merit forgiveness of sins and grace but that we obtain forgiveness and grace only by faith when we believe that we are received into favor for Christ's sake, who alone has been ordained to be the mediator and propitiation through whom the Father is reconciled" (AC, XX, 9). We believe that Jesus Christ is the only way to heaven and that all who die without faith in Him are eternally damned. We believe that those who believe in Christ will enjoy a blissful relationship with Him during the interim between their death and His second coming and that on the last day their bodies will be raised.

We therefore reject the following:

1. That we may operate on the assumption that there may be other ways of salvation than through faith in Jesus Christ;
2. That some persons who lack faith in Christ may be considered "anonymous Christians";
3. That there is no eternal hell for unbelievers and ungodly men.

II. LAW AND GOSPEL

We believe that the two chief doctrines of Holy Scripture, Law and Gospel, must be constantly and diligently proclaimed in the church of God until the end of the world, but with due distinction (FC, SD, V, 24). The Law, as the expression of God's immutable will, is to be used by the church to bring men to a knowledge of their sins as well as to provide Christians with instruction about good works (FC, SD, V, 17–18). The Gospel receives the primary emphasis in the ministry of the New Testament, for it is the message that "God forgives them all their sins through Christ, accepts them for His sake as God's children, and out of pure grace, without any merit of their own, justifies and saves them." (FC, SD, V, 25).

We therefore reject the following:

1. That the Gospel is any message or action which brings good news to a bad situation.
2. That the Gospel is a norm or standard for the Christian life, or that the Gospel, in effect, imposes a new law upon the Christian.
3. That what God's law declares to be sinful (for example, adultery

76

or theft) need not be regarded as sinful in all times and situations.

4. That Christians, as men who have been freed from the curse of the Law, no longer need the instruction of the Law to know what God's will is for their life and conduct.

III. MISSION OF THE CHURCH

We believe, teach, and confess that the primary mission of the church is to make disciples of every nation by bearing witness to Jesus Christ through the preaching of the Gospel and the administration of the sacraments. Other necessary activities of the church, such as ministering to men's physical needs, are to serve the church's primary mission and its goal that men will believe and confess Jesus Christ as their Lord and Savior.

We therefore reject any views of the mission of the church which imply:

That an adequate or complete witness to Jesus Christ can be made without proclaiming or verbalizing the Gospel.

IV. HOLY SCRIPTURE

A. *The Inspiration of Scripture.*

We believe, teach, and confess that all Scripture is given by the inspiration of God the Holy Spirit and that God is therefore the true Author of every word of Scripture. We acknowledge that there is a qualitative difference between the inspired witness of Holy Scripture in all its parts and words and the witness of every other form of human expression, making the Bible a unique book.

We therefore reject the following views:

1. That the Holy Scriptures are inspired only in the sense that all Christians are "inspired" to confess the lordship of Jesus Christ.
2. That the Holy Spirit did not inspire the actual words of the Biblical authors but merely provided these men with special guidance.
3. That only those matters in Holy Scripture were inspired by the Holy Spirit which directly pertain to Jesus Christ and man's salvation.
4. That noncanonical writings in the Christian tradition can be regarded as "inspired" in the same sense as Holy Scripture.
5. That portions of the New Testament witness to Jesus Christ contain imaginative additions which had their origin in the early Christian community and do not present actual facts.

B. *The Purpose of Scripture*

We believe that all Scripture bears witness to Jesus Christ and that its primary purpose is to make men wise unto salvation through faith

77

in Jesus Christ. We therefore affirm that the Scriptures are rightly used only when they are read from the perspective of justification by faith and the proper distinction between Law and Gospel. Since the saving work of Jesus Christ was accomplished through His personal entrance into our history and His genuinely historical life, death, and resurrection, we acknowledge that the recognition of the soteriological purpose of Scripture in no sense permits us to call into question or deny the historicity or factuality of matters recorded in the Bible.

We therefore reject the following views:

1. That knowing the facts and data presented in the Scripture, without relating them to Jesus Christ and His work of salvation, represents an adequate approach to Holy Scripture.
2. That the Old Testament, read on its own terms, does not bear witness to Jesus Christ.
3. That it is permissible to reject the historicity of events or the occurrence of miracles recorded in the Scriptures so long as there is no confusion of Law and Gospel.
4. That recognition of the primary purpose of Scripture makes it irrelevant whether such questions of fact as the following are answered in the affirmative: Were Adam and Eve real historical individuals? Did Israel cross the Red Sea on dry land? Did the brazen serpent miracle actually take place? Was Jesus really born of a virgin? Did Jesus perform all the miracles attributed to Him? Did Jesus' resurrection actually involve the return to life of His dead body?

C. *The Gospel and Holy Scripture* (Material and Formal Principles)

We believe, teach, and confess that the Gospel of the gracious justification of the sinner through faith in Jesus Christ is not only the chief doctrine of Holy Scripture and a basic presupposition for the interpretation of Scripture, but the heart and center of our Christian faith and theology (material principle). We also believe, teach, and confess that only "the Word of God shall establish articles of faith" (SA, II, ii, 15), and that "the prophetic and apostolic writings of the Old and New Testaments are the only rule and norm according to which all doctrines and teachers alike must be appraised and judged" (FC, Ep, Rule and Norm, 1) (formal principle). The Gospel which is the center of our theology is the Gospel to which the *Scriptures* bear witness, while the Scriptures from which we derive our theology direct us steadfastly to the *Gospel* of Jesus Christ.

We reject the following distortions of the relationship between the Gospel and the Bible (the material and formal principles):

1. That acceptance of the Bible as such, rather than the Gospel, is the heart and center of Christian faith and theology, and the way to eternal salvation.
2. That the Gospel, rather than Scripture, is the norm for appraising and judging all doctrines and teachers (as, for example,

when a decision on the permissibility of ordaining women into
the pastoral office is made on the basis of the "Gospel" rather
than on the teaching of Scripture as such).

3. That the historicity or facticity of certain Biblical accounts (such
as the Flood or the Fall) may be questioned, provided this does
not distort the Gospel.

4. That Christians need not accept matters taught in the Scriptures that are not a part of the "Gospel."

D. *The Authority of Scripture*

We believe, teach, and confess that because the Scriptures have
God as their author, they possess both the divine power to make men
wise unto salvation through faith in Jesus Christ (causative authority),
as well as the divine authority to serve as the church's sole standard
of doctrine and life (normative authority). We recognize that the
authority of Scripture can be accepted only through faith and not
merely by rational demonstration. As men of faith, we affirm not only
that Holy Scripture is powerful and efficacious, but also that it is "the
only judge, rule, and norm according to which as the only touchstone
all doctrines should and must be understood and judged as good or
evil, right or wrong." (FC, Ep, Rule and Norm, 7)

We therefore reject the following views:

1. That the authority of Scripture is limited to its efficacy in bringing men to salvation in Jesus Christ.

2. That the authority of Scripture has reference only to what the
Scriptures *do* (as means of grace) rather than to what they *are*
(as the inspired Word of God).

3. That the Scriptures are authoritative for the doctrine and life of
the church, not because of their character as the inspired and
inerrant Word of God but because they are the oldest available
written sources for the history of ancient Israel and for the life
and message of Jesus Christ, or because they were written by
the chosen and appointed leaders of Israel and of the early
church, or because the church declared them to be canonical.

4. That the Christian community in every age is directly inspired by
the Holy Spirit and is therefore free to go beyond the doctrine of
the prophets and apostles in determining the content of certain
aspects of its faith and witness.

E. *The Canonical Text of Scripture*

We believe, teach, and confess that the authoritative Word for the
church today is the *canonical* Word, not precanonical sources, forms,
or traditions—however useful the investigation of these possibilities
may on occasion be for a clearer understanding of what the canonical text intends to say.

We therefore reject the following views:

1. That there are various "meanings" of a Biblical text or pericope
to be discovered at various stages of its precanonical history, or

that the meaning a canonical text has now may differ from the meaning it had when it was first written.

2. That Biblical materials that are judged to be "authentic" (for example, "authentic" words of Jesus, "authentic" books of Paul, or "authentic" ideas of Moses) have greater authority than "non-authentic" Biblical statements.
3. That certain pericopes or passages in the canonical text of Scripture may be regarded as imaginative additions of the Biblical authors or of the early Christian community and therefore need not be accepted as fully authoritative.
4. That extracanonical sources may be used in such a way as to call into question the clear meaning of the canonical text.
5. That the essential theological data of Biblical theology is to be found in the precanonical history of the Biblical text.
6. That certain canonical materials have greater authority than other canonical materials because of their greater antiquity or because they are allegedly more "genuine" or "authentic."
7. That various statements of Jesus recorded in the Gospels may not actually be from Jesus and therefore lack historical factuality or the full measure of His authority.

F. *The Infallibility of Scripture*

With Luther, we confess that "God's Word cannot err" (LC, IV, 57). We therefore believe, teach, and confess that since the Holy Scriptures are the Word of God, they contain no errors or contradictions but that they are in all their parts and words the infallible truth. We hold that the opinion that Scripture contains errors is a violation of the *sola scriptura* principle, for it rests upon the acceptance of some norm or criterion of truth above the Scriptures. We recognize that there are *apparent* contradictions or discrepancies and problems which arise because of uncertainty over the original text.

We reject the following views:

1. That the Scriptures contain theological as well as factual contradictions and errors.
2. That the Scriptures are inerrant only in matters pertaining directly to the Gospel message of salvation.
3. That the Scriptures are only functionally inerrant, that is, that the Scriptures are "inerrant" only in the sense that they accomplish their aim of bringing the Gospel of salvation to men.
4. That the Biblical authors accommodated themselves to using and repeating as true the erroneous notions of their day (for example, the claim that Paul's statements on the role of women in the church are not binding today because they are the culturally conditioned result of the apostle's sharing the views of contemporary Judaism as a child of his time).
5. That statements of Jesus and the New Testament writers concerning the human authorship of portions of the Old Testament

or the historicity of certain Old Testament persons and events need not be regarded as true (for example, the Davidic authorship of Psalm 110, the historicity of Jonah, or the fall of Adam and Eve).

6. That only those aspects of a Biblical statement need to be regarded as true that are in keeping with the alleged *intent* of the passage (for example, that Paul's statement about Adam and Eve in Romans 5 and 1 Corinthians 11 do not prove the historicity of Adam and Eve because this was not the specific intent of the apostle; or that the virgin birth of our Lord may be denied because the infancy narratives in Matthew and Luke did not have the specific intent to discuss a biological miracle).

7. That Jesus did not make some of the statements or perform some of the deeds attributed to him in the Gospels but that they were in fact invented or created by the early Christian community or the evangelists to meet their specific needs.

8. That the Biblical authors sometimes placed statements into the mouths of people who in fact did not make them (for example, the claim that the "Deuteronomist" places a speech in Solomon's mouth which Solomon never actually made), or that they relate events as having actually taken place that did not in fact occur (for example, the fall of Adam and Eve, the crossing of the Red Sea on dry land, the episode of the brazen serpent, Jesus' cursing of the fig tree, John the Baptist's experiences in the wilderness, Jesus' changing water into wine, Jesus' walking on water, or even Jesus' bodily resurrection from the dead or the fact of His empty tomb).

9. That the use of certain "literary forms" necessarily calls into question the historicity of that which is being described (for example, that the alleged midrashic form of the infancy narratives in Matthew and Luke suggests that no virgin birth actually occurred, or that the literary form of Genesis 3 argues against the historicity of the Fall).

G. *The Unity of Scripture*

We believe, teach, and confess that since the same God speaks throughout Holy Scripture, there is an organic unity both within and between the Old and New Testaments. While acknowledging the rich variety of language and style in Scripture and recognizing differences of emphasis in various accounts of the same event or topic, we nevertheless affirm that the same doctrine of the Gospel, in all its articles, is presented throughout the entire Scripture.

We reject the view that Holy Scripture, both within and between its various books and authors, presents us with conflicting or contradictory teachings and theologies. We regard this view not only as violating the Scripture's own understanding of itself but also as making it impossible for the church to have and confess a unified theological position that is truly Biblical and evangelical.

H. *Old Testament Prophecy*

Since the New Testament is the culminating written revelation of God, we affirm that it is decisive in determining the relation between the two Testaments and the meaning of Old Testament prophecies in particular, for the meaning of a prophecy becomes known in full only from its fulfillment. With the Lutheran Confessions, we recognize the presence of Messianic prophecies about Jesus Christ throughout the Old Testament. Accordingly, we acknowledge that the Old Testament "promises that the Messiah will come and promises forgiveness of sins, justification, and eternal life for His sake" (Apology, IV, 5) and that the patriarchs and their descendants comforted themselves with such Messianic promises (cf. FC, SD, V, 23).

We therefore reject the following views:

1. That the New Testament statements about Old Testament texts and events do not establish their meaning (for example, the claim that Jesus' reference to Psalm 110 in Matthew 22:43–44 does not establish either that Psalm's Davidic authorship or its predictive Messianic character).

2. That Old Testament prophecies are to be regarded as Messianic prophecies, not in the sense of being genuinely predictive, but only in the sense that the New Testament later applies them to New Testament events.

3. That the Old Testament prophets never recognized that their prophecies reached beyond their own time to the time of Christ.

I. *Historical Methods of Biblical Interpretation*

Since God is the Lord of history and has revealed Himself by acts in history and has in the person of His Son actually entered into man's history, we acknowledge that the historical framework in which the Gospel message is set in Scripture is an essential part of the Word. Furthermore, we recognize that the inspired Scriptures are historical documents written in various times, places, and circumstances. We therefore believe that the Scriptures invite historical investigation and are to be taken seriously as historical documents. We affirm, however, that the Christian interpreter of Scripture cannot adopt uncritically the presuppositions and canons of the secular historian, but that he will be guided in his use of historical techniques by the presuppositions of his faith in the Lord of history, who reveals Himself in Holy Scripture as the one who creates, sustains, and even enters our history in order to lead it to His end.

We therefore reject the following views:

1. That the question of whether certain events described in the Scripture actually happened is unimportant in view of the purpose and function of Holy Scripture.

2. That methods based on secularistic and naturalistic notions of history, such as the following, may have a valid role in Biblical interpretation:
   a. That the universe is closed to the intervention of God or any supernatural force.
   b. That miracles are to be explained in naturalistic terms whenever possible.
   c. That the principle of the economy of miracles may lead us to deny certain miracles reported in the Scriptures.
   d. That the doctrines of Holy Scripture are the result of a natural development or evolution of ideas and experiences within Israel and the early church.
   e. That the message of Scripture can be adequately measured by laws derived exclusively from empirical data and rational observation.
   f. That man's inability to know the future makes genuine predictive prophecy an impossibility.
3. That our primary concern in Biblical interpretation is not with explaining the meaning of the primary sources, namely, the canonical Scriptures, on the basis of the sources themselves.
4. That if the use of historical methods leads to conclusions at variance with the evident meaning of the Biblical text, such conclusions may be accepted without violating the Lutheran view of Scripture or our commitment to the Lutheran Confessions (for example, the claim that it is permissible to deny the existence of angels or a personal devil because of literary, historical, or theological considerations).

V. ORIGINAL SIN

We believe, teach, and confess that God, by the almighty power of His Word, created all things. We also believe that man, as the principal creature of God, was specially created in the image of God, that is, in a state of righteousness, innocence, and blessedness. We affirm that Adam and Eve were real historical human beings, the first two people in the world, and that their fall was a historical occurrence which brought sin into the world so that "since the fall of Adam all men who are propagated according to nature are born in sin" (AC, II, 1). We confess that man's fall necessitated the gracious redemptive work of Jesus Christ and that fallen man's only hope for salvation from his sin lies in Jesus Christ, His Redeemer and Lord.

We therefore reject the following:
1. All world views, philosophical theories, and exegetical interpretations which pervert these Biblical teachings and thus obscure the Gospel.
2. The notion that man did not come into being through the direct creative action of God, but through a process of evolution from

lower forms of life which in turn developed from matter that is either eternal, autonomous, or self-generating.

3. The opinion that the image of God in which Adam and Eve were created did not consist of concreated righteousness, that is, a perfect relationship to God.

4. The notion that Adam and Eve were not real historical persons and that their fall was not a real historical event which brought sin and death into the world.

5. The opinion that original sin does not deprive all men of their spiritual powers and make it impossible for them to be in the right relationship to God apart from faith in Jesus Christ.

VI. CONFESSIONAL SUBSCRIPTION

We reaffirm our acceptance of the Scriptures as the inspired and inerrant Word of God, and our unconditional subscription to "all the Symbolical Books of the Evangelical Lutheran Church as a true and unadulterated statement and exposition of the Word of God" (Constitution, Article II; cf. also Bylaw 4.21). We accept the Confessions because they are drawn from the Word of God and on that account regard their doctrinal content as a true and binding exposition of Holy Scripture and as authoritative for our work as ministers of Jesus Christ and servants of the Lutheran Church—Missouri Synod.

We accept the following clarifications of the nature of our confessional subscription:

1. We acknowledge that the doctrinal content of the Lutheran Confessions includes not only those doctrines of Holy Scripture explicitly treated in the Confessions but also those Biblical doctrines set forth somewhat indirectly or incidentally, such as the doctrines of Holy Scripture, creation, the Holy Spirit, and eschatology.

2. With the fathers, we recognize that not everything in the Lutheran Confessions is a part of its doctrinal content, but we reject all attempts to abridge the extent of this doctrinal content in an arbitrary or subjective manner. We recognize, for example, that subscription in the Lutheran Confessions does not bind us to all strictly exegetical details contained in the Confessions, or even to the confessional use of certain Bible passages to support a particular theological statement. However, since the Confessions want to be understood as Biblical expositions, we reject the notion that we are not bound by our confessional subscription to the exposition of Scripture contained in the Confessions or to the doctrinal content which the Confessions derive from individual Bible passages.

3. We recognize that the Confessions must be read and studied in terms of the historical situations in which they were written, but we reject the view that our confessional subscription means

only that we regard the Confessions as a historically correct response to the problems encountered by the church when the Confessions were written.

4. We recognize that the doctrinal content of the Confessions centers in Jesus Christ and the Gospel of our justification by grace through faith, but we reject the view that the doctrinal content of the Confessions includes only those confessional statements which explicitly and directly deal with the Gospel of Jesus Christ. Accordingly, we do not accept the idea that our subscription to the Lutheran Confessions permits us to reject such confessional positions as the existence of the devil and of angels or that Adam and Eve were real historical persons whose fall into sin was a real historical event.

5. We recognize that the Lutheran Confessions contain no distinct article on the nature of Holy Scripture and its interpretation, but we acknowledge and accept the confessional understanding of the nature of Holy Scripture and of the proper theological principles for its interpretation.

6. We recognize the Lutheran Confessions as a true exposition of Holy Scripture and therefore reject the opinion that our subscription to the Lutheran Confessions leaves us free to reject any doctrinal statements of the Confessions where we feel there is no supporting Biblical evidence.

7. We acknowledge that our subscription to the Lutheran Confessions pledges us to preach and teach in accordance with the entire Holy Scripture. We therefore reject the opinion that all Biblical matters not explicitly treated in the Lutheran Confessions are open questions.

8. We confess that the Holy Scriptures are the only rule and norm for faith and life, and that other writings "should not be put on a par with Holy Scripture" (FC, Ep, 1-2). We therefore reject the notion that it is legitimate to maintain the doctrinal conclusions of the Confessions without accepting their Biblical basis, or to regard formal confessional subscription as an adequate safeguard against improper exegetical conclusions.

9. Finally, we affirm that our acceptance of the Lutheran Confessions means not only that we tolerate the doctrinal content of the Lutheran Confessions as a viable option for Lutheran Christians today but that we in fact preach, teach, and confess the doctrinal content of the Lutheran Confessions as our very own.

CONCLUSION

The 1971 convention of The Lutheran Church—Missouri Synod reaffirmed the Synod's desire to abide by its doctrinal position as stated in its constitution (Article II). The Synod clearly stated its conviction that its confessional base is as broad as Holy Scripture and that the Synod accepts anything and everything that the Scriptures teach. Moreover, the Synod declared its right as a Synod to apply its confessional base definitively to current issues and thus conserve and promote unity and resist an individualism which breeds schism.

This Statement expresses the Synod's Scriptural and confessional stance on a number of important topics. It is hoped that the endorsement of this Statement will be of assistance to the Synod in the "conservation and promotion of the unity of the true faith" (Constitution, Article III).

Chapter 9

"A STATEMENT"—CRITIQUE

Milwaukee Convention Resolution 2-36 had admonished doctrinal reviewers to be on the alert for "statements that are inadequate, misleading, ambiguous, or lacking in doctrinal clarity." In accordance with this express will of the synod, I catalogued a number of reactions the very day I was in receipt of Dr. Preus' *A Statement*.[1]

First of all, the title impressed me as a brilliant stroke. Preus was about to perform a politically impossible trick in the Missouri Synod. If he was to succeed in controlling the Synod, he would need a document that would define heresy in precise terms. To accomplish this feat he would have to overcome a severe setback suffered by his supporters a little more than a decade earlier. At the Synod's Convention held at San Francisco in 1959, a strongly worded document known as "A Brief Statement" won a status next to the Scriptures and the Lutheran Confessions. But at the very next convention, held in Cleveland in 1962, that decision was declared unconstitutional.

Undaunted, Preus saw in the problem a challenge to his political adroitness. Since the radical right wing in the Missouri Synod was well aware that their only hope of dumping Tietjen and his supporters lay in Preus' hands, Preus knew he could count on their support for any document he might produce which defined "higher criticism" as the root of all their ecclesiastical ills. But the process would take time. First it would be necessary to lay the constitutional groundwork. Part of this he accomplished at Milwaukee (July 9–16, 1971), with a skeletal outline of his strategy presented in his presidential address. Doctrinal purity and managerial efficiency, which formed a unit from his political perspective, were the two main topics.[2]

In the course of the convention business that followed, moderates thought they were being successful in undoing some of the damage done to their cause when President Harms was dumped at Denver in 1969. But Preus outfoxed them by securing passage of the one enabling resolution he needed to clear the way for all-out attack on Tietjen and his faculty.

The crucial paragraph of Resolution 5-24 read: "*Resolved,* that the Synod distinguish between resolutions concerning doctrine formulated and adopted at a convention and more formal statements of belief which are produced by officially authorized groups, and which are then presented to the congregations and clergy of the Synod for study and discussion, *and which are subsequently adopted by a synodical convention* (italics ours)."[3]

Looking down the pike, President Preus could see the New Orleans Convention catapulting him into infallibility in 1973. Nor would the debacle of the Cleveland Convention, 1962, be repeated. Preus' machine would control the votes, and no judgments from a stacked Constitutional Committee would contradict the collectivized will of the Synod and Preus.

The word "principles" in the title of the statement was another skillful choice. On the one hand, it suggested basic matters of belief and therefore appealed to a fundamentalist mindset, as well as to those who viewed principles as doctrinal starting points for theological expression. The latter were to discover, however, that there were no starting points in this document—only concrete finish lines.

Christ As Savior and Lord

There was nothing wrong with the first sentence of Part I.[4] It was lifted out of a basic Lutheran textbook from the sixteenth century, the Augsburg Confession (20,9). The rest of the paragraph left much to be desired, and the second sentence was indefensible. It read: "We believe that Jesus Christ is the only way to heaven and that all who die without faith in Him are eternally damned." The statement was not only typical of anti-semitic strains in sub-Lutheran literature, but it violated Paul's pronouncements in Romans 5 and 2 Corinthians 6. It was totally insensitive to the anguish of Lutheran mothers and fathers, many of whom had relatives who at one time or other had stood at the

88

graveside of an unbaptized infant. It was also extremely restrictive in expressing what the title aimed to assert, namely the Saviorhood and Lordship of Christ, for all emphasis was put on apocalyptic matters, that is, things relative to the after-life. The Bible, however, emphasizes the Lordship of Jesus Christ now as well as in the future. It also takes a dim view of a triumphalist theology that encourages equation of maintenance of pure doctrine with assurance of heaven. But of such biblical perspective and critique there was not a word in Preus' Statement. At the time, this total lack of executive and institutional humility astounded me perhaps more than anything else.

The succeeding list of 'rejects' under the first heading were not very carefully phrased. Preus' first item ("That we may operate on the assumption that there may be other ways of salvation than through faith in Jesus Christ") could easily suggest that faith, rather than God's forgiving love, is the cause of salvation. The point of Acts 4:12 ("There is no other name under heaven given among men whereby we must be saved.") is that Jesus remains the one definitive expression of God's saving intention, will and purpose. Jesus demonstrated the outreach of God's love by associating with the outcasts of society. Rejection of God's own manifestation of Himself is a crime the church can ill afford to commit. All history and all humankind finds its integrity challenged to the depths at the Cross. Rejection of that exposure and of the healing offered there spells the end of opportunity. But the Bible says nothing about those who have not been so exposed. On the contrary, it says that it will be more tolerable for Sodom and Gomorrah in the day of judgment than for those who consider themselves on the inside track with God (Matthew 10:15).

I did not know of any colleague who spoke of "anonymous Christians," so I looked at the third point, with which I agreed wholeheartedly. According to the consistent voice of the New Testament, hell is very necessary. It is the place primarily reserved for the loyal followers of the chief division-maker. In Galatians 5:20–21 St. Paul marshalls alongside fornication and idolatry such church crimes as politicking, splitting up groups by securing a personal following, and dissociating from other groups. A translation designed for unsophisticated readers renders: "arguing, dividing into little groups and thinking the other groups are wrong."[5] And, adds Paul, "those who do such things shall not inherit the Kingdom of God." Preus, as chief pastor of the church, should have stood on the ramparts of Zion and warned all about the possibility that not only professors but other loyal members of the synod could be "unbelievers and ungodly" people.

Law and Gospel

This section began with a reference to the "two chief doctrines" of Holy Scripture: Law and Gospel. The Augsburg Confession, Article IV, clearly refers to "Justification" (clearance of a sinner's guilt before God) as the "main doctrine of Christianity," and Preus correctly emphasized the fact in these words: "The Gospel receives the primary emphasis in the ministry of the New Testament . . ."

The 'rejects' were, however, inadequately expressed. He first used the word "any" ambiguously: "That the Gospel is any message or action which brings good news to a bad situation." The second ("That the Gospel is a norm or standard for the Christian life . . .") was false. St. Paul himself uses the Gospel, the heart of which is Jesus' journey to the cross in humanity's behalf, as a model for Christian community patterns. And what is to be made of Paul's reminders to be imitators of God, who reveals his identity definitively in the Gospel? The third rejection picks up only part of Paul's vice lists ("adultery or theft"). Paul's problems, however, were not so much with fornicators or thieves, as with divisive politics and theological party-strife. Not a word of this in Preus' statement. The fourth point I did not understand, for the term "Law" was far too vague. St. Paul himself appeals to Mosaic Law on occasion (I Corinthians 9:9), and I knew of no colleague who politicked for what was here condemned. Quite obviously when a Christian deserts the path of the Gospel he needs to hear the riot act of the Law, as it is pronounced, for example, in Galatians 5:20–21, recited to him. (See also 1 Timothy 1:8–10). And Christians are certainly not limited to the Ten Commandments in identifying proper conduct. If Preus was attacking the latter view, he had not done his homework. I preferred to conclude that he had erred on the side of misstatement.

Mission of the Church

This was perhaps the most unbiblical paragraph in the whole "statement." Preus stated that "the primary mission of the church is to make disciples of every nation by bearing witness to Jesus Christ through the preaching of the Gospel and the administration of the sacraments." Even a cursory glance at Matthew 28:18–20 would have told Preus that Jesus himself regarded the primary mission of His church as the discipling of all nations 1) by *baptizing* them and 2) *teaching them everything I have commanded you.* Had Preus looked at what Jesus commanded his disciples, especially in the Sermon on the Mount, he would have altered considerably his wording in this paragraph. He would have seen that Matthew 5:16 specifically lays emphasis on the Christian public relations value of "good works." By seeing Christians performing in accordance with their avowed *Principles,* people in general will "see and glorify" the Heavenly Father. All the finest verbalization in the world would have difficulty convincing unbelievers of the truth of the Gospel, if such verbalization were accompanied by scandalous division-making, as was taking place in the Missouri Synod. But of this there was no word from the Chief Pastor in the Missouri Synod. The 'reject' item was again a red herring. I know of no one in the Missouri Synod who declared that "adequate" or "complete witness to Jesus Christ" could be made without verbalizing the Gospel.

The Holy Scripture

No one in the Missouri Synod could or would take exception to the first paragraph. But the 'rejects' again put Preus' meaning into question. The first was irrelevant, for no one among us maintained anything but the uniqueness of the Scriptures. Indeed, the reason we would be less than sympathetic to the elevation of Preus' Statement as a definitive doctrinal expression was our interest in preserving emphasis on the unique character of the Scriptures. Reject 2 took the reader into psychological depths that were beyond my capacity of analysis. I believe that the Bible was inspired in its words, for I consider the Scriptures God's unique miracle in literary history. I knew of no colleague who took a different view. The third reject seemed to backfire on the formulator of the document, for Preus appeared to espouse a canon of Scripture within the canon. That is, he took a liking to some parts, but overlooked others, and such preferential treatment is tantamount to denial of inspiration of certain parts. For such partiality we had long put rationalists and social gospelists under attack. Preus liked all the parts that seemed to talk about pure doctrine but he was allergic to its instruction on division-making. Reject 4 took the reader into technical matters that were beyond the capacity of all but the most sophisticated. Since the Lutheran Church has never defined the canon of Scripture, it was unique to open up such debatable territory in a popular document. Would Preus, for example, challenge a theologian who believed that the Book of Wisdom is inspired? Yet, it is not contained in most Bibles used by Missouri Synod Lutherans. Or did he have reference to books like the *Acts of Paul and Thecla, The Acts of Thomas* and other documents of the post-apostolic community? As to the fifth reject, was Preus denying to the Holy Spirit the right to make imaginative additions, if He so chose? Certainly the Holy Spirit was very active in the early Christian community, and truth is not limited to "actual facts." Personally, I do not think that communities are very imaginative. I do believe the Holy Spirit is responsible for any imagination displayed in the New Testament. To deny the Holy Spirit the right to interpret history, even to the extent of rearranging chronology, is in my judgment tantamount to lese majesty. Ecclesiastical managerial efficiency might not allow for the possibility, but I believe that God is singularly indifferent to any discomfiture theologians might experience in the process of discovery. Any formulation of teaching on inspiration worthy of the name is therefore obligated to record how God has actually seen fit to express Himself, not how he should have done so.

Ultimately Preus' last phrase in the last line of section A was a play to the gallery. What constitutes an "actual fact"? An imaginative addition, even by an uninspired person, is a fact of history. Did Preus' view of inspiration also include the idea that inspiration meant the sifting out of history of everything that might prove disconcerting to a rationalistic approach to Scriptures?

In his summary of "The Purpose of Scripture" Dr. Preus put the saving work of Jesus Christ at the mercy of historical research. No historian in his right mind would deny "historicity" or "factuality" of matters recorded in the Bible. "Historicity" presupposes ability to use the processes of historical research. It is one thing to affirm a matter as a fact, it is far more difficult to establish it to the satisfaction of historians. The universe is a fact. That God did the creating is a matter of belief and cannot be established "historically." It is a fact that the Bible affirms God as the Creator, and it can be determined by historical inquiry that the Bible does so indeed explain the fact of creation. But faith does not rest on ability to prove something historically. If that were the case, only historians could be theologians. That Jesus existed can be demonstrated historically. But that He is the sufficient basis for relationship with God is a matter for faith. Also the affirmation that He is such is a fact recorded in the Bible, and no sane theologian could deny that fact. Preus did indeed have difficulty understanding that faith is a gift of the Holy Spirit, not a work meriting grace.

The 'rejects' cited in connection with the statement of Scriptural purpose were equally irrelevant. The first was patently absurd. Preus had only to ask one of our exegetes what the current developments in biblical studies were and he would have been appraised of the fact that if there is one thing contemporary Biblical scholars affirm, it is the emphasis, especially in New Testament studies, on relationship of biblical data to "Jesus Christ and His work of salvation." I knew of no one on our faculty who affirmed that "the Old Testament, read on its own terms, does not bear witness to Jesus Christ."

The language of the third reject ("That it is permissible to reject the historicity of events or the occurrence of miracles recorded in the Scriptures so long as there is no confusion of Law and Gospel") was so complicated, that only the most sophisticated theologian and historian of dogma could ravel it. Suffice it to say, when it can be established that a given text records a miracle, that is, affirms God's special intervention, the interpreter cannot deny the fact. To assume *a priori* that miracles cannot happen is to adopt a philosophical stance that can be prejudicial to the understanding of a biblical text. Our scholars time and again disclaimed such a narrow use of historical-critical methodology. To confuse the Law and Gospel at any time, as did Preus in this document by in effect making the exercise of the historian's craft a prerequisite for faith, is not to be tolerated without censure in the Church of God.

Neither did the fourth reject advance the cause of reconciliation in the Synod. Evidently Preus meant by the phrase "questions of fact" *not* 'questions concerning the ability to establish something as fact,' but rather questions about stories that everyone in the Missouri Synod understands to be fact. "Were Adam and Eve real historical individuals?" How did they look? Like the pure white Aryans traditionally pictured on Sunday school leaflets in the Missouri Synod? What if it was determined historically that they looked more like Koreans or Nigerians? "Did Israel cross the Red Sea on dry land?" Of course, they did. But how dry was the ground? What instruments at His disposal did Yahweh use? Would it have helped to wear rubbers? What historian knew all the facts? Of this one could be sure, the writer of Exodus, unlike polytheists who relied on mythical description, viewed the screen of history as the place where God projected Himself in mighty deliverance from oppression. Historians' uncertainty about detail could never make Rameses II a less stupid Pharaoh, nor the Deliverance of the Israelites anything less than the other greatest miracle in history for Christians. "Did the brazen serpent miracle actually take place?" Of course, it did, but what was the history of its tradition? "Was Jesus really born of a virgin?" Even his enemies have affirmed that! The question should be asked, "Is it a matter of faith to affirm that the Holy Spirit Fathered Jesus through a virgin?" The answer is unqualifiedly "Yes." "Did it happen in the course of history?" "Yes!" "Can historians prove it?" "No!" "Did Jesus perform all the miracles attributed to Him?" I wrote in the margin: "And many more." "Did Jesus' resurrection actually involve the return to life of His dead body?" Preus' question ran the hazard of turning support of the resurrection of Jesus into a process of mere revivification. With the support of the Third Article we believe much more than that.

Preus' next paragraph, entitled "C. The Gospel and Holy Scripture" started out badly with the parenthetical sub-heading "Material and Formal Principles." Preus had at times complained that we talked over the heads of laypeople. Repeatedly in his Statement he was using terminology and raising complicated lines of thoughts that were far beyond the capacities of the average pew-holder.

Alien Spirit

To go on, however, with this critique, would presume on patience. The criticisms cited above must serve as a sampling of responses that might be made to the document. From these the reader can understand that it would have been embarrassing not only to Dr. Preus, but to the Missouri Synod, to expose all the errors, misstatements, and biblical distortions found in Preus' document. Perhaps he should have gone into secular politics and not exposed himself to theological evaluation nor us to the necessity of rating his document beneath other more serviceable contributions in the history of Christian thought.

Within less than a month our faculty discharged the unwelcome task. In eight or so closely typed pages, we submitted a set of theses and questions for discussion by the clergy of the Missouri Synod. Despite the fact that Preus had gone to the entire church, we continued to go through prescribed channels and discussed the matters with our peers in ordination. As events would later prove, this fidelity to procedure was at the same time our undoing. At New Orleans, Preus' lay supporters would help outvote our clergy sympathizers.

In our response we noted that Dr. Preus had not first shared "his concerns with us and for more than a year has declined repeated invitations to meet with us about concerns we have had about his dealings with us. . . Not until 'A Statement' appeared did we learn what

President Preus thinks the issues at the Seminary are."

We also stated that the positions rejected in President Preus' "Statement" were not "descriptive of our teaching." On the other hand, we said that we were open to correction "We are no strangers to investigation and do not object to being examined. We do object to trial without clear and specific accusation and to judgment without opportunity for defense."

After pointing out irregularities in Dr. Preus' bypassing of the Board of Control we set forth our specific concerns. In connection with Preus' appeal to "the Word of God as we have taught it, understand it, and have applied it heretofore," we asked:

> Does not such a criterion introduce a sectarian principle of tradition? Would this tradition principle allow room for any new insight to be drawn from the Scriptures to correct an imperfect or wrong understanding in The Lutheran Church—Missouri Synod?"

In the concluding sections of our response we declared: " 'A Statement' " has a spirit alien to Lutheran confessional theology." We also said, "The promulgation of 'A Statement' is divisive." To have thought that we could survive in the Synod after Preus' avalanche of print, would have been naive. With Preus' board and commissions increasingly stacked against the faculty, it was a no-win situation, and the outcome was predictable. An honest and scholarly critique by the faculty would either have been construed as further example of intransigent refusal to cooperate with the President of the Synod or would have provided him with a gilt-edged dossier of divergences. With Preus in full possession of the answerbook, it was of no consequence that many of his answers did not even correspond to the questions in our students' manual. All that mattered to Preus was answers, not questions or problems. Apart from Yahweh, our main hope lay in the possibility that District Presidents and clergy would in greater numbers and show of strength recognize the peril to true Lutheranism in the Missouri Synod. If our faculty's critique might be discounted because of alleged partisan pique, those who were interested could read the review published later in *The Cresset,* a Valparaiso University periodical.[6] Even a cursory reading suggested that the biblical-exegetical-theological backing for *A Statement* was about as sound as the securities' base for Kreuger-Toll stock just before the Great Crash in 1929.

95

Chapter 10

"BLUE BOOK"

Moving into higher political gear, Preus produced his second major document, and continued to bulldoze a way for the first. Published on September 1, 1972, it bore the title: "Report of the Synodical President to the Lutheran Church—Missouri Synod." Always eager to comply with Resolutions of the Synod, which obligingly seemed to come up quite regularly with whatever he needed to carry out his objectives, Preus appended the following subtitle: "In compliance with Resolution 2-28 of the 49th Regular Convention of the Synod, held at Milwaukee, Wisconsin, July 9–16, 1971." This Resolution noted that Dr. Preus had submitted the Fact-Finders' report to Concordia Seminary's Board of Control. It further ordered the board to "take appropriate action on the basis of the report, commending or correcting where necessary . . ." and "report progress directly to the President of the Synod and the Board for Higher Education." The President of the Synod was to "report to the Synod on the progress of the Board of Control within one year." [1]

Known as the "Blue Book" from the color of its cover, this report was an ingeniously contrived literary guillotine, in which Preus used the synodical directive as an opener for judgmental and prejudicial attack on the faculty. Most of his book was used for excerpts made from transcripts *appended* to the Board's progress report. Near the end of the book, the equivalent of five out of 160 pages were used to present the Board's actual progress report! The directive of the synod had not requested a minority report from the board, but almost four pages were used for a report signed by Preus' right-hand man, Vice-President E. C. Weber and Walter C. Dissen.[2] A pejorative, unsigned letter, alleged by Preus to contain thirty students' signatures, preceded the two exhibits from the Board of Control.[3] As will be shown in

96

a later chapter, this use of anonymous missiles set a dangerous precedent that would soon blow up in the face of the Synod.

In his explanation of the format of the report, Preus said that instead of quoting the summaries of the interviews and the professors' responses to them, "long sections" were to be cited from the actual interviews themselves and from essays or articles with "preservation of adequate context." "Note also," he stated, "that each professor was given the option of changing or adding to his testimony if he so desired. Also, the transcripts quoted are from copies corrected by the professors themselves." Adding, "every effort had been made to minimize" errors, he assured the church: "Corrections, if validated, will be freely made."[4]

A quick check of material attributed to me through Preus' transparent code designations put the veracity of this preface into immediate question. I was quoted as follows under the title: "Prof. Q Transcript."

COMMITTEE: That's why I'm asking you the question, sir. Do yourself believe that in the Gospels, or in the New Testament in general or in the Old Testament too, if you please, that there are imaginative enlargements? Do you believe this or do you not?
PROF. Q: I think, for example, in the book of Revelation you have many, many cases of imaginative expression. "144 thousand." This is the trouble with a good many witnesses. They go off on a tack, you see, naturally, well let's take, but this is underestimate——"[5]

Now, I may at times engage in superfluous rhetoric but I do try to avoid gibberish. Contrary to the statement he had made in the preface, Preus had not used my corrected transcript in the preparation of his Blue Book. Had he done so, he would have recognized that my own paraphrase at this point suggested a defect in the taping process. In any event, the text here was so bad, he should have checked with me as to the possibility of a slip-up in routine channels. What I did say was: "This is the trouble with a good many of Jehovah's Witnesses. They go off on a tack, you see. Naturally! But this is ——" At this point a member of the Committee interrupted: "Well, let's take two examples you give." Preus or someone else's secretary working on the Fact-Finders' materials attributed part of the committee's words to me, but repeated the phrase "well, let's take" three times, in one case misunderstanding it as "underestimate." In textual criticism we would call this a case of triplography! In a succeeding paragraph another interruption of the committee was attributed to me, and an exchange of

97

the homonym "know" for "no" in a relatively long unpunctuated sentence obscured my point. It was no wonder that one of Preus' followers quipped that professors at Concordia Seminary knew as little about syntax as about theology.

I fared no better under the rubric "Prof. XX," code name reserved by Preus for presentation of alleged errors in my commentary on St. Luke's Gospel. Whether the doubled X was a bit of Preusian humor is difficult to determine. But this is what Preus announced to the Synod:

> XX argues that it is impossible to determine the words of Jesus spoken on any given occasion. He asserts that as Christians pondered on Jesus and His meaning for their time, new sayings of Jesus could be produced, presumably by the community. He includes this type of activity under the umbrella of inspiration. Cf. pp. xviii–xix of his book.
>
> XX applies this idea to Jesus' prophecy concerning the destruction of Jerusalem. On page 212 he claims that the destruction of Jerusalem had already occurred when Luke wrote his Gospel. XX speaks of Luke adding more explicit terms to Jesus' prediction, especially referring to the encirclement by the Roman armies. It is thus evident that XX does not attribute to Christ the details of the prophecy concerning the destruction of Jerusalem. These verses were 'dubbed in' later, after the event."[6]

In all my career as a scholar I had never seen two paragraphs of review writing contain so many errors and distortions. This is what I had, in fact, written on pp. xviii and xix:

> As Lord of the Church, *Jesus* speaks to each succeeding generation. Therefore, it is *impossible to recover without argument* the very words of Jesus spoken on a given historical occasion. The Church possessed a lively awareness of the power of the Spirit in its midst, and this Spirit prompted Christians to ponder the significance of Jesus and his words and actions for their time. Even fresh sayings would be uttered, for the *Lord had not ceased to speak.* Hence, the gospels are not less authoritative or less 'true' than would be a biographical record. The evangelists are not interested in writing biography for biography's sake. Indeed, a biography in the strict sense of the word would be no gospel, and one of the harmful effects of red-letter editions of the New Testament has been to suggest that Jesus' words are somewhat more authoritative than other words in the New Testament. The result is a canon within a canon and a credibility gap in the Church's affirmation of inspiration: '*All* Scripture is inspired by God' (2 Timothy 3:16) . . .[7]

No Recourse

Since Preus' avowed concern in the preface for professors' rights surely could not have gone hand in hand with the kind of misrepresentation expressed in his review of my book, I had to attribute the distortions to one of his advisors. It was, of course, nothing new. I had run into a related kind of rearrangement of the evidence in connection with the Fact-Finders' interview. But this time there was no defense. On Eldon Weisheit's computation, only 2 % in the synod would even notice that I had specifically said that "it is impossible to recover *without argument*" the very words of Jesus. Jesus spoke in Aramaic, but no two scholars agree on the precise Aramaic words underlying a section of Greek text in the gospels. Most of Preus' jury had no inkling of this type of problem faced by biblical interpreters. Yet they would bring in their verdict of guilty at New Orleans. I had placed repeated emphasis on the Holy Spirit. Preus gave his readers no inkling of this stress in my book. Far from asserting the creativity "presumably of the community," as Preus alleged, I emphasized that the *Lord* continued to speak in the church. This was a strong affirmation of Jesus' resurrected presence and His abiding authority in the community. The hypocrisy of the Fact-Finders' critique was all the more apparent in the light of Preus' own affirmation of the "Synodical Position" in his "Blue Book," that Jesus' words may have been modified somewhat by oral tradition in the early church or by the evangelists.[7a]

Apart from the fact that the Fact-Finders' phrase "dubbed in" did not appear anywhere in the context of my book and not to my knowledge in any of my writings, Preus' assumption in the sentence beginning "It is thus evident . . ." ignores a very pointed sentence on page 213 of the commentary: "Luke is at pains to emphasize that Jesus' earlier prediction in his lament over the city found horrible literal fulfillment in days that are but recent memory." As a classical scholar, Preus once learned the importance of noting context. Trusting that Preus would honor his pledge to rectify any errors, I wrote to him concerning the mishandling my commentary had received in his "Blue Book."

Columbus Day, 1972

Dr. J. A. O. Preus
210 North Broadway

Good morning,
Thanks for your good wishes on my publication *Under Investigation*. Unfortunately the price on the latter is set so low that now I am

99

losing money in two directions. I do appreciate your return of the good humor, but believe me, your committee did not share your ability to laugh.

Since my commentary was written especially with laymen in mind also, I used the phrase "without argument" rather than the equivalent French term *a l'unanimite*. Like my wife says: "What you're saying is that we can really believe we have the words of the Lord and don't have to worry whether you scholars can prove it or not." It is incredible to us that your adviser cannot grasp such a simple thing.

Greetings,
Frederick W. Danker

Dr. Preus had wanted clarification of what was meant by my phrase "without argument." After receipt of the following response, however, I knew how hopeless it was to secure justice from the highest echelons of the Synod.

Oct. 16, 1972

The Reverend Dr. Frederick W. Danker
Concordia Seminary
801 De Mun Avenue
Saint Louis, Missouri 63105

Dear Fred:
Your letter of Columbus Day, 1972, was the most patriotic thing that happened to me that whole day. It's so good to be an American. We all stood and sang 'Columbia the Gem of the Ocean' upon receipt of your letter.

By all means raise the price on the "Under Investigation." If it's as good as you say it is, I know that it will sell like hot cakes. We can't have you losing money in two directions.

I think your wife put it better than you do. Maybe she should write the next book.

My adviser and I both send our kindest greetings.

Sincerely

(Signed, Jack)

J.A.O. Preus
President

Preus himself had introduced reference to my *Under Investigation* in our correspondence, and his allusion to the publication reinforced the fact that he would have been better advised to have used it rather than a garbled tape in the preparation of his "Blue Book". His attempt to laugh off the negative impressions he had without cause planted in the minds of his constituency relative to my commentary and my theological position would have been more tasteful had it been accompanied by an apology communicated through one of the many official channels at his command. However, repentance in particulars, as students at the seminary were soon to discover, was not Preus' usual style. More often, pious generalities concerning his "errors," "weaknesses," and "sins" assured the faithful that he considered himself a mere mortal.[8] For them that was enough encroachment on infallibility.

Fact Finding or Fault Finding?

My own experiences with the Fact-Finders and with Dr. Preus' interpretative procedures were only a tip of the monstrous iceberg that was chilling Missouri's ecclesiastical climate.

So biased and unbalanced was the report submitted by the Fact-Finders that Dr. Tietjen addressed to all his brethren in the ministry a response in two parts, entitled: *Fact Finding or Fault Finding? An Analysis of President J. A. O. Preus' Investigation of Concordia Seminary.* Dated September 8, 1972, Tietjen's assessment in the first part aimed to show the following:

1. The fact finding process was conceived in a prejudgment that has shaped the inquiry, predetermined its results, and subjected the seminary to treatment that is *unfair.*
2. The procedures employed by the Fact Finding Committee have produced results that are *unreliable.*
3. The Report is a strange blend of half-truths, misunderstandings, and distortions which make the profile it presents *untrue.*
4. The views of Scripture interpretation which lie behind the investigation and shaped its results are *less than Scriptural.*
5. The theology which lies behind the inquiry and the Report, by whose standard the theology of the faculty was measured, is *un-Lutheran.*[9]

According to Tietjen, President Preus had informed him personally in October 1969, that he considered his election at the Denver Convention to be a mandate to clean house doctrinally. Subsequently, at a

"Meet the President" gathering in Nebraska, on May 13, 1970, when asked whether false doctrine was being taught at the St. Louis Seminary, Preus answered, "Yes".[10] Confronted with the allegation, Preus did not deny it, said Tietjen. Although Preus on several occasions had told the Board of Control that he considered some of the faculty members doctrinally unsound, he had not confronted a specific professor nor entered a specific charge of false doctrine. Despite President Preus' own assurance that "The Committee is merely to ascertain facts . . . and has no legislative, judicial, or executive power," (LWR, Nov. 1, 1970, p.2), summaries of the "stacked" committee included judgmental "observations" and "comments," resulting in a report that "is tendentious and judgmental from the first page to the last." From the manner in which Preus used the Fact-Finders' Report in his "President's Report" to the Milwaukee Convention of the Synod, it appears, said Tietjen, that "the members of the faculty were invited to testify against themselves and to provide the president of the Synod with the proof needed to condemn them."[11]

In connection with Part Two of his response, Tietjen noted that the Fact-Finders were "obsessed" with pointing out the use of historical-critical methodology and based a number of serious charges on incorrect information.

Irritated almost beyond his customary high cool level by the biased character of the Committee's report, his concluding remarks described the underlying "basic thrust" of the Committee's report as *un-Lutheran.* "The Report of the President's Committee," he said, "does such an injustice to the seminary, its faculty, and individual professors that any use or circulation of it constitutes a violation of the Eighth Commandment's prohibition against bearing false witness."[12] He went on to say that his faculty most certainly participated in human frailty. "They know they are not inerrant. But error is not heresy. Only willful, persistent error is. Erroneous views should be corrected, but they are not in themselves evidence of 'differences in doctrine' or of less than whole-hearted commitment to the Scriptures and Confessions."[13] However, he said, "The Committee did not find this commitment to be sufficient. The issue that emerges is whether a professor who is practicing commitment to the Scriptures and the Confessions must be presumed to have departed from that commitment because his method of doing exegesis is different from that of his interrogators."[14]

A final trumpet blast out of the Reformation signalled a point of no return:

To the faculty the Gospel is not one doctrine among others to be found in Scripture, but *the* one doctrine of *all* Scripture which guides and determines all of its teaching and work. Far from being guilty of whatever 'Gospel reductionism' is supposed to mean, the seminary faculty views the Gospel as the one source of life and meaning for the church and therefore the chief accent in its work of preparing students for the ministry. For that, *Sola Dei Gloria!* (God's alone is the glory!).[15]

This was Tietjen's bottom line. Armageddon was to be fought over one issue, and one issue alone: What did it mean to be Lutheran? For similar stakes Luther had held his ground at Worms.

Like the Old Missouri

After Tietjen had circulated his critique of the Fact Finding Committee's report, the seminary's Board proceeded to interview individual professors. I was asked to meet with the Board on October 15, 1972, from 7:30 to 9:00 P.M. Included among their number were William Buege, Harry Krieger, Charles Burmeister, Herman Scherer, Walter Dissen, A. E. Beckemeier, and John Tietjen. The atmosphere of the meeting was totally different from the one I breathed in January of 1971 in the presence of the Fact-Finders. This was more like the old Missouri we all would have liked to see return—Christians meeting without rancour and in mutual respect. I was indeed awed by the presence they communicated, by the sincerity of their dedication, and by their generosity of time contributed out of heavy schedules.

To assist them in coming to a fair decision, I asked whether I might share with them the presuppositions I brought to my teaching task. They welcomed this offer, and I explained to them the theological and scholarly context out of which I did my work at the seminary. Dr. Scherer wanted some clarification of one of my presuppositions, that "neither Caiaphas nor Aristotle determined my interpretive procedures." My allusion to Caiaphas meant to say that Jesus directed his disciples to be loyal to the truth without fear of reprisal from religious authorities. Independence of Aristotle meant that the church could be assured that philosophical presuppositions were not the foundation of sound exegesis. Since ecclesiastical administrators shrink at the mention of Caiaphas, evidently because of the bad press this ancient official received in the four gospels, I added that anyone of us in the room could fall into the role of Caiaphas, who aimed to preserve tradition at all costs. This communal distribution of misplaced managerial efficiency seemed to put everyone at ease.

In respect to the Fact-Finders' report on my theological competence I noted that they had failed to use the corrected version submitted through Dr. Tietjen to the Board. Walter Dissen, an attorney on the Board, queried my ethics in printing the proceedings of my interview.[16] Comparing his uncorrected copy with my published account, he also observed that not everything in his transcript was cited in the published copy. I told him that there was no ethical problem, for a professor's theology ought to be made available to those who pay his salary, and the people's right to know must be honored. On the other hand, the interviewers were entitled to their privacy, and it was sufficient, I indicated, to render the gist of their remarks, some of which might have embarrassed them if seen bare in cold print.

Vice-President Krieger, in his customary pastoral fashion, suggested that part of the trouble developing between us and some of the constituency might be traceable to poor communication. Burmeister tied into this line of discussion by citing my commentary on Luke as a case in point. Fortunately I had copies of the book with me and I passed one to each of the Board members. So as not to stack the deck in my favor, I said, "Pick a page, any page, and show me where I state something unclearly." After some shuffling, he found a page with a word that in his judgment did not seem to communicate adequately. I said, "Read on and you will find it explained. That's the purpose of a commentary." Being himself in charge of Communication Consultants, Inc., a St. Louis-based firm, he gracefully accepted the suggestion and the response. Dr. Buege added the cheering note that he had found the commentary very helpful in his sermonic preparation. It was his antidote to a remark made in the President's "Blue Book":

> "... I am personally convinced that our faculty has more and more isolated itself from the grass roots of everyday church members' thinking and the level of communication receptivity to which they are accustomed."[17]

As I left the meeting, I felt the warmth of the family of God. Mr. Dissen had let in a chill, but one freeze does not a winter make. With more encounters like this, we could have arrived at solutions in true Missourian and Lutheran fashion. Unfortunately, there was not enough Prestone in the world to protect us against the kind of subzero temperatures that were soon to descend on our Synod. But this night I was again proud of my church and I was determined to do nothing to embarrass its expectations of fidelity to Article II of the synodical constitution.

On February 21, 1973 came the long-awaited verdicts. In our mailboxes was the following letter:

Dear Professor_____ :

This is to put in writing the substance of what I reported at the meeting of the faculty yesterday. The Board of Control, in carrying out the directive of Resolution 2-28 of the 1971 Milwaukee Convention of the Synod, has acted to commend you and has thereby concluded that you are not guilty of false doctrine but are teaching in accord with the Scriptures and the Confessions. The board's action was by majority vote. The board intends to arrange for continuing discussion between it and the seminary faculty through further meetings with faculty members. I join with you in thanking God for this decision of our board.

Your fellowservant in Christ,
(Signed) John H. Tietjen
President

That should have been the end of the matter. A long and dreary chapter in Missouri's history ought to have come to an end. The Synod's own official board, after a long series of carefully outlined procedures, had rendered its verdict. The Synod itself had spoken. But ecclesiastical monothelitism, or one-trackedness, is difficult to cure, and this Board had not expressed the will of Dr. Preus nor of the loyal supporters who expected him to implement the Synod's hard line. The Convention at New Orleans was therefore to be faced with some unfinished business, and the question of Authority in the Missouri Synod would have to be decided once and for all.

Chapter 11

"THE WAR IS ON"

"Any kind of efforts at thought-control are always disastrous for human relations. A new kind of spirit prevails also within our church body under the administration of Dr. Harms. There was a time when they were afraid, fearful of what someone might report to higher echelons. In fact, we remember the time when men dreaded to present exegetical papers. Some of them stuck very closely to the words of Dr. Stoeckhardt, to provide a handy recourse just in case some overzealous brother set about trying to earn some 'browny points' for himself. That era has happily come to an end. As a result, a kind of theological renaissance is quietly going on also among us." (Martin Scharlemann)[1]

Well insulated against discontent and unrest in less sophisticated circles, tenants in Concordia Seminary's Gothic towers could not see the mobilization of force that was to terminate the "renaissance." Surely, thought the savants, when it comes to the crunch, the Missouri Synod will always opt for sanity and progress, and *True* Lutheranism.

Realistic evaluation of events since the election of Dr. Preus in 1969 as President of the Lutheran Church-Missouri Synod should, however, have suggested that a less sanguine view was more compatible with facts. To improve vision and rouse academicians out of their specialized slumbers, Dr. Tietjen repeatedly warned: "We're headed for crucifixion!" Had not Missouri's turf already felt the thump of rolling heads, and had not Milwaukee's Convention greased Preus' bid for control of the Missouri Synod, such words might, to paraphrase Scharlemann, have contributed further documentation to the history of synodical pathology.

"The War Is On," wrote Otten on March 13, 1972.[2] Now with the big guns of the Seminary's opposition well in place at the beginning of

1973, the locale of the battle was no secret. Heresy was to be shelled out of existence at New Orleans, with a concentrated bombardment during July 6–13, 1973.

Encouraged by two major propaganda instruments, Preus' elite voting troops could be counted on to make appropriate decision at the zero hour. Herman Otten, editor of *Christian News,* unofficial director of the Synod's decision-making processes, and defined "a 20th century Jeremiah" by one of his adherents,[3] called for the reelection of his Chief of Staff J. A. O. Preus. Prewriting even some of the resolutions, he defined hard-core heresy as maintenance of the following:

1. Moses did not write the first five books of the Bible.
2. Isaiah did not write chapters 40–66.
3. *Almah* in Isaiah 7:14 need not be translated 'virgin' and does not refer to the Virgin Mary.
4. The Book of Jonah does not relate historic fact.
5. The sixth-century prophet Daniel did not write Daniel.

To help his crusaders meet all counter-thrusts of the enemy, Otten supplied convention delegates and others with an arsenal entitled *A Christian Handbook on Vital Issues.* Encased in the color of revolution, this was a veritable encyclopedia of heresy that would in another era have provoked Torquemada to jealousy. The cover cited a long list of topics, with every letter except q, x, and y represented. These he must have omitted for lack of space, for he could easily have included "Quicksand-theology," "X-rated professors" and "Yardstick of Truth."

"Spiritual Treat"

Otten himself described this 854-page digest of choice exhibits from *Christian News* as a "spiritual treat" to celebrate the 10th anniversary of his newspaper.[4] On the rear cover, he carried reviewers' accolades of his other major publication, *Baal or God.* The total impact was one of definitive evidence for the charges leveled week after week against the sponsors of alleged false doctrine in the Missouri Synod and other parts of Christendom. In this book Concordia Seminary's scholars had more than met their match. Here was distilled truth, and the laity especially were to know that the professors were not passing the examinations prepared for them by 'conservatives.' No longer helpless in their delusional systems, for less than four cents per reader Otten's students could take a course in Old Testament criticism and philology at the hand of Robert Dick Wilson's *Is the Higher Criticism Scholarly?*[5] "Clearly attested facts showing that the destructive 'assured results of modern scholarship' are indefensible," read the subheading, followed by the information that Wilson had been professor of Semitic philology at Princeton Theological Seminary. At only a slightly higher cost readers could take a seminar in the meaning of one Hebrew word, *almah,* and have the grandiose experience of knowing more than all living 'liberal' Hebraists put together. No longer could they be ignored and mistreated by arrogant academicians. In a twenty-page blast demonstrating that the American Lutheran Church "can no longer be considered an orthodox Lutheran Church,"[6] Otten concluded with quotations from an equally fearsome barrage levelled in time past by Jacob A. O. Preus against a segment of Lutheranism (ELC, Evangelical Lutheran Church), which later merged with other bodies to form The American Lutheran Church. First spraying the ecumenical terrain, Preus had said: "Catholicism, of course, for centuries has tried to operate with human tradition on an equal plane with Scripture. As an organization Catholicism has been a success; as a church it has been almost total failure. . . ."[7] Then he broached his main complaint: "There does not seem to be a single seminary professor in the ELC who believes that the Pope is THE Antichrist."[8] Proceeding to discourse about women's rights, Preus said, according to Otten: "Another instance of loose practice in which the ELC denies both the authority and clarity of the Word is that of the position of women in the church. A professor at the seminary of the ELC once made it a practice to go about in the congregations, lecturing to them on the merits of women's suffrage. The students at the seminary were told that it was just as well to let the women vote and not to make any trouble over the issue. It was even stated by a seminary professor that women should be allowed to preach".[9]

Delighted with the aggrandisement of their egos through putdowns of eggheads, great church bodies, and fifty per cent of the human race, some of Otten's readers also could find satisfaction in their champion's mastery of appeal to their emotions and prejudice. For example, while claiming interest in the problems of Blacks, Otten described the Rev. Dr. Andrew Schulze, one of Lutheranism's boldest champions of Blacks, as one "associated with some Communist front organizations."[10] With strokes given to racism and fear of 'extremism,' Otten laid out attacks on such Black leaders as the Rev. Albert Cleage and Rap Brown in bombs of varied megaton potential.[11]

Knowledgeable in the intricacies of anxiety syndromes, Otten well knew that his readers would not bother to read all the fine print. In his final dress rehearsal for the Battle of New Orleans, it was important only to maintain the spirit of his troops, so that they might remain impervious to attacks of data which might permit varied explanations.

That there was heresy at Concordia Seminary should have been, to Otten's mind, clear to all. But the delegates required unbending resolution in the face of the parliamentary and oratorical maneuvering that was predictable for the convention at New Orleans. Lest they be misled by the Tokyo Rose-like voices, Otten hammered home his review lesson with captions that required no further eyestrain. The "medium is the massage," said McLuhan, and Otten made a science of it as he set his sights on a global pseudo-community of heresy.

"Evangelical Leader Assails Catholicism, Ecumenism:
Says Rome Worse Today than 450 Years Ago."
"Another Victory of Roman Catholic Liberals"
"Liberals Winning in Rome"
With the prestige of *Reader's Digest* behind another exhibit, Otten's appraisal of the World Council of Churches began with this caption: "Must our Churches Finance Revolution?"[12]

"AntiTrinitarians in the NCC" (National Council of Churches) ran a title heading a protest against Swedenborgianism, a heresy some of his readers might have found difficulty even pronouncing.[13] This was followed by "The NCC's Latest Lawlessness" and "The NCC Anti-Christian Radicals."[14]

In 1925 a minister had set the pace for rhetoric of this type. In a paper read at the Northern Illinois District Convention he fumed: "Modernism, liberal theology, unionism, lodgism, non-attendance at church, lack of Christian education of the children, of love and zeal for the kingdom of God, family worship, the dance, the theater, birth control, entertainments, gambling devices, increasing opposition against the holy Christian Church, also against the preaching of God's Word."[15]

Now reading Otten's jeremiads, the Preus-Otten followers of older vintage felt like singing "Happy Days Are Here Again." Otten did not let them down.

Staid Episcopalians fell before a volley carrying the message "Clergy Assent to 30 Articles Dropped by Anglican Bishops."[16] "Rev. Kinsolving supports pre-marital sex," exploded another.[17] "Are the United Presbyterians Christian?" In a follow-up on a *Newsweek* article another page began, "Anything Now Goes."[18] The United Church of

Canada, Methodists, Eastern Orthodox—all fell before the onslaught of incendiary capitals.

Climaxing his presentation of Baptist views, Otten commented editorially on Southern Baptists' encouragement of pulpit exchanges between Jews and Christians:

> The Bible teaches that Jesus Christ is the only way to heaven and all those who do not recognize that Christ is true God are lost in sin. Anyone, including an unconverted Jew, who does not trust in the merits of Christ for his eternal salvation, will be damned. The unanimously adopted SBC resolution leaves room for the notion that men can be saved without Christ. It attacks the scriptural teaching which forbids worshipping with non-Christians.[19]

This analysis was along the lines of a rebuke administered some pages earlier to Roman Catholic theologian Dr. Rosemary Ruether.[20]

Nor was this the end. Under the headline "Fundamental and Neo-Evangelicalism," such heresies as "millenianism, a general conversion of the Jewish nation, synergism, and predestination to Hell" slumped under the continuing withering fire. Readers who might not have understood all the words nevertheless knew that whatever Otten attacked was bad.

With the combination to orthodoxy safely tucked away in Otten's head, there was no longer any need for "Key '73," an ecumenical program of evangelism. In a deft flanking movement of guilt by association, Otten rounded out this stage of the bombardment with a twenty-fifth section entitled "Cults," in which the first headline ran: "The Jehovah's Witnesses' Bible and the RSV."[21] This attack on the "Cult" was but a lull, and displayed 'conservative' contempt for ecumenism. With readers' antagonisms mounting to explosive pitch and their confidence in Sola Missouri rising to unparalled heights, Otten brought all of Lutheranism into range.

"The Lutheran World Federation Today" read the title to another reprinted lecture.[22] A sub-heading highlighted "Violence and Civil Disobedience."[23] According to an article entitled "The Church of Sweden," citizens of that country were guilty of denial of the supernatural, sponsorship of Communism and numerous other crimes, including militant atheism.[24] "The Lutheran Council in the USA Today"[25] ran another banner, under which a number of iniquities, including entry into the political arena and women's ordination, were cited. Of the Lutheran Church in America, Otten said: "The LCA Allows Denial of

Christ's Deity."[26] Quoting an article by Dr. Robert Preus,[27] brother of President Preus, Otten moved in closer to the capital city of heresy. According to Robert Preus, the Missouri Synod was obligated, in view of the evidence he cited, to suspend fellowship with the American Lutheran Church. The last title, "ALC Snubs Lutheran Church—Missouri Synod"[28] was bound to unleash retaliation for the suffering undergone by a bruised, collective ego.

All this, however, was but warmup for the climactic bombardment of heresy in the Lutheran Church—Missouri Synod. Made all the more effective by the Big Lie of guilt through association, a sub-title like "The Infiltration of Theological Liberalism" [29] suggested sinister, subversive forces, akin to those exposed in the pages that preceded. Among the eminent theologians marked for administrative execution was Martin Marty of the University of Chicago.[30] Dr. Arthur Carl Piepkorn fell under the scornful prose of a fundamentals-oriented teacher at Trinity College, Deerfield, Illinois.[31] In support of his auxiliary forces, Otten reprinted another essay of his in which he spoke as a superior officer reprimanding a corporal:

> While we did urge the election of President Preus, in all candor we must say that we are not entirely pleased with all his actions since his election. We have told him that he erred when he appointed such LCMS liberals as Martin Marty to official LCMS committees. Our president is fast getting the reputation among liberals and conservatives of not being entirely consistent. We have told him that he must speak the truth at all times regardless of the consequences. We have informed him that he can trust us to tell the truth but not to play any political game. God does not bless political maneuvering. Liberals should not be removed from the LCMS through political action or by 'making it miserable' for them. They should be given a fair hearing. We must show them true Christian love. If they refuse to retract their attacks upon Scripture, then and only then should they be asked to leave the LCMS.[32]

Answering the query, "Why don't you leave the Missouri Synod? Isn't the battle hopeless?" he had replied on November 9, 1970, "Christians should not run away from the battle. A soldier in the midst of battle dare not lay down his arms and go to sleep even if he is weary of fighting. . . . Liberals cannot stand up to the truth. Many of them are cowards. . . . My fellow Lutherans, let's not run away from the liberals. We have the truth on our side. We have real scholarship on our side. Above all, God is on our side and he has promised us the victory." [33]

111

Target - Concordia Seminary

After having taken on the world, Otten let loose all his powder in a final brain-shattering bombardment numbered "XXVIII" and entitled "Concordia Seminary, St. Louis." [34]

Complete with Latin captions, his reprinted essay "Why Investigate Concordia Seminary?" warned about an "all-out attack against historic Christianity." [35] He spoke of "treason" and "liberalism," of Jonah and the big fish. He spoke of Moses, Isaiah, Daniel and David as authors of the literary works traditionally ascribed to them, with emphasis on "inerrancy." He lamented the filtering of liberal views into Sunday School materials. He condemned evolution in the same smoke with anathemas on J, E, D and P. He gave top billing to Pete Seeger, Jesse Jackson and the Beatles.[36]

"The War is On," Otten underlined, "and you don't fight a war with spitballs." In bold letters he ordered the troops to "Back Preus!" In the column adjoining this order he submitted a photograph of this headline from the *St. Louis Globe Democrat,* March 7, 1972: Seminary Head Defies Ban Against Teacher.[37]

Having identified the opposing generals, Otten printed in full the formal declaration of war: It was President Preus' "A Statement of Scriptural and Confessional Principles." Then followed headlines like these:

"Fact Finding Committee Finds False Doctrine at Concordia Seminary." [38]

"Problems with the Virgin Birth: Most of St. Louis Seminary Professors 'Caught On' Historicity of Adam and Eve." [39]

In a final appeal to the collective ego of the Missouri Synod, Otten offered his readers a digest of President Preus' report on the Seminary faculty. Editorially, he commented,

All seminary professors who refuse to retract their false doctrine must now be removed from their teaching positions. . . . Orthodox convention resolutions and investigating reports are fine. But they are not enough. Action is needed. . . . THANKS TO THE FFC (Fact-Finding Committee) AND PREUS, BUT NOW LET'S HAVE SOME ACTION BEFORE IT IS TOO LATE." [40]

Filled to overflowing with suspicion of heresy, it is surprising that Otten's readers could take still more. But Otten probed synapses that were inaccessible to the less experienced. Knowing that the name of

112

Tietjen need only be pronounced and the troops would make their dash toward the enemies' fortress, he headlined a succeeding page in huge italics:

" 'Garbage In, Garbage Out'—Tietjen on Seminary Investigation." [41] With his graphic critique of Dr. Preus' investigative effort, Tietjen had touched the Synod's rawest nerve in its collective ego. The President was the epitome of the Synod, which in all its position statements spoke as the Pope did on but very rare occasions, *EX CATHEDRA*. To call that collective will into question was tantamount to defying the Holy Spirit Himself.

After winding up his Handbook with this citation and other references to the seminary's alleged errors and official rebuttals of the same, Otten could afford to rest his troops. During the months of May and June he would merely have to keep up morale while they waited for the signal to close in on Tietjen and his forces.

"Affirm"

On drill in another part of Missouri was an allied army, marching under the banner AFFIRM. Sponsored by "Balance, Inc.," a name that signalled President Preus' increasing concern for sanity and avoidance of extremism, the journal *Affirm* aimed to overcome the disadvantages of notoriety associated with *Christian News*. Much stuffier than Otten's paper, less informative, and more onesided in its presentations, *Affirm* appealed to a clientele who felt that they could now read attacks on heretics without dousing themselves and their environs with airwick. It was the kind of paper one could receive in an unplain wrapper.

The first issue appeared in March, 1971, and among its earliest editors were Dr. Walter A. Maier, Jr., who would become a vice president of the Synod at the New Orleans Convention, 1973, and the Rev. Ewald J. Otto, who would at the same convention be elected to Concordia Seminary's Board of Control and later become its Chairman.

Despite a low-key tone of apparent moderation, a separatistic accent came through unmuffled, even in the earliest issue. Speaking of "the right and duty to *exclude from membership*" in the same breath with the "obligation *to retain and confess everything* which she believes to be an article of faith revealed in God's Word," one of the contributors wrote:

113

> Exclusion from membership means simply that a synod is *serious* about her confession, and cannot in good conscience continue to be identified with those who question and deny her confession, even though they may be Christian.[42]

The last page of the issue left no doubt in anyone's mind as to the ultimate purpose of *Affirm*. Under the caption, "The Sem Inquiry," readers were appraised of President Preus' "equable course" in the face of "critical articles" published in "the secular press." [43] They were also reminded of the "clarity and kindliness" with which Dr. E. C. Weber had refuted Concordia Seminary's open letter of January 5, 1971. With *Christian News,* the editors of *Affirm* were clearly of the view that Preus and Concordia were on collision course.

In the May issue, Dr. Robert Preus, friend of Herman Otten and brother of President Preus, urged suspension of fellowship with the American Lutheran Church at the upcoming Milwaukee convention.[44] Women's ordination and historical criticism came under attack in tones that sounded very much like those of *Christian News.* As in the case of Otten's paper, there was no mistaking the gut feelings of the editors: "The ecclesiastical elites, to which so few of us belong but which derive their power and position and income from us, apparently, item by item, toss orthodox beliefs overboard as so much excess ballast." [45] So ran the front page in June of 1971. "Easily wounded pride," amateur psychologists might have said. But to *Affirm*'s readers the editors wrote out of highest principle.

That *Affirm*'s editors considered the Synod thoroughly polarized long before the New Orleans Convention was clear from the 'pocket dictionary' offered to Milwaukee Convention delegates. Printed in the June, 1971, issue, the 'dictionary' gave two definitions, one entitled 'Liberal' and the other 'Conservative' for a number of key words, from 'Abortion' to 'Youth.' If a delegate knew beforehand whether a given speaker at the convention was 'liberal,' he could easily discover what the speaker meant by looking at the dictionary. If the speaker was not known to the delegate, he was to listen carefully to the speaker's words and then consult his dictionary. At a glance any delegate could see who was on the side of good and who was on the side of evil. Under the word "Investigation" appeared this distinction:

> LIBERAL: An autocratic, dictatorial, and repressive tool used by "Chairman Jao" (President Preus) on the never-to-be-questioned liberal majority in the faculty of Concordia Seminary, St. Louis.
> CONSERVATIVE: "Beloved, do not believe every spirit, but test (investi-

gate) the spirits to see whether they are of God; for many false prophets have gone out into the world." I John 4:1.

The word "Mission" received these definitions:

LIBERAL: "The purpose and work of the Church, i.e., to lift the down-trodden of the world to a higher level of material, social, political and psychological bliss. Occasionally the words 'Jesus' and 'love' are used in connection with this work.
CONSERVATIVE: The purpose and work of Christ's church on earth, i.e., to rescue as many as people as possible everywhere from eternal damnation and for life with Jesus Christ forever. This is accomplished by the Holy Spirit who works through Christ's people in the Gospel. (See 'evangelism,' 'evangelical,' 'Gospel,' and 'revelation.')[46]

Momentum increased over the next two years, and if any heretical, theological growth survived Otten's journalistic napalm, *Affirm*'s editors resolved to double-dose it out of existence. In a thirty-eight page document entitled "Occasional Papers," published in Spring, 1973, *Affirm* torpedoed historical criticism to shreds with a mixture of reason and statements like these:

I believe that practically all our differences and problems in doctrine within our Synod stem from the use of this methodology.[47]

Another wrote:

If the mere label 'methods' automatically guarantees diplomatic immunity from inspection, it will soon be used to smuggle in subversive doctrine! Dr. R. Preus' restriction is surely both methodological and necessary: "Specifically, any literary genre that would in itself be immoral or involve deceit or error is not compatible with Biblical inerrancy and is not to be found in Scripture, for example, myth, etiological tale, midrash, legend, or saga according to the usual designation of these forms."[48]

Close The Seminary?

Under the title, "Some Sobering Reflections on the Use of the Historical-Critical Method," Prof. Martin Scharlemann, of Concordia Seminary, presented a tightly argued case for the importance of recognizing "the dimension of divine intervention into the cause-and-effect chain which keeps so much of life confined and limited." [49] Lucidity had always been a mark of Scharlemann's writing and now it gained from association with other articles. On the other hand, readers who were prejudiced against Concordia Seminary could not fail to find reinforcement for their conviction that historical criticism was *per se* evil.

During the "renaissance" he once spoke of, Scharlemann would have granted his colleagues the same courtesies he had extended to historical-critical scholars at the Pontifical Biblical Institute, Rome, Italy, in a publication that appeared only the year before. In this 1972 publication, Scharlemann had praised the Roman Catholic scholars for their outstanding contributions to biblical studies. "Much to the relief of biblical scholars," he wrote, "the term 'inerrancy' does not occur" in the conciliar document on Divine Revelation.[50] "Roman Catholic Biblical Scholars," he went on to affirm, "are learning well the lessons of *Formgeschichte* (form-criticism) and of *Redaktionsgeschichte* (redaction-criticism)."[51] By way of summary of their work, he quoted a sentence from the conciliar document:

> The interpreter must investigate what meaning the sacred writer intended to express and actually expressed in particular circumstances as he used contemporary literary forms in accordance with the situation of his own time and culture.[52]

After further exposition of inspiration, Scharlemann interpreted 2 Timothy 3:16 (about 'God-breathed' Scripture) in the light of Genesis 2:7 (about man who receives God's breath of life). He concluded his paragraph with these words:

> The point in this connection would be that as man is the product of God's creative work so the Scriptures are the handiwork of the Holy Spirit in all the phases of their coming into being: prophetic utterance, oral tradition, the writings of prophet, apostle and evangelist.[53]

Now, in *Affirm,* all such processes appeared to be illegitimate. Lamented Scharlemann:

> Devotees of the Historical-Critical Method seldom have any stomach for the Reformation principle that the Scriptures are the *sola* (not *prima*) *regula fidei.* (The only, not primary rule of faith, Ed.) For when men begin to analyze texts with the aid of principles of literary and redaction criticism, they find sources of authority not only (if they find

them at all) in the text of Scriptures but also, and even primarily, at various points in the history of the development of the text from oral tradition, literary sources, through various redactions to the final form as given in the canonical text.[54]

Other issues of *Affirm* in March, April and May continued the attack, and the titles of articles seemed to glow with greater intensity:

"The Abyss of Missouri"
  "How to Destroy Orthodox Doctrine in Synod While Appearing to be Orthodox"
    "The Double Standard of Some District Presidents"

With arrival of the June "B" issue it was practically impossible to distinguish the voice of *Affirm's* editors from that of Herman Otten's. "Close the 'Sem' " headlined the front page.[55]

"The solutions proposed by Missourians rule the whole gamut of possibilities," wrote the editors. "Some ask for the resignation of the Seminary's president. Some want a sweeping resignation of the Sem's whole faculty. Some would let just the five faithful remain on the Sem's teaching staff. Some propose that the Board of Control resign since it hasn't controlled the Sem, at least not in the way in which the great majority in Missouri would like to see the Seminary controlled. And some want to close down the Sem. Now. Totally. Perhaps for good. Perhaps for a few years."[56]

Near the end of the editorial, "the most radical of all steps: close the Sem itself" was again offered as last-ditch alternative, with these comments:

> *Affirm* doesn't recommend this course to the New Orleans delegates or to its readers. It urges them all to watch events, to pray, to work toward some solution other than this most radical of all solutions. But it does say that, as the Convention unfolds, all these options must be kept in mind, and if events make it clear that only the most radical of solutions will change the course of Missouri's history and bring her back to the old and tried ways, then the delegates must pray God for wisdom and strength to do what hitherto had been—amongst us all— the unthinkable: close the Sem, for our Lord's honor! [57]

In view of subsequent actions after the New Orleans Convention, including the closing of the synod's other major seminary in Springfield, Illinois, and demolition of the Synod's academically top-ranked Senior

College in Fort Wayne, Indiana, this was no idle threat, but rather the ultimate solution conceived by men who believed as Hitler did about the Jews, that Concordia Seminary was the seedbed of most evil in Missouri.

Chapter 12

BATTLE OF NEW ORLEANS, STAGE 1

In October 1967, one of the Missouri Synod's outstanding theologians wrote: "Under any circumstances, these are exciting days in theology. Whatever signs there are of irresponsibility may in fact be expressions of a radical theology of impatience. It is an age for creative opportunity and blessed is that church body which knows what time it is!"[1]

Many, however, feared that tomorrow might be different from yesterday and they were resolved to protect themselves against the future by turning the clock back at New Orleans in 1973 to Missouri Synod's Standard Time—Seventeenth Century Orthodoxy.

The same theologian also cited the experience of the great critical scholar Father Marie Joseph Lagrange, whose interpretation of the Old Testament had become suspect. He was therefore "relieved of teaching Old Testament subjects and transferred to the field of New Testament studies," apparently considered a less sensitive area by his superiors. "Of course," Dr. Martin Scharlemann reminded his readers, "a church body does not solve any problems this way."[2] It was one of the rare instances in which one of his prophecies proved to be false.

"EVER ONLY ALL FOR THEE"

So ran the theme on the cover of the CONVENTION WORKBOOK (Reports and Overtures) 50th Regular Convention, Lutheran Church—Missouri Synod, New Orleans, Louisiana, July 6–13, 1973.

It is custom in the Missouri Synod to receive proposals for convention action from member congregations. These are then printed for the study in the weeks preceding a convention. The proposals, or overtures, together with the reports from various boards and commissions, are then run through various convention committees, which formulate resolutions for action by the convention.

Sexism appeared high on the list of problem areas. There were repeated pleas to "return to our previous Scriptural position regarding woman suffrage."[3] In 1969 the Denver Convention had reversed the Synod's long-standing tradition against women's right to vote in their church assembly. Now a number of overtures proposed that the Synod rescind that resolution.

More heat began to generate from the overtures listed under the title "Other Concerns." Here came direct attacks on Concordia Seminary's faculty, with pleas to recognize President Preus' definition of "inerrancy" as the Synod's "historic position," "To Affirm Adam and Eve as Historical Beings," "To insist that 'Almah' in Isaiah 7:14 Means Virgin," "To Suspend Professor and Editor of 'CTM' " (the Concordia Theological Monthly, theological journal of Concordia Seminary).[4]

All this, however, was only warmup for the real purpose in assembling at New Orleans, which was to settle "the Seminary problem." The sixty-six pages following the title "3 Seminary Issues" left no doubt on that score.[5] And the manner of presentation suggested the kind of tactics that could be expected in the Convention Hall.

The Board of Control of Concordia Seminary submitted its report in less than two pages.[6] Given equal billing were two minority reports totalling over six pages in length. The first was signed by Walter C. Dissen and E. C. Weber; the second by Eugene E. Fincke and Charles H. Burmeister.[7] These two reports criticized actions and decisions of both Concordia Seminary's president, John H. Tietjen, and the majority of its Board of Control, without opportunity for rebuttal in the workbook by the parties subjected to such unprecedented mode of attack. Pleas for official endorsement of President Preus' A Statement of Scriptural and Confessional Principles were in the same company with demands for rejection, removal, or restriction of historical-critical methodology.[8]

Except for a few overtures favoring commendation of the St. Louis Faculty, most proposed resolutions ranged from demand for removal of an undefined number of professors to suspension of all who signed "Affirmations of Faith" in Part I of Faithful To Our Calling, Faithful To Our Lord. The Board of Control did not fare better. Incompetent, vacillating, uncooperative, negligent, were some of the kinder descriptions. Affirm's suggestions to close the seminary echoed in a number of overtures that appeared to border on hysteria.[9]

What every primed delegate was waiting for came under the heading "Individuals." Hundreds of thousands of dollars, not to speak of an astronomical number of people-hours, had already been spent to bring one man to heel. Close to a million dollars more were about to be spent to make President Preus' wish come true: "Tietjen must go!"

Overtures either called for Tietjen's resignation or simply demanded his removal. And it was not likely that the Convention would ignore the numerous proposals that followed urging the convention to "commend" Dr. Preus, thus in effect reversing the Board of Control's commendation of the faculty.

Inasmuch as the President of the Synod traditionally selects the floor committee, who presents the convention with proposed legislation a few minutes before sessions, the outcome of the convention was subject to almost complete control by an incumbent whose integrity permitted him to make no pretense of leading his church with impartiality.

'Liberals' found themselves doing K.P. on "Stewardship and Finance," "Evangelism," "Special and Sundry Matters" and "Work Program Review." Preus' chief lieutenants manned the heavy mortar installations. "You don't put gangsters on the Supreme Court," commented one delegate in justification of the stacking process. Chairing the committee on "Theology and Church Relations" was Karl Barth, a member of Preus' Fact-Finding Committee. To E. H. Zimmerman of Indiana, Preus had assigned chairmanship of the committee on "Higher Education." Ensuring "Seminary Issues" was L. Niemoeller, a man Preus knew would remain, under heaviest fire, stolidly impervious to the flack of any theological ideas which deviated one jot or tittle from the Synod's past pronouncements. With not a nerve of vacillation in his entire body, Niemoeller's very visage could replace the Rock of Gibraltar as a signature of reliability in the event a nuclear blast were to erase that symbol of permanence from the face of the earth. He was a good man, but with conscience trapped in an evil moment of history.

Keynote

In his opening address, President Preus warmed up the delegates for their first main task—his re-election. His remarks were an invitation to pure triumphalism and were punctuated with words that sounded patronizing and even offensive to minorities. Speaking of the Synod's past, he said: "We are celebrating the 95th anniversary of our

121

entrance into black work this year, and there is no more noble action in the chronicles of our Synod than the decision to minister to these poor, confused, frightened, lonely, unhappy people."[10] Preus had quite evidently not read Dr. Andrew Schulze's *Race Against Time.* No "agitator" himself, Dr. Schulze pointed out in his dossier of synodical prejudice how even Dr. John W. Behnken, long-time president of the synod, had not moved aggressively beyond a pre-election position in which he had stated: "As far as mission work among the Negroes is concerned, our Southern people try to do their part, but we know that it is absolutely impossible for us to sanction social equality."[11] With his one sentence Preus had relieved the guilt of a century.

Latent anti-Semitism received a shot in the arm from sentences that formed part of the conclusion: "As one man has put it, the most tragic man in history is the one who can learn nothing from history. We see the history of the Jewish nation. We see the history of other Christian churches, we see the failures and the catastrophes of human life all around us, when men depart from the Word of the Lord, when they turn their backs on the Lord Jesus Christ and His Gospel and forgiveness. . ."[12] The statements themselves were made without malice, but Preus could lose no votes with words like these. After calling the convention to order with a gavel made from a beam from the Synod's historic log cabin in Perry County, Missouri, President Preus made his official report to the Convention. Against a background of the Synod's long years of success he painted the peril of the moment. Mincing no words over the identity of the combatants in the current struggle, he declared: "It is no secret to any of you that the controversy in our midst on the authority of Holy Scripture has centered largely between the synodical President's office and the administration and faculty of Concordia Seminary in St. Louis, although reverberations and problems in this area exist throughout all parts of the Synod."[13] Anticipating adoption of his own "A Statement of Scriptural Doctrine and Principles," he chose his diction carefully:

> "I affirm before God and in the presence of all of you that I am convinced that the doctrinal position I have set forth and taught is nothing more than the position which has been confessed in our Synod on the basis of God's Word and our Lutheran Confessions for 125 years."[14]

Then, in a bid for a firm mandate he informed the delegates of the terms on which he would accept reappointment. Speaking of "the Synod's position on the Holy Scriptures," he said:

"I say to you in all candor, before you choose the man to occupy the President's chair, that it (The Synod's position) will continue to be my position. . . In fact, I could not in good conscience accept any position in this church body, whether as a pastor, teacher or official, if I were expected to carry out my responsibilities on any other terms."[15]

Then with all the flourish of a presidential candidate with sights on the Oval Office he climaxed this part of his campaign: "For the official position of this great church body is, and by God's grace shall ever remain, the position which I believe, teach and confess with all my heart."[16] Radical Integrity had spoken with all the force of a horizontal conscience. Preus' Will and the Will of the Synod were meshing to perpetuate synodical infallibility.

Only one man posed even a partial threat to Preus' re-election. Unfortunately for the Moderates, this gentleman wished to identify with the good Missouri Synod of yesterday. Up until the campaign for Preus' election at Denver, no open politicking had ever been undertaken to fill the presidential post. Calls were supposed to come from the Lord. In keeping with that tradition, Dr. Oswald J. Hoffmann, successor to Walter A. Maier as Lutheran Hour preacher, refused to commit himself as an avowed candidate. Since a synodical bylaw required a candidate's advance notice of willingness to serve, Hoffmann was ineligible, and an attempt by Moderates to amend the Bylaw lost on a standing vote. Cries for a division of the house fell on deaf ears. It was a test of strength, and Moderates sniffed the first acrid smoke of approaching defeat.

Votes to Spare

With Hoffmann out of the running, Preus had over 40% of the congregations of the Synod behind him, and the announcement of his commanding lead electrified his right-wing followers.

Seated among them were more than fifteen delegates from the Brazil District. According to veteran observers, it was the first documentable case of vote-buying in the history of the Synod. Ordinarily a few Brazilian Lutherans attended the convention of the Synod, but the right-wingers' war chest had made a much larger delegation possible. To Brazilian pastors on very low incomes compared to those of their North American colleagues, the invitation was a great temptation. But in most cases its problematic aspect was easily overcome through the understanding that their presence could very well spell the salvation of the Mother-Church which had in the past been so generous to her Brazilian relative. Others among them recognized an alleged political objective behind the offer of a trip to New Orleans and refused to compromise their consciences.

With his customary polish, President Preus had earlier turned what could have been a disastrous and, as it turned out, unnecessary maneuver, into a political plus. In his presidential report he not only praised the Brazilian delegation, but at the same time scolded his opposition. "On behalf of the Synod," he said, "I want to take this opportunity to publicly apologize to the Brazil delegates, and to all our brethren in the Brazil District, for the unfortunate reference to these brethren as a 'foreign invasion.' "[17]

The ploy paid off. On the very first ballot 606 voters closed their eyes to what many considered the most shameful blot on Missouri's history—the buying of votes in the Church of God. The fact that many had voted for Preus against better knowledge suggested to people concerned about symptoms of moral decay, that the rot had already set in.

Preus' nearest rival was the Rev. William Kohn, a peace-loving churchman, who was more interested in building bridges over troubled waters than in sinking the enemy's fleet. He received 340 votes. Moderates had suffered a disheartening repulse. Offense was now clearly out of the question. They would have to be content with defensive measures.

Voting on the Word of God

Without losing a moment to identify officially the Synod's will with his own brain, Preus attempted to clear the way for the big gun— adoption of a resolution that would make it possible for the Synod legally to adopt doctrinal resolutions by majority vote. Once that had been done, Preus had the delegate machinery to hoist his "A Statement of Scriptural and Confessional Principles" into position. The resolution, numbered 5-03,[18] was designed to clarify Article VIII,C of the Synod's Constitution, which read:

All matters of doctrine and of conscience shall be decided only by the Word of God. All other matters shall be decided by a majority vote. In case of a tie vote the President may cast the deciding vote.

Moderates held that this article precluded any vote in convention on matters involving doctrine. Those to the right of center quoted various synodical fathers in support of a vote. According to C. F. W. Walther and Franz Pieper, two of the Synod's most revered saints, the purpose of a vote on a doctrinal issue was "not to decide the correctness of a doctrine," "but to learn by way of the vote whether *all* have *recognized what is right* and are in agreement with it." Article VIII in turn took care of those who opposed the synodical doctrine. Since it was inconceivable to anyone in the Synod that the Synod could, as a Synod, take an incorrect view of doctrine, a vote meant that those who opposed the Synod's will at a given convention would fall into one of two classifications, depending on the identity of the majority. If traditionalists won, those who publicly opposed or protested Synodical action involving matters of doctrine would be considered rebels, dissenters, and insurgents, with the threat of expulsion hanging over their heads in accordance with Article XIII. If moderates won, radical rightists would consider the majority guilty of false doctrine and would, in lieu of control of the legislative machinery, either enter into a state of confessional protest or reconstitute themselves as an authentic Missouri Synod.

Resolution 5-03, therefore, was a formal declaration of War. Once and for all the Synod was to determine whether it had the right and power to enforce Divine Truth.

Since the Moderates lacked delegate clout, they were compelled to resort to the very parliamentary maneuvering Preus had prophesied in his opening address. "I think it is safe to say," he cautioned, "that the delegates can reasonably expect a great deal of parliamentary maneuvering, points of order, and perhaps even some delaying and diversionary tactics, especially in the opening sessions of the convention."[19] This sentence not only meant that Preus took delight in a challenge of his political expertise, but that he also considered Resolution 5-03, or a reasonable equivalent, a tactical necessity to achieve his immediate strategic objective, the checkmating of John H. Tietjen.

As Moderates were to discover, Preus could not be outwitted in the playing of political games, for he was able to operate with the principle THE END JUSTIFIES THE MEANS to an extent Moderates found uncomfortable for their own consciences. Preus was thoroughly acquainted with secular political strategies, and his originality and claim to a place in church history resided in his ability to bring them into ecclesiastical play to a degree never before seen in the Missouri Synod, nor for that matter perhaps even in pre-Reformation Rome. The most, therefore, that Moderates could hope to achieve was a blunting of the edge of madness that was about to slice through their beloved Synod. If they could get past this convention without material alteration of the Constitutional safeguards, they might be able to appeal to a ground-swell interest in the saner governing methods used by such statesmen of more recent memory as John W. Behnken and Oliver C. Harms.

Under their leadership radicals of any stripe were unsuccessful in controlling the thought processes of the Synod. Efforts were made to maintain balance. If, for example, creative people were employed in the development of educational resource materials, administration made sure that more traditionally oriented people controlled some of the editorial exit routes. Committees and boards always included a mix of what could in popular terms be called liberal and conservative, without suggestion of polarization. If anything, traditionalists remained at all times in firm control of the Synodical machinery, or at least en-joyed respect for their convictions. Eloquent testimony to this fact is the long decades it look to declare that worship and prayer with mem-bers of the American Lutheran Church no longer constituted a doc-trinal and synodical sin. Moreover, to this day the Missouri Synod has joined neither the Lutheran World Federation nor the World Council of Churches. Compared to other progressive denominations in Chris-tendom, the Missouri Synod has in its most alleged liberal moments remained conservative. As a Presbyterian elder reminded one of our members: "With you, it's only a matter of more or less conservative." But those days of sanity were now gone, and there would be no return.

On The Way to Infallibility—2-12

Since Resolution 5-03 was not the most brilliant bit of legislation ever to be put on paper, being even incoherent in spots, the fact that it got mired in slippery parliamentary debate did not phase Preus. Lose some, win some, was the name of the game. Give Resolution 5-03 a temporary rest and introduce another that achieves the same objec-tive! He had outwitted his opposition with such crossfire maneuver at Milwaukee, in 1971. It was time to outflank them again, and surprise, in which he was expert, was of the essence. On Monday, July 9, Reso-lution 2-12, a joint effort of the Committee on Theology and Church Relations and of the Committee on Seminary issues, was presented to the convention.[20]

The aisles were cleared, and President Preus was invited by Chairman Niemoeller to address the convention. In sum, he ordered the delegates to assume for themselves the right to speak *ex cathedra,* with infallible utterance. As the official minutes recorded: "The convention must decide what it wants. Someone ought to have the authority to determine who should supervise doctrine and how our faith should be interpreted. We must retain the authority of the synodical voice and allow our officials to act. We should not delude ourselves as to what is at stake."

Shocked moderates recalled that only once before in her history had Missourians heard such appeal for absolute authority, and they had sent Martin Stephan across the Mississippi for his rebellion against the Reformation. Now an entire delegate convention was being charged to void the Missouri Synod's earliest contract with truth.

Those familiar with ancient Greek culture lifted eyes to heaven with pleas for mercy on Missouri. Greeks knew how *Koros* (satiety) begat *Hybris* (insolence) and *Hybris* begat *Ate* (blindness and delusion). Aghast and helpless, armed, they felt, only with the Word of truth and Robert's Rules of Order, moderates marched to meet the "juggernaut," as they termed the process of the convention. Three-fifths of the convention votes could be counted on by Preus. But a two-thirds majority would be required to "call the question." That is, it would take a two-thirds vote of the assembly to call for a halt to debate and then have the resolution offered for simple majority passage. To moderates, it was like the Maginot line for the French defenders against Hitlerian aggression and like the narrows at Thermopylae when Greece in 480 B.C. fought against the Persian invader under Xerxes.

Unfortunately for the moderates, the parliamentary rule was also a broken reed of Egypt. Hitler simply ignored the Maginot line and outflanked it, and the Persians, aided by an informant who guided the Persians along a mountain pass, succeeded in ambushing the finest warriors of Hellas.

On Tuesday morning, after Resolution 2-12 got bogged down in the two-thirds rule, Dr. Theodore Nickel, who had reached 65 without being retired, quoted sections from Robert's Rules of Order on the rights of the majority. Gilbert LaHaine, Sr., a businessman from Lansing, Michigan, promised to move up a more efficient emplacement on the morrow. He said he was filing notice that on Wednesday he would move that "the standing rules of the convention be changed to provide that following 30 minutes of debate on any motion the chair shall

127

call the previous question and that only a simple majority of registered voters be required to terminate debate and, further, that should the motion to call the previous question fail to secure a majority the chairman shall after 15 more minutes of debate once more put the motion to call the previous question at which time if passed by a simple majority debate shall cease and that this procedure be followed after every 15 minutes of debate."[21] Thus, the entire moderate line that was entrenched behind Robert's Rules could be enfiladed at the will of Preus and his timepiece.

As it turned out, Resolution 2-12 made history before Wednesday. In the person of aging Dr. Theodore Nickel, who was fronting for Preus at the podium, the majority of the delegates saw before them a gentle, gospel-oriented spokesman for the past. Under such and other variations of increasing administrative pressure, moderates began to feel that the political edge of this convention could not be stopped. What hope had they if the majority even declined a proposal to have the chairman lead the convention in prayer before controversial resolutions? The only thing left was to endure. Some moderate sympathizers even thought that the last resolve of Resolution 2-12 protected members of the Synod from tyrannical reprisal. It read: *"Resolved,* That the Synod reaffirm its position (Milwaukee *Proceedings,* Res. 2-21 and 5-24) that such statements, insofar as they are in accord with the Scriptures and the pattern of doctrine set forth in the Lutheran Symbols, are, pursuant to Article II of the Synod's constitution, binding upon all its members. (Cf. also Article VII)"[22] "Insofar as" seemed to be a line no aggressor could cross, and the less politically astute succumbed. They had learned too well their catechism's rejoinder to "put the best construction on everything." Soon they would learn that Preus was through playing games.

Acting with "chaotic vigor," the Synod carried Resolution 2-12 by a vote of 653-381, the largest plurality mustered by Preus' party at this convention. With this adoption the convention, according to the Minutes, stated "that Article II of the Synod's Constitution is to be understood as requiring the formulation and adoption of synodical doctrinal statements."[23] This form of resumé in the official proceedings suggested a stronger magisterial tone than the resolution itself expressed. The *resolve* in question read: "That the Synod understand Article II of its Constitution *as permitting* (italics ours), and at times even requiring, the formulation and adoption of doctrinal statements as definitive of the Synod's position relative to controverted issues . . ."[24] This subtle alteration was probably not intentional, for official minutes are necessarily brief, but it does display the mindset underlying the passage of this resolution.

If there was doubt in anyone's mind as to the ultimate purpose of Resolution 2-12, the session on Tuesday evening, July 10, completely obliterated it.

Adoption of Resolution 3-01 was to be Preus' ultimate gift to church history, for this resolution would declare *"A Statement of Scriptural and Confessional Principles"* to be *in all its parts* (italics ours) Scriptural and in accord with the Lutheran Confessions" and a " 'more formal and comprehensive statement of belief' in the sense of Resolution 5-24 of the 1971 Milwaukee Convention."[25] Preus moved much of the furniture in the heaven and earth of the Missouri Synod to prepare for this moment. Like ancient Roman generals who came back from the wars with kings and princes and slaves in tow, with the produce of many lands trailing behind in heavily laden wagons, Preus was on the verge of winning and celebrating his triumph. Only Robert's Rules of Order stood in the way of infallibility. Despite all his political acumen, Preus could not muster the two-thirds vote necessary to close debate and bring 3-01 to a vote.

Abomination—3-12

Scarcely recuperated from partial survival of Tuesday's ordeal, moderate defenders on Wednesday morning received notice which amounted to unconditional surrender. Printed in the official orders was Resolution 3-12 with these concluding whereases and resolveds.

WHEREAS, Overture 3-182A (CW, pp. 160–161) addressed to the 50th regular convention of The Lutheran Church—Missouri Synod *correctly* observes that the disagreements which presently trouble our Synod are indeed matters of doctrine and conscience; and

WHEREAS, These disagreements especially pertaining to the inspiration, inerrancy, and authority of the Scriptures have been correctly assessed as so fundamental that the alternatives are mutually exclusive (President's Report, p. 25, CTM, November 1972, p. 666); and

WHEREAS, These disagreements pertaining to the doctrine of the Holy Scriptures have far-reaching implications for all of theology (to wit: the doctrines of creation, the fall, the third use of the Law, etc.); and

WHEREAS, These disagreements stem from those in the Synod who disagree with the Synod's position; and

WHEREAS, The faculty of the St. Louis seminary is largely responsible for these disagreements by promulgating doctrine at variance with the Synod's position as this is evidenced not only by the FFC's (Fact-Finding Committee's) Report but also by Part I of the faculty document, *Faithful To Our Calling, etc,*; and

WHEREAS, The president of the St. Louis seminary not only concurs in the doctrinal departures of the faculty from the position of the Synod, but also defends the faculty members and their doctrinal aberrations, and thereby has declared himself opposed to the Synod's position, and therefore unable to exercise doctrinal discipline; and

WHEREAS, The president of Concordia Seminary, St. Louis, is required by Bylaw 6.91 to be the spiritual, academic, and administrative head thereof; and

WHEREAS, Doctor John H. Tietjen as the president of aforesaid seminary has failed in all three categories in that he—

1. Allowed and fostered the teaching and dissemination of doctrine contrary to the Scripture and the Synod's historic confessional stance (Constitution, Article II, and the Charter of Concordia Seminary);
2. Became a principal party and failed to mediate and settle professorial and doctrinal disagreements;
3. Was administratively irresponsible;
4. Presumptuously and wrongfully assumed Board of Control duties and prerogatives;
5. On occasion intimidated Board of Control members;
6. Demeaned the integrity and position of certain faculty members;
7. Demeaned the office of the synodical President and defied the executive authority thereof;
8. Refused to cooperate with the synodical President particularly in doctrinal considerations;
9. Was insubordinate to the authority of the Board for Higher Education;
10. Failed to maintain careful watch over the spiritual welfare, personal life, and conduct of the student body; and

WHEREAS, For more than 2 years, attempts at conciliatory discussions and procedures have proved fruitless and the gravity of the situation calls for immediate action; and

WHEREAS, The *Handbook* of the Synod states, that, "the Synod, its boards and its members shall *first of all* hold him responsible in *all matters* pertaining to the institution" (6.91); therefore be it

RESOLVED, That The Lutheran Church—Missouri Synod in convention assembled, with deep regret, nonetheless, for cause hereinbefore stated, and in the best interests of the Synod, respectfully invite the resignation of Dr. John Tietjen as president and professor of Concordia Seminary, St. Louis, MO., effective August 1, 1973; and be it further

RESOLVED, That should the resignation herein invited not be forthcoming by the time of the adjournment of this convention, it appearing to this convention that a special authorization to the President of the Synod is in the best interests of the Synod, the President of the Synod be and hereby is authorized and empowered pursuant to Article XI, A 2 and B 8, of the Constitution to forthwith dismiss Dr. John H. Tietjen from the office of president and professor of Concordia Seminary, St. Louis; and be it further

RESOLVED, That the Board of Directors of Synod in either event attend to the financial needs of Dr. John H. Tietjen for an appropriate period of time; and be it finally

RESOLVED, That all proper and appropriate steps be taken for the election and calling of a new president of Concordia Seminary, St. Louis, Missouri.[26]

This was a case of pornography according to the fifth commandment (Thou shalt not kill). From the resolution it was apparent that to many in the Synod Tietjen was like the proverbial love of money, the root of all evil in Missouri. Two laymen expressed the feeling succinctly. Asked what the issues were, they said, "Well, this new pastor came in and soon young people were making banners for the sanctuary. And it's all because of that man Tietjen!" This was as rational as a northern pastor's opposition to Preus: "Why, he's not a German but a Norwegian!"

Moderates now felt like the defenders of the Alamo in the last hours of resistance. Deadly fire was pouring in from all directions. To keep the ammunition coming, delegate LaHaine kept his pledge to move for a change of the standing rules for the convention, so that close of debate might take place by simple majority vote. After considerable discussion, debate on his own motion was closed by a vote of 668-333. This meant that moderates were developing battle fatigue, while on the right wing there was some temporary shifting, for the vote to permit closure of debate by a simple majority carried only 548-479.

At that moment the moderates might as well have gone home, for Preus now had all the tanks at his command to run through his erstwhile opposition. But they felt obligated to offer a Christian presence in the face of ruthlessness they felt would come but which they were helpless to oppose. With Robert's Rules of Order torn out of their grasp, they resorted, said one participant, to complete confidence in the promises of the Gospel, and resolved among themselves to mount a stance of moral and spiritual protest against the travesty of constitutional procedures they were witnessing.

In a special address to the convention, Mr. Richard K. Fox, Jr., of

131

the Lutheran Human Relations Association of America, lamented the death especially of Dr. Martin Luther King and fingered racism as the most tragic problem of our times. The convention adopted a resolution urging members of the synod to combat racism and to promote equal opportunity in its own institutions.[27] What many of the Synod's Blacks failed to realize, however, was the intimate connection between racism and the political processes, not to speak of the fact that a number of synodical officials were guests of the Missouri Athletic Club, where full membership had long been limited to whites. Moderates, who had grappled with problems of racism, saw replayed before their very eyes the Synod's patterns of denominational exclusiveness, arrogant sense of superiority in acquisition of truth, and emphasis on master-servant relationships. Here they saw the perennial seedbeds for prejudice, racism and anti-semitism. After ninety-five years not a single Caucasian congregation had a Black minister, and many of the Synod's Black congregations were led by Caucasians. And within a few years, even a resolution such as this one at New Orleans would ring hollow when the Rev. Sterling Belcher, one of the few Black pastors in Missouri, would be cut off from his synodical district's subsidy for supporting moderates in their endeavor to halt the Synod's isolationist trend.

Preus' Hour of Glory—3-01

On Wednesday afternoon, July 11, President Jacob A. O. Preus' big moment came. By a vote of 562-455 on Resolution 3-01, the convention declared "A Statement of Scriptural and Confessional Principles" to be a "more formal and comprehensive statement of belief," and "in *all its parts* (italics ours), to be Scriptural and in accord with the Lutheran Confessions, and therefore a formulation which derives its authority from the Word of God and which expresses the Synod's position on current doctrinal issues."[28] To those familiar with Roman Catholic history the action was tantamount to claiming infallibility for Preus, notwithstanding the guarded disclaimers in the preamble to Resolution 3-01. Right-wingers now could imagine themselves back on the frontier. Like a zealous wagonmaster, Preus had defended his encampment and his ring of wagons against attacking Indians. With the muzzle of 3-01 firmly in place, Missouri's orthodoxy was assured.

As for the moderate forces, from the time of their arrival they had been under the tension of attempting to combat Preus' political machinery. Now that paint-by-number theology was officially in vogue, they were relieved of the necessity of victory and could afford the joy of losing. And what right-wingers saw them do that afternoon was to their way of thinking synodical treason. Ordinarily District Presidents, or Bishops, in the Missouri Synod consider themselves extensions of the synodical will. But that afternoon the Rev. Herman Neunaber, President of the Synod's Southern Illinois District asked that his concern about the resolution be entered into the official record. The Rev. Samuei Roth, who was later to head Evangelical Lutherans in Mission (ELIM), also asked that his objections be recorded. He then invited those who agreed with him to present their names in an orderly way at the Secretary's desk. Nearly 500 delegates, advisory delegates, and visitors moved forward and joined Roth in protest against the Synod's move toward sectarianism by singing over and over the first stanza of "The Church's One Foundation is Jesus Christ, Her Lord." With arms around each other, many wept for what they knew might never return. "It was a devastating experience to me to stand here and watch that happen," President Preus commented later. "I saw many of my friends and former students marching in that line, and it hurt."[29] A visiting pastor, however, said, "It was the most worshipful experience I had during the entire convention." What the Synod had always been on guard against—EXTREMISM—had rolled in with a tide that swept all restraints away. As *Forum* capsuled it:

> The administration's plan was now apparent to all. Equivocations, evasions and statements of denial notwithstanding, delegates realized that "A Statement" would in fact be used as a standard of orthodoxy and as a basis for discipline. The resolution condemning the Concordia Seminary faculty majority on the grounds of "A Statement" was already in hand.[30]

Some indication of the precarious mental balance at the convention was given by the remarks of the Rev. Paul Spitz in Wednesday's evening session. Referring to the demonstration at the close of the afternoon session he pleaded with the delegates to avoid any further maneuvering lest the convention be led into "rash action."[31] If it was Preus who had gotten to Spitz, this warning could have meant: "Tell the moderates to cool it. I'm not sure I can stop these crazies on my right." Was Spitz afraid that Preus' troops would act like the Russians on arriving in Berlin during World War II and roll fellowship with the American Lutheran Church into the Gulf of Mexico? Renounce relations with The Lutheran Council U.S.A.? Disband the English District? Order the closing of Concordia Seminary, a possibility suggested by Ewald Otto in *Affirm?* Or, order the closing of all the Synod's training institutions until a purge of all heretics had been completed?

Chapter 13

THE BATTLE OF NEW ORLEANS, STAGE 2

Frustrated for more than twenty years, the right-wingers had come a long way under Preus. At a convention held in Milwaukee, in 1945, they had been able to muster only a few weak voices against "liberal" proposals. At Cleveland, in 1962, a pastor had told his fellow delegates that he was ready to borrow money, if necessary, to oppose heretical developments in the Synod. In replying to this man's pitiful plea, Dr. Behnken assured him that he did not think such radical steps were necessary.

The Synod had always prized good judgment. But its officials had also worked hard over the years to space out the varieties of mind that a religious community necessarily invites. Now, on Wednesday, July 11, 1973, the Synod had not one, not two, nor even ten weak voices on the floor, but hundreds, and linked with sympathetic brethren they found in Preus a champion to drive evil once and for all out of Missouri's doctrinal paradise. This was their moment in the sun, and Paul Spitz' warning displayed pastoral insight.

Having come thus far, those who were now in the majority would overrule any attempt to rob them of their lawful prey, even if it took what moderates would construe as "ruthless resolution." It mattered not that Preus had reduced them to a statistic that ran anywhere from 550–650. It was a small price to pay for the privilege of saving the Missouri Synod for God.

With all the mightiest weapons in the right-wingers' depot now brought into firing position, the hour Herman Otten, Ewald Otto, and President Preus' brother had been savoring in rhetoric drew near on Wednesday evening, July 11. Forty-five members of Concordia Seminary's faculty were in the crosshair of Resolution 3-09:

135

TO DECLARE FACULTY MAJORITY POSITION IN VIOLATION OF ARTICLE II OF THE CONSTITUTION

This title in effect declared that the faculty reeked of insubordination, rebellion and treason against the Word of God and the very heart of Lutheranism—the Gospel of Jesus Christ. In addition to a "Preamble," the resolution bore an even longer introduction. The whereases spoke of "subversion of the authority of Scripture," of "Gospel reductionism," of a "denial of the third use of the Law," of refusal "on the part of the faculty to acknowledge as true any of the charges of false doctrine," and of "deviations in doctrine."[1] Except that the rhetoric now came from within the Synod rather than from without, these charges were reminiscent of another hysterical time when spies and saboteurs were seen in every German church of the Missouri Synod during World War I. When a seventy-five year old pastor was beaten and tarred in Southern Illinois; when schools and parsonages were painted yellow; and a mob, on the ready with rope, forced a Missouri Synod pastor to leave an Iowa county.[2] But the persecution of their own forbears was forgotten this day in the meeting of the brotherhood at New Orleans. The whereases concluded with this appeal to Lutheran awareness:

> It is in keeping with our Lutheran heritage, specifically our commitment to and under the Lutheran Confessions 'that the opinion of the party in error cannot be tolerated in the church of God, much less be excused and defended' (Formula of Concord, SD, Preface, 9)

Three *resolves* followed. They were

1. That the Synod assert its continuing concern for 'the conservation and promotion of the unity of the true faith' in accord with the Holy Scripture and the Lutheran Confessions.
2. That the Synod repudiate that attitude toward Holy Scripture, particularly as regards its authority and clarity, which reduces to theological opinion or exegetical question matters which are in fact clearly taught in Scripture (e.g., facticity of miracle accounts and their details; historicity of Adam and Eve as real persons; the fall of Adam and Eve into sin as a real event, to which original sin and its imputation upon all succeeding generations of mankind must be traced; the historicity of every detail in the life of Jesus as recorded by the evangelists; predictive prophecies in the Old Testament which are in fact Messianic; the doctrine of angels; the Jonah account, etc.).
3. That the Synod recognize that the theological position defended by the faculty majority of Concordia Seminary, St. Louis, Mo, is in

fact false doctrine running counter to the Holy Scriptures, the Lutheran Confessions, and the synodical stance and for that reason
'cannot be tolerated in the church of God, much less be excused
and defended.' (FC, SD, Preface 9)

In view of the faculty's specific profession of loyalty and disavowal
of the resolution as a description of their position, this resolution
made as much sense as accusing the VFW of plotting to overthrow the
government because some Fourth of July orations did not use approved patriotic rhetoric. On the other hand, the condemnation was
no surprise. As a diagnostician might have described it, through regular doses of LSD (Lutheran Standard Doctrine) handed out by *Christian News, Affirm* and other intermediaries, the Synod had finally hit a
high on pure doctrine. Soldiers under a fog of hallucinogenic drugs
have been known to imagine that their enemies are angels, cows,
spirits or tomatoes, their own gun barrels crooked sugar cane, and
their commanding officer a cook or enemy commander. So members
of the LC-MS seemed to see under every learned utterance a heresy,
and considered their teachers encyclopedists from the day of the
French Revolution, or Reimaruses, Strausses and Semlers out of the
age of rationalism. In their faculty they saw the ghosts who once
haunted the lecture halls of Tübingen, Marburg, and Heidelberg, and
when they saw more clearly they thought they saw forty or more Bult-
manns. In marijuana, the tetrahydrocannabinol content together with
other drugs in the resin produces distortion, impairment of perception
and judgment, and exaggeration of antipathy. "At New Orleans," a
young observer might well have commented, "we saw them stoned on
orthodoxy."
Hoping to salvage something, Concordia Seminary's president took
the floor on a point of personal privilege in defense of his faculty and
the future of the Synod and was granted the right to speak from the
podium. According to the Minutes, Tietjen "rejected the charges of
denying the formal principle of theology, of Gospel reductionism, of
denial of miracles, and rejection of the third use of the Law, and stated
that the faculty of the St. Louis seminary did not regard the description of their position given in the resolution as accurate. He concluded
his remarks with a prayer that the Holy Spirit would lead the convention in finding a better way to deal with the issues than has been proposed."[3]
Prof. Ernst Klug of Concordia Seminary, Springfield, Illinois, responded in the way that past administrations of the Synod had found

137

effective in maintaining credibility of a committee's resolution and assurance of passage by the convention. He said that the committee responsible for the resolution had spent a great deal of time prior to the convention and also during the convention discussing the issues involved. "The committee was convinced that on the basis of its study the statements in the proposed resolution were correct."[4]

Preus did not hesitate to use what to moderates appeared to be questionable political tactics, but he was not stupid, and succeeding developments suggest that he must have assured his right-wing that they could afford to be magnanimous in view of the certainty of the victory that was in the offing. In any case, the delegates voted temporary suspension of their own standing rules and allowed discussion of the resolution to be "held at a more reasonable time with not less than 3 hours allowed for discussion, that the three advisory representatives of the St. Louis seminary faculty be given an opportunity to speak, and that Dr. Tietjen be granted speaking privileges equal to that of the floor committee."[5]

"Accordingly, on Thursday morning, one of the strangest scenes in the history of American Christianity took place as more than 1000 delegates of the Lutheran Church—Missouri Synod in effect conducted a mass heresy trial on the basis of recommendation from a committee handpicked by the faculty's sworn enemy." So wrote the eye-witness editor of *Forum.* "Ironically," he continued, "the task of chairing the grisliest scene in Missouri Synod history fell to the Synod's kindliest official, outgoing first vice-president Roland Wiederaenders."[6] The editor went on to describe how "Wiederaender's gentle guidance of the discussion" was "in striking contrast to the bullying the convention had to put up with on the part of others who chaired the sessions."[7] He would have found support for this appraisal in the observation of a student tourist from Heidelberg, Germany. This student had not known enough about the sides in Missouri to take sides, but as the sessions wore on he began to identify with the moderates. At one point he became so agitated that he rushed out to find the advisory delegate who had befriended him. Venting his spleen over the chairman who happened to be presiding at the time, he complained: "Er hat uns angeschnauzt wie ein Preussischer Unteroffizier." ("He snarled at us like a Prussian corporal.") It was probably a similar reaction that prompted Eldon Weisheit, a *Lutheran Witness* reporter, to comment early in September, "If you found spirituality at New Orleans, you were at a different convention than I was."

"Missouri's historical faith is a faith which works by love," proclaimed Dr. August Suelflow, curator of the Synod's Historical Institute, in the morning devotion on Thursday, July 12.[8] The word "love" was to be interpreted in various ways that day. To Preus' right-wingers, love meant, among other things, obedience to God in suppression of heresy and concern for the heretic that he be properly exposed and dealt with so that he might repent of his evil ways. Love made hate easier. To moderates, love meant, among other things, the prophetic plea of concern for truth and justice. Thus on this weirdest day of all, Missouri's schizophrenia broke apart with love doing battle with love. Professors Edgar Krentz, Robert Bertram, and John Damm represented the faculty and explained from their perspective what actually went on at Concordia Seminary in terms of theological instruction. Tietjen was asked whether he still considered Preus' document "sub-Biblical and not in harmony with the Confessions." He replied to the effect that such statements "had been withdrawn from discussion since they seemed to impugn the character and motives of the President of the Synod." In his response to that point, Preus indicated "that the substance of the charge had not been withdrawn and that he believed that a minority ought not be allowed to impose its theology on the church."[9]

Scharlemann's Rehabilitation

In a climactic effort to prepare the flaming sword for the security of their Eden, the floor committee called on Dr. Martin Scharlemann, member of the faculty minority group, to address the delegates. Having himself praised historical-critical method in years of very recent memory, he now made the following points in favor of the Index of Prohibited Views, as 3-09 would be viewed by history:

"1. The basic question which confronts the convention is one of truth which is determined by facts and not by recognition or failure to recognize the facts on the part of the one who is charged.
2. That there was a refusal to answer questions briefly, directly, and concisely.
3. That there is such a thing as a historical-critical method which undermines the authority of Scripture."[10]

Thereby Scharlemann mortgaged the future of his church's theology to rigid traditionalism.

139

To be under the necessity of recording such "shameless rebuttal," to use *Forum's* phrase,[11] is not an enjoyable task, and especially not when it involves a long-time respected colleague. In view of Scharlemann's physical disability in the early months of 1974, history must painfully record the probability that stress of personal concerns in combination with circumstances and events destroyed for a time Scharlemann's clarity of prophetic vision and his finely-honed theological expertise. In any case, this was not the Scharlemann we had known, some of us for more than two decades. On the other hand, there was political necessity, whether of design or of accident, in Scharlemann's appearance before the convention.

If he was to replace Tietjen in the capacity of administrative head at Concordia Seminary, it was imperative that he be cleared of any taint of heresy that might be clinging to him after his 'confession' at Cleveland in 1962. He had at that time expressed regret for any unrest he had caused, but he had not recanted. Now the Synod itself had heard him trounce the very position the Synod was attacking—historical-critical methodology and its offspring. Since orthodoxy in the Missouri Synod necessarily included also hostility to what the Synod opposed, Scharlemann was now clean.

From Scharlemann's own point of view, in the light of his earlier writing, his critique was not a betrayal of the faculty, but an honest appraisal of the state of theology at that moment in history. Altered circumstances required altered approaches. His gut conviction, therefore, must have been to the effect that the Synod's theology and the practice of interpretive methodology would be safest under his control at the seminary. Ultimately, like Otten and Niemoeller, Scharlemann was more sinned against than sinning.

3-09 and The Faculty

After the three-hour period for discussion of the seminary issues had expired, the standing rules once more went into effect. This meant that Resolution 3-09 could be adopted after only thirty minutes more of debate.

Bent on theological anarchy, so eager were the right-wingers to demolish their target that they failed to note how vulnerable their resolution was on a number of counts. To charge scholars with a crime for interpreting the story of Jonah as a parable made about as much sense as to suggest that a banker must be up to something because he tries to discover more efficient ways to prepare his records for auditors, or that a lawyer must be in league with the Mafia when he explores all legal avenues to arrange the best case for his client. After heated debate the floor committee on resolutions proposed revision of the third resolve and addition of a fourth resolve. The third resolve now read:

> That the Synod recognize that the matters referred to in the second resolved are in fact false doctrine running counter to the Holy Scriptures, the Lutheran Confessions, and the synodical stance and for that reason 'cannot be tolerated in the church of God, much less be excused and defended' (FC, SD, Preface 9)

The fourth read:

> *Resolved,* That these matters be turned over to the Board of Control at Concordia Seminary, St. Louis.[12]

The cure here was worse than the original literary, not to say theological, disease. Resolutions forged with a tincture of hysteria are bound to bear some of the weaknesses of products engendered by a trip with LSD. In this case the third resolve, that "the matters referred to in the second resolved are in fact false doctrine," turned cherished orthodoxy once more into heresy. Among the "matters" referred to in that resolve were "facticity of miracle accounts" down to "the Jonah account" and on through the "etc." which presumably covered everything that Otten had been driving home for years, such as the authorship of Daniel, Isaiah, Ephesians, and whatever else a mind confined to literalism might conjure up. Other Christians would be asking us whether it was now necessary for Seminary professors to teach that lions would eat straw in heaven! (Isaiah 9:7)

Secondly, the phrase "not to be tolerated in the church of God" meant that anyone who defended positions not agreeable to the mind of Preus, Otten, the editors of *Affirm,* and the convention's majority delegation would ultimately have to be expelled from a Christian congregation. Any pastor who heard laypeople propounding or defending such positions openly in his congregation would be obligated to put such a person under discipline, and if the party persisted in informing others that, for example, the story of Jonah was a parable, he or she would be subject to excommunication.

Thirdly, in their zeal to torpedo the 'liberal' faculty, Preus and the framers of 3-09 either failed to take account of, or were unconcerned

141

about, the ecumenical implications of their resolution. In its official form, the resolution served notice on the entire Christian world that interpretation of the story of Jonah as a parable and not as an historical account was intolerable false doctrine. The Lutheran Confessions left no doubt in the matter as to the scope of such indictment. "The church of God" was not a little denomination, such as the Missouri Synod. It was the Church Catholic. In effect, then, the Missouri Synod had proclaimed to the rest of Christendom that a prerequisite for pulpit and altar fellowship and other aspects of joint worship was rejection of all the items singled out by the Missouri Synod in the alleged position of Concordia Seminary's faculty!

From a practical academic ecumenical perspective, the condemnation meant that even if a member of the seminary's faculty did not himself hold one or more of the alleged exegetical no-no's, including those embraced by "etc.", he was nevertheless bound to attest that he rejected the validity of the condemned position also for others. In blunt terms it meant that a faculty member who was also a member, for example, of the Catholic Biblical Association, would be compelled to annul the validity of contraband views held by fellow members in the Association, including Frs. Joseph Jensen, Richard Kugelman, John Hueseman, James Clifton, George Montague, Patrick Skehan, Myles Bourke, Daniel Harrington, Jerome Quinn, Raymond Brown, and a host of other distinguished scholars. In the past it had been the practice of our scholars in the case of recognized controversial points of exegesis and interpretation to help the student develop confidence in judging such matters on the basis of the evidence, without dogmatizing. Now we were required to inform students that it was a dogma of their church that the story of Jonah could not be a parable, and that anyone who held such a view was guilty of an error that could not be tolerated in the Christian Church. Thus once again we were being told that we had to play the reverse name-dropping game, in which the idea is to make friends with someone by calling his enemies nasty names.

Missouri's partners in ecumenical dialogue could well be forgiven if they felt that in the future they were to be dealt treys and fours from the bottom of the deck while the Missouri Synod gave itself all face cards and aces. And if Missourians thought other churchmen were naive enough to think that what happened at New Orleans was strictly a private game, they would have occasion before September was out to reevaluate the intelligence and experience of their partners.

From the added fourth resolve it was apparent that Preus had succeeded in calming down some of his storm troopers. Assured of majority voting strength, Concordia Seminary would indeed be under firm control when the current balance of the Board was tipped in the direction of the convention's mind and will.

When the vote was finally taken on Resolution 3-09, it was clear that the Faculty's representatives and Dr. Tietjen had not made a dent on anyone's skull or heart. "Their minds were made up." "They didn't even listen." So ran the comments. If anything, historical criticism lost a few votes to historical-grammatical method. No one had the nerve to estimate how many votes Jesus Christ lost.

In protest of the resolution, moderates encored a previous moment and moved forward to record their negative vote. While they were doing this, Dr. Paul Bretscher, pastor in Valparaiso, Indiana, read into the record a letter from his father, one of the most respected professors in the Synod's history. To more fully appreciate this letter, it is necessary first to note that its writer, always soft spoken, had the reputation throughout his church of being non-judgmental and unacquainted with malice. These were his words according to *Forum:*

> I am frightfully disturbed by the mad convention resolutions. If it wants to crush forever the one decisive living voice of Lutheranism (the St. Louis seminary), the convention is on the right track—the devil's.[13]

This verdict was straight out of St. John's Gospel in which Jesus had defined theological authorities of his time as children of Satan. The Missouri Synod was not accustomed to language of this sort, not after long years of experience in retailing the theological crimes of others and especially now of the faculty in St. Louis. Besides, Jesus meant Jews, not orthodox Missourians. On the morrow Bretscher and all the rest of his ilk would know who the devil was! For with most of the shelling job now done, there remained only the capture of the opposing general.

3-12A and Tietjen

Resolution 3-12, as noted earlier, had appeared in the orders for Wednesday. This resolution called for the resignation of Dr. Tietjen, but had not been officially before the convention. Since a number of delegates considered its language not only false and inflammatory, but libelous, administration forces urged its replacement with a much briefer one, numbered 3-12A and titled: "To Deal With Dr. John Tietjen Under the Provisions of Synod's 'Handbook' ''.[14] By the time 3-12A was presented, word had gotten around to Preus' right-wing that they had nothing to fear. As a result of the convention's elections, Concordia Seminary's Board now had a new look. Tietjen would be taken care of, and in a completely legal manner. By avoiding rash decision the convention would best achieve its objective in dealing with Tietjen.

Right-wingers therefore entered no protest against the exchange of resolutions. But there was silence also from another quarter. At this point the moderates laid down all their artillery. Facing those who were both accusers and judges, they heeded on their own admission the example of Jesus Christ and made their protest with silence. Like Pontius Pilate, Vice President Weber marveled. Switching from microphone to microphone he waited to hear a dissenting voice. None came. Finally the vote was called: The tally was 513 against Tietjen; 394 for justice.

At this point Tietjen asked for the privilege to address the assembly. He said he had two words for the delegates. One was a "hard word." He said that he had been grievously wronged by the publication of matters relating to overtures for his resignation. He had declined to resign because he believed that the position he held was a call from God. His second word was a "good word," a word of forgiveness. He said that he did not believe the convention knew what it was doing. His word therefore was a word of forgiveness because of the suffering and death of Jesus Christ. He stated that he felt no ill will toward anyone and prayed that God's love might surround the delegates and that they might know his peace.

From a political standpoint his speech, which revealed a perpendicular conscience, was a mistake. Forgiveness of the Synod was the last thing the majority in convention wanted to hear. To receive forgiveness meant a demand for acknowledgment of sin, and that ran counter to the collective synodical ego. Confession was a one-way street. The Synod had expected Tietjen, as Scharlemann had done in 1962, to acknowledge that the Synod was right.

At the conclusion of his pastoral absolution, minority members of the Synod surrounded him and applauded for more than five minutes before leaving the Hall to celebrate Holy Communion outside. To the music of rousing Lutheran hymns, members of the Press heard Tietjen disclaim any interest in taking his church to court or in heading a schismatic movement.

It was difficult for non-conventioneers to understand that the merrymakers around the Lord's Table were the losers, not the winners, at this convention, which had made it possible for many to become part of Luther's script at Worms.

Throughout the history of God's people, victory over the enemy was a cause for great rejoicing. After the Reed Sea had been filled with Pharaoh's finest troops, Miriam led the people of Israel in a victory dance. In the face of Caiaphas' oppressive measures, the believers in Jerusalem were filled with joyful boldness. One might therefore have expected those who felt themselves trampled by historical-critical method and robbed of their Bibles by the "great scholars" to have filled the air with hallelujahs. Instead, it was the losers who made the city of New Orleans peal with praise. "Theology without doxology," someone has said, "is *tedium;* with doxology *Te Deum.*" Only one moderate was heard to put a damper on the celebration; he said, "I'm so tired of hearing about Jonah, I've lost my taste for fish." Clearly, historical-critical method had not diminished the reality of the Lord's resurrection for the Moderates. And again others asked, "Who indeed were the losers at New Orleans?"

In defense of their publication of 3-12, the floor committee on Seminary Issues read into the record that they had acted in good faith, but had been impeded in carrying out their work. "We are therefore grieved," they concluded, "that we are accused of having grievously wronged Dr. Tietjen for presenting certain facts in *Today's Business.* The Convention has been likewise accused. Brethren, we regret this unfair condemnation of the Convention and the Committee."[15]

To Moderates, this self-defence was again symptomatic of the basic issue confronting their Synod. The Synod could do no wrong. Pleas for due process were themselves construed as judgmental accusations. Committees appeared to be infallibly right. Their members seemed incapable of enduring criticism. The fact that this mindset had traditional roots did not alter the Synod's obligation to grant a person his day in court. And a delegate convention was not the best atmosphere for conducting a heresy trial. Defenders of orthodoxy saw it from a different angle. Said one veteran of the old dormitory hazing tradition: "I'd say you liberals got your butt waxed."[16]

During the Synod's brief renaissance, one of her scholars had made this observation about the hazard of mating powerful ego with the collective will:

"It may well be that the battle for the new will be lost," he wrote. "In fact, it is rather likely; for, oddly enough, the redemptive works of

145

God move through history, with the muffled stride of One who chose to empty Himself, specifically rejecting all claim to the use of political power, quite probably because He saw rather clearly that the practice of power and the redemption of men can not be embodied in one person without jeopardizing and even destroying the latter."[17]

Succeeding months would prove that once again Scharlemann had spoken truth. New Orleans had been the site of depressing battle, but it was not yet Armageddon.

Chapter 14

PROTEST

When Dr. Tietjen arrived in St. Louis, airline personnel and passengers awaiting flights at Lambert Airport could not believe that a man who had just gone through so much with his church could beam with a look that spelled victory and receive such a hero's welcome. "The Church's One Foundation is Jesus Christ, Her Lord" for a few minutes drowned out announcements. Banners and signs were everywhere. One read

WELCOME! JOHN, THE BELOVED

Lending support to him for the days ahead were words such as these:

16 July 1973
Dr. John Tietjen
Concordia Seminary
St. Louis, MO 63105

Dear John:
I just wanted to drop a note to thank you for the poignant witness to the gospel of our Lord Jesus Christ you made on Friday the 13th. Your two "words" of Law and Gospel were the only ones that were appropriate.
You and your faculty have given us all a living exposition of the gospel. While you are earthen vessels, you carry your precious content with zeal that can only come from the Lord. I commend you to his continuing care in the face of uncertainty. While our witness may at times appear to be nothing more than pearls before swine, or decibels that will not register in the deaf ear, we know that our God will

sustain and protect those who place their trust in Him alone. In that confidence and faith we can continue to witness to His love and mercy. The only unity we can have is that which He gives, the unity of the Body of Christ. May this blessing, which I have composed, be yours and that of the faculty:

Get Hold!
He comes blessing!
No mere vocable.
No providential writ of insurancestability.
No papa's sigh over sleeping babes.
But rush of Spirit Power.

His Blessing first was Word in flesh,
    Christ's hammered flesh, then raised;
He came to rip, redeem and bless.
And blesses now through upraised flesh
    with pulsing force of Comforter,
    Backbone Stiffener.
In tumult of fire and freedom,
    The Final Blessing.

Cock both ears for hearing!
One echoes with accusation
But faith-full ear
Hears
Whisper of grace, His words of love.

Go then, winded,
To world of smut and smokestack
To be His breath
Where men breathe.
You are dis-missled.

    Pow men.
As ever,
John F. Groh, Asst. Prof. of History

Our faculty needed such encouragement and much more. Whether New Orleans would go down in history as the site of Missouri's Armageddon, or whether the climactic battle would be postponed, depended to some extent on the morale of Concordia Seminary's battle-worn faculty and the political efficiency of Preus.

On July 17 our faculty majority met in St. Louis and discussed possibilities relative to the actions taken at New Orleans. It was a foregone conclusion that no truce was possible between officially infallible Missouri and a theological line of inquiry that insisted on being fettered only by the Bible and the confessional standard of the Lutheran Church. Mass resignation was suggested, but a vote on such a measure would have imposed pressure on those who might have considered other options equally compelling, and it would have left the students hanging. Another course was simply to admit defeat and leave, as each saw fit. No longer would we meet as a group to ponder ways of bringing the Missouri Synod back to life. If our church did not give a damn; if the majority of the Bishops would not see that the plumbing was stopped up, the roofs leaking, the plaster falling, the windows broken out; if the laity who had contributed their millions would not blink an eye as they looked at the rubble of what was once their great Missouri Synod; if ministers still felt that it was best not to "disturb the people," why should we linger in the graveyard?

But where was theology worth the name in such thinking? Gospel meant resurrection. Instead of taking action, we were reacting and feeling sorry for ourselves. All our tons of print, our highly-pitched theological rhetoric, our clever political counterplays had failed. It was hard for us to admit that we were indeed humbled to dependence on the Gospel which spelled out acceptance of disaster in the interests of freedom for every person. Tietjen had been right all along—we were beginning to realize as never before what it meant to be Lutheran. Besides, we were not really so reduced in ranks. At New Orleans hundreds had stood up and were willing to be counted. They were now marked men and women! It would be tragic to permit such courage and resolution to be dissipated for want of a clear call back to the colors. If bishops, supported by their clergy and laity, were to restrain the fury unleashed at New Orleans and turn their church away from sectarian directions, it was necessary for them to act in the next few crucial weeks. To aid them in their recruitment the faculty would hoist high a banner under which mutual conversation and free assembly for defining the goals and tasks of the church might take place. It would be important to do this, however, before Preus retook the initiative and closed the school or vacated the office of the presidency of Concordia Seminary. In such event a joint witness would be greatly jeopardized and its effectiveness substantially blunted along the detour of reaction rather than action.

Therefore, on July 24, 1973, we published

A DECLARATION OF PROTEST AND CONFESSION

In the fear of God and mindful that this may be our final opportunity to speak with one voice we, members of the faculty and staff of Concordia Seminary, St. Louis, Missouri, take courage from our Lord Jesus Christ to protest actions of the New Orleans Convention of The Lutheran Church—Missouri Synod and to make a confession to our church.

WE PROTEST

We protest the convention's judgment that we teach false doctrine which "cannot be tolerated in the church of God." The evidence cited in support of the judgment misrepresents and distorts our teaching. We teach what the Scriptures teach, and it is that teaching which the convention has misrepresented and condemned.

We protest the convention's violation of the procedures for evangelical discipline clearly outlined in the Synod's constitution and bylaws. We were accused, tried and condemned without due process even though the seminary's Board of Control had already examined us and declared us not guilty of false doctrine.

We protest the convention's breach of contract in judging and condemning us by a doctrinal standard different from the doctrinal article of the Constitution (Article II), the platform on which all members of the Synod have taken their stand together.

We protest the convention's violation of the principle of *Sola Scriptura* (Scripture Alone) in elevating tradition above Scripture. The convention fettered the Scriptures by requiring members of the Synod to interpret them in accord with a presumed synodical tradition, which the convention defined through the adoption of *A Statement of Scriptural and Confessional Principles.* Like Luther we stand for an open Bible which we are free to read on its own terms, limited only by our voluntary commitment to the Lutheran Confessions.

We protest the convention's use of coercive power to establish the true doctrine of the Scriptures. The truth of God cannot be imposed through convention action in adopting doctrinal statements but can only be recognized and confessed by means of the Holy Spirit working faith through the Word of God.

We protest the convention's unconstitutional act of altering the Synod's confessional standard by expanding the doctrinal article of the Constitution (Article II) to include doctrinal statements adopted by the Synod and by making such statements binding upon all of the Synod's members.

WE CONFESS

We confess before God and all to whom these words come that we repent of what we have done to bring God's judgment upon our church. We ask God and His church for forgiveness.

PROTEST

We confess our longing for peace and unity in the church. We seek to forgive as we have been forgiven and to foster the unity of the Spirit in the bond of peace. We earnestly desire to work in harmony with our brothers and sisters in the Synod and stand ready to enter into discussion with them.

We confess once again our ordination vow. Together with the Synod and every member of the Synod we accept *without reservation:*

> The Scriptures of the Old and New Testament as the written Word of God and the only rule and norm of faith and of practice;
>
> All the Symbolical Books of the Evangelical Lutheran Church as a true and unadulterated statement and exposition of the Word of God.
>
> (Article II, Constitution of The Lutheran Church—Missouri Synod)

We confess that we accept no other doctrinal standard as binding on our consciences even though we may have to suffer for our stand.

We confess an open Bible unfettered by any human rules. With Luther we "acknowledge no fixed rules for the interpretation of the Word of God"—whether historical-critical, grammatical-historical, or any other—"since the Word of God, which teaches freedom in all other matters, must not be bound." ("The Freedom of a Christian," *Luther's Works,* American Edition, Vol. 31, p. 341)

We confess our determination to oppose any teaching which is less than the full Law and Gospel which our Lutheran Confessions affirm to be the doctrine of the Sacred Scriptures.

We confess our resolution to continue to carry out our solemn call to teach the doctrine of the Scriptures and to prepare students for the Ministry of Word and Sacrament, as long as God gives us the grace to do so.

AN APPEAL

Our church confronts a crisis. The Gospel is at stake. Our church is in danger of losing its truly Lutheran character and of becoming a sect. In issuing this *Declaration of Protest and Confession* we join with those delegates to the New Orleans Convention who stood together to protest convention actions and to confess the Bible's Gospel. We call upon our brothers and sisters to join in a common movement of protest and confession within the Synod.

We need to stand together in our concern to be truly Lutheran.

We need to stand together in our concern to be the church.

We need to stand together in our concern for a free and open Bible.

We need to stand together in our concern for the Gospel.

THE CHURCH'S ONE FOUNDATION IS JESUS CHRIST, HER LORD!

Members of the Faculty and Staff
Concordia Seminary, St. Louis, Mo.
July 24, 1973

MEMBERS OF FACULTY AND STAFF OF CONCORDIA SEMINARY, ST. LOUIS
WHO AFFIXED THEIR SIGNATURES TO
"A DECLARATION OF PROTEST AND CONFESSION"

Gilbert Amadeus Thiele
Herbert J. A. Bouman
Robert W. Bertram
Paul F. Goetting
Arlis John Ehlen
Robert J. Werberig
Walter Wegner
Thomas C. Rick
Arthur M. Vincent
Mark R. Roock
Holland H. Jones
Richard R. Caemmerer, Sr.
Edgar M. Krentz
Erwin L. Lueker
Edward H. Schroeder
John H. Tietjen
Robert H. Smith
Herbert T. Mayer
David C. Dahline
Kenneth H. Breimeier
Donald F. Hinchey
George W. Hoyer
Alfred von Rohr Sauer
Carl Graesser, Jr.
Larry Neeb

Everett R. Kalin
Carl R. Sachtleben
John W. Constable
Alfred O. Fuerbringer
Andrew M. Weyermann
John S. Damm
David J. Heino
Robert A. Grunow
Mark P. Bangert
David E. Deppe
Arthur Carl Piepkorn
Robert R. Bergt
Norman C. Habel
Frederick W. Danker
Carl A. Volz
Kenneth J. Siess
David C. Yagow
Duane P. Mehl
W. J. Danker
Lucille Hager
Kenneth M. Ruppar
Arthur C. Repp
Leonhard C. Wuerffel
Ralph W. Klein

From the number of signatures attached to the Protest it was impossible to dismiss this statement as an emotional outrage of a few malcontents who might have felt themselves contracted for elimination by New Orleans Resolutions. Except for the members of the self-styled "Minority," Professors Ralph Bohlmann, Richard Klann, Robert Preus, Martin Scharlemann, and Lorenz Wunderlich, this list composed the faculty and staff which had already serviced thousands of congregations with ministers and was even then in the business of teaching and administrating a student body ranging between 600 and 700 men and women. Nor was the content of the protest extraordinary. A quarter century earlier one of the seminary's most respected and quoted theologians took his synod to task in a document which was reprinted in 1965. Commenting on the Synod's trend to give "undue weight to the opinions of the fathers" including Luther, Walther, Pieper, and synodical essays, he said, "I challenge anyone to look into the literature of any church but our own to find anything parallel to this situation. . . . The method is absolutely unique . . . The idea is that we are not only without flaw or error in all our past applications of Holy Writ—we shall even regard ourselves in duty bound to pass the same judgment, no matter what the change may be in the situation." Disqualifying himself for the task, he said: "There is urgent need . . . of psychoanalyzing the Missouri Synod."[1]

It was not always so in Missouri, Theodore Graebner reminded his reader. Dr. Franz Pieper himself admitted: "Also in the Missouri Synod we have not in every respect and in every place spoken correctly on Election and Conversion." "But," sighed Graebner, "that was thirty-five years ago. Since then we have added Dr. Pieper to the immortals." He then pointed out that when the question of women's suffrage arose at a convention in 1938, the delegates placed on record the fact that according to Dr. Pieper "it is *the accepted position* and practice of Synod that women shall not be granted voting membership in the Christian congregation." "I wonder," mused Graebner, "where outside the Roman Catholic Church any resolution containing such appeal to authority would be found in all Christendom."[2]

"Twenty years ago," he noted, "the demand that women be silent in the church was interpreted by Dr. Pfotenhauer [president of the Synod at that time] as including the reports of women missionaries, zenana [harem] workers, and missionaries' wives, who accordingly were permitted to address only women and children. Today they address mixed audiences the length and breadth of our Synod. No admission has ever been made that the former ruling went beyond the intention of Paul's prohibition."[3] Graebner went on to cite how the Missouri Synod forgot that the official *Handbook* of the Synod had in 1937 condemned refusal to worship in the church nearest one as "sectarian in tendency." In connection with faculty statements on controversial issues during the early 1940's, he said: "From this point of view (inadmissibility of change) it will be understood why such a panic spread through the conferences five or six years ago when the story was peddled around that the 'The faculty—The Faculty!—*is not united !*' "[4] In other words, the record of collective infallibility was broken!

Adding to his list of prize examples of ecclesiastical blunders, he pointed out that the Fort Wayne and Milwaukee preparatory academies had once been split over the question of theater attendance. The Milwaukee college permitted students to see Julius Caesar and Macbeth. Fort Wayne, in deference to Dr. Walther, did not. Conference resolutions, he pointed out, especially prohibited the appearance of Luther among the characters in pageants on the ground that "he is a sacred personage, being the subject of prophecy!" Graebner ended his paper with these words: "There is only one remedy for the conditions here described: Biblical scholarship."[5]

This one remedy the Synod had riddled with whereases and resolveds at New Orleans, and we had done the impolitic deed on July 24 of questioning decisions of the Synod in the public forum. A legislative body that had ignored democratic process at the New Orleans Convention by denying continuance of the two-thirds rule for closing debate could not be expected to indulge such free speech. The Synod had prescribed channels for people who found themselves in disagreement with others in the Synod. But, as we were to discover, channels were to be followed by those who *disagreed with approved policy.* Others, like the editors of *Affirm,* could continue to express themselves publicly with impunity, for they were in *approved disagreement* with other members of the Synod.[6] With such a double standard for freedom of speech prevailing, it was inevitable that the war which had been encouraged at New Orleans should break out with fresh intensity.

ELIM Organized

Reactions and actions in response to the events at New Orleans came swiftly. Under the date of August 8, 1973, concerned members of the faculty of Concordia Teachers College, River Forest, Illinois, sent out the following invitation:

August 8, 1973

Dear Colleague:
    Since New Orleans, a number of us have been talking informally about our concerns, fears, hopes, etc. Some of us who were there are

naturally a little more anxious than others. But there is a general interest among a number of colleagues that some forum be established to evaluate the convention, and perhaps respond in some formal way to those events.

After considerable "table talk" a small group of us have decided to invite a few colleagues to a meeting off-campus to discuss our mutual concern. We view the agenda as follows:

a. Is some corporate response to the events of Synod's Convention appropriate at this time? Necessary?

b. Are there areas of information and assistance to colleagues in the event of possible actions at our own institute? (No fear tactics intended, just attempting to view realistically the possibilities of the next year.)

c. How can we sustain, encourage and support each other, especially those vulnerable because of specific teaching areas, eg. theology?

This invitation is being sent to about twenty-five of your colleagues. We do not wish to raise anxiety. Consider the invitation a matter of private concern. We want to encourage your participation, but do not want in any way to pressure your decision. Feel free to accept or decline as your feelings dictate.

Place: Steve Schmidt's
        807 N. 5th Avenue
        Maywood, Illinois

Time: 7:30

Date: Tuesday, August 14

We'll provide the beer and pretzels and space. Hopefully the evening together can be useful and healing.
Sincerely,
John Groh
Steve Schmidt
Jim Kracht
Wayne Lucht

The proposals for this scheduled forum reflected much of the thinking that lay behind a letter sent out a week earlier by the Rev. Bertwin Frey, formerly president of the Missouri Synod's English District, and F. Dean Lueking, minister at Grace Lutheran Church, which adjoins the River Forest College.

155

Box 151
River Forest, Ill. 60305
August 1, 1973

Friends and Fellow Christians:

This letter is going out to approximately one thousand clergy and laity in our Synod. We hope you will share its contents with everyone you know to whom its message pertains.

First, thanks tremendously to all who have worked hard in the circuits, districts, and at the Convention in New Orleans. Your labors are not in vain. Whatever is done in Christ's name is never lost. People have witnessed, worked, prayed, wept and laughed together. We are not despondent or in disarray. We are men and women in Christ who have learned that "the testing of faith produces steadfastness."

Second, and more important, we now look forward not backward, facing the serious problems and hidden blessings that are before us all in our Synod. Our immediate concern is the Seminary faculty in St. Louis and their fate at the hands of the newly-elected Board of Control. The stirring "Declaration of Protest and Confession", issued by the faculty July 25, appeals to all of us to join in voicing our consciences in protest of Convention actions which threaten our Synod with becoming a sect and losing our truly Lutheran character as a church. We want to heed that appeal, since *our* consciences are involved, too.

Therefore a *"Conference on Evangelical Lutheranism"* will be held on August 28, 10 A.M. through August 29, 4 P.M. at the O'Hare Inn, Higgins and Mannheim, Des Plaines, Ill. (adjoining Chicago's International Airport, O'Hare Field). Please come. Use the enclosed card to register. Send it directly to O'Hare Inn. We wish we had funds to cover your travel and lodging expenses. We do not. But in this crisis moment in our Synod, we ask you to find ways to get here because you are needed now. Those who come from greatest distances, and who must have some help, should receive equalization assistance which will be worked out here. If staying with a host family will help by eliminating lodging costs, please write immediately to Rev. Eugene Roeder, 1110 Westchester Blvd., Westchester, Illinois 60153. Each person attending the conference is asked to pay a program fee of $5.00. The Conference is open to all clergy, teachers, and laity who are interested in practical steps necessary in a movement of protest and profession of the faith we hold as Lutheran Christians.

Program participants will include President John Tietjen of the Seminary. Synodical President Jacob Preus has been invited to speak his concerns to us and receive ours in return. ALC and LCA leadership representation is invited to come, since close contact with both sister churches is increasingly important. An inclusive statement of protest will be ready, as well as materials that will help parishioners get into the issues and be equipped for appropriate action.

Instead of being mesmerized by the present turmoil, we are summoned by the power of Christ our Lord in His Gospel to believe that God is indeed able to do far more above all that we ask or think. Take heart from His Word which tells us that though afflicted, we are not crushed, perplexed we are not in despair, persecuted we are not forsaken, struck down we are not destroyed. (II Cor. 4:8–9)
Fraternally, in our Lord,
BERTWIN L. FREY
F. DEAN LUEKING

Anticipating future developments with accurate prophetic vision, Professors Groh and Schmidt encouraged their colleagues to take a vital interest in the conference that was to be held later in the month. On August 9 they wrote:

Dear Colleague:
The enclosed letter of invitation to the August 28–29 Conference on Evangelical Lutheranism is being sent to you upon our request. If you can become involved, we encourage your attendance. However, if your position is not in sympathy with the conference goals, we in no way wish to pressure you into actions not in accord with your conscience. Consider the invitation one of colleagial concern. Feel free to share this correspondence with other members of the faculty.

A number of us feel that the issues in the church today call for commitment, participation and decision. As professors of the church we share responsibility for leading the church in theology and practice. We must be involved in crucial decisions. Unordained teachers are especially encouraged to participate. The conference is an opportunity to speak, pray, act and *VOTE* on policies which may significantly effect our future ministries.

If you have any questions or personal concerns, please share them with us.

We look forward to your involvement.
Sincerely,
(Signed John)
John Groh
(Signed Steve)
Steve Schmidt

Owing to such quality of leadership and coordination of resources, attendance at the Conference exceeded expectations and the results of the business sessions clearly signalled fresh directions for Missourians.

ELIM Assembly

On August 28–29, 1973, a total of 812 concerned laity and clergy met at O'Hare Airport, Chicago, Illinois. Out of this meeting emerged the organization known as EVANGELICAL LUTHERANS IN MISSION. The assembly elected ten people (five clergymen and five laypeople) from five regions of the country to serve as a Board of Directors. Five additional members were to be selected by the Board so as to ensure minority and special interest representation. The Board members, as first constituted, included: Elwyn Ewald, a missionary teacher and administrator, who had recently returned from New Guinea, chairman of the Board; William Carter, Boulder, Colorado, Vice-President; Patricia Nissen, Ann Arbor, Michigan, Secretary; Vernon Nuss, Great Bend, Kansas, Treasurer. Other Board members included Viola Coleman, St. Louis, Missouri; Will Herzfeld, Oakland, California; Alfred E. Jordan, Shawnee Mission, Kansas; F. Dean Lueking, River Forest, Illinois; Kenneth E. Markworth, Springfield, Illinois; Martin E. Marty, Riverside, Illinois; Raymond C. Schulze, New York City, New York; Flora Seefeldt, Milwaukee, Wisconsin; John H. Tietjen, St. Louis, Missouri; and Alton F. Wedel, Minneapolis, Minnesota. One Board member, Harold Kieschnick, submitted his resignation, at the request of his congregational Board of Education. Wilbert Krause, of Dallas, Texas, replaced him.[7]

Choice of Elwyn Ewald as general manager for the new organization itself indicated how members of ELIM understood themselves in relation to official policies in the Missouri Synod. Ewald was a no-nonsense, up-to-the-front-of-the-bus champion.

He viewed himself as an organizational facilitator, not an ideological transformer. Younger Blacks and women immediately recognized that he stood for a confessional movement in which minorities were not to be patronized nor used for political clout, but evaluated for their actual and potential contributions to the total well-being of the church and of society. Those who felt that their civil rights might have been infringed by convention actions were confident that he would implement the assembly's concern for justice, through legal channels if necessary.

No sponsor of the dependency syndrome, Ewald had encouraged the New Guinea mission to become self-supporting and in charge of its own structural destiny. From illiterate subsistence farmers he attracted substantial financial support for the school in their district. He helped a local community establish its own program for community health, including the building of clinics and the introduction of a much-needed community-health-insurance program. Under his direction, the Wabag Lutheran Church developed local leadership to such an extent that the New Guinea mission outstripped all other synodical mission ventures in the speed with which it gained a footing of equality with the sending church.

The selection of Ewald, in sum, meant that ELIM was committed to a balance of traditional Missouri God-talk and social sensitivity, with a high premium placed on respect for human beings in the richness of their diversity. Sound doctrine and integrity in one's relations with people came out of Ewald's Bible as a single package.

Since Preus had determined to solve the Synod's problems with political imbalance, Ewald was under orders to *add balance.* Having come to New Orleans with only a semblance of corporate political strength, Moderates were now to engage in precinct-level work. With Preus determined to oust those who posed obstacles, Ewald was to administer a program of maintenance and support of those whose positions or persons were threatened by Preus' managerial efficiency program. To combat the diet of theological pablum perpetrated on the synod, structures were to be set up for theological study. In an attempt to halt the Synod's headlong dash toward isolationism and exclusivism, provision was made for exploration of inter-Lutheran relations. Matching Preus' awakening of the laity, involvement of lay members on all decision-making and action levels was to be high on ELIM's agenda.

The Rev. Frank Starr prepared a report on the Assembly for the *Lutheran Witness,* official organ of the Missouri Synod. President Preus and his appointed doctrinal censor ("reviewer" in the Synod's terminology) endeavored to prevent or at least shape the form of the article. Starr retained his journalistic integrity. After meetings with *Witness* personnel, Dr. Preus finally agreed to the publication but demanded the opportunity for instant rebuttal on the next page. Thus it happened that Starr's report took up page 22 and Preus' reply, "Meeting of Insurgents Deplored," covered page 23. Even the layout suggested that the President's message was to be the point of focus for the reader.[8] With words like "insurgent" and "rebellion," Preus could count on hundreds of thousands of readers of the official paper to suspect that the Synod had indeed been invaded by subversive forces. It was a stratagem unworthy of his high office, for he himself had declined the opportunity to counsel the Assembly personally.

Madness in Missouri

As the first issue of *Missouri In Perspective,* the publication developed by ELIM, reported it, Preus had shown himself unable "to respond pastorally to the concerns and frustrations of thousands" of the Synod's members.

The paper documented this grave charge in a number of statements; among them the following:

1. Preus' response reveals intolerance to the feelings and opinions of others in the family of faith.
2. By innuendo he suggests that the Evangelicals are so permissive that they are guilty of denying miracles, rejecting the Virgin Birth of our Lord, and, he says, "similar matters."
3. He misreads Article 8C of the Synod's Constitution by interpreting "interpret and witness" to mean, in effect, the right to bind the consciences of her members.
4. He misinterprets the Evangelicals' dissent about the authority of "popes, bishops, or councils" as a threat to the authority of the Scriptures and the Gospel.
5. He illogically concludes that a faculty not bound by the Synod will bind the consciences of the people by what it teaches the future pastors of the church. Thereby he overstates the influence of a faculty in a responsible, theological and academic setting controlled by the Lutheran Confessions and the ordination vows of every member.

Concluding its editorial, *MIP* said:

The madness which has gripped our Synod these past few years under such a legalistic approach to faith and life can be documented in the growing number of casualties among our administrators, professors and pastors—many of them long-time servants of our church; it is evident in the flurry of activities since New Orleans to "clean house" as soon as possible; and in the abandonment of Missouri's traditionally Evangelical practice of discipline and patient fraternal discussion in favor of the heat of angry debate and the application of bald administrative and political power. As the list of good men who are charged and threatened and unfrocked grows, we see the fruits of the spirit behind such an un-Lutheran use of both Scripture and Evangelical practice. No parish pastor would survive, either in terms of an effective Gospel ministry or in terms of congregational support, were he to be so unsympathetic and insensitive to a substantial minority in his congregation or if he were to employ such heavy-handed methods of demanding conformity or purging dissent.

The Bible is not really at stake—despite the oft-repeated threat that "they are taking our Bible away from us." What is at stake is the very thing the Bible was inspired by God to communicate—that undergirding all of faith and life is a loving God who "calls, gathers, enlightens, sanctifies, and preserves through the Gospel." When the primary methods become inhibitive by resorting to Synodical resolutions, appeals to the Constitution, a re-writing of bylaws to increase power of administrators and boards, and when the imposition of non-Gospel criteria becomes a threat to the confession and mission of the church, then Evangelicals must raise their voices in dissent and, whether branded insurgents or rebels, re-affirm the historic position of the Lutheran Confessions and the glorious liberty of our Lord Jesus Christ.[9]

Catholic Biblical Association Intervenes

Many Missourians considered the battle in Missouri as strictly Missouri's affair. They were surprised, therefore, to read in the public press a critique of the convention's actions by Roman Catholics.

Whereas Lutherans had traditionally associated Roman Catholics with an institutionalized interpretation of the Bible, now it was Lutherans who were imposing official interpretations of Scripture not only on Lutherans but Christians everywhere. For according to New Orleans Resolution 3-09 anyone who held to the condemned points expressed in the resolution was guilty of holding an error that was not to be "tolerated in the church of God."[10] Thus the Missouri Synod was in effect lecturing the ecumenical world.

As respects number of official interpretations, the Missouri Synod at one convention may have made more specific interpretations of Bible passages binding on its members than the Roman Catholic church had imposed on its membership in fourteen hundred years. Such a magisterial approach appeared to nullify avowed ecumenical interests on the part of Missouri.

The Catholic Biblical Association did not appreciate either the implicit attack on Concordia Seminary's biblical scholars through New Orleans Resolution 3-09, nor the indictment of historical-critical methodology expressed explicitly in the resolution. Knowing full well the political implications of any pronouncements it might make, the Catholic Biblical Association preferred to put moral and scholarly integrity ahead of expediency in a way that shamed us at Concordia Seminary.

To my knowledge and memory, we had never spoken up in behalf of scholars who had been fair game in our church, very often without even the courtesy of being read.

As a faculty we had never been horrified by this statement made in *The Abiding Word,* a part of the Missouri Synod's Centennial celebration, and which to this day has not been retracted:

> A congregation or a denomination becomes a sect when it persists in false doctrine in spite of admonition. The Papacy is the worst example of a sect. But even in this corrupt group some Scriptural doctrines are still in evidence, though not in their purity . . . The Roman Church is full of damnable errors, and a Christian should know these errors, to be able to bear witness to the truth. . . . The Papacy and unionism are the two most dangerous forces. The Pope makes salvation doubtful; unionism makes truth doubtful. Let us be filled with a holy hatred against the Pope and against unionism . . . A Christian is called to battle and controversy . . . Finally, we must not overlook the fact that not only error, but also errorists are *not to be tolerated.* (Italics ours)[11]

The Catholic Biblical Association's rejoinder to divisive activities in the ranks of the Roman Catholic Church as well as outside the Roman fellowship took first the form of a resolution:

> that as they (the members of the Association) look forward to the observance of the thirtieth anniversary of the promulgation, on September 30, 1943, of the magistral encyclical of Pope Pius XII, *Divino Afflante Spiritu,* rightly regarded as the magna carta of modern Catholic scientific biblical studies, they reaffirm their grateful devotion to the See of Peter for this and many other signs of its interest in and support of the dedicated labors of so many loyal sons and daughters of the Church further to open up the treasures of God's Word; and that *they emphatically reiterate their fraternal support of those fellow biblical scholars,* some of them honored members of their Association, *who have been and are being made the target of irresponsible and totally unfounded attacks* in the press and elsewhere, often precisely because they have tried to follow the lines of scientific investigation laid down and warmly recommended in *Divino Afflante Spiritu.*

A letter framing this resolution of the Catholic Biblical Association went on to speak about matters we Lutherans considered our private domain. We had always had, we thought, the best lexicographers and grammarians, openness in scholarship, and concern for the "true liberty of the children of God." We Lutherans had always encouraged Bible study at the hand of an open Bible. Now Roman Catholics were reminded that Pope Pius XII had insisted on all these things.

In the concluding paragraphs of his public letter of September 14, the Executive Secretary of *The Catholic Biblical Association,* Fr. Joseph Jensen, O.S.B., wrote:

> That control of a Christian community can be gained by militant fundamentalists is witnessed by recent events in the Lutheran Church—Missouri Synod; if the new leadership succeeds in ousting from Concordia Theological Seminary those committed to critical scientific scholarship and remaking the institution along fundamentalist lines, that segment of Christianity will be effectively diminished and ecumenical dialogue will be hindered.

Addressing himself then to attacks launched by *alter egos* of the *Christian News,* such as *The Wanderer,* he continued:

> Seeking to discredit and destroy solid, moderate scholarship, their attacks cause confusion among the Catholic laity and threaten the freedom of responsible scholars to speak out. Such attacks ultimately threaten the ecumenical movement, both because they make any talk of a Catholic consensus impossible and because they tend to destroy the confidence of large groups of Catholics in those who should be their spokesmen in ecumenical dialogue.
>
> As responsible Catholic scholars we will continue to avoid both a fundamentalism alien to the Church's interpretation of the Scriptures and an extreme liberalism that would effectively deny their inspired and normative character. We are grateful that you have always followed the injunction of *Divino Afflante Spiritu* to the bishops of 'encouraging all those initiatives by which men, filled with apostolic zeal, laudably strive to excite and foster among Catholics a greater knowledge of and love for the Sacred Books' (#51). We trust that we will always enjoy your support and confidence and that you will not permit those who labor for the advancement of Catholic truth, in union with the Magisterium and in conformity with Church directives, to be labeled as perverters of the faith. We earnestly hope the Bishops will find it possible to indicate to the faithful that these uncharitable voices speak for their own convictions and do not represent the views of the Magisterium.

Right-wingers among both Roman Catholics and Lutherans would say in reaction to Jensen that he did not know the difference between fundamentalism and the doctrinal position of the Missouri Synod. The term "Fundamentalism" was originally used to describe a species of Protestantism that flourished in the United States from 1909 on. In the face of what they considered a rising tide of liberalism, conservative leaders from various denominations stressed primarily the inspiration and inerrancy of Scripture, the virgin birth, vicarious atonement, and the bodily resurrection and second coming of Jesus. The movement found support, among many others, in William Jennings Bryan, J. Gresham Machen, Oswald T. Allis, Robert Dick Wilson, Benjamin J. Warfield, James Orr, and Melvin Grove Kyle. Fundamentalists also found great encouragement in the sermons of Dr. Walter A. Maier, famed Lutheran Hour speaker.

It is true that Fundamentalists in the earliest sense of the term could be distinguished from Lutherans and others in the catholic tradition by virtue especially of their lack of emphasis on the holy sacraments. But the term gradually came to be applied to any doctrinal position with a rigid view of inerrancy of the Bible, maintenance of traditional positions on date and authorship of biblical books, and a strong strain of apologetics, with special reference to supernatural aspects and specifically the historicity of miracles.

Inasmuch as the Missouri Synod's description of false doctrine that was not to be tolerated in the Church of God (New Orleans Resolution 3-09) covered almost everything that Herman Otten and fundamentalists of earlier and later variety had stressed, Jensen's application of the term to phenomena in a broader ecclesiastical circle followed the normal development of language. Moreover, he stressed the main point which Lutherans have traditionally held against Fundamentalism: isolation from the church catholic. At New Orleans, the Missouri Synod's concentration on a rigid view of inerrancy and other topics dear to fundamentalists was leading to the very *apartheid* Jensen lamented in his letter. Fundamentalism, minus sacramental laxity and fanciful speculations associated with the last times, had indeed invaded Missouri.

Right-wingers might further have charged that the Catholic Biblical Association had misread the happenings at New Orleans. Not a single biblical scholar at Concordia Seminary, they might have argued, had been charged with false doctrine. It is fact, however, that the preamble and the whereases were adopted at New Orleans and form part of the total resolution known as 3-09.[12] In the third and fourth *whereases,* reference is made to the "faculty majority," and the two books containing the names of the majority members are specifically cited in the fourth whereas. That Preus' supporters at the convention understood Resolution 3-09 to be not only condemnation of a position but a charge of false doctrine against identifiable faculty members is clear from Herman Otten's pronouncements subsequent to the convention. He wrote editorially: "The Lutheran Church—Missouri Synod's New

Orleans convention adopted an excellent resolution declaring that the majority of faculty members at this seminary is guilty of false doctrine . . . " Preus and his administrative associates tried to emphasize the letter of the law and said, "Only the faculty's *position* was condemned." It was a case of the visible faculty and the invisible heresy, a paradox readily recognized by Missouri's more astute dogmaticians. The man on the street knew better. "It's people who take positions. When you condemn a position, you condemn the people who hold it. At New Orleans we condemned the liberals, the majority faculty."

Chapter 15

ABORTED SUSPENSION

Herman Otten, who had scored heavily at New Orleans, continued to assume for himself direction of proceedings. "Officials don't have too much time before school starts in September," he wrote editorially. "They may even have to forfeit their vacations but they should immediately ask each member of the St. Louis faculty if he retracts his false doctrine and if he now subscribes to *A Statement of Scriptural and Confessional Principles.* Those who refuse to retract their false doctrine should not be allowed to continue teaching. Arrangements will have to be made to get loyal teachers to take their place."[1]

As far as Otten was concerned, the faculty had failed his correspondence course. The " 'The great scholars,' " he said, "should have stayed home and done some serious homework. They should have tried to answer our questions on *almah* and Dr. Robert Dick Wilson's questions on the J-E-D-P source hypothesis. We still haven't received any answers to these questions from the 'great scholars' at Concordia Seminary, St. Louis,"[2]

Since Preus and company had in a number of vital issues been following Otten's agenda, faculty and staff at Concordia Seminary did not need a crystal ball to know what was in the offing.

Two weeks after the convention, members of the Board of Control who were antagonistic to John Tietjen called for a special Board Meeting for August 17-18, among other things, to take action on resolutions made at the New Orleans Convention. Approximately a week later, the Rev. Leonard Buelow and the Rev. Harlan Harnapp, two members of the very committee (number 3) that formulated the harsh resolutions against the seminary, sent formal charges, not to Tietjen, but to the Board of Control. The wording of their accusations followed Resolution 3-12 word for word. Tietjen objected that the charges were submitted a week after the proposed agenda. The majority on the Board of Control overruled his objections and used the charges against Tietjen as leverage to act on the recommendations of the New Orleans convention.

According to the Synod's own precise guidelines for due process in the case of charges filed against a faculty member, the Board was bound to follow these two initial steps:

1. When a Board of Control receives a charge, it should have the complainant "communicate directly with the person against whom he has a complaint and attempt to find a peaceful and amicable resolution of the matter."

2. If the complainant wishes to pursue the matter, he is to "notify the Board of Control and present the charge in writing, formulated with reasonable definiteness, and the evidence . . . Charges against the president of the institution shall be dealt with by the Chairman of the Board of Control."[3]

Without even first reviewing the convention's actions and recommendation, the Board majority, shortly after 12 o'clock noon on August 17, entertained a resolution based on the charges made by the two ministers, Buelow and Harnapp. In his resolution, Walter Dissen, Secretary of the Board, directed Tietjen to meet with the complainants and to report the results of that meeting by 3:00 P.M. that afternoon. So far everything was strictly according to the rules, except for the deadline to carry out Jesus' instructions on dealing with fellow Christians (Matthew 18). With one of the complainants living in Wisconsin, and the other in Nebraska, Tietjen suggested that an immediate meeting with the complainants might be a bit difficult. Dissen replied that they were in town at his own invitation. This coincidence, explained Tietjen in a subsequent declaration, was "clear evidence of collusion between the complainants and the members of the Board majority."[4]

After further discussion, an amended resolution arranged for a meeting between Tietjen and his two accusers at 7:00 P.M. that same evening. The three men met from 7:00 to 8:15 P.M. and Tietjen agreed to answer their charges in a subsequent meeting, "as soon as," he said, "I had opportunity to gather my thoughts and my materials." No discussion of the substance of the charges took place, according to Tietjen. On the next morning, the complainants presented a letter to the Board's Chairman in which they asserted that they had been unable to reach a peaceful and amicable resolution. ('We did what we were supposed to do, but got nowhere.') They were now ready to

167

move into the second step specified in the Bylaws, which meant that the Board Majority could direct the Board's Chairman and Tietjen to meet with the two ministers. This they did forthwith and Chairman Otto, with his supporters overruling a challenge, immediately declared a recess. Evidently the complainants were as anxious as Otto to get the Bylaws over with and suspend Tietjen as quickly as possible, for Otto explained that the two ministers were still in St. Louis awaiting instructions. "Further clear evidence of collusion between the complainants and members of the Board majority," said Tietjen.

After a forty-five minute meeting in Tietjen's office, and without any discussion of the "substance of the charges," the chairman announced that his efforts as an arbiter had been unsuccessful!

Now the Board majority was at paragraph "d" in Bylaw 6.79. Otto and his supporters had decided "to proceed." At this point they had two options. In the case of a theological question, they could refer the charge to the Synod's Commission on Theology and Church Relations "for an advisory theological opinion."[5] At the same time, if "the Board decides that the charge is serious enough to threaten immediate harm to the accused or others by his continuance as a member of the faculty, the board may suspend the faculty member from his teaching duties; contractual obligations of the institution, however, shall continue until the charge is resolved."[6]

Again, without specifying either charges brought against him or spelling out alleged "harm" being averted, the Board majority voted to suspend Tietjen from his office as president and professor.

A Little Slower, Please

In less than thirty-six hours the very Synod's Bylaws which had been designed under the nose of the Association of Theological Schools to protect workers in the church against improper attacks were used to catapult Tietjen into suspension. In commenting on the ordeal, Tietjen said that the conditions under which he was tried could "best be described as a kangaroo court" with "predetermined objective to remove me from office and from the pastoral ministry of the Synod."[7]

Tietjen refused, however, to go into academic limbo under such *ultra vires* violation of the Bylaws and denied the validity of the suspension. Less certain now of the legality of their action, the Board majority decided not to implement the suspension until legal and constitutional opinions could be obtained with reference to the actions taken.

Reaction

Newspeople were perplexed. The *St. Louis Post-Dispatch* headline, page 1, on Sunday, August 19, 1973 read: CONCORDIA'S PRESIDENT SUSPENDED. The *St. Louis Globe-Democrat,* on Monday, August 20, read: *TIETJEN SUSPENDED. OR WAS HE?*

Robert H. Duesenberg and his brother Richard, eminent attorneys, and graduates of Valparaiso University, Indiana, and also respectively of Harvard and Yale, were not perplexed. On August 31, 1973, Robert served notice of indignation and demand for prompt redress in a letter addressed

ROBERT H. DUESENBERG
Attorney at Law
400 South Fourth Street
Saint Louis, Missouri 63102
Tel. (314) 621-5400

August 31, 1973

ALL DISTRICT PRESIDENTS

Gentlemen:

In the course of recent years our Church, the Lutheran Church-Missouri Synod, has struggled with internecine conflicts most frequently represented to the laity to be of doctrinal concern. The observing layman has perceived more.

Let me advise you now that I do not comment upon or commit myself to one side or the other in this debate, if, in fact, there be any clearly defined issues. Neither is that matter here germane. I address to you a concern that focuses alone on conduct of officials and a Board of Synod illegal and tragically reprehensible.

I have for some time witnessed the President and other officers of Synod with disapproving judgment. This past weekend the Board of Control of Concordia Seminary suspended the President of that institution from teaching and his administrative office. That event and the machinations up to it are the nadir in my long observation and the reason for this letter.

While the suspension represents the struggle in progress, it was a good deal more: a near denouement of that struggle executed in bold disregard of applicable by-laws, and, in that sense, an arrogant act that must not be tolerated, and which, if not reversed, threatens to split our Church asunder.

I assume you are versed in the facts. To state a few is essential, however, for these premises.

169

Commencing at New Orleans, amendments to Synod By-Laws were adopted providing in detail procedures for dealing with faculty termination of tenure and dismissal. At the same time, a resolution was offered to take action regarding the President of the Seminary and then withdrawn in favor of a resolution that "The matter of Dr. John H. Tietjen as President and Professor . . . be dealt with in such manner as is permitted under . . . provisions of the *Handbook*." (Res. 3-12 and 3-12A). In addition, at New Orleans President Preus accomplished election to the Seminary Board of Control personnel he could count upon to pursue suspending Dr. Tietjen.

After New Orleans and by July 30 the Preus majority on the Board acted to call a special meeting of the Board to take action in regard to the faculty, including, it is clear, Dr. Tietjen. At this time no charges were outstanding let alone charges to support a removal from office.

The meeting was held on August 17 and 18. Less than two days before commencement of the meeting a letter of charges was delivered to Dr. Tietjen. At the meeting, and without confrontation between the accused and accusers prior to the meeting, by majority vote of the Board Dr. Tietjen was suspended from teaching and administrative office. In a strategy no more artful than guileful trickery Dr.Tietjen's two accusers were brought to St. Louis so that the Board might be able to direct Dr. Tietjen's immediate meeting with them and thereby in some minor manner make colorable compliance with one step in the by-laws procedures.

Once accomplished, this author's brother telephoned the counsel for the Seminary to admonish strongly concerning the action and warn of its legal implications, a matter which he and I, out of concern for the Lutheran Church-Missouri Synod, had previously, on our own volition, made a subject of intense research and study. The result was suspension of the suspending resolution.

I will not labor you with the legal analysis except to advise you also that the action of the Board, indeed, presents a justiciable matter. It violates Dr. Tietjen's tenure rights and it is in offense of the By-Laws, particularly Section 6.79 thereof, and, though likely a non-legal matter, it is aberrant of any respectable moral standard. You can accept that conclusion, and if you will—it coming from individuals with qualifying credentials, the point and petition of this letter, which is being sent to all District Presidents, can be reached.

It is hard to imagine any circumstance of more imperious conduct than has been fashioned to suspend Dr. Tietjen. Arrogant, while at the same time seemingly guided by almost puerile counsel (as evidenced by the accusers' happenstance appearance in St. Louis), that proceeding should be the last move of its kind you will tolerate from the Synod's President. It is time the officers in this Church act to make its leadership conduct itself aright. No president, no council or board in this body is above its rules, procedural or substantive.

As a layman I, and many with me, loathe the apparent sinister, divisive force that is at hand, the malevolent notion that seeks fulfillment without regard to law, without effort at reconciliation, without concern for the effect in the larger sense the relentless pursuit will have. As a lawyer I look with disdain upon acts and practices of such gross impropriety particularly where a great wrong is done to a man, and a man who is one among us.

I warn you, Gentlemen, we are headed for a lasting fracture, not the mere expungement of a few the present administration cannot accept. While there may be apathy within the laity of the Church on the issues you fight over, there will not be passive resistance where the Church or its boards act in egregious error. While my brother and I have framed the legal issues, we are not in a position to assume advocacy. I can tell you though that that matter is arranged. The counsel is selected and I have reviewed the issues and the law with them. At the same time I have admonished the counsel, even as we tried to implore the Board of Control, that litigation is not the course to be desired, but to be assumed only if forced.

The petition is addressed, therefore, that you see to it for the benefit of us all that the actions of the weekend a fortnight ago are reversed, that the heat of bitterness is put away, the work of reconciliation and understanding begun, and procedures and attitudes of hate supplanted by pastoral and evangelical concern. I tell you again, a great part of your laity will have it in their Church no other way.

I cannot help reflecting upon the demise of another Synod at the hand of Dr. Preus. He is in our midst from a later day. We welcome him among us. But his hand must not be permitted a divisive force again. Let us demand that end, but in a forgiving spirit.

Sincerely yours,

Robert H. Duesenberg

RHD:dw

This letter helped preserve a measure of decency and semblance of justice during what appeared to be the lowest moral ebb period since the time of Martin Stephan.

Embarrassed by the unseemly haste taken by the Board majority and the two ministers in going through the Bylaw provisions, the Synod's Commission on Constitutional Matters advised the board to do more slowly what they did too quickly on August 17. "Somewhat like a first grader who slams the door being told by the teacher to come back and close the door right," commented Tietjen.[8] On September 20, in a special meeting, the Board reverted back to its

171

position prior to August 18 by resolving that the Board of Control's resolution of August 18, suspending Dr. John H. Tietjen, be vacated without prejudice.[9] This was in effect, however, an admission that the process in August 18-19 had been illegal. Yet, even with the Board slowed down a bit, Preus' prophecy "Tietjen must go!" could be fulfilled before the year was out.

Faculty Identity Crisis

By Oct. 18, 1973, it was evident that Tietjen's removal was non-negotiable. If synodical administration and the faculty majority were to work out a mutually acceptable proposal for coexistence, it would have to be without Tietjen. Thus, the pressure was on the faculty to advise Tietjen to resign, or face the consequences of a potentially harsh replacement for Tietjen. Any delay in Tietjen's resignation could also work to Preus' own further advantage, for Preus could project the line that Tietjen himself prevented dialogue between the majority and the minority on the faculty. Along this route the day of accounting for the faculty would merely be postponed, and Tietjen would come off looking even worse.

Preus' mating net was indeed closing in. Three ways to meet the threat were therefore open to the faculty. One, they could advise Tietjen to resign and enter into immediate dialogue with Preus and the minority faculty. That way the church could see that the faculty was interested in negotiations. On the other hand, the faculty had nothing to gain in I'm O.K.-you're not O.K. encounter except a repetition of the invitation to their own lynching in the publication of *Faithful To Our Calling, Faithful To Our Lord*. For dialogue in the context envisaged by Preus would mean that the minority would have elegant opportunity to finger disagreements with their own "orthodox" position as established at New Orleans through Resolution 3-09. No real discussion of "the issues" could take place under such monolithic conditions.

Two, the faculty could ask Tietjen not to resign, and yet attempt to enter into dialogue with Preus and company in an effort to effect some kind of compromise for coexistence. Such a plan, however, involved a basic contradiction, for insistence on the retention of Tietjen would nullify any avowed effort at compromise. If indeed compromise was what we wanted to achieve, then we were bound to urge Tietjen's resignation. For Tietjen recognized and projected himself as the last official barrier of protection for the synodical rights of his faculty. In the

172

face of further encroachment on those rights and of attacks on the confessional position of the faculty majority, Tietjen would have to stand firm as he had at New Orleans and throughout the investigation of his faculty. Thus, nothing would be achieved by urging Tietjen to remain. On the contrary, such urging would be construed as an act of defiance, bound only to hasten the faculty's day of synodical sentence. As for the practicality of compromise with Preus and company, the faculty had only to recall their agreement to participate in the Fact-Finding process under Tietjen's own urging. The end of that was "garbage in and garbage out." Could the faculty also forget that Tietjen had tried compromise in the case of Ehlen? Did it work? And soon Paul Goetting. Would they want to "compromise" this colleague out of the seminary? And, if we were later to tell Preus, "We gave you Tietjen, and we gave you Goetting, we give no more," could we really ignore the fact that at least eight to ten bodies would have to be rolled out of the brotherhood to satisfy the expectations of right-wingers who had passed Resolution 3-09? Would we be so blind as not to see Preus baring his 'wounds of Sebastian' with the lament that despite all his efforts of conciliation with the faculty, he was continually rebuffed? Who did we think we were? What syndrome of arrogance suggested that we were capable of playing on Preus' terrain?

Thus, we had to face up to the question: "Was compromise without sacrifice of principle even possible when dealing with the synodical administration?"

A third option remained. The faculty could sit tight, ask Tietjen not to resign and resolve to be a paradigm for the rest of the church. That is, they could on the one hand set an example of continuing protest against what many in the Synod were convinced was a departure from the Gospel and flagrant violation of the Judeo-Christian tradition of basic justice and right of conscience. Thereby, they could continue to make a positive contribution toward a broader synod-wide movement of moderation in tune with the principles enunciated at the August meeting of ELIM. On the other hand, by taking such a sit-tight stance without compromise, the faculty majority could be sure that the crushing weight of the Synod's administrative machinery would move against them and bulldoze them out of their academic Eden. In such case, all other professors, also ministers, teachers, bishops and administrators and board and staff members of the Missouri Synod who mounted any firm protest, could count on the steamroller likewise to move them out of the brotherhood for such rebellious and subversive activity.

173

Any way we chose to write the script, political realities read TRAG-EDY. Neither conscience nor history are, however, well served by a lesser choice. Therefore, we opted for the third. There was nothing especially heroic about this choice. The worst they could do to us was deprive us of our good names, but these they had for the most part already destroyed. They could also take our monthly incomes and our pension and medical security. In the civilized United States thought-control was done humanely. There were no cold guns at our heads. No visible thumbscrews. No recognizable stand-up cells. No literal tiger cages. No state-sanctioned secret police demanding a confession. No geographical ovens of Belsen or Auschwitz awaited us. There was merely the cold choice which, we as theologians, expected any Missourian to make, namely, to be faithful to avowed principles under the Gospel, the constitution of the Synod, and the constitution of the United States. One could not expect God to send a note of congratulations for each doing of the thing that must be done. It was as simple as that.

Always there remained, we consoled ourselves, the possibility that God might yet cure the madness of Missouri before it was too late. If only enough people would realize how they were being swindled out of their church, to use our colleague Richard Caemmerer's phrase, it might be possible, we thought, to reverse the impact of New Orleans. If only more District Presidents would accept their responsibility to be faithful to Article II of the synodical constitution, and if only more pastors would inform their congregations and urge them to reclaim what was properly theirs, then Preus and company would be compelled to recognize political, if not moral and theological realities. But what if none of this happened and our stance should continue to be construed as rebellion against synodical authority? The question required no answer, for all theology narrowed at that point to a cross on Golgotha. We had passed our identity crisis. If there was to be a barbecue, Preus would have no Judas goats.

Chapter 16

THE GOETTING CASE

Since one member of the Board majority could not be present at the October 15 meeting of the Board of Control, Tietjen's complainants postponed report of their alleged inability to reach an amicable settlement until November 19. This evaluation of their efforts was reached after only two, two-hour sessions with Tietjen, on October 10 and 26. And in these two meetings they discussed only two of the ten accusations made against Tietjen. Nor did they discuss a single item of ten pages of discussion material presented to the complainants in order to deal with the issues in their charges of false doctrine.

In a letter to the Board of Control dated November 13, 1973, the two complainants included twelve charges, two of which they had never discussed with Tietjen. They were therefore in violation of the provisions of the first step prescribed by Bylaw 6.79. Despite their knowledge that this provision had not been fulfilled, the Board majority on November 19 determined to proceed to the next step in the suspension process, namely, to involve the complainant and Tietjen with the chairman of the Board. So secure were the majority members in their mandate from the convention at New Orleans that they confessed to arrangement of the agenda for the meeting and had agreed on major resolutions in advance of the meeting. "Innumerable telephone calls," reported Tietjen, "were made by the Chairman of the Board of Control to the two complainants, to other majority members of the Board, and to synodical headquarters during October, November, and December." "This," he said, "was further evidence of the collusion in carrying out the 6.79 Bylaw procedure."

On November 28, 1973, Chairman Otto convened a meeting between Tietjen and the two complainants, but refused to honor Tietjen's request that the complainants discuss with him personally all the

175

material they had presented to the Board, including the large amount of material they had not previously discussed with Tietjen.

After this perfunctory compliance with the synodical handbook regulations, Otto reported by letter to the Board of Control that he had not been successful and had achieved nothing of substance in carrying out his responsibilities under Bylaw 6.79b. It was clear, said Tietjen, that "his only purpose in convening the meeting on November 28, 1973 had been to satisfy the letter of the 6.79b Bylaw so that the Board could get to the next step in the disciplinary process," the suspension of Tietjen from office. "If it is not possible even for minority board members to get a hearing from the majority board members, I surely cannot expect to receive one," concluded Tietjen.[1]

That this assessment was not unrealistic is suggested by the following facts: The Rev. Ewald Otto, Chairman of the Board, was an editor of *Affirm* and himself had called for the ouster of Tietjen. Mr. Alfred Briel, elected at New Orleans to serve on the Board, was on record in the public press as condemning Tietjen. Both he and Edwin C. Weber, vice president of the Board, were members of Committee 3, which had condemned Tietjen in a resolution so infamous it had to be withdrawn. Together with Weber, Mr. Eugene Fincke and Mr. Charles Burmeister had submitted accusations about Tietjen's doctrinal position and administrative work. These were included in the Convention Workbook as Reports 301 B and C and served as the basis for accusations in Resolution 3-12 and in the charges of Buelow and Harnapp. To those interested in a recapitulation view of history, Pastors Buelow and Harnapp were in a way replaying script out of Matthew 26:60 and acting as agents for the processing of charges initiated actually by members of the majority Board of Control. In effect, the majority members sat in judgment on the validity of charges which they themselves had submitted in evidence. Yet they were, in keeping with the Handbook regulations of the Synod, to be impartial judges.

Immediately after the convention Tietjen told reporters that he did not expect to be president of Concordia Seminary much longer. Preus had made his own prophecy concerning Tietjen much earlier. "By the end of the year," some heard him say.

Professor Goetting, Get Lost!

Given the strategy adopted by Preus' forces at New Orleans the Board's movement against Tietjen was in the realm of the rational and the expected. A similar evaluation could not be made in the case of the Board majority's parallel move against Professor Paul Goetting. Repeatedly Preus and company informed the Missouri Synod that only the faculty's position, not individual faculty members, had been condemned at New Orleans. In doing so, they ran counter to the contrary interpretation publicized by *Christian News,* which had earlier generated the hostility against the faculty expressed in Resolution 3-09. Evidently there was a conflict between what delegates thought they were saying at New Orleans and what officials then *interpreted* them having said. But an even more eloquent contradiction of the official interpretation came from Preus' own right wing in connection with what came to be known as "The Goetting Case."

If any proof were needed that the actions at New Orleans made every member of the teaching staff at Concordia Seminary vulnerable to arbitrary dismissal, it was the experience of Prof. Paul Goetting.

By no stretch of the imagination could Goetting have been accused of being a historical critic, for his work was in subjects relating to the Seminarian's practical ministerial tasks. Immediately after his interview with the Fact Finding Committee in 1971 President Preus had asked him, "How are things going?" "Awful," replied Goetting. Two days later Preus said to a friend of Goetting, "Tell Goetting he has nothing to worry about." Since he was, according to official interpretation, also not condemned at New Orleans, he was clean on Jonah, the meaning of *almah* (virgin) in Is. 7:14; the authorship of Isaiah, Daniel, and in all probability most of the "etc." cited in Resolution 3-09. "They'll never conk *you,"* said Goetting's Black supporters.

Shortly after the New Orleans convention Goetting received an invitation from the seven-member Federation of Evangelical Lutheran Churches of South India (FELC) to assist them in a major research effort they were conducting in cooperation with the Lutheran World Federation (LWF). The India Lutheran Church (IELC), a sister church of the Lutheran Church-Missouri Synod and member of the FELC, helped channel the invitation to the stateside board through the Rev. James Mayer, executive representative of the Missouri Synod in Asia. The Missouri Synod board endorsed the request but instructed the staff, specifically James Mayer, to secure some other person for the assignment, that is, someone who was not from Concordia Seminary.

Since the Missouri Synod was unwilling to fund Goetting, Indian church leaders resolved to appeal to the LWF for money and sought a three-month leave of absence for Goetting from his seminary responsibilities. There was not much time left, but Goetting received word that LWF money would be available and private gifts from people in the states would make up any deficit.

By September the Board of Control had received Goetting's petition for a three-month leave to assist the churches of South India during the Winter Quarter. In the Seminary Board's October meeting the petition was debated, but a tie vote left Goetting hanging. To break the tie, the Board agreed to convene a committee to decide the matter. Ewald Otto and John. H. Tietjen were to represent the seminary's interests, and William Kohn and Waldo Werning, the Synod's Board of Mission. According to Goetting, Otto made no effort to convene the committee. His delay, however, gave the people in India opportunity to cable Otto directly, and, according to Goetting, it may have become obvious through their cables that it could be embarrassing to Otto if his refusal was made public. One day, in any event, Otto is alleged to have phoned Tietjen with a very brief noncommittal message: "Tell Goetting to get out of the country." This message was relayed to Goetting about the first week in November, about a month before his scheduled departure. Otto could now tell India, without having committed the Synod to official approval of Goetting, that Goetting was on the way. The decision was worthy of the mind of Preus.

At the same time the deadline was drawing near for action on Goetting's contract. On the night of the Board's November meeting, Dr. John Damm, Academic Dean, telephoned Goetting that the Board had voted neither to interview nor to renew his contract. This meant that Goetting's contract with Concordia Seminary would automatically expire in June, 1974.

The next morning Goetting went to his seminary office, sat down and asked himself, "What do I do now?" During his dialogue with himself the telephone rang—it was Geneva, Switzerland calling. "The Lutheran World Federation is happy to announce that you are the recipient of a grant to serve the Federation of Evangelical Lutheran Churches in India," said the voice on the other end. Additional monies donated from private sources made it possible for Goetting and his family to leave for India on December 1, 1973. But they knew that on return to the States, they would have but four months to find new quarters and new employment.

In reviewing the data relating to Goetting's case, more than one observer has remarked, "Things just don't add up." It seemed like a 'whodunit' with one of the vital clues missing. "It's really irrational," explained Goetting. "I was told by a military man that any commander who hates his enemy loses rational capacity for entertaining viable alternatives. New Orleans generated hate, and I was first in the line of fire." In editorial comment, Moderates said, "Paul Goetting and also his family deserve better from so-called *fellow* Christians than to be 'unceremoniously dumped' *without even the benefit of a hearing or the courtesy of a reason.*"[2]

Through its action the Board majority in reality confessed that doctrine was not the chief issue. By dismissing one of the faculty's most evangelical and conservative professors, the Board was signalling a pogrom that was soon to make a shambles of Concordia Seminary at 801 De Mun Avenue, St. Louis, Missouri.

Mass Retirement

As though determined to grease their excursion into academic suicide, the Board majority on November 19 resolved that seven professors were to be scheduled for retirement or modified service, effective February, 1974. Those affected were: Richard Caemmerer, Arthur Carl Piepkorn, Herbert Boumann, Alfred von Rohr Sauer, Lorenz Wunderlich, Arthur C. Repp, Alfred O. Fuerbringer. According to Bylaw 6.82 of the Synod, "e. Faculty members *may* (italics ours) be honorably retired or transferred to modified service by action of the Board of Control at the age of 65 or any year thereafter and *shall be* (italics ours) retired at the age of 75. f. Service loads and conditions of service after age 65 shall be modified according to individual capacity and shall be determined by the Board of Control."

In previous years the Board of Control discussed retirement plans with professors and took into account age and physical capacity. At this November meeting, however, Erwin Roschke, a member of the Board was so depressed by the lack of human concern that he left the meeting prior to adjournment, saying that he could not in good conscience remain.

The mere fact of retirement did not cause Piepkorn so much indignation as did the accompanying description: *honorable.* "It's an insult," he said. "They have no theological competence. How then can they retire me *honorably?* What does that say for my theology? I want to be retired *dishonorably.*"

Again, the fact that seven were to be retired "honorably" revealed what some construed as basic hypocrisy implicit in the procedures and resolutions adopted at New Orleans. Six of the professors were part of the faculty majority, and the Board had, in effect, simply determined, without interviews after New Orleans, that these six men were not guilty of the position condemned at New Orleans. Moreover, these six men had signed the statement of protest on July 24. Yet they were retired honorably without retracting their protest. It was not difficult therefore to discern the political, rather than high doctrinal concern, in the major resolutions adopted at New Orleans. Conscientious pastors and laymen who voted for them out of the depth of convictions and agony of their minds, were being betrayed by their own leaders. Otten, writing in *Christian News,* called for more honest treatment: "Even if older professors . . . are 'retired,' it should be stated that they are not being permitted to continue as professors in the LCMS because they are guilty of defending false doctrine."[3] If it was Otto's intention really to "Close the Sem," he was on a sure-fire course. By attacking at the same time three different parties, namely Tietjen, the very non-controversial professor Goetting, and seven men near or in their 65th year, Otto had opened the door to fresh appraisals by conscience.

In addition to their avowed dedication to theological principle and appreciation for the contributions Tietjen had made to their spiritual and academic life, the students now could think in terms of arbitrary procedures that threatened their own careers to the very roots: Some of the seminary's best professors were disappearing before their very eyes, and without show of cause.

With One Voice

In response to the action of the Seminary Board in their meeting of November 19, the students of the seminary addressed themselves to the pastors and teachers in a document entitled WITH ONE VOICE, An Appeal by the Students of Concordia Seminary. Their accompanying letter read:

December 12, 1973

Fellow Members of the Body of Christ,

During the past year, thousands of words have been spoken and written about the "faculty majority" of Concordia Seminary, St. Louis, Missouri. Some of them have been words of praise, but many of them have been words of accusation, words which accuse these men of teaching false doctrine and leading many astray.

As students at Concordia Seminary, we are deeply affected by these words. For the accusations which are being brought against these men are being brought against men whom we deeply love and respect, men who are instructing us in the faith and equipping us for a ministry of Word and sacrament.

In the enclosed letter of appeal, we defend these men and indicate that we are not about to let these accusations go by unchallenged. We appeal specifically to The Seminary Board of Control to reconsider some of its past decisions regarding members of the "faculty majority," and we appeal in general to all of the members of our Synod for their support and fervent intercessions.

We are sending this letter of appeal throughout our Synod not because we desire to divide it, but because we feel that it is important for pastors, teachers and laymen to know how we feel.

A large number of students have already endorsed this appeal, and their names are included in this mailing.

In the Name of Jesus Christ and for His Church,

The Student Administrative Council
Concordia Seminary, St. Louis, Missouri

WITH ONE VOICE
An Appeal by the Students of Concordia Seminary

In the fear of God and mindful of this opportunity to speak with one voice we, the members of the student body of Concordia Seminary, St. Louis, take courage from our Lord Jesus Christ to make this statement.

"God has so adjusted the body . . . that there may be no discord in the body, but that the members may have the same care for one another. If one member suffers, all suffer together; if one member is honored, all rejoice together. Now you are the body of Christ and individually members of it." (I Cor. 12:24–27)

As members of the Body of Christ and students at Concordia Seminary, we stand with the faculty majority of Concordia Seminary, St. Louis.

Because they have been unjustly condemned as false teachers "not to be tolerated in the Church of God" and because they confess faithful allegiance to "the Scriptures of the Old and New Testaments as the written word of God and the only rule and norm of faith and practice" and "all the Symbolical Books of the Evangelical Lutheran Church as a true and unadulterated statement and exposition of the word of God", and because they are faithful to their ordination vows, we stand with them.

Because as members of the Body of Christ we do not suffer alone but together, we understand the condemnation of the faculty majority of Concordia Seminary to apply also to us.

We face this condemnation and the crisis it has created in our church in faith, and we will act accordingly and respond appropriately.

There are no easy solutions to our problems and, in fact, we may not be able to resolve the current crisis at Concordia Seminary and in our church. But we will no longer be silent. We will work to redeem this situation by a faithful witness to our Lord and Savior Jesus Christ. In Him alone are we free to be the church in this place at this time.

Therefore, we appeal to the Board of Control of Concordia Seminary, St. Louis, to reconsider the decisions made at its November 19, 1973 meeting, to renew the contract of Professor Paul Goetting, and to revoke the new retirement policy. We believe these decisions of the Board of Control to be unfair and contrary to good pastoral practice and good Christian conduct. If the Board of Control does not reconsider its decisions it will have proceeded against all the members of the student body.

We believe that the Church ought to know that we are individually struggling with our Christian commitments to the Lutheran Church-Missouri Synod. We do not know what the decisions of the Board of Control mean for our continuing theological education and our future ministry in the Church.

In the face of this uncertainty, we confess our loyalty to Christ Jesus as our Savior and our Hope, and our commitment to the Scriptures of the Old and New Testaments and to all the Symbolical Books of the Evangelical Lutheran Church.

We appeal to the Church, to our brothers and sisters in the faith, to our pastors and teachers, to the President of the Synod, to the District Presidents, to the Board of Control, and to all Christians into whose hand this statement comes for their support and for their fervent intercessions.

In the Name of Jesus Christ and for His Church,

SIGNATURES

I YEAR

Paul Appel
Wayne Bacus
Jack Bailey
Wayne Basch
Allen Belanger
Robert Bjornstad
William Bordonaro
Charles Bohning
Jerome Burce
Vernon Burger
Robert Day
Steven Dietrich

Brent Duesenberg
Rodney Eberhardt
Charles Erzkus
Triffel Felske
Don Flaxbart
Lawrence Frederick
Wayne Freund
Richard Gall
Frank Gervascio
Donald Gold
Tom Hadley
William Hartfelder

THE GOETTING CASE

Duane Heckman
Jonathan Heerboth
Mark Helge
John Helmers
Kevin Hilgendorf
Gary Hill
Robert Hingst
John Hitzeroth
Paul Hunsicker
Jon Imme
Paul Jaster
Mark Kastens
Gregory Kaufmann
Steven Kenney
Paul Kersten
Dale Koehneke
Victor Kolch
Jonathan Kosec
Robert Kuppler
Jerrold Lamb
Goerge Loewer
Clifford Lohmann
Michael A. Malinsky
Kenneth Mann
Bruce Modahl
Craig Moeller
Edward Mohme
Charles J. Molnar
Terry Moore
Mark Nieting

David Olson
David Osborne
Janith Otte
Mark Patzke
Carl Pihl
David Preisinger
John Priest
Philip Quardokus
Ernst Rex
Walter Rice
Gerry Rickel
Jerry G. Rossow
John Ryding
Edgar Schambach
Donald Scherling
George Scheurich
Curtis Schneider
M. Samuel Sherouse
William Shimkus
Keith Sievers
William Singleton
Paul Sodtke
Darrell Stuehrenberg
George Tilley
Vernon Vansteenburg
Richard Wolf
Michael Zehnder
Douglas Zike
Richard Zuch

II YEAR

Steven Albertin
Michael Averyt
David Baker
Robert Bartel
Tom Beavers
James Bickel
Dennis Bux
Kim Campbell
William Clements
James Cottingham
Larry Courson
James Couser
Duane Daeke
Norman Dake

Kim DeVries
Roger Dramstad
Allen Dundek
Richard Dunker
Thomas Duval
Donald Duy
David Elseroad
Robert Farlee
Boyd Faust
Dan Flaxbart
Michael Fox
Ronald Friedrich
Daniel Gerken
John Gosswein

Paul Gross
Patrick Hahn
Frank Hamil
Thomas Hartley
Jack Hartman
Timothy Hartner
Ronald Hatch
Jeffrey Hering
Frederick Hertwig
Terry Herzberg
Thomas Hiller
Roland Hornbostel
Steven Hummel
Paul Jagusch
LaVerne Janssen
Keith Johnson
Philip Jordan
Tony Kluender
Justin Kollmeyer
Steven Kosberg
David Drueger
Andrew Leahy
Michael Lohmann
Marcus Lohrmann
Thomas Ludwig
Dany Manullang
Matthew Martens
Robert McConnell
Larry McCormick
Waldemar Meyer
Lloyd Miller
Jacquelyn Mize
Kjell Omahr Mørk
Charles Muse
Lee R. Nelson
Marlin Otte

Thomas Piel
Robert Porisch
Kyle Radcliffe
David Rebeck
James Rehder
Leroy Rehrer
Fred Rengstorf
Robert Rimbo
Richard Rist
Edward Rivett
Donald Romsa
Leon G. Rosenthal
Timothy Rothfuss
William Ruth
Kent Schaufelberger
Reinold Schlak
John Schmelzer
Timothy Seeber
Paul Sieveking
James Stein
James Strasen
Roger K. Straub
Mark Strietelmeier
Eugene Stueve
Paul Theiss
James Thomas
William Triebe
Adolph Wachsmann
Lynn D. Waggoner
Charles Werth
Blake Wolf
Gordon Young
William Zabel
Arthur Ziemann
Reid Zimmermann

IV YEAR [4]

David G. Abrahamson
Philip Backman
Mark Bartels
David Beckmann
Paul Bierlein
Barry Brandt
Daniel Comsia

Martin Dasler
David Doroh
David Dudley
Dennis Fakes
Duane Feldmann
John Flaxbeard
Daniel Gensch

THE GOETTING CASE

John Glamann
Robert Gnuse
Roger Harms
Frederick Hedt
Robert Heiliger
Stephen Helmreich
Keith Holste
Roland Jank
Lance Jennings
David Keller
Paul Kellert
David Krause
Daniel Kriefall
John Langewisch
Paul Langohr
Loren Leapaldt
Norman Lentz
Guy Leppich
Steven Liechti
Elwyn Luber
Barry Ludwig
Larry Mackay
Gerald Mansholt
Carroll Marohl
Charles McCrum
Thomas McElwey
Arthur Meyer
Duane Meyer
Stanley Meyer
David Meyers
Gerald Miller
Brian Moran
Richard Mueller
Donald Mulfinger
Steven Myers
Gregory Naeser
James Navta
Ronald Neustadt
James P. Nickols
Steven Olson

Vernon Oestmann
Barry Pfanstiel
John Prohl
David Reichert
Daryl Robarge
Dennis Rock
Kenton Rohrberg
William R. Roper
David Roschke
Ronald Roschke
Donald Schaefer
Kenneth Schamber
Jonathan Schedler
Norman Schmoock
Dell Schomburg
Jerry Schultz
Paul A. Schwan
Glen Segond
Thomas Seim
Paul Spangenberg
James Spilos
Kenneth Storck
Frederick Strickert
Paul Terhune
Gary Teske
Norman Timmermann
Charles Vogeley
Walter Vosicka
Dwight Wascom
Kent Wendorf
Daniel Wenger
Eric Westmark
Arthur Wienandt
Keith Wiens
James P. Wind
Lee Woolery
Clifford Zeckser
Marvin Ziprick
Ray Zischang

GRAD STUDENT

Jerry Dykstra
Lieselotte K. Hanna
Dale R. Kuhn
Richard G. Herbel

Joan Lundgren
Mary Mittlestaedt
Sieg Schroeder
Leslie F. Weber

185

Michael T. Clifford
Richard E. Hoffmann
Paul G. Theiss
Aaron L. Uitti
Michael P. Rowold
Ted Schroeder

Jim Geuder
Thomas R. McQueen
J. Paul Rajashekar
Gwen B. Sayler
Robert C. Wiemken

After Goetting's dismissal, the students received a further preview of their academic future when it was announced that the Board of Control had on January 7, 1974, eliminated nineteen courses from the Seminary's catalog, pending review by a special committee. Pointing to Academic Dean Damm, one of the Board members said, "See this course on world hunger? That's how they're wasting Synod's money!" (Laughter) In view of the Synod's avowed interest in foreign missions, it came as a surprise to Dr. Wi Jo Kang, the seminary's chief expert in Eastern affairs, when his course on "The Christian West and the People's Republic of China" was excised. Nor was the Synod, after leaving most of the ghetto to itself, interested in learning about "The Church and the City in History." Also, after Preus' involvement in the 'Brazil Connection,' a story best left to oral tradition, it was a foregone conclusion that "The Church's Involvement in Economic Activities" would not be a world-beater. In fairness to the Board it must be granted that they may not have understood the catalog description, or they would not have questioned "Christian Anthropology and Models of Man in Contemporary Social Sciences." Old Testament offerings were gutted. Courses on creation theology and implications for environmental concern hit the block. Etc. Etc. New Testament interpreters were aghast at the possible implications for the quality of their own theology; none of their courses were among the favored 19, not even "Paul and Wisdom" and "Readings in the Thought World of the New Testament."

If the Board had any intention of interesting the students in the way they planned to run the Seminary, they certainly succeeded in keeping their counsel. In any case, the catalog represented to some extent a contract with the student, and the axing of 19 courses without consulting the consumers was not calculated to win their affections. Also, the Board's failure to submit questions about particular courses to the chairmen of the departments was a gross violation of academic professionalism. Concordia Seminary was well on its way to becoming a third-rate Bible College.

Chapter 17

MISSION UNDER FIRE

Missouri's battle lines in January and February of 1974 were spread out across the world. If members of the Synod thought that Concordia Seminary was the seat of their problem, they had only to start a body count at the mission headquarters of the Lutheran Church—Missouri Synod.

The Rev. James Mayer, for seventeen years a missionary in India, had been engaged for almost a decade more in synodical mission planning. On Saturday, January 12, 1973, the Synod's Board for Missions terminated his services without granting Mayer's request for a statement of the reasons.

Tension between the missions staff and the Synod's Board had been building up especially since 1971 when The Rev. Dr. Waldo Werning, a hardline traditionalist, moved into the chairmanship of the Board.

He and his associates were not happy with the *Mission Affirmations,* which the Synod had adopted with a near unanimous vote in 1965.[1] One of the resolves asked, "That we repent of our individual and corporate selfcenteredness and disobedience, whenever it has caused us to regard our local congregations or our Synod as ends in themselves and moved us to give self-preservation priority over God's mission . . . ." To a church congenitally accustomed to being always in the right this was a hard saying, yet it had passed. But it meant that the Synod henceforth could be subject to critique.

Another resolve stated that "Christians will approach men of other faiths in humility and love. They joyfully acknowledge that God is active in the lives of all men through his continued creative and providential concern, through the law written in their hearts, and through God's revelation of himself in creation and nature. Christians affirm a common humanity with all men. They confess a common sinfulness.

They rejoice over a universal redemption won for all in Jesus Christ. . . ."

Such words made obsolete the favorite illustration recited on mission Sundays about the number of souls per minute going to hell. This paragraph suggested that God might yet have mercy on those who died before the Missouri Synod or some other group could reach them. It was the first major blow that had ever been struck in Missouri for divine executive privilege.

Another resolve asserted that "the Evangelical Lutheran Church is chiefly a confessional movement within the total body of Christ rather than a denomination emphasizing institutional barriers of separation." To the minds of moderates this one sentence drew the curtain off Missouri's ecumenical poker game in which the Synod's representatives came to the conference table dealing themselves all high cards of pure doctrine and the opposition low cards of unionism, liberalism, social gospelism, and historical-critical methodism, with the winner maintaining the *status quo*. However, to discourage any thought that the Missouri Synod was about to run downhill smack into ecumenism, the next resolve balanced things with a proviso that cooperation was to be refused "when it would deny God's Word." All this was expressed in the spirit that was typical of the Missouri Synod in days when the collective ego balanced happily between tradition and expectations of the future.

Werning and associates might even have been willing to live with this document without supplementary interpretation, had not most of the Synod's mission staff taken the document so seriously as to implement the resolves at every opportunity. The result was that Missouri Synod Lutherans now found official support for prayer with other Christians on the mission field and could go to the Lord's Supper with at least Lutheran non-Missourians, without waiting for a convention twenty or thirty years in the future to grant permission. To traditionalists steeped in the rhetoric of antagonism toward others who were deficient in doctrine, such actions were heresy, and those who encouraged them in the name of the Mission Affirmations would have to pay the consequences.

How would President Preus handle the explosive situation? Preus was too politically astute to let Werning come too close to him, but he had to accept the political reality of the clout Werning carried in the Middle West. Werning had helped Preus win at Denver, and Preus counted on a large share of the financial support that came from "Mainstream" Missouri.

Mission Money

This mainstream area of the Missouri Synod raised a large percentage of the money for the $24,000,000 + operation of all the Synod's enterprises. So far as the people were concerned, everything contributed by them to the Synod's work was a contribution for "missions." "Mission money" supported the Synod's vast bureaucracy and educational system, which supplied teachers and ministers to carry out the church's mission. Only a comparatively small percentage actually went into the support of foreign mission installations and personnel. The word "mission" was therefore a powerful political term. Were the people to lose confidence in their Synod's mission program, the entire structure of the Synod could collapse with the catastrophic force of an earthquake in an area covered by mud huts.

Thus Werning posed for Preus both an asset as well as a potential liability, and the latter loomed large on the weekend of January 10–12, 1974.

To pull off both the suspension of Tietjen later on in the month and now the termination of Mayer meant that Preus would be involved in a war on two major fronts. It would take all the political sophistication he could muster to come out of it with his church substantially intact. True enough, people of the Missouri Synod, long accustomed to unquestioning and uncritical obedience, might weather the temporary storm, but there were less hazardous routes to attain the purification objective.

Therefore, prior to the Board's meeting, Preus had urged its members not to make any "changes at this time."[2] But Werning chose either to forget or to ignore the fact that Preus did not relish being blistered in the mail and went on to encourage Mayer's dismissal. At a subsequent convention, Anaheim, California, 1975, he would pay for this indiscretion by being the sole loser out of 131 candidates endorsed by the right-wing journal *Affirm*.

In a unanimous denunciation of the termination of their colleague, seventeen full-time staff members of the Synod's world mission agency confronted Dr. Preus with their concerns.

Like the Fact-Finding Committee, the Mission Board's committee responsible for reviewing Mayer's service record was composed exclusively of so-called "conservatives." About a year earlier the cosponsor of the Mission Affirmations, Dr. Martin Kretzmann, had been terminated without show of cause. The fact that he had reached the age of 65 was irrelevant in view of the further fact that the Synodical headquarters had numerous people over 65 serving in various capacities.

In the wake of the action against Kretzmann, the dismissal of Mayer appeared to the staff to be a sympton of "a much deeper problem that threatens to reverse the forward thrust of missions" which the Synod had enjoyed, they said. "The repeated downgrading of co-workers in mission and the allegations of unionism, lack of evangelistic fervor, inefficiency, complacency and mismanagement follow the same pattern of negative premises and judgmental evaluations which the leadership of the Board for Missions has directed against missionaries and Missions staff." Denying the Board's implication of differences in theology (which in Missourianese meant that the accused were guilty of false doctrine), the staff said: "The issue is a difference in the philosophy by which the Word of God is practiced—an evangelical orientation vs. legalism. Polarization, political maneuverings, and the intemperate use of power have frequently replaced Christian love and fair play." In a climactic appeal to Dr. Preus, the staff reminded him, "That our church is committed in many Synodical statements to relate to districts and sister churches in a manner that frees and enables them to be zealous proclaimers of the Gospel and to deal with them in a climate of trust rather than of paternalism and control."[3]

The letter was signed by

William H. Kohn, Executive Secretary
H. W. Rohe, Ministry to Deaf
Dorris J. Lamb, Medical Missions
J. W. Mayer, South Asia
Paul Heerboth, Personnel Services
James C. Cross, North America—Church and Community
Paul H. Strege, East Asia
Reuben J. Schmidt, North America and Special Ministries
Walter H. Meyer, North America -Congregation and Community
Phyllis N. Kersten, Mission Interpretation
William F. Reinking, Africa and Middle East
W. J. Fields, Campus Ministry
William T. Seeber, Assistant to the Executive Secretary
Fred J. Pankow, Latin America
Marion Kretzschmar, Designated Gifts
Wolfgang F. Bulle, M.D., Medical Missions
Herman H. Koppelman, World Areas

Instead of finding his financial base strengthened, Preus was shortly to be faced with its steady erosion. On January 28, 1974, the Board of

Evangelical Lutherans in Mission (ELIM) issued a direct challenge to the leadership of Preus. After sketching the world-wide respect the Missouri Synod had enjoyed for 25 years after World War II, their statement said:

> Since 1969 all that has changed. The current synodical administration combines dogmatic rigidity with legalistic political leadership. Our church has lost the respect of much of the Christian world and is a source of embarrassment, suffering, and distress to her members, who are now set over against each other.
>
> Today the growth has ended. The international missionary staff, reflecting also the discontent of the large majority of our missionaries, unanimously dissents against the new policies encouraged and established by the administration.

The statement went on to speak of the "paralyzed" educational system and of the "controlled" media which make it impossible for the church's members to "receive balanced accounts on the basis of which to make up their minds in a spirit of fairness about the Synod's problems."

"President Preus' effort to direct Dr. Tietjen into ministry in a synodical parish even while under serious charges of false doctrine showed," the statement said, "that Preus was 'capable of tolerating false doctrine.' "

After pointing out that the question of Preus' "resignation" might well be raised, the statement looked with hope to the District Presidents for leadership in the task of working for "renewal, unity, and growth in our beloved Church." "Out of the chaos and ashes of our present Synod," the ELIM Board concluded, "God can effect a new creation in Jesus Christ. It is then still possible that we can, through it, serve Him and our fellow humans in ways that can give us all together a joy worthy of our destiny as his children."

Underwriting this statement, the ELIM Board resolved: 1. To encourage the establishment of an independent mission society, 2. To support efforts to continue theological education for St. Louis seminary students through possible alternate methods, and 3. To assist by all means those whose ministries had been terminated or threatened by the current synodical crisis.[4]

With his action against James Mayer, Werning had indeed begun to line the bottom of the coffers of ELIM. Preus' Seminary Board of Control would ensure the filling.

191

Chapter 18

MORATORIUM

After months of trial and error, the Board of Control of Concordia Seminary finally succeeded in suspending Dr. John H. Tietjen from the presidency of the school at about 9:30 P.M., on January 20, 1974.

Victor Bryant, in charge of public relations for President Preus and the Synod, had come on the campus in the late afternoon of the same day. "I thought something might happen," he casually remarked in explanation of his presence to a colleague in the newsgathering business. Unfortunately for synodical credibility, his news release, apparently drawn up before the event, included reference to Tietjen's alleged "malfeasance in performing the duties of the office" of President. The Board had, however, not made this particular judgment prior to the issuance of Bryant's news release on the next day, Monday. But Bryant's certainty about the outcome was of a piece with Preus' announcement made six months earlier, "Tietjen must go!" "Obvious collusion," said the Seminary's PR man, Larry Neeb. With the help of Preus, Bryant could compete with St. John the Revelator and write the scenario for Armageddon before the charge began. Reaction was swift. Concordia's communication network pulsated at its highest frequency. By midnight, shortly after Dr. Martin H. Scharlemann had been declared Acting President, a majority of the student body knew they would be meeting in special assembly after only a few hours sleep.

The students' publication *With One Voice*[1] in December should have alerted the Board of Control to the implications of action against Tietjen. Preparing for the worst, a special committee, Students Concerned for Reconciliation under the Gospel (SCRUG), with the support of the Student Advisory Committee (SAC), had convened a meeting in Sieck Hall, Room 102, on Saturday, the 19th. Refurbishing Bryant's words, seminarian John Dornheim later commented, "I suppose we all expected John Tietjen to get the axe at the Board of Control meeting which was being held that weekend."

Besides members of student committees and other seminarians, invited guests included campus chaplains, two representatives from Concordia Teachers College, River Forest, Illinois, Steve Harms from Concordia Senior College, Fort Wayne, Indiana, and ELIM's president, Samuel Roth. Dr. Martin J. Marty had another commitment and was unable to accept the invitation extended to him. Instead, he communicated by video tape and urged the students to do well whatever they planned to do.

In a special interview Dornheim described the proceedings:

> "In the course of the meeting Roth cited reasons for the birth of ELIM. *Missouri in Perspective,* he said, was an effective tool to inform the Missouri Synod's constituency. Numerous people were in jeopardy because of synodical actions, and a recent anti-ELIM ruling of the Synod's Commission on Constitutional Matters confirmed the probability of bad prospects for the future. But ELIM was committed, he said, to support both emotionally and financially the victims of 'creeping legalism,' which substituted the Law for the Gospel. Roth also informed the group about developments on the mission scene and expressed the view that whatever happened at Concordia Seminary would have a serious effect on the entire church.
>
> "Steve Harms addressed himself to the problem of the general lack of information at the Senior College. He said that he would be willing to work with other students in disseminating information at the Senior College as well as at other synodical schools.
>
> "One of the campus ministers spoke about the problems of fellowship between Missouri Synod people and members of other church bodies. He thought it was necessary to affirm a stance that was in accord with the best of Missouri's tradition, as expressed in the *Mission Affirmations.* Taking a charitable view, he felt that there was indeed a spirit of legalism afoot, but not the spirit of Anti-Christ, and he looked for continuance of positive courses of action. Another participant urged that a grapevine network be set up.
>
> "The assembly then explored possibilities in the event of Tietjen's dismissal. But none competed seriously with the proposal to close the seminary for one week, two weeks, or an indefinite period of time. We felt that we could not get a decent education and that our future ministry was in jeopardy if we continued under the threat of Board of Control actions.
>
> "I guess we never really got past this issue. Apparently none of us could see any alternative. If we did, I don't remember. Oh, there were trivial suggestions, like holding a prayer vigil in the quad below the

board room, but they never really got off the ground. So the moratorium was the major agenda item. We all felt that John's suspension was pivotal. Until that happened, we couldn't do anything.

"It is possible that we had justification to act before John was suspended, especially on the grounds of the termination of Goetting and the 'Retirees.' But we felt that any action would have confirmed the notion that John was incompetent for not being able to control his students, a criticism that was actually levelled against him. So, it was a matter of how we were going to pull it off.

"There are those who still contend that guys on the faculty were calling the shots. If that was true, I never knew it. Sure, the moratorium was not an idea which just popped up on January 19. All of us there were committed to it. Yet, we were all sensitive to the needs and anxieties of our peers. This tempered greatly our discussion. Our two major concerns were Tietjen and the other students. Most of us wanted a full indefinite moratorium. Classes, all classes, would stop. We would do everything we could to convince the others. We felt it would be ineffective to have half of the student body still going to class.

"Any sizeable percentage would hurt our effort. We had to deal with students who had minority profs. The faculty majority we were sure would go along. But we had to deal with students who would agree to strike only to get out of classes. There were also some in the meeting who felt that a partial moratorium would be sufficient. But by the end of the day it appeared that consensus was unanimous.

"On Saturday evening the resolution for moratorium was phrased by a special committee. We reconvened on Sunday afternoon at 1:00 P.M. and spent considerable time discussing it and putting it into final shape.

"Then after dinner on Sunday evening, Jon Kosec and I met in the Academic Dean's office with John Damm. We felt that it would be necessary to let someone know what had transpired. Midway through the meeting, the phone rang. Before it was answered, the three of us knew, almost instinctively, that John Tietjen had gotten the axe. Kosec and I immediately began telephoning faculty members with the news, telling them that an emergency meeting would be held. We also called the student leaders. Within a short time everyone in the community knew and Tietjen spoke briefly in the chapel at 10:00 P.M."

Later the same evening Gerald Miller, president of the student body, went to see Tietjen. Already two months earlier Miller had himself composed a draft resolution of moratorium, but in the "sincere hope," he said, that it would not be found necessary. The resolution that came out of the students' committee on Sunday afternoon was a refinement of his draft, and it was the finished version that he presented to Tietjen. "He was quite surprised to see me," said Miller in recollection of the visit. "I shared with him the draft of our moratorium resolution, but he expressed no special elation. He did, however, underline the seriousness of what we were about to do. It has been said that he pushed us, but this is simply not true."

No "Business as Usual"

On Monday morning, January 21, the entire seminary community met for devotions in the chapel-auditorium, in Wyneken Hall. Shortly thereafter two meetings would be in progress. About 50 yards away Concordia's regents were to resume sessions at 10:30 A.M. In the chapel, two hours earlier, Gerald Miller, fourth-year student and president of the student body, raised his gavel.

On February 6, Dr. Martin E. Marty, professor of Church History at the University of Chicago, would publish a memorial message in *The Christian Century.* In the form of a tombstone inscription, with cross, it read in appropriate Gothic: "In Memoriam, Concordia Seminary, St. Louis, December 9, 1839–January 20, 1974. R.I.P." (may it rest in peace)

Apprehending the threat of rigor mortis, the students accepted their responsibility to history, came to order, and heard their chairman ask:

> "How long can we continue to go on with business as usual. I personally have had all that I can take. A man of God is being taken away from us because he has dared to disagree with those who are over him. Our life and work in this place is being disrupted and turned into a farce. Many people in the church are looking to us for leadership. If we fail to act now, I'm afraid that we will never act. The wind is blowing in our favor. The Spirit of God is resting upon us and is alive in this place.
>
> I believe we need to call a halt to our theological education under this Board of Control until it has given an account of itself, until it has proved to the church that it has been dealing justly and evangelically with its responsibilities in this place. We have outlined how they might do that in 'A Student Resolution.' "

Prayer for the Accusers

After the meeting got underway, outsiders heard thunderous applause emanating from Wyneken Hall. In a time of low popularity ratings for administrators of educational institutions, it would have been difficult for them to infer that the students were cheering a school president.

Dr. Tietjen waited for the ovation to subside and then read to the assembly a statement which he planned to give to the press at 10:00 the same morning.

Shocked into total disbelief, the students heard what seemed to many a script out of Watergate. Unnamed "agents" of Preus had been in contact with Tietjen "for the past two months" in order to "arrange a deal." The proposal included these terms, he said, "If I would agree to accept a Call (to serve as pastor in some congregation), arrangements for which were being sought through friendly district presidents, Professor Goetting," (whose contract had not been renewed in November, 1973)[2] "would be re-engaged, a one-year moratorium would be declared on all efforts to remove faculty members, and the charges preferred against me would not be pursued. I was informed that unless I agreed to the proposal, my suspension was inevitable, the decision not to renew Professor Goetting's contract would stand, the Board would proceed to implement its new retirement policy, and additional procedures would be invoked against the faculty.

"In response, I made it clear again and again that I would not be party to such a 'deal' and could not even consider another call as long as the present charges against me remain in force. I consider the proposed 'deal' to be immoral. In the first place, it turns faculty members and their families into pawns in pursuit of political objectives. Devoid of any integrity, it plays with people's lives. In the second place, it clearly demonstrates that the charges against me are nothing more than tools to remove me from my position. If there is any substance at all to the charge that I am a teacher of false doctrine, then it is immoral to arrange a Call for me and to inflict me on another community of Christian people. The proposed deal makes a mockery of God's truth and of the church's obligation to safeguard it.

> "I will not participate in such evil in order thereby to spare myself or to pursue some false hope of protecting faculty members. In the face of such evil I cannot remain silent. I am well aware that what I say will be denied and attacked, but it is the truth. The members of our Synod must become aware of the moral bankruptcy of the actions of the present leadership of our Synod and of the Seminary's Board of Control. Such evil, if allowed to continue, will bring the judgment of God's wrath on us all."

He then informed the student body that legal counsel had advised him

> "to challenge the suspension action of the Board of Control by asking for an injunction against it in civil court. I have been assured on the basis of considerable evidence that the action of the Board of Control is illegal and that I have sufficient grounds for bringing suit against the majority members of the Board of Control and the president of the Synod.
> "I have done a great deal of soul-searching over whether or not to challenge the legality of the Board's action. I am fully aware not only of the consequence of that decision for the seminary, the Synod, and myself, but also of the significance of that decision for many others who are committed to contend against the oppressive legalism that has become dominant in our Synod.
> "I have decided not to institute legal proceedings in my own behalf. Though I would gladly go to court to insure the rights of others, I prefer to endure injustice than to contend for my rights against my own church body in secular court. My decision is a consequence of my understanding of what it means to be a follower of the Lord Jesus Christ. In the Sermon on the Mount our Lord Jesus tells us, 'If any one strikes you on the right cheek, turn to him the other also; and if any would sue you and take your coat, let him have your cloak as well' (Matthew 5:39–40). The president of the Synod and the Board of Control are determined to take my present position from me through a process which will also force me out of the pastoral ministry of the Synod. In accord with our Lord's injunction I will not make use of the legal process of the secular courts in order to stop them."

Declaring his resolve also to take no further action in response to remaining procedures the Board of Control would have to follow before it could legally remove him from office, Dr. Tietjen said:

> "I stand committed to my ordination vow, reaffirmed at the time of my installation into my present office. I accept without reservation the Scriptures of the Old and the New Testaments as the written Word of God and the only rule and norm of faith and of practice and the Lutheran symbols comprising the Book of Concord as a correct and unadulterated statement and exposition of the Word of God. I also stand committed to my pledge to carry out the responsibilities of my office as seminary president. I do not object to evaluation of either my faithfulness to my confessional commitment or to my performance in office. I have no doubts about the outcome of a fair and impartial evaluation.
> "However, the present proceedings being conducted by the Board of Control on the basis of Bylaw 6.79 offer no possibility of a fair and

impartial judgment. They are the result of collusion between the president of the Synod, the six majority members of the Board of Control, and my two accusers [Pastors Leonard Buelow and Harlan Harnapp]. They are a charade in which my two accusers and the majority members of the Board are seeking to fulfill the letter of the Bylaws for the purpose of reaching a predetermined objective, already publicly announced by the president of the Synod [a reference to Dr. Preus' statement in 1973, "Tietjen must go"], to remove me from office and from the pastoral ministry of the synod. . . .

"In conclusion, I should like to point out that there is little point in participating in proceedings whose outcome has already been determined. When people refuse to hear, there is no point in speaking. When your accusers are also your judge and jury, you already know the verdict of the trial. My respect for the Bylaws of Synod is too high to permit me to engage in proceedings which by a show of right make a mockery of that Bylaw whose purpose is to assure due process. Though I will gladly give a reason for the hope that is in me to anyone who asks, I will remain silent in further proceedings based on Bylaw 6.79. I pray that God may bless my accusers and judges with His forgiveness and love. I commit myself to the Righteous Judge and trust his grace and mercy because of the atoning death of Jesus Christ on the Cross."

After reading his statement, Dr. Tietjen left the meeting. His exit was symbolic of his style of administration. Frequently the charge has been leveled that faculty members brainwashed the students into rash decisions. The fact is that faculty and staff made every effort to keep themselves out of strictly students' business, and for the reporting of the rest of this meeting I am dependent on students' personal notes and observations. As one of them indicated, ". . . to the best of my knowledge, only one faculty member and one executive person were present at the student body meeting, and neither of these men spoke."

After his departure, a proposal of resolution was handed out by students to their peers for consideration and possible adoption. It read in the form published later the same day:

A STUDENT RESOLUTION
by students of Concordia Seminary, St. Louis, Missouri
1. Because members of the "faculty majority" of Concordia Seminary have been publicly accused of teaching doctrine which is "not to be tolerated in the Church of God,"
2. Because members of the "faculty majority" have publicly protested these accusations and have declared that they "teach what the Scriptures teach,"

MORATORIUM

3. Because Dr. John H. Tietjen, who defended the "faculty majority" against these accusations, has now been suspended from his office as president of Concordia Seminary,
4. Because the members of the "faculty majority" are either guilty of teaching false doctrine and, therefore, not fit to be our teachers or innocent of these accusations and, therefore, worthy of exoneration,
5. Because the Seminary Board of Control has not yet decided which, if any, of the members of the "faculty majority" are guilty of teaching false doctrine,
6. Because we, as students of Concordia Seminary, are currently being taught by members of the "faculty majority,"
7. Because we, as students, have the right to know which members of the "faculty majority," if any, are false teachers and what Scriptural and Confessional principles, if any, have been violated, before we continue our theological training,
8. And because our whole theological education has been seriously disrupted and jeopardized because these issues have not been resolved,

We, the undersigned students of Concordia Seminary, therefore resolve:

I. To declare a moratorium on all classes until such time as the Seminary Board of Control officially and publicly declares which members of the faculty, if any, are to be considered as false teachers and what Scriptural and Confessional principles, if any, have been violated.
II. To spend our class hours, until the Seminary Board of Control informs us of its decisions, communicating to the Board of Control and to the synod at large what we have been taught at this seminary, especially the Gospel of our Lord Jesus Christ.
III. To complete our academic requirements for those classes which we will miss according to procedures which are acceptable to those who are responsible for course accreditation.

We make this resolve mindful of the possible consequences of our actions and asking God's blessings upon our labors.

copies to: Dean Kenneth Breimeier
Dr. John H. Tietjen
The members of the Seminary Board of Control
President J.A.O. Preus
Monday, January 21, 1974

Someone moved adoption and vigorous discussion followed, especially of the items numbered 5 to 8, with emphasis on number 7. A vote to close discussion ("calling of the question") failed 180-181. This kind of tally meant that the assembled students participated in the

199

spirit of the "Old Missouri". Everyone was to have his say. This was not a run-away freight "like the one at New Orleans," commented one of the participants.

Someone then announced that the Board of Control had decided to retire Dr. Arthur C. Repp without provision for modified service. "That should swing fifty votes," said a second-year man.

The students went on to consider the possible consequences of the proposed action: One said, "The Board of Control could adjourn, leave town, and we would be left high and dry." Another observed, "The moratorium could last for weeks, even months. Where does that put us in our education?" A fourth-year man commented, "In four months my parents are supposed to be down for my graduation. What am I going to tell them? And what about our calls into the ministry?"

At approximately 10:00 A.M. that same January 21, the students made their first test of depth in the Reed Sea. Two hundred and seventy-four voted YES. Ninety-two voted NO, but not all in salute of Acting President Scharlemann. Fifteen abstained. Concordia's classrooms were to feel the silence of such a decisive vote. One student who disagreed with the majority's vote broke into tears, but a few days later, as the horror of the event became more pronounced, he signed the moratorium. One of the 274 said, "It was with deep and tearful sorrow that I voted at this point in time to call a halt to my theological education as I have known it. I considered the cost which I might ultimately be asked to pay as a result of my actions: (1) My further theological education and preparation for the ministry in the LC-MS at Concordia Seminary. (2) My graduation in May. (3) My call into the ministry of the LC-MS. Mindful of these possible repercussions to myself and my wife I stand ready to pay whatever price I am called upon to pay as a result of my action."

Little did this man realize at the moment how high the price for many would be. Theoretically, he knew that Jesus had warned his disciples that they would be put out of the assemblies, brought before authorities and condemned, and that fathers and mothers would disown sons and daughters who left the security of tradition for the "Madman of Nazareth," but pressure would shortly be on when students telephoned their parents, some of whom had scrimped for ten years since grammar school to put their children through the seminary. Who would have the nerve to tell his mother or his father (in many cases, a minister): I may not graduate on schedule. "Get back into the classroom. And that's an order," some would hear. "Who are you to tell the Synod what to do?" "Side with Tietjen, and you might as well never come home again!" The harassment and pressure would take many forms, and some who underestimated the cost of traveling in the future would in a few weeks have second thoughts about completing the crossing of the Reed Sea. Most of them, however, were agreed that Preus and the Board were treating them like pieces of machinery that could be used or discarded at will.

"Speak softly, but carry a big stick," was Scharlemann's instruction from Headquarters. Undoubtedly recollecting Julius Caesar's self-styled clemency, the "General," as students affectionately called him, wisely waited with his proposals to roll back "liberalism" at Concordia. In a gesture of Hannibal-Patton-like courtesy he ordered a suspension of classes for Tuesday—to "give them time to get over their emotional jag." He was never more wrong.

This student body was not an undisciplined hoard such as he, in his mind's eye, had seen burning down buildings and shouting obscenities at law enforcement agents in the Sixties. Nor had they gathered to mug television cameras. On the contrary, one of them had grabbed one reporter's camera who had zoomed in on a row of students near the rear of the chapel, and soon thereafter the chapel-auditorium was evacuated of news personnel.

Clearly the seminarians had much to learn about dealing with the media. Sheltered behind their three foot Gothic walls, they were hesitant to come out into the blinding light of the world. But their motivation was transparent. And except for the cameraman who could not understand why a student would not want the world to know about his protest, members of the media corps were generally sensitive to the students' concern that issues should take precedence over notoriety.

In keeping with the seminarians' maturity of discipline was their ability as a group to distinguish policy and administration. This clarity of judgment, in striking contrast to the bewilderment of the faculty, preserved them from irrelevant debate and made it possible for them to meet the attack on Tietjen and the faculty with their terse resolution of moratorium, while reserving the rest of the day for discussion of detailed implementation.

"Bring Us Some Milkshakes"

To students who might have had second thoughts about their decision in favor of the moratorium, the majority Board members themselves provided a failproof antidote. Shortly after the students' vote had been taken, Intelligence announced that the Board of Control had decided to implement Dr. Alfred von Rohr Sauer's retirement at the end of the Winter quarter.

Typical of the insensitivity perpetrated during Concordia's holocaust was the way in which Sauer learned of his academic demise. Slipped under his door was a note from Scharlemann informing the eminent archaeologist and Old Testament scholar of two items: (1) Dr. Scharlemann had tried to call Dr. Sauer, but was unable to reach him. (2) Dr. Sauer was to be retired from the faculty.

The point was not lost on the students, who, from the standpoint of the Board, were in no position to really know what was going on. Their Board had messy business to handle. Better to spill all the blood with one gash, be done with the inevitably bad publicity, and then get on with business. The world, deluged with headlines of atrocities, would soon forget, and tranquility would once more pervade the campus of Concordia Seminary. In short, this was Blitzkrieg. To effect it, Preus and the Board had promoted a one-star Brigadier General to five-star status.

With no less acumen in tactics, coupled with a profound grasp of strategy, the students had made their decision, and at 11:00 A.M., the day after Tietjen's suspension, President Miller himself hand-delivered the Resolution of Moratorium to the Board Room. He managed to get inside and deposited it in Chairman Otto's hand. Otto asked, "How many voted for it?" Miller told him, but Otto made no comment.

It was Miller's second visit to the Board Room, and with similar frustration in dialogue. Several weeks earlier, on Saturday, January 5, he had asked for an audience with the Board of Control, with a view to emphasizing that the Board's first responsibility was to the students. Chairman Otto informed him that he could come at 11:15 and would have about five minutes to present his case, but to bring along nine malted milks. Miller went to a hamburger shack near by, bought the malteds and knocked on the board-room door. After being admitted, he was paid by board-member Fincke, but before he could deliver his message the malted milks were going down the hatch. The Rev. Kurt Biel said, "You made a mistake. You gave them their food first." Miller asked whether it might be possible for the students to engage in further dialogue on the issues troubling the seminary. There was no response. "They weren't at all communicative," said Miller. "It was so frustrating." Miller's cohorts were not too happy either about the impasse in communication. The board majority appeared to close their eyes to the fact that within four months Miller and more than a hundred others would be the professional peers of some of the men in the room. They also may have forgotten that Concordia Seminary had not been established to educate hewers of wood and bearers of burgers.

After the resolution on moratorium had been delivered to Otto, copies went to President Preus, to Kenneth Breimeier, Dean of Students, and to Tietjen. Then the community celebrated the Holy Eucharist and assembled at the Luther statue where Miller, with Reformation pitch in his voice, read the resolution to the world.

For such public utterance the students were bound to face criticism. Moses had declared to Israel, "You shall judge your fellow countrymen with strict justice. You shall not go about spreading slander among your father's kind" (New English Bible, Leviticus 19:15–16). The students, a generation that took the Bible very seriously, thought the world should now know that there were some in the Lutheran Church—Missouri Synod who still upheld law and order, and that they did not sanction injustice. The "radicals," the destroyers of civilized structures and edifying institutions, were not, in the judgment of many, standing in front of Luther statue that day. From the students' viewpoint, Scharlemann had, like Caiaphas, prophesied correctly, albeit with different intent, when he warned about sinister forces at work on the campus. A huge question therefore remained: Would the Lutheran Church—Missouri Synod repent of its wrong, first done to Tietjen in official synodical assembly and now repeated through its own elected Board? Would the "old Missouri" cry for a halt to bigotry and the senseless destruction of a distinguished seminary? Or, like those who smelled the peculiar aroma of Auschwitz, would they turn their noses the other way and climb back on the teeter-totter, desirous of hearing again "the other side?" Or would some even agree with Scharlemann, who told the Board of Control, "The way to handle rebellion is to *crush* it!" These and related questions were on the students' minds and lips on January 21, 1974. Some began to sense fresh meaning in Exodus 7. And all were wondering, "What will the faculty do?"

Chapter 19

INDECISION

On an airplane in June, 1973, a prominent synodical administrator told Elwyn Ewald, later Executive Secretary of Evangelical Lutherans in Mission (ELIM), "The faculty won't do anything." Had not President Preus predicted, "With Tietjen out of the way, the faculty will fold"? "It'll all be over by Christmas after the removal of some key personnel," Preus had assured supporters. Piepkorn's unconscionable arrogance of dying at the wrong time had somewhat punctured administrative infallibility, one was heard to say, but what was four weeks' delay in church history? Had not Preus been to Rome, seen the Pope and the splendor of weathered centuries? After the "rhetoric" (one of Preus' favorite terms) died down, emotions would sag back to normal, sheer economics would dictate directions for conscience, Tietjen would be buried, the Missouri Synod could put a few pieces of sod back into place, the kingdom of the right hand and the kingdom of the left hand of God would reign with balanced grace, and the church could get on with the job of spreading the wonderful news of the loving and compassionate Savior, Jesus Christ, and redeem the world for justice and for truth.

For a while it seemed as though Preus' political instincts would steer a safe course through the crisis. The faculty had no clear sense of direction. Later charges of long, careful planning for a breakaway seminary were patently slanderous and false. The fact is, we did not know what to do. Our responsibility was to train future ministers for the LC-MS. A profound sense of obligation to remain faithful to that task governed everyone on the faculty and supporting staff. The big question was: How?

Fortunately Preus always managed to undermine his own political savvy with built-in tripwires for his own disaster. By triggering some of

204

these, the Board had made the students' decision easy; the very force of the explosions was beginning to clear for us a way through boulders of indecision.

The suspension of Tietjen began to loom larger as an atrocious violation of basic American, not to speak of Jewish and Christian, principles of justice. To be charged with harboring theological criminals, without identification of the criminals allegedly harbored, was a denial of a basic doctrine of Western jurisprudence—the writ of *habeas corpus*. Nor was there an escape from official culpability for the Board. Preus' own Press Secretary, Victor Bryant, had declared that Tietjen had been charged by the Board with "failure to take action against faculty members who hold positions contrary to the clear words of Scripture." At a minimum, two faculty members should have been cited for promoting teaching contrary to Christian doctrine. Yet the Board refused to name one. And when the students on Monday, January 21, asked the Board to clear the name of the deceased Dr. Arthur Carl Piepkorn, they were told that such action would be impossible, for no individual faculty members had been named in Resolution 3-09 adopted at the Convention held in New Orleans in 1973.

Scharlemann—Acting President

Majoring in volatility, the Board had in the judgment of many observers compounded basic injustice with total insensitivity by appointing Dr. Martin Scharlemann as Acting President of Concordia Seminary. It was impossible to construe the appointment as anything else than a reward for Scharlemann's loyal minority voice and for his instigation of the campaign against the majority faculty. As the Dean of Physical Education, Eldon Pederson, later rebuked the Board, "it was like waving a red flag." The fact that Scharlemann was a "gutsy" man, hired to clean house at Concordia, was of minor consequence as we reviewed for ourselves some of the recent history involving our long-esteemed colleagues.

Many on our faculty, including those who had been retired without a word of explanation, had defended Dr. Scharlemann against attacks on his theological position. The editor of *Christian News* had consistently complained that theological problems at Concordia Seminary had begun around 1955. This was precisely the time when Scharlemann had "come out of the bushes." His retraction at Cleveland in 1962 was short lived, for in 1967–1968 he published a series of articles in *The Lutheran Scholar* in favor of interpretive procedures which were very similar to the methodology for which John Tietjen was condemned. He said in connection with a study on the Transfiguration:

> "We have spent so much time on a single pericope (namely, the account of the Transfiguration) to show what can be done with the method of historical criticism. The point we are trying to make is that the method of Fundamentalism will not yield the results presented here, for the simple reason that its exponents reject the means by which this is done. . . ." [1]

Earlier in the same article he said this about the offspring of Fundamentalism:

> "Moreover, it became the instrument by which lesser lights saw their opportunity to get attention especially by means of heresy trials, resolutions to assemblies of churches, bitter articles in the press, and other ways of disseminating hatred and division. Very soon the theological outlook of Fundamentalism shrank to rather narrow interests and perspectives; and 'fundamentalism' became a word of opprobrium. While it is still a complex phenomenon, it can be described not so much as an independent movement with a doctrine of its own, but rather as a vigorous and often poorly informed spirit of protest against liberalism, historical criticism, and ecumenism. Its effects are felt in every denomination; and in Biblical interpretation it stands for a rather extreme emphasis on literalism, a rejection of everything that smacks of literary or historical criticism, and a defense of what is called 'the old-time religion.' " [2]

As late as 1972, two years after Dr. Tietjen had said that biblical scholars cannot do biblical interpretation without historical criticism, Scharlemann contributed further high praise to modern developments in the use of this methodology. His remarks appeared in a volume of tribute to Dr. F. Wilbur Gingrich, collaborator with Dr. William Arndt in the translation of Professor Walter Bauer's dictionary of Greek New Testament words. In his article, Dr. Scharlemann praised Roman Catholic scholars for putting behind them the "fundamentalist notion of inerrancy," which, he said, was "the product of a false rationalization, constituting the conclusion of a syllogism in which the minor premise uses an understanding of truth quite different from that of the conclusion, as follows:

Major premise: The Scriptures are inspired by God.
Minor premise: God does not lie.
Conclusion: Therefore the Scriptures are inerrant."

Rather, he argued, inspiration means that "as man is the product of God's creative work so the Scriptures are the handiwork of the Holy Spirit in all the phases of their coming into being: prophetic utterance, oral tradition, the writing of prophet, apostle and evangelist." [3] For less than that our entire Biblical department was being pilloried!

There is no syllogism dearer to radical conservatives in the Missouri Synod than the syllogism cited by Scharlemann. But no one on the faculty ever went further than did Scharlemann in attacking a major support base of the Synod's fundamentalism. Yet, Tietjen had just been suspended, apparently, in the absence of any specific charges, for harboring the very same kinds of views expressed in clear print by one who was made Acting President in his place.

Dr. Tietjen had also been periodically attacked for condoning historical criticism, and even declaring that it "must" be used in scholarly interpretation of the Bible. Of course, he did not mean that a scholar at Concordia would have to use it under penalty of academic censure. He meant that historical criticism is as necessary to technical scholarly inquiry into ancient texts as study of anatomy is to a pre-medical student. Scharlemann, however, could write with impunity: ". . . the exegete (Biblical interpreter) must engage in the art of form criticism as a method of reaching some understanding of how the Holy Spirit was at work among the people of God, guiding its life and enlightening the minds of prophet, apostle and evangelist for the work of creating the sacred text as the authoritative witness to God's saving activity." [4] Now any first-year seminarian knows that form criticism and the name of Rudolf Bultmann go hand in hand, and that form criticism is a primary aspect of historical criticism. But after Scharlemann said it "must" be used as a method, he received a promotion; when Tietjen used the same language, he received the ecclesiastical boot. Scharlemann went on to characterize older Roman Catholic scholarship in words that could just as well have been applied to pre-critical Missouri Synod Lutheran scholarship: "Their scholarship was almost totally devoid of critical analyses, and interpretations of Scriptural texts hardly amounted to more than pious devotional talk that was not permitted to come to grips with the real profundities of God's written word. That time is past. . . . We have to read these works (the products of the new critical investigation) because they are by experts who are now free to use contemporary methods of biblical interpretation." [5] No one on the faculty at Concordia Seminary was saying or writing anything out of line with the scholarly standards to which Scharlemann accorded his paeans of praise. Yet he was made Acting

President and Dr. Tietjen was given the axe for trying to maintain a seminary in respectable academic, and theologically Lutheran directions. Nor was it very convincing to be told that there were other reasons. In such case the Board would have been better advised to concentrate on those than to frame Tietjen under a smokescreen of theological accusation.

Such were the thoughts and utterances among us on Monday afternoon, January 21, 1974, when we met as the Faculty Majority. Of one thing we were certain: It would be extremely difficult to conduct academic business and practice theology in what any objective observer could conclude was an ambiguous, if not hypocritical, context of ecclesiastical administration. To such point of unity Preus and the Board had brought us. But what were the options? High on the agenda was the report of the students' resolution declaring a moratorium on academic work. At the same moment we were hearing it, students were reading it aloud to staff people at the headquarters of the Missouri Synod, 500 North Broadway.

To his credit, as someone said, Dr. Preus does not gloat publicly when his political guillotine is in action. According to subsequent reports, he was nowhere to be seen during the reading of the students' declaration.

Without the need of further discussion, each of us envisaged problems in the face of their resolution. Students were on assignment, as part of their practical training, throughout the city. Ministries in hospitals, schools, and in other institutions would be affected. Then there were the foreign students, who like Simon of Cyrene, just happened to be on the scene when the crucifixion took place. Some of them were on limited visas. We were also sensitive to the rights of students who had not voted for the moratorium. Also, Tietjen had been suspended, not fired. And above all, we were called to teach.

Honorable Heretics

The end of decision-road was still out of sight, but data that began to filter in were destined to make the ultimate choice easier. Like the Scandinavian lemmings who make their annual dash to the North Sea in a desperate attempt at self-destruction, the Board of Control developed expertise in decisive bungling, or, as the editor of *Christian News* observed in a different connection, ability to extract defeat out of the jaws of victory. Garnishing the platter that held Tietjen's head were

208

the scalps of three other administrators, Drs. Alfred O. Fuerbringer, Alfred von Rohr Sauer, and Arthur C. Repp. Their salaries would cease on February 28, 1974, and their services would terminate six days earlier. One month's notice to three of the Synod's most loyal and distinguished servants! Again "stupid!" was the coach's word to the Board after his return from sabbatical. Later on the retirees would be told that they might well have expected their termination in view of the action taken at the Board's meeting in November, 1973. For the present, a note sufficed to inform them of their termination.

Such administrative style was totally foreign to anyone in the room. To the expectation of callousness we had, to be sure, grown accustomed. It was the content of the notes that stirred our theological bile. For each of the three was informed that he had gone into "honorable" retirement. This either meant that investigation of the heresy harbored at Concordia could now be narrowed down to three fewer suspects, or that heresy was not really the issue at all, in which case again our president, Dr. Tietjen, had been officially and ecclesiastically framed. Everyone knew that Dr. Sauer practiced historical criticism and held the view that the story of Jonah could be understood as a parable without committing theological suicide. Yet he was retired honorably, after a convention had declared such a view intolerable in the church of God. All of us were convinced that Tietjen was right. The administration of the Synod refused to discuss the real issues!

Au Revoir!

To top off the Board's adventure in moral brinkmanship, it voted to retain three other men who also had been slated for retirement. They were Drs. Richard Caemmerer, Herbert Bouman, and Lorenz Wunderlich. That trimmed the number of suspects to 39. It was also a demonstration of Old Missouri's teeter-tottering. Preus knew that Caemmerer had trained most of the preaching clergy in the LC-MS, Bouman appeared to be a bridge between warring parties, and Wunderlich had been one of the loyal five, voting with Drs. Robert Preus, Scharlemann, Klann and Bohlmann. Three balancing three. The world was to know how fair this Board was. What the world could not know was the fact that Dr. Sauer, as chairman of the exegetical department, the hot bed of historical criticism, "had to go"; that Dr. Repp had once been told by President Preus, at a meeting with the faculty, "You don't speak in a very conciliatory tone," and because of his forthright questioning of synodical procedures he too "had to go"; and that Dr. Fuer-bringer had to be spanked with the "big stick" for putting the LC-MS into the awkward position of having to adopt a hard line to shell out alleged liberalism at Concordia Seminary where he had presided as president since 1953, numbering among his achievements the preser-vation of Scharlemann's scalp at Cleveland in 1962.

Dr. Norman Habel, professor of Old Testament, exposed an action which someone described as a "nugget of brainless churchmanship." He was scheduled for business with the Board and had scarcely en-tered the meeting room when the Rev. Ewald J. Otto, chairman of the Board, said to him, "Sit down. Talk. That's what you're here for." Habel then asked for a three year's leave of absence (leaves of ab-sence were not unusual), and immediately the "junta," as the majority Board members were increasingly termed, voted to release him from his call. He asked them for reasons, and they told him, "You're under indictment with the rest."

The faculty was being urged to return to the classroom. How was that possible if we were all under indictment? As one of the colleagues observed, "even Hitler would have blushed at the use of such Blitz-krieg rhetoric."

Another member of the Board lost no time in wishing him "God-speed." Habel asked them, "Does that mean 'peaceful dismissal'? " The junta said, "No." It was apparent, reported Dr. Habel, that "they had decided the situation in advance." What struck us most blatantly, however, was the immorality of their action. Repeatedly the synod had been informed that no faculty members were condemned at New Or-leans. The convention, it was said, has only condemned the "position" of the faculty.[6] Yet our colleague was informed during a few minutes of official meeting time that he, as well as we, were "under indictment." Honorable retirement for some, but no peaceful dismissal for Habel. Yet all of us were supposed to be party to the false doctrine allegedly harbored by Tietjen. There appeared to be no doubt in anyone's mind that the students were justified in asking for speedy clearance of the names of their professors. Spending only a few minutes of time, the Board had cleared or indicted seven specific individuals. Such official actions could not take place without collusion, we concluded. Before the last plane would leave from Lambert Field, the members of the Board should be able, we felt, to go through the rest of the list. At their present rate of performance, it would not have taken more than fifteen minutes. We were tired of asking "Is it you?"

Some spirits were lifted by the report of Elwyn Ewald that many lay-persons were indignant over Preus' unfair tactics. "Men in fifteen countries," he deplored, "are being charged with praying with Christians who do not belong to the LC-MS or affiliated churches." His point, of course, was that our present experience was of a piece with ecclesiastical disaster perpetrated throughout the world under Preus' leadership.

Unanimity as to a course of action respecting our teaching responsibilities still remained in the distance, and instructions were given to the Faculty Advisory Committee to bring in a report at a special meeting scheduled for 8:30 in the evening.

Monday Evening, January 21, 1974

Since more than our own theological and professional responsibility was involved, our meetings had begun to take on a more familial round-table atmosphere. Participating with us in our decision-making process were our wives, who would be bearing with us the consequences of our actions.

As the first order of business for the evening, we were told that the faculty meeting scheduled for Tuesday afternoon was cancelled. Evidently the "General" was beginning to recuperate from his rash Varus-like tactics, and classical scholar that he was, now adopted Fabius' delaying strategy.

In our afternoon meeting, colleague Habel had reported that the Board for Higher Education (BHE) had informed Concordia Seminary's Board of Control on or about Wednesday, January 16, that the seminary's financial situation could be jeopardized unless its Board took action in the matter of Tietjen. This administrative maneuver was, in effect, a Preusian green light, yet without personal injection of the Synod's presidential office in the affairs of the seminary. In effect, two goals were achieved.

First, Preus obeyed the letter of a major requirement to ultimately secure and maintain unblotched accreditation by the Association of Theological Schools. One of the purposes of the New Orleans convention was to secure removal of ATS criticism of undue interference by the administration of the Synod in the affairs of the seminary. To that end the convention had revised the Bylaws of the Missouri Synod so as to define clearly jurisdictional limits. However, under Bylaw 6.05, the Board for Higher Education, easily controlled under Preus' managerial efficiency program, had almost absolute power to express the presidential will, being bound to "a.) Supervise the execution of all rules, regulations, and resolutions of the Synod, relating to its educational system or its institutions; b.) Determine, direct, and supervise, within the intent and resolutions of the Synod, the educational and administrative standards, policies, and procedures of the Synod's educational system and institutions . . ." What Dr. Ziegler of the ATS received from one hand was taken back by another political hand. Similarly, Bylaw 6.75 appeared to guarantee the rights of faculty members against undue synodical interference by giving final adjudication to the board of the institution, with "a record of the proceedings to be filed with the Board for Higher Education." However, this rubric applied only to "controversies and disagreements" among members of the faculty, for the Bylaw made specific reference to the exceptions set forth in Bylaw 6.81. In turn, this Bylaw made reference to Bylaw 6.80 which states that "a faculty member who is a clergy or teacher member of the Synod is under the ecclesiastical supervision of the Synod. In cases in which such a faculty member is charged with false doctrine or conduct unbecoming a Christian and in which the complainant finds unacceptable the decision of the Board of Control not to pursue the charge, he may be dealt with by the District President *or the synodical President* (italics ours) and be removed from membership in the Synod and therefore from office in harmony with the provision of the Constitution and Bylaws of the Synod. . . ." Since most controversies and disagreements in the synod have historically revolved on points of doctrine, these provisions gave Preus every legal cover to move against anyone whom he deemed a roadblock to his and the synodical Board of Directors' concept of managerial efficiency. Some discerning delegates at the New Orleans convention sensed the political mind concealed in the verbiage of these Bylaws, but the proposal of an amendment to delete the words "or the synodical President" failed to make a dent on the Juggernaut.

The second goal achieved by the injection of the Board for Higher Education into the events of January was the solidification of voting power in the Board of Control. Totalitarianism of any kind breeds a deficiency in independent judgment. The lackey must wait for the master's signal. A pencil dropped on a board-room table may be the high sign for the loyal corps to take suggested action. In August, members of the seminary Board were terrified lest they be struck with lawsuits, and they quickly unsuspended Tietjen. Mindful of that debacle, Herman Otten had insisted in his editorial cited in Chapter One, that Preus must be present at the meeting on January 20. Apparently he hoped that men committed to the Synod's will might respond with appropriate decision and not be cowed into anxiety about personal legal liability. Certainly they could trust the superior wisdom and resources of the "collective will of the Synod," to cite a phrase from Bylaw 1.09. Naturally, Preus was not personally present, but the full weight of the Synod's concentration of will and power in the Presidential office was present in the message of the Board for Higher Education. Tietjen discovered, as have many under related-type regimes in totalitarian countries, that there is no escape from such inexorable movement of the collective will.

Now in our evening session, one of our colleagues reported that Charles Mueller, president of the Synod's Southeastern District, would be willing to testify that funds were indeed to be cut off unless Tietjen was suspended. It was becoming increasingly clear that, so far as the synodical administration was concerned, economics and civil law, rather than objective discussion of issues, would decide the destinies of students and faculty. We could resolve to stay on without pay and teach outside the classrooms, but the Board could get an injunction and lock us out of all the seminary's other facilities.

After floundering for more than an hour and a half, we finally received a report from colleague Robert Smith, member of the Faculty Advisory Committee. He presented an outline of the type of public response we might make to the suspension of Dr. Teitjen and at the same time communicate our intentions respecting the moratorium declared by the students.

Prudent politics would have suggested that we content ourselves with applauding the students for their churchmanship, accept the present situation as tentative, pursue all legal channels available for due process, and in the meantime follow the instructions of officially constituted authority and return to the classrooms. But we were first people with responsibility before God, not politicians, and the political indiscretions of the Board kept sharpening our resolve not to be participants in the further erosion of justice and truth within the Missouri Synod. On this we were all united, single, married, and spouses, and we knew well that the decision we were making would leave us all economically and legally vulnerable.

Even as we were reflecting on the consequences of our possible action, Dean Damm reported that the *Post-Dispatch* was carrying the news that four replacements had been found for the heads of departments. In possession of two doctorates, Scharlemann was to wear two administrative hats. Besides serving as Acting President, he would chair the exegetical department. "Radical orthodoxy," as he described his own brand of historical criticism, was firmly in charge. Dr. Robert Preus, brother of the president of the Missouri Synod, was, with his double doctorate, now head of the Historical Department and declared Vice President of Academic Affairs. From the latter appointment some concluded that Dr. Scharlemann would be in for early retirement as chief administrator of Concordia Seminary.

Dr. Richard Klann replaced Dr. Bertram as head of the Systematics Department and was given the prestigious task of serving as Coordinator of Course Description for the seminary's catalog. The students could be sure that they would be spared courses dealing with "The Christian and Race Issues," or "World Hunger." Professor Arthur Vincent, a member of our majority, heard his name read as replacement for the head of the Practical Department. Looking as though he were in a state of outraged shock at the Board's tactics, he exclaimed, "I decline. I don't know how I got into that company. I prefer the company I'm in right now." He had not even been consulted by the Board and his quick response reflected the mood of us all. Preus' people would not succeed in making deals with anyone in this room. Much less would they be able to divide our theological witness with cheap political tricks such as the ones we had been continually encountering.

But we still had no document. If some reason was to be sought for our inability to respond earlier with a clear-cut statement, it could be summarized in the admonition addressed to us by one of our advisers:

> "I want to make one thing perfectly clear: your doctrinal rhetoric and theologumena bypass the noetic capacities of your intended receptors, and I counsel and advise your forthwith adopting a more lay-oriented and intelligible manner of discourse so that the justiciable and litiginous characteristics of the current circumstances for which a prima facie case is extraordinarily apparent may facilitate interaction with and illumination among the cortical synapses of your audience."

Trained longer than the students in the processes of synodical decision making, that is, being more adept at loquacious teeter-tottering and theological tightroping, we were bound to move more slowly than the students. They had already made history. On the morrow we would add a few footnotes.

Chapter 20

MORATORIUM ENDORSED

At 10:00 A.M. Tuesday, January 22, 1974 the Faculty Majority reassembled in Pritzlaff Hall. We were accustomed to think of the Communist system as expert in thought control, but again Concordia Seminary's Board outdid the masters of the art. In short order we heard that students who had attached their names to a protest statement entitled "One Voice" were to be given *opportunity* to explain why they signed the document. Faculty members, on the other hand, would be *required* to explain their participation in the protest of New Orleans resolution 3-09 on July 24, 1973. We were, according to Dr. Scharlemann, "in rebellion," and, as stated earlier, he had been given instructions by his Board to walk softly but to carry a big stick.

Heartened by reports of mobilization in farflung parts of Missouri's empire, we resolved to send the following letter to Dr. Preus:

January 22, 1974

The Reverend J. A. O. Preus, President
Lutheran Church—Missouri Synod
500 North Broadway
Saint Louis, Missouri 63102

Dear President Preus:
   The Board of Control of Concordia Seminary has emptied the classrooms and silenced the teaching of the Word of God on our campus. The Board did this when it suspended John H. Tietjen from his duties as president and professor at the seminary on charges of false doctrine and malfeasance of administration

The charges of malfeasance are absurd—a piece of harassment and propaganda. The charge of false doctrine is trumped-up because President Tietjen accepts, without reservation, as we do, the Scriptures of the Old and New Testaments as the written Word of God and the only rule and norm of teaching and practice and the Lutheran Confessions as a correct exposition of the Word of God. He reaffirmed that stand when he was installed as our president.

By condemning President Tietjen's confessional stand and suspending him from office, the Board of Control has condemned our own confession and has suspended all of us from our duties as teachers and executive staff members.

We address you, President Preus, because the Board of Control has now for months ignored our communications.

How can classes and teaching resume at Concordia Seminary? There are two possibilities:

(1) Publicly declare your agreement with the Board of Control. Then you would have to direct the Board to press the case against us and provide the evidence that the doctrine we teach is in fact false. If that happens, then we should be dismissed from our positions by due process according to the provisions of the *Handbook*. New teachers could then be sought to enter the classrooms and begin teaching. But would they teach the doctrine of the Scriptures and Confessions or some new doctrine?

(2) Take the lead in clearing us—John Tietjen and all the rest of us—of the charge of false doctrine. If that happens, we will be freed to return to our classrooms. We pledge to make up all classes that have been missed in the interim.

Until the present uncertainty regarding our confession and teaching is cleared up, there will be empty classrooms at Concordia Seminary. You, President Preus, have it in your power to lift the silence that has descended upon the campus. Not only we of the faculty and executive staff but also the whole Synod await your reply.

Sincerely,

Members of the Faculty and Executive Staff:

Mark P. Bangert	David E. Deppe
Robert R. Bergt	Alfred O. Fuerbringer
Robert W. Bertram	Carl Graesser Jr.
Herbert J. A. Bouman	Robert A. Grunow
Kenneth H. Breimeier	Norman C. Habel
Richard R. Caemmerer Sr.	H. Lucille Hager
Robert L. Conrad	George W. Hoyer
John W. Constable	Holland H. Jones
John S. Damm	Everett R. Kalin
Frederick W. Danker	Wi Jo Kang
William J. Danker	Ralph W. Klein

Paul G. Lessmann	Carl A. Volz
Erwin L. Lueker	Robert J. Werberig
Herbert T. Mayer	Andrew M. Weyermann
Duane P. Mehl	Leonhard C. Wuerffel
Eldon E. Pederson	Donald Hinchey
Arthur C. Repp	Larry Neeb
Alfred von Rohr Sauer	Karl Reko
Edward H. Schroeder	Thomas C. Rick
Kenneth J. Siess	Mark Roock
Robert H. Smith	Kenneth Ruppar
Gilbert A. Thiele	Carl Sachtleben
Arthur M. Vincent	David C. Yagow

Forty-six of our faculty and staff signed the document. Despite Dr. Preus' numerous attempts to divide us, not one had defected. It was one thing, however, to say we considered ourselves suspended. To face the results of our decision was another matter. Were administrators to cease issuing memos? How were we to respond to Scharlemann's orders? Should we answer calls to faculty meetings? What about response to students and their problems?

Qualifying his query with a protective clause, "I don't want to appear paranoid," one of the colleagues asked whether we might legitimately be locked out of our offices? Another alleged that when Preus became president of Concordia Theological Seminary, Springfield, he had the locks changed and gained access to an increased number of files. Springfield's Academic Dean, Dr. Lorman Peterson, changed a changed lock, he said, leaving "Jack" incensed. We took this as a bit of comic relief. Preus had a few defects, such as malnutrition in his understanding of the church and allergy to sustained appreciation of basic apostolic theology, but executive snooping on such a scale appeared beyond belief, and history must record that the administration which replaced Tietjen for the most part honored the privacy and possessions of the faculty and staff.

After the vote on our letter to Preus was taken, one thing was clear: We had taken a step that could in all probability terminate our paychecks and affect the pensions of many among us; for what we termed our "suspension" would undoubtedly be construed as resignation. But Jesus had invited his followers to the carefree existence of the lilies of the field. Our theology had passed one of the acid tests, and it was comforting to know that when so much is spent one can no longer afford to be intimidated. Reminded of the magnitude of the injustice that had been perpetrated, we all took fresh heart. What moral

217

difference is there, we were asked by attorney Richard Duesenberg, friend of the faculty, between wholesale condemnation of 45 people or a nation of two million? What is left of due process when a lawyer on the Board "just happened" to have two men present with accusations on the day that John H. Tietjen was to be charged in August of 1973? Thirty-six hours to determine the fate of the head of a great religious institution! Can anyone justify the substitution of an anti-Tietjen agenda of 19 pages for one of nine at the November 21, 1973 meeting of the Board of Control, he asked, with the result that members of the Board who were hostile to Tietjen were privy to information not in the hands of the minority? In disgust, one dissenting member of the Board had said, "We expect this kind of thing in the business world, but not here in the church!" He found himself corrected, "This would *never* happen in the business world." "I am a very conservative lawyer," concluded Mr. Duesenberg, "and I react aggressively to destruction of democratic principles." Such counsel would help improve communications.

We met again at 3:00 P.M. Student President Gerald Miller reported to us that in his judgment things were going "very well . . . The students are happy about your document. They only fear that you might break up . . . One hundred seventeen vicars (referring to third-year men gaining experience in parishes across the country) have endorsed the moratorium through phone conversations."

A colleague reported that the students had invited us to attend their next meeting on Wednesday morning, at 8:30. The seniors especially showed signs of nervousness, he said, but 30 students rose up in a meeting held earlier in the day and identified with the rest.

Reports were coming in from distant points in the Synod. On the preceding evening, 30 to 40 pastors in the area of Buffalo, New York, entered a request for the resignation of President Preus and of four vice presidents "for not taking care of the faculty":

> Dr. Jacob Preus is a charming and personable individual. He has many other God-given talents. However, to our great regret, Dr. Jacob Preus has abundantly manifested his unfitness for the high and responsible office of president of The Lutheran Church—Missouri Synod.
>
> He has failed to supervise doctrine in person, as he should. In four and one-half years he has met with the faculty of Concordia Seminary, St. Louis, for extended theological discussion only twice.
>
> He has failed to carry out his presidential duties to protect pastors and others in the synod as they carry out their calling.

218

He has failed in the role of chief pastor of the church. He has failed to deal evangelically as good pastoral practice demands, relying instead on legalism and compulsion.

He has failed to unite the Lutheran Church—Missouri Synod. Instead he has polarized it as never before by the introduction of political methods never before witnessed on such a scale nor exercised so brazenly. Though often adopting the stance of deploring all party movements and pressure groups, he has confessed that Balance, Inc., which campaigned successfully for his election as president, was organized in his own home.

Above all, Dr. Jacob Preus lacks the essential integrity of character which the office of the presidency requires. Numerous persons and groups have been shocked by his lack of truthfulness and honesty. One recent instance contributed to the launching of the student moratorium:

The senior class of Concordia Seminary invited him to meet them on January 18. A student committee met with him to draft the ground rules. Dr. Preus himself insisted that no faculty members should be present. He agreed with the students that this meant Dr. Ralph Bohlmann, a faculty member on leave, should also not attend. However, on the appointed day Dr. Preus not only brought Dr. Bohlmann into the meeting but insisted that he remain.

Numerous persons have had similar experiences. Dr. Preus from time to time may make a comment or proposal to an individual privately and follow it with the comment: "If you quote me, I'll deny it."

This frequent lack of truthfulness and integrity, which many of us have long recognized and experienced, compels us in spite of our distaste for such a duty, to demand at long last the resignation of Dr. Jacob Preus as President of the Lutheran Church—Missouri Synod.

We also must express our deep disappointment with the vice presidents who have served with Dr. Preus especially since the New Orleans convention. They have done nothing effectively about the situation we describe. And above all, they have failed to tell the church. The synod has been left in ignorance of the true character of its president, and for this reason lay people and clergy are unable to deal with the troubles his failings have brought upon it. Therefore, with great reluctance we must also demand the resignation of the following vice presidents: Dr. Edwin Weber, Dr. Theodore Nickel, Dr. Guido Merkens, and Dr. Walter Maier.

Without integrity, fairness and honesty we cannot expect to remain in the truth of Christ which alone can set us free.

Jim Cross of the Synod's Mission Staff reported that a minimum of eight districts were developing back-up plans for students in the moratorium. Around fifteen hundred people would assemble in Sacramento, California, on the weekend and register their protest against the actions of Preus' Board. Dr. Alfred Heugli, President of Valparaiso University rejoiced over the "integrity" of the faculty.

Tietjen, who had laid everything on the line for his faculty, told us: "You are magnificent. It's a fantastic action which cannot help but speak to those who have ears . . ." But he acknowledged that there were "difficulties." He was not discouraged about placement of 1974 candidates, but he warned us that we had better be prepared for "mobility," with possibilities of interim employment in the Districts. Dr. Arthur Repp, Vice President of Academic Affairs, indicated that a number of districts were thinking of establishing continuing education bureaus.

"No Confidence"

One major item remained—our relation to the Acting President, whose appointment had revealed the Lutheran Church—Missouri Synod with all disguises removed. The following resolution took care of the matter:

STATEMENT OF THE FACULTY MAJORITY
ON ACTING PRESIDENT MARTIN SCHARLEMANN

Dr. Martin Scharlemann in 1957 took the lead in introducing up-to-date, progressive methods of Bible interpretation to Concordia Seminary, St. Louis. He was then widely attacked and denounced. His colleagues on this faculty stood by him, defended him, spoke well of him and urged people and pastors in our Synod to put the best construction on everything. The Seminary's defense of Dr. Martin Scharlemann was costly in terms of the wide support it had previously enjoyed among pastors and people in the Lutheran Church—Missouri Synod. But Dr. Scharlemann remained in his teaching position.

In 1969 he actively sought the presidency of Concordia Seminary. When Dr. John H. Tietjen was called, Dr. Martin Scharlemann displayed his disappointment. Even before Dr. Tietjen was installed as president of the seminary Dr. Scharlemann publicly attacked the newly elected president and his theological statements.

In 1970 he sent a letter to President J. A. O. Preus of The Lutheran Church—Missouri Synod requesting an official investigation of the same seminary faculty which had staunchly supported him in his time of trouble. Dr. Martin Scharlemann's actions contributed to the downfall of President John Tietjen and this faculty. He publicly in the presence of the faculty rejected the efforts of former President Fuerbringer who had faithfully and steadily defended him against dismissal from his professorship.

Now Dr. Scharlemann's efforts and those of other foes of Dr. Tietjen have succeeded. Dr. Tietjen was suspended by the Board of Control on January 20, 1974.

We, the faculty majority, know and believe that Concordia Seminary was wrongly deprived of the able and faithful services of its rightful president, Dr. John Tietjen. His confessional Lutheran faith is also our own.

Therefore, we call upon our colleague, Dr. Martin Scharlemann, to resign as acting president.

We further call upon President J. A. O. Preus and the people and pastors of The Lutheran Church—Missouri Synod to demand that the Board of Control reinstate President John Tietjen in the position to which he was divinely and properly called.

We, furthermore, appeal to President Preus, Dr. Scharlemann and all the pastors and people of The Lutheran Church—Missouri Synod to understand the grave injustice perpetrated here. This is why we of the faculty majority cannot in good conscience or even in a spirit of fair play recognize Dr. Martin Scharlemann as our acting president.

An attendant resolution called for delivery of the document to Scharlemann between 4:30 and 5:00. Informed that he was engaged in other business we decided to wait until 5:15 and give him every opportunity for personal encounter. He never came. The next day we received his explanation:

January 23, 1974

Dear Colleague,

Mr. Robert Smith invited me last evening to meet with you. I told him that I was not in control of my schedule, and that I could not be sure of being able to do so. A later word indicated that you would wait in your meeting until 5:15.

My second interview for TV lasted just beyond that. So I did not come. But I want herewith to indicate in substance what I had in mind to say; namely,

1. I had asked Dr. Damm to cancel the regular faculty meeting for yesterday afternoon;
2. That there will be a faculty meeting next Tuesday afternoon provided we are all back at work and classes resume, as announced, Monday morning.
3. I could consider a response to your letter at that time and in that context.

We shall, therefore, await developments. My hope is that you will meet the responsibilities laid upon you by your call and by your position. To be more explicit, I trust you will resume your regular work on

Monday next to meet the students whose desire it is to get on with their work of preparation for the ministry.

Sincerely yours,

MARTIN H. SCHARLEMANN

Acting President

Student Session—January 22

The students had begun their own session on the morning of Tuesday, the 22nd, with a resolution to declare their meeting open. This meant that the media were welcome. Announcement of Professor Vincent's declination of the chairmanship of the Practical Department received an ovation. Correspondingly, incredulity and exasperation registered at the news of the Board's refusal to clear the besmirched name of Dr. Arthur C. Piepkorn. The refusal etched even more indelibly on the students' minds what more and more were recognizing as patent hypocrisy. Tietjen had been indicted for protecting false doctrine. Yet the ground for refusal to clear Piepkorn was the fact that his name was not mentioned in New Orleans Resolution 3-09. The Board had double-talked itself out of about thirty more votes that now moved to the "yes" side of the moratorium. At the Board's present rate of "Grade A action and Grade C brains," as Professor Caemmerer phrased it, the entire student body would soon be out.

Our resolutions of the evening of January 21, including our declaration of pride in the student body, gratitude for their solidarity, and willingness to support their moratorium, lifted their spirits. At one point one of the students had asked Bertram whether the faculty might break up. He answered, "We would no sooner desert you than we would our own families."

If for some reason anyone might have been tempted to falter along the way, the seminarians could count on the Board of Control to stiffen weak knees. In the rare communication from the Board, the students were assured that their action would have no effect on their certification for the ministry. This was an exceptional display of amnesty. (One of their professors, Paul Goetting, had not fared so well after engaging in a related statement of protest on July 24, 1973.) The Board of Control, they were told, would act with all deliberate haste in resolving the implications of New Orleans resolution 3-09 as it applied to the faculty; meetings were to be held with faculty members on an individual basis. On February 17, the communication went on, the Board would meet with the District Presidents. Then came the clincher, which struck the students at the very heart of their professional anticipation: Dr. Richard Klann was to be Chairman of the Systematics Department. That drove the Black vote hard into the affirmative column. Dr. Robert Preus was to manage history, and Dr. Martin Scharlemann was to chair the Biblical (or Exegetical) Department. The only good news, so far as the students were concerned, was the announcement of Professor Vincent's refusal to be a part of academic "travesty."

Encouraged by developments, and incensed at the Board's trifling with their future in the interests of political advantage, the students resolved to affix their names to the declaration of moratorium. Almost any fate would be better than the intellectual torture that would have been theirs under the directives of Resolution 3-09. That way the Board would be able to determine which students were interested in knowing the identity of their alleged false teachers. Otherwise the Board would later respond in Dissenese (the rhetoric named after Mr. Dissen, a member of the Board) to the effect that they could scarcely reply to students hidden in anonymity. It was a virtue soon forgotten by their executive officer.

During the small-group discussions that followed, I, II, and IV-year students shared ideas and concerns and viewed a video-taped message by Dr. Martin Marty.

At 1:00 P.M. the students reassembled for the latest up-date. Their agenda sheet concluded with Psalm 43:5: "Why are you cast down, O my soul, and why are you disquieted within me? Hope in God; for I shall again praise him, my help and my God." Dr. Scharlemann had called a student assembly for Wednesday, at 10:00 A.M. Evidently forgetting that Gerald Miller had announced on Monday, that business as usual had come to a halt and that a moratorium was in progress, Scharlemann had acted unilaterally, another mistake that could merely have stiffened resistance had not the student body responded in a manner they considered to be dictated by the Gospel. They resolved to invite Dr. Scharlemann to speak to the student body at a mutually agreeable time. Not wishing to box him in, they gave him considerable latitude for option, anywhere from 9:00 A.M. to 1:00 P.M. on January 23, 1974. In contrast to Scharlemann's practice of depositing important decisions and information in mailboxes, the students urged conveyance to Scharlemann personally. Still impervious to realities, Scharlemann issued an announcement that classes would

223

resume on Wednesday, January 23. The students responded by inviting the faculty to their next meeting, which was to begin at 8:30 A.M. on the morrow.

Organization

Some further indication of reasons for the solidarity of the student body was given in the function and quality of the committees that reported. The students were well aware of the possible consequences of their action, and the tensions and anxieties that accompanied disruption of their normal routines had to be faced. The fact that many of them had working wives, some of whom were supporting children in addition to paying their husbands' tuition, compounded urgency of intelligent commitment on the part of the Worship and Spiritual Life Committee, consisting of Robert Rimbo, Charles Boerger, Michael Rowold, and David Beckmann. Their job was to help maintain corporate health and unity under the ONE HEAD, Jesus Christ. Quick intelligence of operation was guaranteed by the Internal Communications Committee, headed by Michael Lohmann, with David Reichert in an advisory capacity, and John Langwisch in charge of the Emergency Phone Network. A constant stream of vital information and official documents kept flowing from the Publications Committee, directed by Jacquelyn Mize, Skip Wachsmann, Leon Rosenthal, and Donald Schaefer. Entrusted to the Materials Development Committee, led by Gerald Miller, aided by Dave Abrahamson and James Wind, were research projects having to do with the history of the controversy, fact sheets and other matter pertinent to the interpretation of the students' response to Preus' actions. Deployment of the human resources of the community for communication to the church at large required a Travel Committee, under direction of Leslie Weber. All of the operations demanded money, which was managed by the Financial Committee, led by George Schelter and Don Duy, advised by Boyd Faust. Secretaries were Robert Heiliger and John Kosec. And at the telephone, monitoring rumor and endeavoring to circulate accurate information, was John Fredrick Christian Dornheim XIX, who accepted his responsibility with devotion akin to that of the centurian who held his post in Pompeii while Mt. Vesuvius buried him in ashes.

A high level of trust meshing with initiative born of Gospel-oriented freedom gave to this community extraordinary mobility and dispatch in responsible decision. I thought, as I marvelled at their operations

224

through the preceding two days, how envious colleague Scharlemann must be to see an army functioning so efficiently, and without a discernible central command post. If only, I said to myself, the college and university students of the sixties had shown even a small percentage of the self-discipline here displayed, how different would have been the future of the United States and of the world. Theirs had been to a large extent an orgy of self-indulgence and disoriented reaction; these young men and women moved with rational and dedicated purpose, and on a trajectory of fine theological discernment. As Professor Bertram aptly put it, "You're beautiful, and we just bust our buttons."

To Change or Not to Change

Out of all that was happening, newscasters in St. Louis isolated one of the decisive issues: Is it the church's task to accommodate or to withstand change? Jim Murphy on KMOX-TV, in interviews with the principals, asked whether the church was a bed-rock of truth to which people adapt, or something that adapts to people. In answer to the suggestion that change might compromise truth, Tietjen said, "It's not *our* truth, it's *God's* truth" that is at stake. When we box the church into tradition, change is necessary in order to let the truth be the truth, he observed.

On the same newscast, Scharlemann expressed the view that the church's responsibility is to *withstand* change. He had seen the present crisis developing "for a long time," he said. "I've paid attention to it especially for the last four years (that would be during Tietjen's incumbency). The emphasis has been on social concerns instead of the main message—the Gospel!" (This last sentence would be an important key for historians who sought later to ravel the mystery of Scharlemann the alleged liberal turned Preusist conservative.) On another channel, Professor Bertram, faculty spokesman, admitted that the job market was in short supply, "but we have counted the cost."

"Friends of the Seminary"

That same evening a crowded fieldhouse served notice to the world that Tietjen, the students, and the faculty were being joined by thousands of clergy and laity in protest against the intrusion of Gospel-

225

breaking tactics in the church. Sponsored by "Friends of the Seminary," the meeting began at 8:00 with a rousing period of singing led by a peppy group under the pastoral direction of Sterling Belcher. Gerald Miller announced that 412 students had endorsed the moratorium, and that many of them would be participating in Operation Outreach, beginning Friday, January 25, and extending through Thursday, the 31st. The Lutheran Church—Missouri Synod, from California to New York, from Canada to the bottom of Florida and Texas, was to learn why education had come to a halt at Concordia Seminary. "The Board of Control," Miller proclaimed, "must show it is dealing justly and fairly with the people in this place." John Damm, still the Academic Dean, reported that "the faculty finally came around today, at 11:00 A.M."

Robert Bertram declared in words to this effect: "The biggest hazard to the church to which we belong is not the injustice, the cruel oppression, the bad example we are giving to the world, but that the Word of God is being silenced in our midst. But the situation need not go to waste. There will be more new opportunities to say what the Word of God is. President Tietjen has been suspended for teaching the Word of God. Thus they have attempted to silence his voice. Yet the Word of God surfaces again in his confessional stance which is the same as ours. If he is suspended, then we are too, for the Word we proclaim is the same for which *he* was suspended. Not we, but the Board have silenced our classrooms. They can, however, be unsilenced. How? In one of two ways. President Preus can acknowledge the error of the Board in condemning faculty members without first preferring charges (in reference to the fact that Tietjen was suspended for "failure to take action against faculty members who hold positions contrary to the clear words of Scripture.") Or, he can clear us of charges of false doctrine, in which case we would be free to return to our classrooms. They cannot put us under condemnation and at the same time ask us to remain in the classrooms. We have nothing to hide."

After a standing show of support, Bertram continued, "Perhaps you thought of our families. Our wives and youngsters sat with us in deliberations. Most of us had consulted with our kids and received their encouragement. Nor have we any illusions that the current silencing of the Word is confined to our campus. We happen to be the eye of the storm. Other places will soon feel the weight of suppression. We are so proud of our students. They have shown themselves most churchmanlike and responsible future ministers."

As an Amen to Bertram's speech we sang "A Mighty Fortress is our God," after which James Mayer, one of the victims of the Synod's bombardment against the mission staff, took to the rostrum. "We have to repent today," he opened, "because *we* are the enemy. It seems we can't be galvanized into action until we see the blood flowing in the streets. Efforts are afoot to bring overseas ministry, campus ministry, and other specialized ministries under complete and total control from Synod's headquarters. Things came to a head on January 10–12. The Mission Board completely ignored recommendations of the mission field and renewed the contracts of three staff members, but not mine. Various missions had made over 50 recommendations, but the report containing them was rejected. . . . What can you do? You can send letters of dissent in support of the rights of workers. You can speak out in favor of fair play. And you can emphasize a loving concern to speak the word of judgment and forgiveness. Anything short of that is not in accord with our heritage!" This last Lutheran reminder stirred a round of clapping. He then cautioned, "Don't *withhold* funds. You can't hurt synodical headquarters. We are in the process of organizing a Mission Committee to channel monies in the most efficient and cheapest ways. Finally, we need to learn to love. That means to be *for*, but also *against* something." With that he received a standing ovation.

The next speaker was the Rev. Samuel Roth, President of Evangelical Lutherans in Mission (ELIM). "Dr. Martin Scharlemann," he began, "claims that the students are on an emotional jag. If so, it will dissipate quickly. But I think it is much more than that. . . . To have a share in their commitment you need to lay yourselves on the line. First, speak out against the wrong-doing, both at *home* and in your *congregation*. Second, say, 'We stand with them and their faculty. Their cause is our cause. If they are guilty, so are we.' Third, withhold funds from the support of those who are corrupt. We must support those who are in need. Evangelical Lutherans in Mission has been organized for this very purpose. We must all remember that we live by faith."

A Matter of Ethics

Attorney Richard Duesenberg, an enemy of theological mystification through obfuscating rhetoric, brought down the house with his opening Nixonian statement, "I want it made perfectly clear . . ." Continuing, he said, "I have been performing services to Dr. Tietjen without malice to anyone. I am not interested in running anyone out of the Synod, but we do want to avert a travesty that is about to befall our Synod . . . Our laity will not be aroused by theological disputes. As a lawyer, I pride myself in the American concept of the value of the individual. We must govern ourselves by the rules and principles that we adopt. If we do not, then we have no reason to exist. Can we as a Christian denomination tolerate such violation of principle? . . .Most lawyers have a sense of due process. . . . This denomination did not make it at the November meeting of the Board of Control. In a substituted agenda, material not available to the minority on the Board of Control was in the hands of the majority members. . . . In this morning's *Globe-Democrat* a charge of malfeasance against Dr. Tietjen was noted in connection with the organization of FLUTE (Fund for Lutheran Theological Education) . . . This fund, officials say, could be held to be in competition with Synod's funds. They claim that $50,000 was in it. Well, the truth is, *I* organized FLUTE and wrote in detail to Synod's Board of Directors expressly to preserve Dr. Tietjen from conflict of interest. And no one has any information about any $50,-000! I want to hold our beloved synod together. If there is one message you take back to your people it should be this: *Live according to the principles of Christian ethics.* I have advised pastors of congregations to urge withholding of funds from the central office. Withhold them until we get a firm commitment. What has happened in the last six months must not be repeated."

Standing for the Gospel

This manifesto earned a long clapping, after which a three minute standing ovation greeted the announcement of Dr. Tietjen's turn on the podium. "Bless you," he greeted the assembly, "for letting us be identified with you. After the action of the Board of Control, I, students, and faculty took our stand. Now we are all standing together tonight . . . They think your stand will crumple. They *don't know YOU!* (clapping). Among other things, they said that some of the faculty would resign. I told them that they grossly misjudged Concordia Seminary, that they grossly misunderstood our level of conviction. Their misreading stems from cynicism, thinking that we engage in 'mere words' that will crumple in the face of hard economics." Their cynicism may in fact flow from a *lack* of commitment for the Gospel.

228

"We are *standing for the Gospel!* We are opposed to additions, accretions of human ideas or traditions no matter even how right they may be. The Gospel is *all* we have. The Gospel means too much to us to permit it to be diminished. We are prepared to risk *all* for it. And you must trust the Gospel as you stand for it. At my installation I preached a sermon on Counting the Cost. The general (followed by a roar of laughter at an unpremeditated suggestion of the military atmosphere engendered by Scharlemann's tactics)—the general drift of it was that one must never underestimate the possibilities of the Gospel. I counted the cost, for I applied to myself the words of Jesus about building the tower and encountering the enemies' forces. But after the night comes the dawn. Resurrection comes out of crucifixion. God is a God of justice who brings his salvation to bear no matter how great the catastrophe. God has all kinds of surprises. He doesn't do what you expect him to do. But he will do what is right and good for his church. Some may tell you IV-year men here that you won't be graduated. But they can't stop you from entering the ministry. They can't stop us from preaching! We can count on God to overcome the evil in our lives and turn it to good. Reporters ask me what I'm going to do next. I answer: 'Live one day at a time. Try it, it's a great way to live.' (Laughter) One of a number of telegrams I received cited Hebrews 13: 5–6: 'Keep your lives free from the love of money . . . God has said, I will never abandon you . . . I will never fear what man can do to me.' " To the tune of that closing thought the fieldhouse trembled with long and joyous clapping.

Joy

Return to tradition as Preus, Scharlemann, and the Board of Control knew it evidently spelled gloom. "We had no joy," traditionalist delegates were heard to say at the close of the New Orleans convention in 1973. This assembly wanted the joy of the Gospel, the disciplined freedom of the Lord who loved to party with his friends. "Losing is beautiful!" one said. Long years of suppressed emotion under the rubrics of Teutonic ecclesiastical order broke out in ecstatic paeans of thanksgiving this night. Preus was beaten, I said to myself, with this replay of Acts 4:23–31. The past was a shadow. The morning would bring fresh realities of encounter—but there would be no turning back. Some had accused us of not believing in the miracle at the Reed Sea. Soon they would discover how firmly imbedded in our minds

229

were the words of Moses to the Israelites as Pharaoh's chariots moved in on them at the water's edge: "Stand firm and see the deliverance that the Lord will bring you this day; for as sure as you see the Egyptians now, you will never see them again. The Lord will fight for you; so hold your peace . . . The Lord said to Moses, 'Tell the Israelites to strike camp. And you shall raise high your staff, stretch out your hand over the sea and cleave it in two, so that the Israelites can pass through the sea on dry ground. For my part I will make the Egyptians obstinate and they will come after you . . .' " (Exodus 14:13–17) Had we not believed in miracles, we would never have come to this day in the history of Concordia Seminary and of the church. To assure the crossing, we could count on the Lord's hardening of Pharaoh.

Chapter 21

SHOWDOWN

"Snoopy says, 'Love is a moratorium.'" With this announcement, student body president Gerald Miller opened the students' meeting, which faculty and press were free to attend, on Wednesday, January 23, 1974.

In the right-hand corner of their moratorium agenda for the day were these words: "Keep your life free from love of money, and be content with what you have; for he has said, 'I will never fail you nor forsake you.' Hence we can confidently say, 'The Lord is my helper, I will not be afraid; what can man do to me.'"

Looking at the gaunt faces of his friends who had assembled at 8:00 A.M. to take care of unfinished business, he informed them that the County Health nurse would be on hand that evening to speak on nutrition. "Advice on nutritious, but cheap meals," he said, "should be welcome to our wives." The wave of laughter that followed loosened up the assembly for an encounter that could not be postponed much longer.

First Retreat

On the preceding evening Dr. Scharlemann received a hand-delivered letter courteously offering alternate times for meeting with the students. Typical of the frustration experienced by the students was the fact that up to 10:30 P.M. they had received no formal reply. Finally Miller called Scharlemann and asked him, "Can you come at 9:15 A.M.?" This was the time cleared on the moratorium agenda for a "Report from the Board of Control—Dr. Scharlemann (and questions of clarification on the report)." Scharlemann said, "I'll be in the chapel to speak at 10:00!" Miller asked, "You are not recognizing the moratorium?" "Yes, I recognize the moratorium. I will be there at 10:00."

In the face of this information two proposals came to the floor. One suggested: We adjourn at 10:00 and do not meet with him. The other: We will meet with him, but only to recognize him as a member of the Board of Control.

Students clapped and many came to their feet when one of their number said, "I suggest we do not meet with him at 10:00. But let us choose the time as men who can think for ourselves."

In answer to a query Miller said, "Yes, the note was given to him directly."

Jacqueline Mize, a minority member of the student body, summarized her view of the take-over strategy: "If we meet him at 10:00, there is no way we can refuse to recognize him as our executive officer. . . . He is coming to address you as little boys."

"But," cautioned another, "we must not cut off communications. We are servants of the gospel. Let us show ourselves to be servants of Jesus Christ."

"I am against recognition of Dr. Scharlemann as head of this institution," came a rejoinder.

Someone wanted to know whether the language of the students' letter was clearly polite. "Yes," replied Miller, "the letter said, we *'invite'* Dr. Scharlemann. But he did *not* honor our R.S.V.P. I had to see him personally."

"We have been slighted," mourned one, "but let us do as Christ did. Bend a little."

"No," came the answer from another part of the floor. "The Fourth Year class agreed to meet last Friday (January 18) with the President of the Synod, with no one else in attendance. But the President deceived us and brought someone else anyway. Out of respect for him we gave in. Now Dr. Scharlemann is trying to change the rules under which this moratorium operates."

In support, another observed: "Once we submit to his time we recognize his authority."

The chapel clock now read 9:35 A.M. Reflecting the basic mood of fairness in the assembly, a speaker read part of the faculty's resolution requesting Scharlemann's resignation and concluded: "We should listen to him."

A motion not to recognize Dr. Scharlemann as President of the Seminary, but nevertheless to meet with him at 10:00, lacked the 2/3 majority to which the student body had bound itself in this matter. A new motion, to set a different time, now held the floor.

"Maybe he's being pig-headed, and perhaps we are being pig-headed too," boomed a voice at one of the microphones.

It was now close to 9:45 A.M. as the television cameras converged on the reader of a resolution not to meet with Dr. Scharlemann under the present circumstances, but that a committee work out with him a mutually agreeable time for a future meeting, inasmuch as the student body desired to hear him.

All were wondering whether Scharlemann might already be on his way over. Should they stay in the room? A motion to remain in the chapel required a head count. It was defeated. Scharlemann must have gotten wind of the way things were going. "Dr. Scharlemann says he is not coming," came the news. "He says he will meet at 11:00 this morning with anyone who wishes in Koburg Dining Hall," announced Miller.

Thus did Professor Scharlemann make his first retreat in the week of January 20.

Check the Rumors

In keeping with their scholarly standards, the students were reminded: "Check your rumor service. Dial 727-9902." This concern for the truth-factor was one of the primary reasons for the maintenance of community cohesion in the face of divisive tactics by opposition forces. Separation of fact from fantasy was all the more necessary since many of the facts that surfaced during this week themselves appeared so incredible that only approved demonstration of veracity could be assured a hearing. Repeatedly it was said, "People will find it hard to believe that a church would pull stuff like this."

To maximize flow of accurate news, the students' Internal Communications Committee announced that the Student Administration Office would be the only source for information from 8:00 A.M. to 10:00 P.M. No information would be given out unless it was first verified by a source "who is in a position to know the facts." After 10:00 P.M. student David Reichert would be available at his home. Moratorium information and documents of interest to the community would be posted on the bulletin board of the main dormitory, Loeber Hall. A process was already set up, the students were told, to assemble the student body for emergency session, "should one prove necessary."

233

According to the Publications Committee materials were in the process of being printed. The Materials Development Committee reported that a suggested form for presentation by students to groups or congregations was being developed.

"Operation Outreach" is being set up, assured the Travel Committee. Students able to leave the St. Louis area would depart on Friday morning, January 25, to carry to the Synod at large the message of what had happened. They would be gone for approximately one week. "Moratorium Travel Service" read one of the brochures. "See the U.S.A."

Constantly aware of the powerful clout packed by money, the Financial Committee reported that a specific fund was being set up.

Undergirding all the wholeness was the expectation of celebrating with the Great Liberator in a Eucharistic service at 7:30 P.M. on Thursday. Concordia Seminary's troops moved with heart as well as with head.

So that they might not be in doubt as to what their professors were doing and thinking, the students forwarded a plea to the faculty that Professor Robert Bertram be the pipeline for information from that sector.

Problems of Recognition

Soon he appeared, and with cameras focused on him, Bertram first addressed a personal note to the students: "I am pleased to see that you are not only holding but advancing your consensus. You are not frightened by differences in viewpoints or approaches. . . . I want to thank you for being who you are!" In respect to the moratorium, "we were helped in reaching our position," he said, "by *your first* reaching your position. This is not just ritualistic exchange of praise. . . . We wondered whether it would interfere with your interests if we stayed out of the classrooms. A committee of yours said, 'If our action frees you up for freedom from consideration of us, then we have achieved what we set out to do.' "

Speaking of their obligation to Scharlemann, he said, "Lutherans are fond of making distinctions between a man and his office. You meant no rancour. You were concerned about a Christian brother. But you *do* have to deal with him as an official figure."

It was now 10:20 A.M. when Bertram read the Faculty Majority's resolution of request for Scharlemann's resignation. Coming to the end he

234

said, "I guess that's all, Mr. Chairman." Three minutes of clapping, followed by stanza one of "The Church's One Foundation Is Jesus Christ, Her Lord" thunderclapped the future.

After the music died down Bertram continued: "It is a fact that we cannot deny he is an official head." Continuing in his dialectical manner that mesmerized students into metaphysical trances, he queried: "How can we ask him to resign and at the same time *not recognize* him? Why Not? Because we cannot in good conscience do so!"

"How do you plan to disseminate your resolution?" asked a student. "It's being done right now," replied Bertram.

"Why was Scharlemann's apology (to the Synod in 1962) not mentioned in your document?" asked a student. Professor Richard Caemmerer was given the floor and received an ovation. Apologizing for being retained on the faculty, he said, "The Board probably kept me on because I refused to be *honorably* retired." He then explained the omission: "His (Scharlemann's) apology did not include any retraction of any of his teachings."

A student wanted to know whether efforts were being made to divide the faculty and staff as well as the student body? "Yes," said Caemmerer in response to the first part. Prof. Arthur Vincent's aborted appointment as head of the Practical Department was a case in point. "And there are efforts being made to divide *you*," he added. "The efforts are quite transparent."

In encouragement of his peers one gentleman said, "I got a call from my mother last night. She said, 'The District is behind you. Don't compromise until those conservatives come clean.'" Someone else wet-blanketed that with the information that he was told, "Why don't you quit bothering us so we can go back to sleep."

Group Meetings

In the small group meetings held later at 11:15 A.M., faculty and students engaged in rap sessions, but it was the students' show. Their leaders had let it be known that the moratorium was the students' idea, but faculty members were welcome to listen to their dialogue. Fourteen persons were in our group. My brother, Missiologist William Danker, and I were the two faculty guests in this particular section. William asked, "What are your minimum requests?" Answer: Our official resolution says we want them to name names, tell us who the false teachers are, and state the charges. When you guys are back teaching we'll go back. Our resolution was based on the suspension of Dr. Tietjen. That brought things to a head. Among the people most wronged were the retirees. Then there's Prof. Paul Goetting who was not re-hired. But naturally we would like to get back to class as soon as possible.

Someone observed: The faculty majority has declared its stance. The five dissenters have not. (A reference to the faculty minority: R. Bohlmann, M. Scharlemann, R. Preus, R. Klann, L. Wunderlich.)

Adding to the number of supportive votes coming from all over the world, one of the group informed us that three pastors located in Fort Wayne, Indiana, had submitted their identification with Tietjen's suspension.

The news was of a piece with the bulletin in the Great Bend, Kansas *Tribune,* which on the same day quoted the Rev. Robert H. Studtman's criticism of President Preus for his "high-handed manner." "In fact," said Pastor Studtmann, "Dr. Preus has stated: 'If it's too hot in the kitchen, get out.' We do not treat Christians in our congregations in such unloving ways and we do not feel that it is proper for a man who has been in 'our kitchen' for little more than a decade to come in, turn on the heat, and invite us to get out of our own kitchen. . . . It is shocking. . . to see such authoritarian methods used in a Church that has so much of God's love to offer the world."

"The Bataks (a group of Lutherans in Indonesia)," my brother observed, "have 250 ordained pastors. In 1846 they had two missionaries eaten. We can think of a few who make contemporary bill of fare." On this cheerful note, that digestible heretics would most certainly guarantee the future of the church, we adjourned for lunch.

Scharlemann Dialogues

While our small groups were in meeting, Scharlemann was answering questions in Koburg Dining Hall. He had announced that he would be there at 11:00, and according to information he was not one second late. Thirty-five were present at the beginning, and at 11:18 there were seventy-five, of whom about thirty were students, according to seminarian Patrick Kiefert. James Adams of the *Post-Dispatch* ended with a count of about 110, a figure that included press and visitors, as well as students. Rumor control now had battle fatigue, but the statistics should have been an ominous forecast to Scharlemann. Any way things went, he would not be long in his present job. Astute politician that he was in many ways, President Preus could not ignore the eloquence of the tally. But how many acting presidents could Concordia Seminary marshall before the Preus machine could finally fire Tietjen?

Colossians 3:12 was the text for Scharlemann's meeting. The Apostle wrote: "Put on the garments that suit God's chosen people, his own, his beloved: compassion, humility, gentleness, patience." Scharlemann then proceeded to inform the students that he was operating the Seminary and would not meet on anyone's terms but his own, and that Robert Preus had the same policy. "Will the Sem be in operation?" he was asked. Scharlemann replied that he thought about 120 students would be interested in learning, and that the burden of disruption would rest on those who neither came to teach nor to learn. The Board is determined, he said, to implement New Orleans Resolution 3–09, and it will not be impressed by pressure tactics. Truth is not decided by vote. Professors and students are expected to return to the classrooms forthwith, on Monday, January 28. Visiting colleague David Truemper sized up the rhetoric: "The General delights in affirming what shall be and decrees that it shall be so."

In reply to a question, Why was our school allowed to open last September if the faculty were false teachers?" Robert Preus replied, "I disagree with your logic. Why did you come in September? Do you expect the Board to drop things in midstream?" The student did not press the point that students had come in September precisely because the Board of Control had been unable legally to suspend Tietjen at the time. As for the agenda of the Board, some were asking themselves, why did they start with the retirees instead of the rest of the faculty? But that question would come up on the morrow.

James Thomas asked, "How can you justify a racist on this faculty?" Scharlemann did not enter into details but assured the student, "My office is always open."

When asked about the matter of the "deal" offered to Tietjen, Scharlemann said that a "deal" means to "discuss a problem and offer a solution." This was a sample of the new hermeneutics that had invaded Missouri. He did not explain how the riders attached to the trade-off of Tietjen's resignation for a call into the ministry fell under his definition. Part of the "deal" was that Professor Goetting would be rehired and the retirees would not be summarily dismissed from their chosen tasks. Both faculty and students found such perversion of people into negotiable items obscene. There still remained the further fact, moreover, that it could scarcely be called a Christian "solution" to put an alleged shelterer of false teaching over people in a congre-

237

gation who were less sophisticated than students in sorting out truth from error. It was like removing a bear as overseer of foxes and making him administrator of a fish pond.

A reporter asked, "Doesn't your position polarize by hardening positions?" Scharlemann's reply to such and related questions was: "The question is, who runs the institution?"

I expressed my regrets to a student that I did not hear personally everything that went on in Koburg Dining Hall. He assured me that I would probably be hearing the same script on Thursday.

January 23, 3:30 P.M.

At 3:30 P.M. Wednesday afternoon, our faculty majority met. We discovered that apart from committee work and meetings, many of the students were bewildered as to how they might best spend their time. Some were clearly upset, not knowing how things were going to turn out. They were worried about the disruption of chapel services, accreditation, completion of their courses, certification for entry into the ministry, and eventual placement. Professor Andrew Weyermann assured us that the appropriate task force would bring in a report soon.

Administrative HDQ began to realize that the students on this campus were not boys and girls but men and women who knew what to do when they had to do it. Wisely from their point of view, but ineffectually, a decision was handed down that there was to be no more printing except by permission of Scharlemann and Business Manager Alvar Lindgren. I remarked to a colleague that students had once erected barbed wire to protest shootings at Kent University, and that Scharlemann had been indignant at the students' action. Now, with power on his side, *he* was attempting to inhibit free communication.

At this point, Bertram issued a bulletin from the Oklahoma District of the LC-MS. Members of the District were asking that out of $300,000 for the work of the Synod as a whole, $100,000 was to be earmarked "for our oppressed workers." Other groups also promised to beat back economic threats with assurances of funding.

According to the *Omaha World-Herald,* Theophil Janzow, President of Concordia College in Seward, Nebraska, a teacher-training institution in the LC-MS, had made a statement in favor of the Moderate cause.

The Faculty Advisory Committee, we were assured, would shortly be sending out a letter from Tietjen, a letter from Bertram with our majority's action included, and a letter from Gerald Miller with the students' resolution.

Professor Everett Kalin wanted to know more about "The Deal." "Can you say who the participants are?" Tietjen answered that he didn't intend to reveal confidences if he didn't have to. Professor John Constable asked, "Wasn't there a deal offered you at New Orleans?" "Yes," replied Tietjen, and "there is verification for the *truth* of what I have said."

Tietjen then went on to share the news that a former congressman had called from Washington, D. C. to say that congressmen were beginning to talk about events at Concordia Seminary, and that he had informed President Preus that it was imperative to do something. The congressman had proposed to Preus the appointment of a panel of mediators and asked for Tietjen's reaction. Tietjen said, "I told him, 'I will be very frank and blunt with you, Preus will appoint those who are favorable to him.' " What then would Tietjen suggest? "Screening by people like yourself to make sure of a proper panel." The congressman said he would serve at his own expense. "There's no way," Tietjen emphasized, "to turn down a proposal for mediation. . . but it is necessary to insist that it be independent. I would not consider any panel but a top-level group, including university professors and jurists."

Historian Herbert Mayer laid perhaps the biggest prophetic egg: "Pat Wolbrecht (head of The Lutheran School of Theology at Chicago) offers any help he can give." That promise would hatch in May.

John Constable, his colleague in the department of historical theology, said that all was rumor at Concordia Theological Seminary in Springfield, Illinois, but that there seemed to be little hope for the Moderates on the faculty.

Andrew Weyermann wanted to know how many were prepared to go on Outreach if students invited them. Six or so raised their hands. Tietjen, who had no anxieties about the quality of his student body, cautioned us that it would be expensive for faculty members to participate. "We must husband our resources of finances and time," he cautioned. Obviously he was not one to exercise the heavy-handed administrative role caricatured by the Board of Control's massive dossier of allegations against him.

Chapter 22

DISMISSED!

"There are four things which we need to do now. (I am going to read so that it is precise.) I will read to you the resolution of the Board of Control applying to the student resolution on the moratorium. After that I want to attach a few thoughts of my own within the context of the present situation. Before we start, let me make an announcement for Dr. Robert Preus, the new Vice-President for Academic Affairs, that he will meet any students that want to come next Tuesday night at 7:30 in Sieck Hall, Room 201."

With this for an opener, Dr. Martin Scharlemann proceeded to address the faculty and students in the presence of the media at 9:30 A.M. on Thursday, January 24, 1974.

Here is the way the Board of Control formulated its motion in response to the student resolution:

In answer to the student resolution dated 1/21/74 the Board Resolved:

a. Students will be certified in the usual manner by the existing faculty under Bylaw 6.163c.
b. The Board of Control pledges itself to make all deliberate haste in resolving the implication of Resolution 3-09 of New Orleans over against the faculty.
c. The Board of Control asks that professors and students return to their classes forthwith.

This motion was carried. Now for an interpretation:

a. On the question of certification let me note first of all that the term itself does not occur in the student resolution. However, this is obviously a major concern for many of us. The problem itself had been brought before the Board previously and it had agreed on the principle expressed by the statement contained in their present resolution.

There are two aspects to this part of the resolution. The first consists of saying that the Synodical Statement [a reference to Dr. Jacob Preus' *A Statement of Scriptural and Confessional Principles*] will not be used as part of the process of certification. Secondly, I think you ought to know that congregations may raise the question; district presidents and vicar supervisors may inquire into this issue. However, that is not part of the certification process here at the seminary.

    b. I think it would be helpful if we all took the time actually to read Resolution 3-09; for some of the apparent assumptions in the student resolution cannot be based on the actual wording of the resolution.

The resolution in the *Convention Proceedings*[1] deals with 'the faculty'. The resolution itself is a long one. On page 138 we read:

'It now becomes evident that by: (1) the subverting of the Scriptural Word as the formal principle, or touchstone, by which all teachers and all teaching are to be judged; (2) by introducing a Gospel-reductionism (by whatever definition it is considered); (3) by adopting neo-Lutheranism's rejection of the third use of the Law; the faculty has in effect and in fact put itself in opposition to Article II of the Synod's Constitution. . . .' The wording was carefully chosen. The resolution does not deal with the faculty majority, nor with the minority, nor with an individual. It addresses itself to the problem of 'the faculty' as a corporate entity. Now, according to that resolution, it is the assignment of the Board of Control to see to what degree and in what way the irregularities described by Synod Committee 3 apply to 'the faculty.' It is the intention of the Board to get to this matter in the very near future. Just what the procedure will be is impossible to indicate at this point. I must simply ask for a manifestation of charity and understanding at this point. The Board might have closed down the seminary in July. But in the interest of making it possible for you to be here, it resisted that temptation.

    c. The word 'forthwith' I am now interpreting to mean next Monday morning. Monday morning, classes will resume; students are asked to go to their regular classes; and professors are asked to be present in those classes to teach them. I would urge all of you very strongly to do so. I have just prepared a letter for each faculty person on this matter. I have asked them to transcend the present situation and manifest a Christ-like example by returning to the job to which they were called.[2]

It is the Board's approach and mine that we are dealing with mature and responsible persons. You might be interested, therefore, in knowing that the Board did not even wish to discuss any alternatives, in the form of some kind of pressure and threat. It has refused, and I refuse, to go beyond this assumption.

And now for a few reflections of mine on the present situation: The expression 'body of Christ' is a rather favorite one on campus, I see. That is a good Pauline expression. Let us reflect on the meaning of this unique terminology. It underlines our need to serve others rather than ourselves.

I know that we have some 120 students, roughly speaking, who want to get on with the work that they began this year. They have so expressed themselves. And so I am asking you for their sake to return to the classroom. I would like to put this on the conscience of each one of you. These people are anxious to take up the courses for which they signed up, and which they will be kept from completing by failure of classes to go on beginning next Monday.

Let me put that another way. The program of instruction which I am asking you to resume, in the name of the Board, is the one agreed on when registration took place. The only way this objective can be met is for all of us to go back to work. If this should not happen, then the burden for disruption will lie squarely on the shoulders of those who do not return to the classroom and who, therefore, make it impossible to resume our normal schedule. I am putting it that way because the time has come to get things the right way around. The Board of Control is not the disruptive force; nor is the newly appointed administration of the seminary. The onus of disruption will be on persons who make the resumption of our work schedule impossible.

I cannot make up your mind for you in this matter. The final decision is for each one of you to make. As you reflect on what has happened during the past few days, you may wish to keep in mind the following points:

a. The Board of Control is determined to carry out the assignment and the intent of the New Orleans Convention. That expresses the will of the church body which operates this institution through the Board of Control.

b. No kind of extra-curricular activities, including those of the moratorium, will change the mind of the Board. In fact, if I may say so, it is my firm conviction that their determination will become even more firm with any new developments that may suggest some kind of disrespect or indifference to its resolutions.

c. In weighing the various factors which pertain to the present situation, it may be well to keep in mind such possibilities as the following:

1. Situations of this kind create rumors. You have heard the rumor that I asked the Board of Control for authority to impound student funds. That is sheer invention. I never even thought of the subject; and the Board never discussed it. You have also heard that we had said something about a cut-off date for faculty salaries as of February 1. That is pure fabrication. I have never talked about the subject; and it simply had not entered my mind, if for no other reason than that I am working on the assumption that as responsible persons we will all go back to work.

2. You ought also to consider the possibility that you are being

242

used. There are abroad all kinds of people who are willing to cheer others on without the necessity of committing their own careers. I say this as an item from life in general. I have no one specifically in mind here.

3. You ought to allow for the distinct possibility that some agitation could be going on here for purposes other than the welfare of this institution and the church body which runs it. There are abroad in society today spirits of anarchy and lawlessness whose interest is none other than to create disorder and disruption.

4. I want to make a promise to those students who want to go back to work. Somehow they will be taken care of in their educational progress.

5. This is a time for the testing of our faith. Many of you have suffered inconvenience and anguish. While this always hurts, it can serve a constructive purpose. It may bring out the measure of our commitment to the Lord of the Church who has promised to stand by us even under the most adverse circumstances.

After his signature he added the following:

P.S. There just came to my attention the announcement that the facilities of Eden Seminary and of the St. Louis University Divinity School will be available on Monday for those who want to continue their work under professors from here. May I take this way of saying that such is not the road for certification in the LC-MS. You may want to weigh that factor.

Behind the Rhetoric

It was pure Scharlemannian rhetoric and a relief from some of the ghost written stuff to which the Synod had been exposed. But as I looked around me during the reading of it, I could see by the varying reactions that registered on the students' faces how unpersuasive and unconvincing the speech was in many of its parts:

1. The word about certification was not encouraging. Granted that the seminary might not at this time have required subscription of its graduates to Dr. Preus' *A Statement,* Scharlemann's words about district presidents and vicar supervisors did not inspire hope. Even before the events at New Orleans, the orthodoxy of some graduates had been questioned in congregations simply because they had studied under "that liberal faculty." What would happen now after the accusatory resolution 3-09 had been aimed at nine-tenths of their faculty?

243

2. Partly to protest this very cloud, threatening to mar the first phases of their ministry, the students had declared the moratorium. Instead of speaking to the issue, Scharlemann had compounded student anxieties. Nor did his questionable interpretation of the phrase "the faculty" appear to pick up any votes. These students were trained in Techniques of Biblical Exegesis (Interpretation), with emphasis on contextual signals in a body of text. Most of them knew well the phraseology of New Orleans Resolution 3-09. Not only does this resolution refer specifically to documents which contained the signatures of "the faculty" mentioned in the resolution, but it specifically interprets "the faculty" in question with the clause "excluding the 'minority five.'"

Moreover, in the paragraph quoted by Scharlemann, beginning with the words "It now becomes evident . . . " the term "the faculty" is followed ten lines later by a sentence beginning, "The faculty majority exults in the 'freedom of the Gospel,' . . . " No one, whether in or out of his right mind at New Orleans, would have understood the terms "the faculty" and "the faculty majority", in the context in which they occur, as including the "minority five" (Professors Klann, Scharlemann, R. Preus, Wunderlich, Bohlmann).

3. In his reference to the Board's resistance of a temptation to close the seminary in July of 1973, Scharlemann exposed the fragility of any feeling of security at Concordia Seminary. The future of an entire community had rested on "resistance of temptation." How fortunate! But on January 20 the Board had given into temptation and had in effect closed the school! How many more cases of such weakness could a student body endure?

4. There were raised eyebrows over the statement that the Board "did not even wish to discuss any alternatives in the form of some kind of pressure and threat." That they had come up appeared evident; that they had not been formally discussed appeared probable. That they would be implemented appeared certain from Scharlemann's subsequent warning that the "Board . . . will become even more firm with any new developments that may suggest some kind of disrespect or indifference to its resolutions." If this was not pressure and threat, language ceased to have meaning.

5. The reaction to Scharlemann's diction, including such terms as "disruptive" and "spirits of anarchy and lawlessness" was one of sheer consternation. The students could not believe that Scharlemann's head was still back in the Sixties.

Was he thinking of some S.D.S.-type plot? If he thought that this moratorium was of a piece with some of the mindless and unoriented activity of that decade they were faced not only with ambiguous morality in the suspension of Tietjen but paranoia in high administrative echelons.

6. His reference to "rumor" indicated how out of touch he was with the administration of the moratorium, for the students themselves had a built-in antidote to unverifiable rumor.

7. The lack of any touch of remorse for actions taken at official levels appeared to make a strong negative impression.

8. A 'does-he-think-we-are-still-kids look' was a rather general registration during the entire speech. Scharlemann spoke as though these men and women did not know their own minds, but instead were being led down a primrose path of disobedience to authority by some kind of Pied Piper. It was not only an erroneous rumor to which he had given credence, but a woeful misreading of the very "commitment" of which Scharlemann had spoken in his second last sentence. The fact that this base rumor would be repeated by synodical officials and others in the Synod would not help improve understanding of developments in the week following January 20, 1974.

Question-Answer Session

In the questioning period that followed Scharlemann's speech, some of these reactions took on verbal form.

QUESTION: "Will Dr. Repp or Dr. Sauer be allowed to teach?"

ANSWER: "The Board of Control says 'No.' It is under no obligation to give reasons." The atmosphere in the room was of the variety one would associate with the receipt of an official mandate from an occupation force.

QUESTION: "New Orleans Resolution 3-09 names no one in particular. Yet faculty members have been dismissed."

ANSWER: "No one has been dismissed as yet under 3-09. I don't know why they are being dismissed. I wish I had some facts."

QUESTION: "If the Board of Control wants to handle 3-09 speedily, why did they handle retirement first?"

ANSWER: "I shall ask them. I don't know their priorities."

At this point the Rev. Richard E. Hoffmann went to the microphone. Scharlemann offhanded him with "You're not a student." Hoffmann countered, "I am enrolled in the graduate school," and went on: "There was a member of this faculty who, contrary to the Handbook of the Synod, brought information against faculty members in a letter to

President Preus. What about that?" Scharlemann agreed, "Yes, I sent that letter, and I'm glad you asked that question." The Acting President then went on to say that he had "discovered over a period of six months" that no headway was being made in dealing with the theological problems at Concordia Seminary. "The TERC report," he said, "hit me between the eyes." (This was in reference to a report on "Theological Education for Today" carried out under the direction of the Theological Education Research Committee of the Board for Higher Education of the Missouri Synod.) "I presented my misgivings," he continued, "but it didn't seem to matter what I said. These things were ignored. Finally as a pastor in the Missouri Synod I took the matter to the President of Synod."

Hoffmann countered: "Even in the military the first order of business would have been to take the matter to your immediate supervisor, in this case Dr. Tietjen, then the Board of Control and on down the line." Scharlemann assured him that as an officer in the Air Force he could speak from experience. He went on to explain that when a member of the military does not receive satisfaction he can take the matter to the Inspector General. However, he said, when Dr. Tietjen brought in the resolution from the Board of Control that things were to be channeled through the Board, I followed that procedure.

"Please read the title of Resolution 3-09," requested Hoffmann, handing Scharlemann a copy of the New Orleans Proceedings. Scharlemann read: "To Declare Faculty Majority Position in Violation of Article II of the Constitution" and curtly dismissed the issue: "The heading is wrong."

In allusion to Scharlemann's interpretation that the entire faculty came under the purview of Resolution 3-09, Hoffmann asked: "If you are part of the indicted faculty under 3-09 how are you functioning as an executive officer?" "Same as the others," came the answer.

"If there was sufficient evidence from the Fact Finding Committee, why was 3-09 necessary?" In his reply to Hoffmann, Scharlemann observed that in addition to theology malfeasance in office was involved. On the basis of the release from the Department of Public Relations, he pointed out that Tietjen had altered Board of Control minutes; had discussed with faculty members the contents of letters addressed to the Board by synodical officials before delivering the letters to the Board; had spent $12,000 without authorization; and was ineffective in dealing with students, especially in the matter of the student publication *Spectrum,* which, he said, had "published slanderous editorials against the leadership of the Synod."

In answer to a request for explanation of the phrase, "people will be taken care of who wish to get on with their education," he said in effect, "We aim to carry out our end of the contract."

Typical of the gracious manners of the seminarians was Patrick Kiefert's contribution to the discussion: "We're happy to have you appear," he said. This was no mere *captatio benevolentiae*, or rhetorical softsoaping. As another gentleman observed, who saw more votes entering the plus side of the moratorium with every additional Scharlemannian paragraph, "We ought to have him come more often." But you should know, Kiefert continued, that "no actions here compromise our interest in students' education. We have not forced them out. . . . I would also like to point out a discrepancy in your figures. There were seventy-five people in Koburg Dining Hall yesterday. Only thirty of these were students." "Very few students," he said, were not participating in the moratorium.

In his reply to Kiefert, Scharlemann warned that the disruption would be squarely on the shoulders of those who continued to disrupt. The "outcome," he said "will not be determined by your interpretation."

Kiefert then asked about the "injustice" that had been perpetrated. Scharlemann, never losing his cool, told him that they didn't have all the facts. "I read you only a few," he said. "Why don't you let the Lord judge the case?"

After declaring "Truth is *not* decided by majority vote," Scharlemann received such an ovation that he must have thought the battle of the moratorium was over. Unfortunately for him, he had forgotten that these troops in front of him were not some newly arrived boot-camp trainees. They knew how Article VIII C of the Constitution of the Lutheran Church-Missouri Synod read: "All matters of doctrine and of conscience shall be decided only by the Word of God. All other matters shall be decided by a majority vote . . . " That, they concluded, put Resolution 3-09 and the suspension of Tietjen in legal limbo.

Marxist Philosophy

Somewhere along the line Scharlemann must have referred to "those in authority." A questioner therefore took him up on his statement that the students did not have all the facts to form judgments of the kind they were making, and asked him who was "running the show" so that they could get some answers. He was told that the

Board of Control had the information the students needed, but that it could not as yet be released. This was too much for most of the audience, and they suppressed with difficulty their indignation at the official clampdown on information, for they had long been accustomed to openness and trust in their community. Especially were they nonplussed because Scharlemann had often criticized Marxist philosophy and the student movements of the Sixties as a threat to the free and open society enjoyed in the United States. Now, at this moment, students found themselves in support of free dissemination of ideas, whereas an officer of the church bound himself to the support of the suspension of a man who had encouraged "free course" for the Gospel and the maintenance of basic American freedoms. Therefore I marvelled all the more at their discipline. Before groans could become voices of voluble protest, a student could be heard saying "Shh" to a neighboring student. "Let him talk," went the whispers. "If he keeps this up, we'll invite him back."

Even the most conservative students could not take it. One of them, Fred Storteboom, asked for the floor and with firm courtesy stared down the barrel of the cannon and informed Scharlemann that he "had better acquaint himself with the depth of conviction of this student body. I did not sign *One Voice*," he said, "but I did sign the Moratorium."

One of the editors of the student publication, *The Spectrum,* addressed himself to Scharlemann's statement about "slanderous" items in that publication. "I am an editor of *The Spectrum*," he said, "but I never heard from the Board." Another student took the floor and remarked to Scharlemann, "When we committed blunders, Dr. Tietjen did not condone our blunders."

Someone asked whether Preus' *A Statement* would be used later on in determining a student's credentials. Scharlemann answered: "No."

Another observed that at the Synod's convention in Cleveland, Ohio, in 1962, charges had been brought against Scharlemann. "Did you apologize or retract? Were the faculty members supportive?"

"I'll be very glad to answer," replied Scharlemann. Then he went on to explain that it was an entirely different matter. "I was working in a field that had not been entered into before," he said. "I wrote exploratory essays. People were saying 'we don't explore theology, we know it,' " he went on to explain. But, he assured the students, it wasn't like questioning "the Third use of the Law," a doctrine, he said, which is covered in the Formula of Concord, Solid Declaration, Article VI. "I followed the creative Australians on creative approach to the problem of 'inerrancy.' " He then pointed out that it was impossible to maintain a discussion at the time because the "air was filled with charges of false doctrine" in committee at Cleveland. In defense of his approach to his colleagues, he explained that it is his custom to identify with issues, not first of all with the person. "I have always tried to be very careful," he said. "I have talked not about people, but about issues."

"You say you did not retract your essays at Cleveland. Shouldn't you retract them now?" someone queried, apparently in reference to the fact that the faculty had been criticized for maintaining views that Scharlemann had himself espoused in his essays.

Scharlemann, who had said at Cleveland that he would withdraw his essays, now unwittingly restored them for discussion: "You will find no false doctrine there!" he exclaimed.

"You said that we were misled," said another. Scharlemann corrected him and said that he had referred to the "danger" of being used.

One of them wanted to know whether Professor Goetting and the retirees had really been dealt with in an evangelical and Christian manner. Scharlemann said that he didn't know.

When asked whether he considered their intended Outreach a "threat to the body of Christ," he said, "Yes," and explained that it was their obligation to live under authorized administration.

James Reginal Thomas entered into the dialogue at this point saying that he had attended Scharlemann's meeting the day before and had made reference to a "racist and bigot on the faculty." He went on to say that this faculty member had written in the periodical *Affirm* the preceeding summer. "I wrote to him," he said, "on the 14th of July, but received no answer. On my return I found my letter in *Christian News*. It was the only copy, and yet it ended up in *Christian News*. Can we really be sure that our private correspondence will be honored? I wonder about his fitness for the office." Scharlemann assured Thomas that "there are procedures."

Thomas hung on. "I will give you a copy of *Christian News* in which John C. Baur called me a garrulous black agitator.' Now who told him that?" [4]

Scharlemann tried to console him saying that he had been "in this business" a long time. But, he explained, whether the letter was sent out by "the head of the Systematics Department remains to be determined."

Scharlemann had told students the day before, "If there are obstacles they must be removed." Someone now moved that "we follow the orders of the day." This was the politest way the troops could say to the 'General': *Dismissed!*

Dr. Alfred Fuerbringer, Tietjen's predecessor in administration of Concordia Seminary, summed the matter: "I have always tried to be a peacemaker, but there comes a time when we must react positively against injustice and unmercifulness. It comes with ill grace that those who have changed the rules of the Bylaws and have arbitrarily dismissed us without concern for economics, should say that we must simply abide by their decision. It also comes with ill grace on the part of disrupters of the Synod to say that if we do *not* do certain things on a certain day that *we* will be guilty of *disruption*."

Thunderous clapping punctuated these words. Among the "orders for the day" was lunch. But before disbanding, the students received this advice on television exposure: "A Jewish friend says some of you are over-reacting to the light. Be spontaneous."

Chapter 23

"NO DEAL!"

At our faculty meeting on January 24 we appended an explanatory letter to the letter we had sent out earlier on January 22 to President Preus.[1] The two documents were to form part of Dr. Tietjen's general communication on January 25 to our colleagues in the ministry. The explanatory document read:

Dear Friends:

On the next page you will read the letter which our faculty and staff have addressed to President Preus, asking him—as we have so often before—please, in God's name, to stop. To stop what? To stop the suicide course on which he is leading our church. To stop his silencing of the Word of God.

Specifically, what we are asking is this. Are we to teach? Or are we not? Our opponents on the Board of Control, all of them in cahoots with President Preus, insist that we be in our classrooms teaching. Yet they also claim that *what* we teach, when we are in the classrooms, is "false doctrine which is not to be tolerated in the church of God." Now which is it going to be? If we really are false teachers, how can we be commanded to teach? Either prove the heresy charges against us and replace us. Or clear us of those charges so that we may return to our classrooms. But President Preus and his loyalists have been afraid to be that open. Instead they have been quietly removing teachers from their classrooms—and not only classrooms at this seminary, and not only teachers but also missionaries from their posts and pastors from their pulpits—without daring to admit why.

But now, at last, with their suspension of President Tietjen, they have been forced by legal procedures to make at least a show of fac-

251

ing him with charges of false doctrine. And to that, we his colleagues now want to say: you have suspended him for his confessional stand, which is the same as ours; thereby you have suspended us as well, and for the same confessional reason. Our reason, in short, is not our personal loyalty to John Tietjen (which is immense) but our loyalty to that Word of God for which he and all loyal Lutherans are standing up and being counted, regardless of the cost.

Of course, President Preus and his followers may well try to evade this issue once again. They may claim that it is we who have suspended ourselves. They may misrepresent our action as a strike or as insubordination—anything to avoid facing the confessional issue of the Word of God, that Word which threatens to expose legalism in high places. But really, as we wish to say to them, they have nothing to fear. God's *other* Word, His Gospel, is a Word of reconciling and mutual forgiveness and working out our differences as brothers and sisters in Christ. That is His last Word. And that is what we are asking to have un-silenced in the classrooms of Concordia Seminary and in

the Synod everywhere.
Yours in Christ,
Robert W. Bertram
for the "Faculty Majority" and Executive Staff,
Concordia Seminary, Saint Louis

President Preus was not sitting on his mail either. On January 24, President Preus sent the following letter in identical form, except for the name and address, to each of the signatories to our letter of January 22. My copy, Certified Mail, No. 667517, read:

Professor Frederick W. Danker
61 Ridgemoor
Saint Louis, Missouri 63105

Dear Brother Danker:
Grace be unto you and peace from God our Father and Our Lord Jesus Christ.

I share with you your grief and anguish over the recent events occurring at Concordia Seminary.

Your letter of January 22 is at hand. I am sending you an individual copy of this letter in the hope that you will not only discuss this in your meetings but also in the privacy of your home and your prayer closet.

As the report of the Fact Finding Committee indicated, many of you are in no way at odds in your personal confession of faith with the doctrinal position which your church has espoused.

You say in the third paragraph of your letter, ". . . the Board of Control has condemned our own confession and suspended all of us from our duties as teachers and executive staff members." I am uncertain as to the meaning of the word "confession" in this paragraph, but, for the moment, would prefer to concentrate on the fact that this statement of yours in saying the Board "suspended all of us" is not literally correct. You have not been suspended. Therefore the statement, since not literally true, is unclear to me as to its intent.

Let me ask you a question to which I believe the church and the Board of Control are entitled to a categorical "yes" or "no" answer. Do you still regard yourself to be a member of the faculty or executive staff of Concordia Seminary? If your answer is "no" the rest of your letter is for the moment at least purely academic. If your answer is "yes" then I am disturbed over your statement that you will not teach or carry out your staff duties.

Your Synod annually gives over a million dollars for subsidy for Concordia Seminary. This money, contributed by the labors and with the prayers of our people, goes largely for salaries to pay you to carry out the duties of the high and holy profession to which you have been called and which you have agreed to perform, namely, to educate and prepare the future pastors of our church.

If you do not teach or exercise your executive staff duties, you are not carrying out the responsibilities of your call, and the future pastors will not be prepared.

Surely you realize that the two possibilities you give me as your suggested solution to the problem are both matters which require enormous outlays of time.

Possibility 1. The process you suggest might take a number of years to complete. Are no classes to be taught during that period? And if not, what is our Synod going to do about the need for pastors and missionaries?

Possibility 2. The Synod's judgment that certain teachings are false stands unless a future convention of the Synod reverses the resolutions. Will you force the unfortunate students who, whatever their personal views, are between two disagreeing elements, and that without fault on their part, to wait until future conventions before they can return to class?

You know as well as I do that neither you nor I have the authority to annul a resolution of the synodical convention.

Thus I ask you in the sight of God and His church, do you still regard yourself to be a member of the faculty or executive staff of Concordia Seminary? If you do, please return to your teaching or staff duties as quickly as possible and trust that the procedures your church has established for dealing with doctrinal supervision and discipline will be dealt with in all deliberate haste.

I shall encourage the Board of Control to give your concerns prompt and careful attention. I shall also encourage the Board to exercise fairness, justice, and consideration for your feelings in all of its dealings with you.

For the sake of the students, their distraught parents, wives, and families, their congregations and the church at large, I pray God that He will move your hearts to heed this solemn and brotherly request: Please resume your duties.

Sincerely,
(Signed)
J. A. O. Preus
President

JAOP/jb

c.c. Board of Control of Concordia Seminary
Board for Higher Education
Board of Directors of the Synod
District Presidents of the Synod
Doctor Martin H. Scharlemann
Presidents, Colleges and Seminaries
Mr. Gerald Miller, Student Body President

Colleague Carl Volz informed us in our meeting on Thursday, January 24, that a very well-known M.D. in the Synod had advised him, "What you are doing is very serious. It could split the church. I have talked to President Preus. The plan is, if you are not in class Monday, you will be fired, and any student who does not return to classes will be dismissed." Through such routing of "possibilities" it was perhaps expected that we would cave in to the pressures of sheer economics and the bearing of responsibility for the fate of hundreds of students. At the same time, Preus could quite naturally claim that he had suggested nothing of the kind and that we were the victims of idle rumors, which merely complicated his task of trying to chart a safe and serene course for the ship of the church. In any event, Professor Volz was not a dreamer of dreams, and the conversation fitted into a pattern we had observed developing: unmerciful actions, pleas, threats expressed in legal terminology, promises of due process, and further reminders of the consequences if we did not comply.

Caemmerer, still refusing to be honorably retired, said that Dr. Preus' letter "maintains the misunderstanding that we are in *revolt* against articles of faith held in the Missouri Synod and reenunciated at New Orleans. That's not true. We are *protesting* indictment without charges of guilt being made. This is a diversion of issues on his part. We are seeing a ghastly operation of politics and of malfeasance in office."

Then Mr. James Cross of the Synod's Mission staff reported that a press conference had been scheduled for 10:00 that morning. Preus, however, "besought, threatened, cajoled" and otherwise pleaded for cancellation until further discussions could be held. No other staff, except possibly the Board for Parish Education, "will stand with us," he said. But a "groundswell" is developing.

William Danker underwrote the missionaries' concerns: "I was moved very deeply this afternoon by an African student. He was thinking of transferring. Tears were rolling down his cheeks at the prospect of leaving Concordia." He added that the Rev. Richard Jeske had called to say that his tri-Lutheran congregation in Lawrence, Kansas would be devoting the next Sunday evening to study of the seminary crisis.

With the addition of the names attached to the following communication, practically 90% of the population of Concordia Seminary was in protest against the disruption of their facilities by Preus and the Board of Control.

CONCORDIA SEMINARY, St. Louis, Missouri 63105

Date: 23 January 1974

To: Dr. John H. Tietjen
      The Faculty Majority
      Students of Concordia Seminary
   We of the Clerical, Secretarial, and Professional Staff of Concordia Seminary applaud your Christian witness and your actions against injustices.
   These were not only actions involving the Church, but also totally immoral actions. And we, as fellow human beings, cannot sit idly by without expressing our support and dedication to you. Should the time come when our immediate supervisors are dismissed we have no choice but to leave with them.

Yours in Christ,

cc: Board of Control, St. Louis
    President Jacob A. O. Preus
    Dr. Martin Scharlemann

The following persons affixed their names to this statement.

Nancy Rimkus, Administrative Assistant to the Registrar
Verna Renner, Graduate School Secretary
Dorothy Carmack, Development Administrative Secretary

Thelda Bertram, Library Staff
Margarete Wuerffel, Clinic Assistant-Secretary
Marsha Straub, Secretary to the Director of Admissions
Linda Goggin, Secretary to the Director of Financial Aid and Housing
Paula Liechti, Secretary to C.T.M.
Joann Toedebusch, Secretary to Director of Placement, coordinator
    of C.P.E. and Director of Graduate Program in Pastoral Counseling
Laura Brusick, Instructional Media Center Secretary
Barbara J. Morris, Secretary to the Academic Dean
Carol Bauer, Secretary to Director of Field Education
Diane Hageman, Secretary to Registrar
Maggie Germann, Secretary to Dean of Students
Carolyn Rapp, Secretary, Director of Resident Field Education
Karen O. Ludwig, Secretary to Profs. Bertram, Bangert, E.
    Schroeder, F. Danker, and Habel
Kathleen Wind, Secretary to Profs. Volz, Bergt, Constable, Werberig,
    Sauer, and Goetting
Nellie Turner, Secretary to Profs. Mehl, Repp, Krentz, Bouman,
    Lueker
Rosemary Lipka, Director of Secretarial Services
Jeannette Bauermeister, Administrative Assistant to the Academic
    Dean
Lydia Volz, Library Staff
Ann Vendt, Fieldhouse
Anna Constable, Library Staff
Mary Bischoff, Library Staff
Eleanore Sauer, Library Staff
Elizabeth Danker, Library Staff

Continuing the momentum of good cheer was a telegram that read: "They can't fire you. Slaves have to be sold!"

Someone asked what the Missouri Synod's bishops (district presidents) were doing. Paul Lessmann said that twenty-four of them were meeting in Orlando, Florida and were preparing to serve an ultimatum.

Dr. John Hollar, Concordia alumnus and academic field editor at Fortress Press, communicated through Professor Everett Kalin the "friendship and total support of himself, Norman Hjelm [Director and Senior Editor], and Fortress Press."

"The students are keeping the faith both at home and out [in reference to the vicarage class]," was colleague Werberig's word of consolation.

In view of the increasing heavy artillery of legal terminology that was coming our way from Synodical bases, we needed an attorney to advise us about our tenured and contractual rights. Our Defense Committee and Faculty Advisory Committee reported that we had available some of the best legal counsel.

Our Outreach Committee recommended that the students should go out on their own, but that we "support them fully" in their undertaking. We endorsed this, fully cognizant of the consequences—that we would probably be asked to write a letter of explanation to the Board.

According to Pastor Alfred Buls of Bethel Lutheran Church, which was attended by many faculty, staff, and students, about a hundred St. Louis area pastors had signed a letter that was to be read on Sunday, January 28.[2]

A PASTORAL LETTER REGARDING THE SEMINARY CONTROVERSY TO THE METROPOLITAN ST. LOUIS LUTHERAN COMMUNITY

I

An emergency situation exists in our Synod. As you are aware from the events of recent days, the life of our St. Louis seminary hangs in the balance. The crisis on that campus is symptomatic of the serious situation in other areas of our Synod, such as the Division of Missions, where both staff and policy are under attack. The crisis reaches all the way to our local congregations, and affects us all.

As of this moment, Concordia Seminary is closed. The student body has declared a moratorium and the faculty has declared itself suspended by the Board of Control. Both of these actions came as a response to the suspension of President John Tietjen on Sunday, January 20.

These are drastic actions. The people most directly involved—students and faculty—are thereby indicating the depth of their disagreement with the action of the Board of Control, and the strength and solidity of their support for Dr. Tietjen's position. Their intensity should convey to us the urgent need for action on our part.

It is our responsibility to become informed on this issue if we are not already, and to act immediately and responsibly in accord with our own convictions. This is a matter for the whole Synod, and we are the Synod. The necessity for us in this metropolitan area to act is even more pressing because Concordia Seminary is part of our immediate community, and the brothers and sisters involved are members of our congregations.

II

We are prepared to state our own convictions. We are compelled to do so, even though we realize the issues are controversial.

257

Remaining silent only compounds the problem and permits wrongdoing to continue without opposition. We pray that those who hear our words will understand that they come out of hearts concerned pastorally for people on both sides of the issue, and mindful of our own sins and weaknesses.

It is apparent to us that the Board of Control has proceeded along a course of action contrary to Christian ethics. To carry out a predetermined objective, the Board majority has misused the bylaws of our Synod which are intended to provide due process for a peaceful settlement of differences.

Already prior to the New Orleans convention, the president of the Synod declared publicly, "John Tietjen must go." The present Board of Control, with a new majority elected at the convention, has pursued and accomplished that goal with utmost haste. In the process, the Board majority has employed tactics of collusion, secrecy and dishonesty. Evidence to support this judgment is now available to all.

We are convinced that the Board of Control majority is guilty of wrongdoing. Their actions are symptomatic of the legalistic spirit which now permeates much of our synodical administration.

III

We accept without reservation the Sacred Scriptures as the written Word of God and the historic Lutheran confessions named in Article II of our Synod's constitution as a true exposition of that Word.

So does the faculty of Concordia Seminary, including the majority of 43 (out of 48) who have been accused of false teaching.

We reject that accusation as untrue, and stand with the faculty majority in their confession of faith. They are no more false teachers than we are.

We do not make that statement lightly, but in the confidence that they are faithful to their ordination vow, as we are faithful to ours.

IV

We therefore appeal to the congregations for prompt action in this crisis. We request congregational officers to call special meetings immediately, devoted to the discussion of the issues and events described, and leading to action which will help correct wrongs that have been done.

We live by the gospel of the forgiveness of sins. We know this is our only hope for healing. We therefore pray for a repentant spirit on the part of all, that together we may rejoice in God's grace.

"The body does not consist of one member but of many . . . If one member suffers, all suffer together; if one member is honored, all rejoice together." (I Corinthians 12:14, 26)

These are the names of the greater St. Louis area clergy who had signed the enclosed pastoral letter by the time it had been prepared for mailing.

Justus C. Kretzmann
Richard D. LaBore
John Gugel
Leland Lochhaas
David S. Luecke
Robert Hoyer
John Koch
Thomas Teske
Werner Boos
Ervin Brese
Gil Busarow
Alvin Kollmann
Alan Wyneken
Walter Grotrian
John Kovac
Elmer Schwartzkopf
Walter M. Schoedel
Alfred Buls
Kenneth C. Haugk
Paul Hutchinson
Norman C. Meyer
Paul A. Beins
Paul C. Dorn
Paul A. Metzler
Norman R. Gardels
Robert Trautmann
Arnold Bringewatt
Robert Rosenberg
Warren W. Gritzke
Jack Geistlinger
Wm. H. Hansen
Paul Ihlenfeldt
Paul Pallmeyer
Tim Brunn
David A. Peters
Robert M. Zorn
Robert Fiedler
James Fackler
Gary H. Heide
Daniel Jungkuntz
Neil F. Pape
King Schoenfeld

Edmund Lammert
L. E. Eifert
David E. Wobrock
Edw. M. Hummel
Robert Myers
Arden Mead
Arthur H. Strege
Alvin H. Sasse
Gary P. Kubista
Donald D. Kasischke
Milton E. Stohs
Paul J. Haberstock
Leo E. Wehrspann
Luther G. Albrecht
Albert H. Schroeder
Ronald J. Schlegel
Paul R. Heckmann
Roy A. Moeller
Arno E. Krentz
Paul Weinhold
George H. Fehl
Paul E. Hinrichs
Harold Fleischhauer
Ronald E. Duer
Barry Hong
Richard Brendel
Eugene A. Koene
Arthur E. Otto
Erwin H. Meinzen
G. K. Schmidt
Wesley A. Bartels
Norman E. Porath
Roger Arnholt
Thomas Stephan
Earl Feddersen
Bernard Asen
David F. C. Wurster
Richard E. Hoffmann
Josef Mensing
Mark Wegener
Samuel J. Roth
Art Erb

Ronald Bronemann
Milton F. Drumm
Francis M. Lieb
James R. Lillie
Dan Deutsch
Jack Amen
Wm. E. Schmidt
Vernon Wiehe
Alfred Peuster
Robt. C. Wiemken

Robert Preece
Williard Mueller
Aaron L. Uitti
Walter Diekroger
H. A. Rehwalt
Alfred J. F. Meier
Wm. H. Winkler
Paul Koch
Richard G. Herbel

The Rev. Alfred Buls followed up this reassuring statement of support with the information that Dr. Herman Scherer, President of the Missouri District, would be asked to call a meeting of the district immediately. Some, he added, are strongly in favor of withholding funds for the Synod's work.

Preus Seeks A Truce

President Preus was beginning to see that things were not going as he had anticipated; we were informed that he was in the process of inviting clergymen and laymen in the Synod to serve on an *Advisory Committee on Doctrine and Conciliation.* On the same day we were meeting he sent out the following letter to the men he had chosen:

To the Advisory Committee on Doctrine and Conciliation
You probably have heard that I have discussed with the Council of Presidents, the Board of Directors, and the CTCR, the possibility of establishing an Advisory Committee on Doctrine and Conciliation. This idea has been discussed in many different quarters and by many different people for the past several years. It has been proposed to me in letters from all parts of the church and from all elements of the church.

Doctor Wiederaenders also made reference to an idea of this kind in one of the recent Council of Presidents meetings.

I asked the Council of Presidents in the meeting in Tampa to send me names of men they would propose for such a committee and about ten or twelve of them have given me some very excellent suggestions.

The committee will consist of 14 members who have been chosen not only because they represent the diverse theological positions held within the Synod, but because of their ability to communicate their convictions and concerns with those who disagree. In addition, there will be a moderator whose sole task is to chair the meetings, and also a journalistic consultant who shall assist in the reporting process to the church and also, by committee request, aid in the formulation of statements.

The following tasks are assigned to the committee: (1) delineate the issues, and (2) develop proposals for dealing with the issues in such a way that the Synod can under God and by His grace achieve doctrinal consensus.

By delineating the issues, I do not mean simply listing such items as the historical-critical method, Gospel reductionism, the third use of the Law, inerrancy of Scripture, relation of Gospel and Scripture, etc., but rather, systematically setting forth the point at issue in each of these items. For example, it is not enough to say that we are in disagreement concerning the use of the historical-critical method. We need first to define the term; then we must delineate where we agree and where we disagree point by point. These points must be set forth in a manner which is comprehensible to everyone in the church.

The members of this committee must be absolutely agreed that no statement shall be issued by them as to what the issues are unless *all* agree on the wording and on the issues. That is to say, all need to agree that a certain point is at issue and all need to agree as to the way in which the point at issue is to be formulated. We need to understand the positions with which we disagree and be able to describe them as well as we do our own. This must be done unanimously.

The work of the committee is to supplement the duties of the CTCR and other agencies which have been assigned doctrinal responsibilities in the Constitution and Bylaws of the Synod. Such agencies will continue to exercise their stated responsibilities as before. Likewise, the resolutions adopted by conventions of the Synod remain intact.

The committee can do much in creating a climate favorable to the solution of controversy.

I am asking you to serve as a member of this committee. I am very hopeful that the committee can complete its work by the 1st of January, 1975, to enable us to make concrete proposals for the 1975 convention in the hope that by that time we can draw down the curtain on this unhappy chapter in our Synod's history.

You might be interested to know who the other people are who have been asked to serve. I am enclosing a list for your consideration and also making public the names of the individuals as a way of informing the church and developing confidence in the work of the committee.

I want to thank you in advance for your willingness to serve.

Sincerely,

J. A. O. Preus

President

JAOP/jb

P.S. The first meeting of the committee will be held on February 19, 1974.

Members of the Committee:

Chairman: The Reverend Doctor Arnold Kuntz, President of the Southern California District

Journalistic Consultant: The Reverend Frank Starr, Associate Editor, *The Lutheran Witness/Reporter*

The Reverend Karl L. Barth, President of the South Wisconsin District

The Reverend Doctor Richard Caemmerer, Professor, Concordia Seminary, Saint Louis

The Reverend William Eggers, Wauwatosa, Wisconsin

The Reverend Doctor Carl Gaertner, Pastor, Zion Lutheran Church, Dallas, Texas

The Reverend Doctor Lloyd H. Goetz, President of the North Wisconsin District

The Reverend Arthur Graudin, Pastor, St. Luke's Lutheran Church, Claremont, California

Mr. Robert W. Hirsch, Yankton, South Dakota

Mr. Les Kuhlman, Saint Louis, Missouri

The Reverend Doctor Richard Lischer, Pastor, Emmaus Lutheran Church, Dorsey, Illinois

The Reverend Doctor Armin Moellering, Pastor, Grace Lutheran Church, Palisades Park, New Jersey

The Reverend Doctor Robert Preus, Professor, Concordia Seminary, Saint Louis

The Reverend Samuel J. Roth, Pastor, Zion Lutheran Church, Ferguson, Missouri

The Reverend Doctor Robert Smith, Professor, Concordia Seminary, Saint Louis

The Reverend Doctor Lorenz Wunderlich, Professor, Concordia Seminary, Saint Louis

The 'Deal'

Before adjournment, Tietjen said that a number of telephone calls had come in asking about the 'deal' that he had laid out before the student body on Monday morning. "Can you make it stick?" he was asked. "Yes. Take a look at Vic Bryant's statement." It read:

"NO DEAL!"

From: The Lutheran Church-Missouri Synod
Department of Public Relations
Victor W. Bryant, Director
500 North Broadway
St. Louis, Mo. 63102

1/24/74 - 9
IMMEDIATE RELEASE

Sᴛ. Louis, Mo.—Mr. Vic Bryant, public relations director of The Lutheran Church-Missouri Synod, has issued the following statement:

For the past two years I have tried to be honest and impartial, reporting without editorial comment actions of both "sides" of the doctrinal controversy that has hindered the major work of my church. I believed, and still do, that this is the proper role of the public relations department.

Now, however, I feel compelled to share some information with you because I believe I might well be one of the "agents of the president of the Synod" referred to Monday by Dr. John H. Tietjen, the suspended president of Concordia Seminary, St. Louis.

Dr. Tietjen was described to me by a member of the media as "one of the seven PR wonders of the world." And having worked for some 15 years in public relations, I do, of course, respect his abilities in this area. But I cannot condone the use of half-truths.

Semantics is a large part of the game being played. I would use the word "conciliation" rather than "deal." And I am ready to stand before my Lord to let Him judge if my efforts toward conciliation, to bring an end to the bitter strife in our church, are indeed immoral and evil or represent moral bankruptcy!

Early last fall, in a brief phone conversation with Dr. Tietjen, I asked where we were all headed. John replied, "to disaster." I asked if there were no other way. He replied, "No *honorable* way."

I relayed this conversation over lunch with Larry Neeb in late fall. (Larry is on leave from Concordia Seminary, where he is director of communications.) I also told Larry of a brief paragraph which vividly describes for me what has happened to The Lutheran Church-Missouri Synod. It was written by Dr. Roland Wiederaenders shortly before the New Orleans convention and describes what happened to the church after he had presented a paper in 1963 to the Council of Presidents and seminary faculties, stating the need for clear theology. That paper of December 2, 1963, said in part:

Despite repeated efforts we have not dealt honestly with our pastors and people. We have refused to state our changing theological position in open, honest, forthright, simple and clear words. Over and over again we said that nothing was changing when all the while we were aware of changes taking place. Either we should have informed our pastors and people that changes

263

were taking place and, if possible, convinced them from Scripture that these changes were in full harmony with "Thus saith the Lord'" or we should have stopped playing games as we gave assurance that no changes were taking place. With increasing measure the synodical trumpet has been given an uncertain sound.

Dr Wiederaenders then describes the steps that occurred over the following ten years:

Quite generally our pastors and almost entirely our laity became more and more confused. Confusion led to uncertainty. Uncertainty led to polarization. Polarization destroyed credibility. Loss of credibility destroyed the possibility for meaningful discussion. The loss of meaningful discussion set the stage for a head-on collision.

I expressed concern to Larry as to how the process could be reversed. How can we get back to meaningful discussion? After considerable—and, I felt, meaningful—discussion, we mutually agreed that an honorable way might be possible if John would accept a call. Larry wondered if this would be acceptable to LCMS President Preus. We decided to discuss such a possibility with the two men (he with John, I with Jack) and regroup. Both men indicated a willingness to listen.

The result was countless phone calls with Larry, Missouri District president Herman Scherer and Atlantic District president Rudolph Ressmeyer, who in turn discussed the possibilities with English District president John Baumgaertner.

During this period of some weeks I was repeatedly told that John was willing to listen but had not reached a decision. Some of the items listed in John's statement were broached by me, others by Larry. All were raised as possibilities in an effort to obtain meaningful discussion with and by John. I, of course, had no authority to make a "deal." (And neither, for that matter, did President Preus.) My request to Larry was to ask John if he would put in writing his requirements for reconciliation for discussion with the chairman of the seminary board, the only body which would have the authority. A final phone call stated that John had decided he would not accept a call. The meaningful discussion had ended.

"There's more to come," added Tietjen.

One of the gross deficiencies in Bryant's rejoinder was, of course, the absence of any reference to the negotiable faculty pawns, Paul Goetting and the six retired professors. Even by way of mere suggestion that the Board might reconsider its action against them in the event of Tietjen's acceptance of a call elsewhere, the pressure would be heavy on Tietjen to weigh his own conception of honor against the careers of seven men, not to speak of the rest of the faculty.

That Bryant should have conveyed to Tietjen the suggestion of accepting a call was not at all out of line on Bryant's part. And since ministers in the Missouri Synod are not in the habit of giving a categorical "No" when asked if they might consider a call elsewhere, it was proper for Tietjen to at least participate in exploration of such a possibility. Tietjen never declined an honest effort at reconciliation, and he often encouraged us, no matter how weary we were of fighting against insuperable odds, to accept invitations to dialogue. Undoubtedly Bryant did not personally include the trade-off as incentive to Tietjen to accept a call, for he knew Tietjen better than that. Tietjen did not barter people. But that President Preus might put pressure on the Board of Control to rehire Goetting and the retirees and drop charges against Tietjen in the event he accepted a call elsewhere was well within the realm of Preus' political pattern. The Board would be rid of the conservatives' Enemy Number 1, yet without any bloodshed. Clergy and laity to the right and to the left would be grateful for such wisdom and churchmanship on all sides. How could Tietjen, who wrote *Which Way To Lutheran Unity?* refuse?

That such was the probable script found confirmation in A STATEMENT REGARDING THE 'TIETJEN DEAL' issued by Larry W. Neeb, Director of Communications (on leave), January 27, 1974:

A STATEMENT REGARDING THE "TIETJEN DEAL"
January 27, 1974
Larry W. Neeb, Director of Communications (on leave)

In a statement following his suspension from the presidency of Concordia Seminary on January 20, Dr. John H. Tietjen made reference to a "deal" stating that he had been told that certain arrangements had been offered if he would agree to accept a call.

Since that time his statement has been attacked by both President J. A. O. Preus as well as the chairman of the Board of Control of Concordia Seminary, the Rev. E. J. Otto.

A statement issued by Mr. Vic Bryant, Public Relations Director for The Lutheran Church-Missouri Synod and a report in the St. Louis Post Dispatch referred to me as one of the people involved and I want to set forth the facts from my personal knowledge.

I want to confirm that I relayed to Dr. Tietjen a conversation which I had with Mr. Vic Bryant on the evening of December 8. In that conversation he told me of a phone call which was made by Dr. Preus and synodical vice-president E. C. Weber, to the Rev. E. J. Otto, chairman of the Board of Control of Concordia Seminary. He told me that in that conversation Rev. Otto had been "fully informed" of the things we had been talking about and agreed that if Dr. Tietjen would agree to take a call that it would be possible to drop the charges of false doctrine against him, Professor Paul Goetting could be rehired, the six professors who had been retired in the November Board meeting would be able to continue work, and that during a certain period of time there would be some protection for the rest of the faculty.

This conversation came near the end of a series of discussions I had with Mr. Bryant during the four weeks prior to a scheduled meeting of the seminary Board of Control in December. These conversations began a search for a way to avoid what seemed like certain destruction of the Synod when the Board of Control carried out its intention to suspend Dr. Tietjen from office. Mr. Bryant repeatedly expressed his hope that there might be some way to "get dialog going," but that the way things were going a head-on clash seemed unavoidable. We agreed that if Dr. Tietjen received a call, it might serve as a way of avoiding that tragedy.

Throughout these conversations Mr. Bryant told me of contacts with district presidents, between district presidents and between Dr. Preus and some district presidents. Though asked, I made no contacts with other members of the seminary staff or members of the church. It was understood that he was relaying his information to Dr. Preus and that I was speaking with Dr. Tietjen.

From the outset, Dr. Tietjen told me that he was "willing to listen" but that he really didn't see how he could take a call when charges of false doctrine were pending against him. Efforts to bring Dr. Tietjen a call were not successful and after one district president did, in fact, call him to inquire about his openness to a call, Dr. Tietjen explained to that district president that he couldn't consider a call while there were charges against him. After that call from a district president, Dr. Tietjen called me and asked that I specifically call Mr. Bryant and say that no further efforts should be made in that direction. He did not feel that he could possibly be qualified for service in another parish of the Synod while there were charges of false doctrine against him. He said that he had faced an "easy way" out when Dr. Preus asked him to resign during the New Orleans convention and that he had said no. He preferred to stand for what he thought was right. He said that the future of the church was in their hands.

I conveyed this information to Mr. Bryant and we concluded that there appeared to be no further point in seeking a call or in our discussions.

It was a long day and reporters had been very busy. Some critics of the Seminary had complained that Tietjen and the faculty were overly news conscious. But the faces of Dr. Scharlemann and President Preus on both Channels 4 (CBS) and 5 (NBC) that same evening gave the lie to the rumor that Tietjen, faculty and students were hogging the media or that the media were unfair in their coverage.

Newsman Jim Murphy wanted to know how Scharlemann had managed finally to meet with the student body. He answered that the time had been "negotiated."

Preus, in answer to the question whether there were any contingency plans, said that there were two or three possibilities, but that nothing he said was to be construed as an answer. Alternatives could presumably include bringing in people to teach, or even to close the seminary.

Scharlemann, still sniffing out Marxists, said, "Some agitation could be going on here that has nothing to do with education."

Ms. Lee Sheppard observed that the students scarcely looked like radicals; they were so "well-behaved during Dr. Scharlemann's speech; but they did seem to respond vociferously to some answers."

John Damm, Academic Dean, said, "In the event things go along their present course, we have a responsibility to these students to see to it that they complete their courses of study. Some may go to other Lutheran seminaries. Here in St. Louis arrangements are being made through members of our consortium, Eden Seminary and St. Louis University's Divinity School."

Attorney Richard Duesenberg told one of the reporters that he had given "much energy to this dispute." He said he loved the Lutheran Church-Missouri Synod, which has done so much in so many ways, but he indicated that he was very much disturbed that his church's "actions did not conform with avowed principles."

When asked on Channel 5 whether he thought the professors would return to classes, President Preus declared: "I don't know what they're thinking." In answer to the suggestion that the church seemed to be in quite an uproar over the events of the week, Preus commented, "St. Louis is not the Missouri Synod." His questioner was unaware of the ominous tone in Preus' answer. It was evident that the media had no inkling of the massive artillery build-up taking place with the help of the printing presses at Concordia Publishing House, source of all synodically approved reading material.

Chapter 24

OUTREACH

If one of the primary virtues of an academic president is to be fiscally responsible, Dr. John Tietjen could make first claim. According to the minutes of the Student Body's meeting, held on Outreach Day, Friday, January 25, 1974, he was about to undergo a sixth audit of Concordia Seminary's books by administrators of the Synod who had hoped to find something to make their charge of malfeasance stick. "They ought to be able to find a few stamps unaccounted for," said one of our colleagues.

Tietjen's financial competence was matched by the students, who reported $2,154.04 in their fund known as "Seminarians Concerned." Preferring to remain anonymous, a member of the United Church of Christ had augmented their treasury with a $1,000.00 check.

Despite administrative efforts to curtail the flow of unauthorized information to the faculty and students, mimeographed memos and reports were in as great abundance on this day as before. Through the grapevine a woman, who also did not want her left hand to know what the right one was doing, informed a student that she had a garage filled with paper for duplicating. The students were welcome to it. For one particularly sensitive publication they loaded a car down so heavily the springs were dragging, but made it to Prince of Peace Church, where they printed the material; then hauled it to Zion Church in Ferguson to run the folding machine. The springs still held out. Like the widow's flow of oil during Elisha's visit, the students' paper supply continued for the duration and beyond.

On Thursday, Professor Vincent had jocularly pleaded with the faculty to "coordinate our rumors with theirs." As a back-up system to rumor control, which supplied a recorded three-minute update of information, the community could put through a request for specific information by calling the Office of Student Government on the seminary's phone. Students on intern leave (vicarage) could phone from distant states and then relay first-hand information to peers in their geographical vicinity. With such resources of basic communications media at their disposal, the students looked forward to their Outreach effort.

All the focus of Friday, January 25 was on the Service of Commissioning held at 11:00 A.M. in the chapel for the benefit of the students involved in OPERATION OUTREACH, designed to bring the news of what was really going on at Concordia Seminary to the grassroots of the Missouri Synod. I had originally been assigned months before to deliver the address for the chapel service regularly scheduled on this day. My text was to be I Corinthians 12:3–13, and I had chosen as the theme, "Who's in Charge?" But I put it back in the barrel. It was more appropriate that Dr. Tietjen himself handle the message this day, which he did outside in front of Luther Statue after the chapel service.

Revealing no ill effects of suspensionitis, in a few simple sentences he told the students, who were preparing to go to almost every state in the Union, to attest what they had been taught at Concordia Seminary. "Tell the people of our Synod that they have nothing to fear except the Evil One (an allusion to the First Epistle of John)." Far from being told what to say, and what not to say, as alleged by some of their adversaries, Tietjen encouraged them to tell the truth. The faculty had nothing to hide, and we were not worried about out students' answers, for freedom is , next to love, the best antidote against fear. As an anonymous sage put it, "Only liars require good memories."

Each of the student teams then drove up to receive a blessing for a safe journey from Dr. Tietjen. Even this religious concern on their part ran into jaundiced criticism. The editor of *Christian News* claimed that they were driving back and forth before the television cameras.[1]

Twenty-four hours earlier the students had sent out "A Letter to the Church." It read:

Dear fellow members of the body of Christ,
 By now you have probably heard and read all sorts of things about the recent actions of The Board of Control of Concordia Seminary, its students and its faculty and staff majority. I'm sure that you are deeply concerned about these actions and are interested in knowing as much about them as you possibly can. It is with this concern in

mind that I would like to address you in behalf of the students of Concordia Seminary.

As you probably already know, students at Concordia Seminary have declared a moratorium on all classes. The number of students in support of this moratorium represents about 80% of the total student enrollment. Our reasons for calling this moratorium can be summed up in some very simple words: We feel that it is time for The Seminary Board of Control to give an account of itself and to prove once and for all that it is dealing justly and evangelically with its responsibilities in this place. As students at Concordia, we have every right to demand this of The Board of Control, for ultimate responsibility for the most meaningful and efficient operation of the whole seminary rests with The Board of Control.

At the present moment, however, we find it very difficult to believe that the Board of Control is carrying out its responsibilities as it should. We find it difficult to believe that the Board is dealing justly and evangelically with Dr. John H. Tietjen and the faculty and staff majority. In the opinion of many students, Dr. Tietjen's statement of Jan. 21, 1974, is enough evidence to prove that justice is something which we can no longer take for granted in the Lutheran Church-Missouri Synod. The blitzkrieg-like fashion in which The Board of Control replaced one department head after another at its January 20–21 meeting, without even consulting with the men who headed these departments or explaining its reasons for doing so, is unbelievable in a church which calls itself "evangelical."

We have called a moratorium at Concordia Seminary because we feel that the issues which are at stake are important enough to warrant such action. Our church body can no longer afford to ignore the serious nature of those problems which confront us. There is no way in which the unjust and unevangelical actions which are taking place in our synod can be justified. The issue is not who has the authority to make certain decisions, but rather how we reach decisions in a Christian community.

We know that some people have been saying that The Seminary Board of Control has the right to do what they have been doing out of a concern for doctrinal purity. To that we simply say: If The Seminary Board of Control has anything against any of the professors or staff members at Concordia Seminary, then let them bring specific charges against them and convince the people of our church that these men are indeed "false teachers." If they cannot do this, then they owe it to the church to exonerate these men immediately and to treat them as innocent of all such charges.

As long as The Seminary Board of Control refuses to do so, as long as it treats people as guilty until proven innocent, students have not only a right, but also a responsibility, to refuse to go to classes. We pray that in your own way, you also will urge the Seminary Board of Control to carry out its responsibilities in a just and evangelical way.

When this has been done, there will be no need for a student moratorium.

Your brother in Christ Jesus,
Gerald A. Miller
Student Body President

Could their church ignore their expression of conscience? Surely this plea must help to open doors on their Outreach.

Can We Get a Fair Hearing?

Earlier the same morning the faculty assembled to hear a few words from Dr. Herman Scherer, President of our Missouri District, and a member of the Board of Control, but who, like Nicodemus, "had not consented to their purpose and deed."

"Dr. Scherer has assured us of having a fair hearing," said Robert Bertram, by way of introduction. "He will now interpret how he understands 'fair treatment.' "

In his brief remarks Scherer pointed out that "tragedy began at New Orleans" and that as the result of recent events some who had been in sympathy with us were becoming angrier each day the seminary remained closed. He pleaded with us to study Dr. Preus' letter of January 24 and to respond in direct fashion with a delegation, indicating when we would be willing to reenter the classrooms. Another delegation should have a hearing with the Board of Control, he said. Although he had not as yet succeeded in gaining us a fair hearing, he promised that he would go to bat for us if we came with a delegation.

Dr. Tietjen expressed the esteem of all in the room: "In your presence I say, I am deeply appreciative of your support as a Board member and as a District President. You have done everything humanly possible."

Since 'calls' into parishes are channeled through the office of the district president, Tietjen wanted to clear anyone's mind of the notion that Dr. Scherer might have been participant in any aspect of Preus' "deal," designed to exchange the continuance of the teaching careers of a number of the faculty in return for Tietjen's voluntary resignation prior to January 1974. "Bryant (head of the Synod's Public Relations) was the agent," said Tietjen. "The only role of Dr. Scherer was the correct function of seeking a call."

271

Colleague Erwin Lueker endorsed Dr. Scherer's honesty and integrity. But, he said, "John Tietjen's suspension *must* be lifted. He is *conservative* and an example of what an administrator ought to be. . . . The only fault I can find with Dr. Tietjen is that he did *for us* what the President of Synod should have done for us. . . . When his suspension is lifted, then mine will be lifted."

"You don't have to convince me, "said Dr. Scherer, "but you will have difficulty to convince the Board of Control of that."

By way of suggestion to the Faculty Advisory Committee I had written earlier:

> Our previous relations with Dr. J. A. O. Preus have made it clear to us that his word cannot be trusted. His committee appointments bear the marks of a "stacked deck." The present committee he has suggested for conciliation is further evidence thereof, for it includes his own brother and a member of his Fact Finding Committee. We, as the faculty, might propose that the Council of Presidents order into being two committees, with instructions that said committees publish their report to the entire church on the basis of their own ground rules. Conciliation Committee No. 1 is to consist of 8 appointees, two each from the four seminaries with whom the LC-MS is affiliated (Capitol, Dubuque, Luther, and Springfield). The members of this committee are to be appointed by majority vote of their respective faculties. This committee is to examine the present conflict in the light of the question: "What is Lutheran and what is not Lutheran in the theological issues that have been raised?" Conciliation Committee No. 2 is to consist of the following: 1 member of the National Education Association; 1 of the American Association of University Professors; 1 from the American Association of Theological Schools; 2 from the AFL-CIO; 1 from the NAACP; 1 from the American Civil Liberties Union; and 1 from the Anti-Defamation League. This committee is to concern itself with the moral aspects of the situation and the question of justice as viewed by outsiders.
>
> The Church has the right to know, and the world has the right to know that we are willing to live according to the principles we claim to stand for as Christians.

Lueker encouraged something along the same lines, with a view to "scrutinizing the entire picture and the work of the Fact Finding Committee."

Someone else, however, thought that Scherer's suggestion should be followed, lest we seem to adopt an 'obdurate' position. "After all," the colleague said, "we are not in opposition to the Synod."

Arthur Repp, appropriately forgetting that he had been retired, said he saw no way for his return "until John H. Tietjen is reinstated." Dr. Scherer replied, "Unless the seminary is opened, we will have an impasse." Scharlemann had put it another way the day before, but the message was the same.

Two members of the Board had now in effect told us that we were on a one-way street named 'Unconditional Surrender.' Any talk of dialogue was a verbal fiction. Power meant monologue.

Alfred Fuerbringer, Tietjen's predecessor in the presidency of Concordia Seminary, emphasized "that our faculty had again and again tried to meet with Dr. Preus, but without success," and that he himself was denied an audience with the Board concerning his retirement.

Scherer replied that when the matter of Fuerbringer's retirement had come up, he tried to insist that Fuerbringer, along with Alfred von Rohr Sauer and Arthur Repp, be present. "But they would have none of it," he said.

Paul Lessmann said he preferred to entrust himself to the Faculty Advisory Committee. "Since New Orleans," he observed, "the basic principle is: People are guilty until proved innocent. We, on our part, must insist: (1) a man is innocent until proved guilty; (2) *we* are considered innocent until proved guilty; (3) *our product* is innocent until proved guilty."

Academic Dean John Damm entreated Scherer: "The Holy Spirit can move the hearts of people. And we know that the Holy Spirit is pleading with us, through you, that we please be reasonable. But some evangelical persuasion must be brought to bear on the other side.... *Please* do not force us into a confessional room where they hold all the cards and we stand naked."

Historian Herbert Mayer observed that we were in a very difficult position because of the politicization of the Synod. Although we were a part of the church, we were forced to defend a moral principle in the face of attack from other sectors of the church. This would render our position unpopular in the eyes of a number of constituents who might think that authority could not err.

Refusal to Affirm the Obvious

President Preus' letter addressed to us the day before (January 24) in response to our communication of January 22 had already etched the truth of Mayer's evaluation.

273

Comparison of his reply with the problems and questions we had raised in our briefer letter of January 22 suggest how difficult it was to awaken openness to the central issue. ". . . Many of you are in no way at odds . . ." Preus had written. The word "many" ought to have lowered the number of suspects for "heresy" to a very small percentage out of 45. The same word also suggested that the highest officials of the synod knew who the alleged heretics were, but were not telling. Yet without charges, the suspension of Dr. Tietjen on the allegation of "failing to take action against faculty members who hold positions contrary to the clear words of Scripture" was in effect a kangaroo court condemnation of the sort one might expect from an obsessed vigilante squad. Dr. Preus, however, appeared to be completely insensitive to the immorality of such a travesty of justice.

Further, his statement that "the process" we envisaged, "might take a number of years to complete" was belied by events that had already taken place. Six men who had earlier identified with Tietjen and had signed a statement of protest *against* New Orleans Resolution 3-09, which had condemned the alleged "position" of the faculty majority, had been retired *honorably*. It did not even take one hour to terminate Professor Goetting's contract. Professor Norman Habel was sent on his way in less than five minutes, but at least with greater grace of consistency, namely, minus a peaceful dismissal.

"Totally irrelevant, absurd, and dust in the eyes of his jury," was the general reaction to Preus' statement: "The Synod's judgment that certain teachings are false stands until a future convention of the Synod reverses the resolutions." It was absurd, because the false teaching described in the resolution was of a nature "not to be tolerated in the church of God." How in the world could a future convention of Synod even consider revocation of such a resolution, and make such teachings once more tolerable? Did not the Synod's constitution irrevocably state that matters of doctrine are *not* decided by majority vote? It would have been like asking a synodical convention to decide whether the church should continue to pray and honor the Holy Trinity.

Further, it was irrelevant because Preus was speaking of condemnation of "certain teachings." In our letter to him we had not questioned the Synod's right to condemn false doctrine. Rather, we had indicated that none of us had been *charged* with teaching any false doctrine and that Dr. Tietjen's suspension on such grounds was therefore at the same time an indictment of ourselves which we refused to recognize. It was a very reasonable and simple request we had directed to the President of the Synod. In no way could it have compromised his position. All he had to do was affirm the obvious: No charges of false doctrine have been levelled against any members of the faculty, therefore the suspension of Dr. Tietjen on such grounds is invalid. First establish the guilt of a specific professor or professors and then see whether Tietjen will or will not take action. Such procedure would have been in accordance with the Bylaws of the Synod and would have met the requirements of the accrediting agency.

Our united reply to President Preus took the following form:

26 January 1974
The Reverend Dr. Jacob A. O. Preus
President
The Lutheran Church—Missouri Synod
500 North Broadway
St. Louis, Missouri 63102

Dear President Preus,

We are herewith responding to your January 24 response to our letter of January 22.

First of all, to your question we say categorically, "Yes, we are members of the faculty and executive staff of Concordia Seminary." We are eager to get back into the classroom and resume our normal teaching and other duties. We did not cause the present disruption and nothing could please us more than to see it ended. In suspending John H. Tietjen, the Board of Control suspended us.

You, the Board of Control, and the whole synod should know furthermore that we are not shirking our teaching duties. We are teaching right now, but not in the classroom and not in the usual fashion. We have taken our stand precisely in order to teach our students and to witness to the synod that playing cynical games with people's lives is incompatible with the Gospel we love and profess and with that righteousness and justice demanded by the prophets and by our Lord.

To be teachers and ministers in the church is a high and holy calling and is not merely a form of employment. We do not see ourselves as functionaries drawing paychecks. Even if our salaries were cut off, we would be conscience bound to continue protesting the injustice which has been dealt to President Tietjen and to continue professing and teaching by words and actions the glorious Gospel of Jesus Christ. Anything less would be an abdication of responsibility.

As we have frequently told you and the church, our teaching is the Scriptural Gospel, and we are not guilty of the charges leveled against us at New Orleans in Resolution 3-09. We are not saying that the doctrine of the Missouri Synod (Article II of the Constitution of the

Lutheran Church—Missouri Synod) is wrong; we are saying that the charges of our violating the doctrine of the Missouri Synod are wrong. We are not protesting the doctrine of the Missouri Synod; we are protesting the action of the New Orleans Convention in charging us that we deny that doctrine.

Our letter of January 22 set two possible actions before you: 1) that you declare your agreement with the Board of Control, press the case against us by due process, and eventually dismiss us, or 2) that you take the lead in clearing us of the charge of false doctrine.

You reply that 1) we are to get back into the classroom and teach, and 2) that the judgment of synod stands until a future convention reverses Resolution 3-09 which in wholesale fashion condemned our teaching as "false doctrine not to be tolerated in the church of God."

You seem to contradict yourself, President Preus, or to be caught on the horns of a dilemma. 1) If you insist on our going back into the classroom and teaching (and we desire nothing more than to do that) then you are contradicting Resolution 3-09, which we also disown. But you also claim not to have the power to rescind 3-09 or to make it inoperative. 2) You state that synod's resolutions, including 3-09, do stand, and yet you instruct us, condemned as false teachers by that resolution, to go back to our duties as teachers and executive staff. Are you admitting that the present struggle is largely political rather than doctrinal?

We are one in confession and suspension with our three colleagues who were so rudely retired (Alfred O. Fuerbringer, Arthur C. Repp, and Alfred von Rohr Sauer), with Paul Goetting whose contract was not renewed, and with John H. Tietjen and his administration who were suspended and removed last Sunday. How can we go back to the classrooms as long as these actions stand and as long as the conditions which resulted in these actions remain unchanged?

Finally, we applaud your offer to urge the Board of Control to be fair, just and considerate of our feelings. They must begin by dealing satisfactorily with the evidence presented by President Tietjen:

1. "that the proceedings being conducted by the Board of Control of Concordia Seminary, St. Louis, . . . offer no possibility of a fair and impartial judgment;"

2. "that they are the result of collusion between the President of the Synod, the six majority members of the Board of Control, and the two pastors who have preferred charges;"

3. "that they are a charade in which the two accusers and the majority members of the Board of Control are seeking to fulfill the letter of the Bylaws for the purpose of reaching a predetermined objective, already publicly announced by the president of the Synod."

Yes, we are still the faculty. We are *now* teaching our students. We desire to reenter the classrooms. We are as eager as ever to dialogue and communicate with you face to face to find a way out of the

276

present impasse. You have yet the opportunity to be pastor to the entire church by repudiating all injustices committed by any board or person action in an official capacity.

Our unanimous endorsement of this letter represents our collective and individual response to your letter of January 24.

Fraternally yours,

(Signed)

Andrew M. Weyermann
For, The Faculty Majority and Executive Staff at Concordia Seminary

The students would learn of our letter in their afternoon meeting at 4:00. They would also be heartened by the news that the Buffalo, New York, Pastors' Conference had issued a protest on behalf of the seminary. "We declare the office of the President of Synod vacant," read their message.

Before adjourning, Coach Pederson announced that "The Preachers" (our basketball team) had lost the night before. Someone behind me said, "And Sunday, Monday, Tuesday, Wednesday, Thursday, too." We had little doubt that on Monday next we would have to ponder a reply by Dr. Preus, who had a recognized reputation for answering his mail promptly, and that our losing record would remain unbroken.

"Some Bible passages," I had heard a student say, "are assuming fresh significance for me." He was thinking especially of Jesus' words in St. Luke's Gospel about leaving even father and mother, if need be, for the sake of the Gospel. We ourselves were now close to Jericho, where once the walls had tumbled down. That Golgatha was only three weeks away, we did not know.

Presbyterian Hospitality

On Sunday evening, January 27, our colleague Robert Werberig gave us all a fresh perspective. We gathered as a community, student and faculty families, at Second Presbyterian Church in the heart of St. Louis.

Unlike a great many of St. Louis' churches which have moved out to the suburbs, "Second Pres" as everyone in St. Louis knows it, has a backbone composed of members who saw a future in failing ecclesiastical fortunes and stuck it out in the inner city. Believing in the literal truth of Jesus' words about "turning the other cheek," Second Pres ignored the fact that Missouri Synod Lutherans have always treated 'The Reformed' as second-class ecclesiastical citizens. Looking on us as refugees from oppression, of which they had seen many varieties, they generously assured us the use of their facilities when it became increasingly difficult to find unlocked meeting rooms at Concordia Seminary.

In his introduction of our colleague Robert Werberig, who had been invited to preach on the evening of the 27th, Orville Brotherton, one of the several pastors at Second Pres, said: "We are accustomed to conflict. . . . We love you and we know the anguish that you feel. . . . Christian love is not bound by denominational lines, and as Christians sharing a dilemma we welcome Professor Werberig to our pulpit this evening. . . . It is an important time in Christendom, but let us be glad and rejoice."

Put To The Test

"Experiences are our faithfinders and directors for the future," proclaimed Werberig. "I and my brothers have been put to the test over the past four and a half years," he said, adding that it had been a "liberating experience," in the realization of "both Crucifixion and Resurrection." "I am a man of peace," he affirmed, and in the same breath expressed appreciation for his synod's heritage with its emphasis on the Gospel. "But when that same Gospel is jeopardized, then one's personal well-being is irrelevant." With sound of sorrow in his voice, he said, "I share in the astonishment of many at a great church on the brink of greatness sliding into fear and retreat from responsibility in the present. . . . We live under a cloud of suspicion and adverse judgment concerning matters not covered by our Lutheran Confessions. Our books, articles, degree documents, tapes of our interviews—all have been thoroughly analyzed, and we were declared innocent by our Board of Control. Yet our president has been suspended on the charge of harboring false teachers." Recoiling at the very thought, he said with heavy tremor: "To be called a false teacher means to be a LIAR BEFORE GOD! . . . We have therefore elected suspension for ourselves until we are either declared innocent or guilty of charges." He then explained that even though the charges had not been lifted, the faculty had been told to return to classes on Monday, January 28.

Entering into personal implications, Werberig said he had discovered during the past week and over the past four and one half years what "a wonderful thing" it was to be associated with his faculty. "I must confess to personal disillusionment at first when I saw what was happening to my church, but they handled me with care, and we have grown profoundly in the process."

"The Resurrection morning is showing," he rejoiced, "and support is coming in from all corners of the Church. . . . Those who seek to *bend* us into *silence* belong to the Old Age. The pressures have bent us, but not beaten us, and they have driven us to a solitary dependence on God in Jesus Christ, to give us wisdom and love. . . . "

"We receive His mission and are in mission. . . . In a sense the mission is already accomplished through Jesus Christ who left behind on the wood some pieces of paper and mapped out a new future that transcends denominational lives with an all-encompassing love. . . . "

"God's pilgrims love one another. You and I need one another. You need us. But we are happy to have found the freedom to say, we need you. . . . When we were kids we used to eat baked potatoes around a camp fire. We shared what we had with each other. We are all pilgrims and on the way we learn to share our bread with one another. We know a little more about that now, thanks to you, YOU PRESBYTERI-ANS!"

With that way to confession of past Lutheran ecclesiastical arrogance we all enjoyed the absolution of knowing Presbyterian smiles.

Chapter 25

THE CASE OF APPENDIX 6

While awaiting the return of their friends from Operation Outreach, the student body of Concordia Seminary displayed increasing concern about the future of their education. When asked about the prospects of the Spring quarter, the Registrar, David Yagow, announced at an update on January 29, 1974, that he considered himself suspended. At the same time he scotched a rumor that transcripts had been removed from campus and assured the students that he knew where each one was in his program.

Sensitive to the heavy burdens borne by their president, the students shelved for a moment their own anxieties and presented Gerald Miller with an assortment of medicinal commodities. The list included Excedrin ("to kill the pain"), No-Doz ("to stay alert for the next atrocity"), coffee ("Brazilian, that is") and a bottle of *Jack* Daniels.

This display of good humor served further notice on President Jack Preus that serious discussion concerning academic matters was not to be construed as a sign of weakening will.

Robert Preus, newly appointed Academic Dean, apparently did not receive the message, for he sent out a report that was obviously calculated to halt the forward motion of the moratorium. Students would receive a passing grade of "S" in all courses not currently meeting. Letter grades would be given for the few courses actually being taught. Students could either switch to such courses or take a reading course in order to receive a letter grade. Graduate students would have similar options. A student interviewed on KMOX commented: "It sounds like the same old political game of divide-and-conquer. It hasn't worked before, and I don't think it will work now."

Students at the chief supply center for Concordia Seminary, Concordia Senior College, Fort Wayne, Indiana, apparently shared his view. According to visiting Professor Rusch, the Senior class had voted 120 to 30 not to come to the seminary "if the situation was not solved."

Robert Grunow, in charge of Development, reported to the faculty on January 30 that some of the District Presidents told him that President Preus' 'game plan' had not included a student moratorium. Nor had 'Jack' anticipated that the faculty would actually be willing to risk their jobs. "Jack has everything to lose. He's in deep trouble on missions."

But anyone who thought that President Preus would falter now had failed to take the measure of the man's determination or the depth of the Synod's deterioration. Echoing what surely was the official line, Dr. Martin Scharlemann, now in his tenth day as Acting President of Concordia Seminary, agreed that registration for the Spring quarter would have to be postponed. That would leave the seminary about $250,000 in the red. "But," said he, with the confidence of a general whose stalled tank forces were awaiting fresh supplies of gasoline, "we will get all the money we need. We will move right ahead to see this thing through."

Preus' Message to the Church

The arrival of President Preus' 32-page "Message to the Church" admitted no doubt as to the meaning of Scharlemann's words and clarified Preus' earlier reminder to a reporter that the Missouri Synod was not limited to St. Louis.

Prefacing the document was a one-page letter, dated January 28, intended for reading in every congregation on February 3, 1974. A nine-page letter followed, addressed to pastors, teachers, congregational officers, lay members of synodical boards, and lay delegates to the New Orleans convention. This long letter was designed to be read in association with the other letters and documents that followed it. The power of the entire parcel to affect the nerve centers of the synod's constituency was matched only by its skillful maneuvering around the issues and by the deadly effect of its innuendos.

The fact that the student body had declared a moratorium because, among other things, professors had been put under a cloud by the suspension of Dr. Tietjen, received little mention. Instead, Dr. Preus maintained that the dissenting faculty members were inconsistent in returning to the classrooms after the New Orleans convention and then refusing to do so after Dr. Tietjen's suspension. Is the faculty's action "largely political rather than a matter of principle, a political action taken in response to the suspension of Dr. Tietjen?" asked Preus, the politician.

What he failed to acknowledge was that his own official news release had stated that Dr. Tietjen had been charged by the Board of Control with "failure to take action against faculty members who hold positions contrary to the clear words of Scripture." This meant that not only Dr. Tietjen but the Board of Control could presumably know who the alleged false teachers were. But the Synod's own Board of Control had given all members of the faculty a certificate of clean doctrinal health early in 1973. Therefore Dr. Tietjen could be excused for not reopening the matter. That would indeed have been executive "malfeasance," a favorite term in Preus' document. This left only the Board of Control with knowledge of the culprits' identity, and the Board was not handing out the names! All this President Preus ignored in his "Message."

As to the innuendo of political motivation for refusal to return to the classrooms, several points are to be kept in mind. The faculty had displayed extraordinary patience, first of all in its response to the President's request for cooperation with the Fact Finding Committee. Few academic communities would have tolerated what has appeared to many secular academicians as unwarranted intrusion in the business of running an educational institution. We could have protested in 1971 and 1972 in some dramatic fashion against the inquisitional procedure, but we were confident that submission to the process could, despite the personal cost, best serve the interests of the Seminary and the Lutheran Church-Missouri Synod. Tietjen's track record also was certainly not one of "defiance," as Preus repeatedly asserted in his Message, for Tietjen had urged us to respond positively to President Preus' investigative process. Even our protest, issued in July, 1973, was mild in comparison with what might have been said in response to the actions taken at New Orleans.

Going into September we were still hopeful that the Synod would recover from the disasters generated at New Orleans, so we returned to class. But we kept asking ourselves, how much are we to take? At what point do we say, "No more!" Patience and obedience do have a bottom line, and that line was drawn on January 20, when Preus' majority on the Board of Control suspended Dr. Tietjen. This action meant that Preus and company were deadly serious about implementing the New Orleans resolutions.

In view of what we knew the future was certain to bring, did Dr. Preus really expect us to abdicate all responsibility to the theological task? Did he really think that academicians working at comparatively low salaries would play political games at the risk of their families' livelihood? Did he really harbor such a low estimate of principle? Did he really expect us to come off in history as the gutless wonders of the Christian church in the Twentieth Century? It was therefore ungallant of Preus to condemn us before the entire church for not displaying less patience in September 1973, while urging us at the same time to "let the processes of the Synod proceed." After New Orleans we knew what that could mean!

Insinuations

Preus' paragraph concerning arrangements "being made for the students to continue their education at Eden Seminary (of the United Church of Christ) and St. Louis University Divinity School (a Roman Catholic institution)" carried insinuations that lingered for months despite clarifications to the contrary. It was a cheap shot.

Eldon Weisheit, at the time a member of the editorial staff of the Synod's paper, once estimated that only about 2% of the Synod's members were theologically literate. Preus' sentence therefore conveyed to them: "Do you realize that many students will now be studying theology at the feet of United Church of Christ professors and Roman Catholic priests?" The students would, in fact, continue their studies with the same curriculum, under their previous instructors. Only the location of theological instruction would be changed.

To further discourage any sympathy or support for the continuance of the students' education off the campus of Concordia Seminary, Dr. Preus stated in his letter that he was "reliably informed that ELIM has about $200,000 in its treasury," and that such a small amount would "support a faculty or a school for only a small portion of a year." This was tantamount to saying that the faculty at Concordia Seminary was off its rocker to even think of alternative procedures for education.

Preus' put-down of the students' departure for Outreach as "largely a theatrical production" was compounded by his innuendo that the students were being "used." This was an insult to a student body composed of men and women, many of whom were rearing families and were perfectly capable of making major decisions on their own.

The fact that they had helped the faculty to see the light more clearly should not have prompted Preus to negate the power of their witness to what they considered truth and justice. His innuendo that they were driving cars from one parking lot to another for the benefit of the television cameras was a further indication of Preus' lack of understanding of the students' depth of commitment. Worship was an important part of the Seminarians' lives. Prayers and blessings before departure for holidays or special events were features of the chapel services. The fact is that there was not room enough in Luther Square to accommodate all the cars whose occupants were receiving the blessing for a safe and profitable journey.

Evidently Preus had been reminded that his Acting President at Concordia Seminary had once been in difficulty with the Synod. In his letter, Preus granted this fact, but said: "The difference lies in the fact that Doctor Scharlemann asked the forgiveness of his church and received a rising ovation and the heartfelt love and affection of the church. This was genuine reconciliation. Doctor Tietjen, on the other hand, by contrast, forgave the church and charged his church with 'grievous wrong.' "

Preus again was ignoring significant data. Scharlemann had indeed expressed his regret and sorrow for the part *he* played in contributing to unrest in the Synod, and had expressly confirmed his commitment to "the doctrine of the verbal inspiration of the Sacred Scriptures." But in answer to some protesting queries, President Behnken gave the floor to the committee in charge of the report on Scharlemann. "We have been assured," said the committee, "by those who have the responsibility for supervision, that charges of false doctrine made against Dr. Scharlemann have not been sustained to date." By contrast, the New Orleans Convention condemned as "position" of the faculty what Dr. Tietjen and other representatives of the faculty refused to recognize as valid description of the faculty's stance. Dr. Tietjen could have taken the Synod to court. Instead, he followed the Scriptural admonition to "turn the other cheek" in the face of what he forthrightly exposed as "grievous wrong," and he forgave his church. For this 'crime' he was now pilloried by Preus. Yet had he sued his church, Preus would have cited 1 Corinthians 6:6 against him: "Brother goes to court against brother, and in the presence of non-Christians at that!" Incredibly, Preus seemed to sponsor a viewpoint most citizens find repulsive, namely, that forces of justice should favor the assailant more than the victim.

But the frosting on the cake was Preus' grumbling over Tietjen's alleged fiscal management. First, he complained: "Had the faculty, under his leadership, given help to the Synod in delineating the issues and bringing forth in a quiet and dignified manner helpful solutions to these problems, we would have applauded them and called them blessed. This unwillingness has been perhaps the greatest of all charges that could be levelled against the president of the seminary." Then in the very next paragraph he wrote: "In the area of malfeasance I would only ask our pastors and laymen how many of them would dare to spend $12,000 without the authorization of their governing board. This was done, however, by Doctor Tietjen." Two years later he himself would be asked at a District conference how he would explain his own unauthorized expenditure of far more than $12,000 in the mailing of a thirty-two page document to more than 50,000 address-ees. But such details did not stand in the way of rhetorical demands at a time when Preus' political future in the Lutheran Church-Missouri Synod was at stake.

Apart from their inconsistency, it must be granted that the juxta-position of thoughts was filled with misrepresentation.

The Other Side

The fact is that the $12,000 cited by Preus had, in fact, covered the production and distribution of the faculty's Affirmation: *Faithful To Our Calling, Faithful To Our Lord.* We had been asked by members of the Council of District Presidents to declare plainly what we believed and taught. We thought this was an invitation to proceed through proper channels. Since we had nothing to hide, and believing in the free dissemination of ideas and the peoples' right to know, Dr. Tietjen offered for public distribution our printed confessional statements and suggestions for discussion. Much of the cost of the printing was recov-ered from the sale of the two booklets. That could scarcely be said of Preus' thirty-two page document, which had been mailed at first class rate. We were under the impression that the entire procedure be-longed to the order of "quiet and dignified manner," and was in the direction of "helpful solutions." Instead, the President of the LC-MS was now turning what the faculty considered a major and reasonable contribution to discussion of the real issues into an opportunity for a charge of "malfeasance" against Tietjen!

Preus also made a big point of Dr. Tietjen's contribution to the for-mulation of Bylaw 6.79 adopted by the synod. This Bylaw dealt with the due process procedures for faculty members.

285

Recipients of Preus' summary might well have inferred that Bylaw 6.79 did, in his words, "insure that the President of the Synod and the Board for Higher Education did not exert undue influence on the Board of Control." Few of the addressees, however, would have noted that Preus' summary failed to mention that the last paragraph of Bylaw 6.79 declares that "a faculty member" can lose "his membership in the Synod through the ecclesiastical route." Bylaw 6.80 clarifies what is meant by the "ecclesiastical route": "A faculty member who is a clergy or teacher member of the Synod is under the ecclesiastical supervision of the Synod. In cases in which such a faculty member is charged with false doctrine or conduct unbecoming a Christian and in which the complainant finds unacceptable the decision of the Board of Control not to pursue the charge, he may be dealt with by the District President or the synodical President and be removed from membership in the Synod and therefore from office in harmony with the provision of the Constitution and Bylaws of the Synod" (here follow references to constitutional and bylaw provisions). In short, Preus still retained control even over decisions of the Board of Control.

Again there was no denying Preus' political expertise. He had outwitted the national accrediting agency, known at the time as AATS, and because of Preus' modesty in overt assessment of his political accomplishments, few of the recipients of Preus' "Message" grasped the scope of his achievement.

To supplement his basic indictment of Tietjen and the faculty, Preus included four pieces of correspondence between the faculty and himself. In a letter dated January 22, and signed by 44 members of the faculty and executive staff,[1] Preus was told that Tietjen's suspension was tantamount to a suspension of all the signers. If Tietjen was guilty of false doctrine, then we were also guilty of false doctrine, for we shared the same confessional stand. In that case, Preus had two choices: 1. To publicly declare agreement with the Board's decision and press the case against us, or 2. "Take the lead in clearing us— John Tietjen and all the rest of us—of the charge of false doctrine. If that happens, we will be freed to return to our classrooms. We pledge to make up all classes that have been missed in the interim." This request appeared to us perfectly reasonable. If we were being asked to return to the classrooms, evidently we were not guilty of false doctrine. At the same time we affirmed that we were all guilty of Dr. Tietjen's alleged false doctrine.

A back-to-work order was in effect tantamount to clearing both

286

Tietjen and us of any dereliction in doctrinal responsibility. Could the Board and Preus in good conscience have it both ways? In his reply of January 24, Preus preferred not to discuss the word "confession," although the question of our confessional stand involved a huge constitutional issue and was the point of the faculty's move after Tietjen's suspension.

Instead of endeavoring to understand what it meant that we considered ourselves suspended with Dr. Tietjen, Preus resorted to linguistic maneuvers and belabored the obvious by declaring our statement "not literally correct."

Ignoring the faculty's point that to return to the classrooms under present circumstances would be a denial of truth and principle in view of Dr. Tietjen's suspension under allegation of false doctrine within the faculty, Preus spent the rest of his letter urging the faculty to continue the task of education. His observation that the "process" we requested "might take a number of years to complete" was patently irrelevant.

Preus was writing to the church about "certain teachings," and all that we requested was a statement of specific charges so that we might know who, if any, among us were responsible for the dismissal of Tietjen on the ground of protecting faculty members who are allegedly guilty of false doctrine. Why was the Board or Preus so reluctant to give out that information?

We were entitled to our day in court, and we wanted it now so that we and the students could return to the classrooms without living under a constant cloud of suspicion. We had repeated these concerns in a reply to Preus dated January 26, in which we emphasized that our present stance was a protest not only against New Orleans Resolution 3-09 but against the procedural steps that led to the suspension of Tietjen. In his reply of January 28, Preus again appealed to literalness as the only criterion of truth, thus in effect calling us liars before the entire church. On the same grounds he might have alleged that Paul had not really died when he said that he had died with Christ, for Paul was still bodily very much alive. But we were up against the monolithic hermeneutic of the LC-MS, which was very wary of figurative language. Yet, whether Preus liked it or not, we considered ourselves very much suspended with Tietjen, and we thought it unpastoral of Preus to tell us *how* we *should* be dealing with matters of conscience. Once again dismissing our dual Affirmation, *Faithful To Our Calling, Faithful To Our Lord* as "hastily drawn up and briefly discussed material," he complained about "the preparation of more public relations

287

material, the staging of more theatricals, the devising of ways to trick people, for example, in phone conversations by setting up tape recorders to trap them into 'deals.' "

Despite the fact that at New Orleans Tietjen and our faculty representatives vigorously disassociated the faculty from the charges of false doctrine leveled against them in resolution 3-09, Preus asked us to further study "Resolution 3-09 and the faculty material on which it is based and then approach the Board of Control and inform them that you no longer wish to be associated with the theological vagaries condemned therein and that your teaching and confession will be in accord with what your Synod asks you to teach, as it understands Article II of the Synod's Constitution in the formulation of and adoption of synodical doctrinal statements."

Here Preus tipped his hand and revealed the basic reason for the impasse between himself and the faculty. We had been called to teach according to the provisions of Article II of the Synodical constitution. This was the basis on which we had accepted calls to our positions at Concordia Seminary, and this was the standard explicitly set forth at the time of our ordinations. All pastors and teachers in the Synod bound themselves to that standard of orthodoxy. Now Preus was himself modifying the constitution of the Synod in a "Message" that was being delivered to every congregation in the Synod. No longer were we bound only to the Scriptures and the Lutheran Confessions, but each time we entered the classroom we were expected to be in accord with every formulation and interpretation given in Synodical doctrinal statements. What if these were in conflict with the Scriptures and our Confessions? In his letter of January 24, Preus himself admitted that a future convention might conceivably reverse its judgment about the doctrines cited in 3-09. Were we then to teach as doctrine what the LC-MS later might decide was a non-doctrine? Where, then, did this put us relative to the constitution which states that doctrine is not to be decided by majority vote? Luther himself had emphasized that Popes and Councils could err, and when they did so he taught and proclaimed publicly what he found in the Scriptures. Were we now to agree against Luther that tradition was of equal importance with Scripture? What was distinctively Lutheran about such a position?

Reverting again to Dr. Tietjen, among other charges Preus complained that Tietjen had published transcripts of his meetings with Buelow, Harnapp, and Otto, terming the action "as fine an example of 'moral bankruptcy' as this tragic case has yet revealed."

Readers of that sentence who did not know the principals might have thought that Tietjen was guilty of betrayal of confidence during an investigation by Buelow, Harnapp, and Otto. Of course, it was the other way around. Buelow, Harnapp, and Otto had questioned Tietjen's theology. If Tietjen was embarrassing anyone with his transcripts, it was himself.

Never one to hide the evidence that involved himself or his colleagues, he told the church, "Here it is. I have nothing to hide. Read it yourself. These were the questions or observations, and here are my replies." Why should Preus have considered reprehensible Tietjen's refusal to engage in a cover-up of his own theological position? Since when was candor about one's theological stance a sin?

Again, Preus could not have it both ways. On the one hand he accused the faculty of having tried to "change the theology of the church without telling the church what we were doing," and now he was complaining about Tietjen's and the faculty's openness in declaring publicly what we were actually thinking theologically.

Appendix 5 in Preus' message consisted of Victor Bryant's explanation of his endeavor to arrange meaningful discussions. Appendix 7 described the formation of an "Advisory Committee on Doctrine and Conciliation" which was to delineate the issues in controversy and discuss proposals for dealing with them.

In Appendix 8, Preus submitted a selection of "Pertinent Portions from the Synodical Bylaws." But the blast that shook Preus' world and ultimately jelled Concordia Seminary into Seminex was Appendix 6.

Disastrous Appendix

Few documents in history have succeeded so well in accomplishing their objectives with such disasterous and unexpected side effects. Backed against the wall politically and seeking desperate expedients, both Preus and Scharlemann failed to evaluate the variable impact potential of their missive. To many in and outside the seminary it was bound to have the effect of a *Playboy* centerfold sent out for solicitation of funds to a mailing list of Mothers United for Girl Scout Sunday. The Appendix is here presented in its entirety:

APPENDIX 6

Concordia Seminary
Saint Louis, Missouri
January 26, 1974

Dear Fellow Lutherans,

You have heard much about the problems of Concordia Seminary. Permit us to add some items. Let us say, first of all, that we are students committed to completing our study for the ministry according to the principles adopted at New Orleans. We stand solidly with President Preus and the new Seminary administration.

For years we have been harassed and bullied by those who call themselves evangelical. We have experienced various acts of intimidation. Here are a few examples:

1. A student was ejected from a class for refusal to accept the ideological orientation of the professors, being forced to take the course again the following term.
2. Students have failed classes or have had grades lowered for theological disagreement with professors who were themselves engaging in doctrinal aberrations.
3. The former president of the Seminary told students (who are now in the fourth year class) that they would be taught the Historical-Critical Method despite the accepted position of the Synod. Students have been required to use this method if they wished to pass their courses.
4. Students have been compelled to accept the ideology of persons who use educational devices to keep students from reaching the proper scholarly conclusions of Lutheran doctrine.
5. Liberal professors have advocated openly or implicitly the revolutionary technique of change for change sake, showing themselves to be insensitive to the consciences of individual students.
6. Class time and even public chapel exercises have been consistently used for ridiculing the expected activities and accepted responsibilities of the synodical administration.
7. Students have been exposed to such aberrations as universalism, denial of personal devil, the refusal to say that anyone will go to hell, etc. These aberrations have not been clearly and emphatically rejected.
8. In teaching theology, professors have often avoided making personal commitments in the classroom in terms of doctrine and faith and have presented the orthodox position pejoratively or at best as only another alternative.
9. Professors have frequently denegrated the traditional orthodox doctrine of the Lutheran Church as well as its heritage by snide remarks, cynical observations, and by broad innuendo.

Classes in the history of Lutheranism have been often turned into parties of ridicule.

10. There has been an almost unceasing ridicule of the simple child-like faith of the laity. In fact, the laity of the church is often described as being so ignorant that they become the pastors' adversary.

11. The counseling services of the Seminary have been used deliberately for purposes of brainwashing. For example, conservative professors have consistently been by-passed and have not automatically been given advisees. Therefore conservative students have risked labeling themselves by asking for conservative professors as advisors.

During this current academic year many of the above mentioned practices of harassment have continued. Even in these last days we have experienced some incredible cases of intimidation. Here are just a few examples:

1. In a given course, the traditional orthodox doctrine of creation was ridiculed as being unscholarly, if not totally stupid. Proponents of the orthodox view were portrayed as being fearful to present their views for scholarly review.

2. During a recent presentation by the acting president to the student body, a liberal professor left his seat on the main floor of the chapel and proceeded to the balcony where it was generally known that conservative students sat. He proceeded to call the acting president obscene names.

3. In class the New Orleans Convention has been described as being devoid of the Spirit of God and conservative delegates were described as being barbaric.

4. Chapel exercises have been devoted perversely to such matters as compromising the prayer life of students by forcing them to participate without warning in prayers that violate their theological position. Devotional periods were turned into entertainment or political rallies.

5. Contrary to the specific requirements of Scripture, professors have slandered persons in classes prior to chapel and then have proceeded immediately to the celebration of Holy Communion. Contrary to the practice of our church body, closed communion is no longer practiced on this campus.

6. Upon resumption of the classes this fall, a professor expressed refusal to abide by synodical resolutions passed at New Orleans and stated that those in disagreement should register for other classes.

7. The Gospel has consistently been turned into a new Law, destroying the Gospel which, in its Lutheran sense, is the pure proclamation of the forgiveness of sins.

8. During this past week of student moratorium assemblies, we have repeatedly been subjected to false rumors voiced as ac-

291

cusations with the apparent intent of encouraging further student rebellion against the new seminary administration. For example, it was publicly announced that an attempt was made to "impound student funds." In another speech given by a liberal professor, students were told that the Board of Control "changed the *Handbook*" in their dismissal of certain professors. It was also stated that in the history of our Synod, professors have never been dismissed in this manner. We have since found that these and numerous other rumors and accusations to be totally without substance.

We could cite many more instances and are willing to do so upon request. We have set forth these items to give you an idea of the oppressive climate and theological perversion that has been promulgated under the guise of the Gospel at Concordia Seminary.

Because of this climate it is imperative, at this time, that we, as students, withhold our names. However, our names are on file in the office of the acting president of Concordia Seminary and this letter is being written with his authorization.

(Received by
Martin H. Scharlemann
Acting President)

Diagnoses

Had Preus sent out his message without this appendix, he might have won his war that very week, for the student body still registered a large number of students who had not signed the moratorium. But on Thursday, January 31, 1974, the tide began to shift. The *Globe-Democrat* that morning reported Dr. Scharlemann as saying "I worked with them on this [Appendix 6]." Outraged by the anonymity of the document and the irresponsibility of the charges, the students began themselves to clarify the issues. With respect to the charge that a professor had urged those in disagreement with his position to "register for other classes," a student went back to the primary source and reported that "Dr. Piepkorn had told his class: 'In July my own church declared me a heretic, unfit to teach. If you do not care to be taught by a heretic, please register in another course.' " The student's report rang true, for two days before he died Dr. Piepkorn had told me that he was going to write to Dr. Preus and counsel him that the "greatest service he could render the Missouri Synod would be to resign."

Professor Alfred von Rohr Sauer volunteered information about the alleged "obscenities." He said, "I was in the balcony that morning when Martin Scharlemann spoke, and I said *'There* is a traitor, a Benedict Arnold.' That's what Appendix 6 called *obscene."*

In a long letter dated January 31, 1974, and addressed to Dr. Preus, with many copies to many others, seminarian Gary Phelps, self-styled conservative, refuted charges of harassment by faculty members. One of his professors had given him B's instead of A's, but Phelps thought he deserved what he got and learned in the process. "In my class experience, and in public chapel exercises," he wrote, "I have never in all my time at the seminary ever seen ridicule of 'the expected activities and accepted responsibilities of the synodical administration.' "

"As far as the 'simple child-like faith of the laity' is concerned, never from any professor, whether moderate or conservative, have I heard, seen, or even encountered the slightest innuendo as a subject for ridicule. In fact, my professors have told me on many occasions that the child-like faith of any laity is one of the pillars of the church, and the greatest part of a pastor's ministry."

With respect to alleged "brainwashing" by the Seminary's counselling services, Phelps asked why, if the aim was to brainwash him, he had been sent to a conservative congregation which was in total support of President Preus and to a pastoral supervisor who was also conservative. Phelps went on to say that one of his professors had indeed criticized a favorite hymn of many people; it was "Lord of the Dance," but on the ground that it was "inadequate, and un-Lutheran." Blasting charges of alleged Gospel reductionism, that is, emphasizing the Gospel above all else, he said, "Prof. Deppe made me rewrite a sermon because it lacked law, and too much Gospel—'no balance' he said." Of the devotions, Phelps said that they "were not subject to entertainment or political maneuvers." Referring to the allegations that a professor had claimed that the Board of Control "*changed* the Handbook," Phelps said that this was "a misquote. The Professor stated that the Board '*did not follow* the Handbook.' " On the anonymity of Appendix 6 he said, "I can assure you that when I write something, I sign it." He also emphasized that he would have liked to react to Appendix 6 by talking to the authors. Moderate and conservative students, he said, "submit their resolutions for open discussion." In view of President Preus' inclusion of Appendix 6, Phelps said that he was now withdrawing the parenthetical remark, "with many serious reservations," which followed his signature on the declaration of moratorium.

Similar clarifications concerning other charges, especially of harassment, were volunteered by numerous students. A Filipino student avowed: "I did not sign the moratorium. But now Dr. Prues' appendix puts all of us foreign students under a cloud. This thing that just came in is *ridiculous.*" His accent on the last word doubled up the assembly. "No one has harrassed me," he assured the group, "no one told me to sign the moratorium. I did not sign it simply because this is an internal affair of the LC-MS. The only one who harassed me was Ed Schroeder (professor of Systematic Theology), who told me it's bad for me to smoke. If that's harassment, give me some more." After another wave of laughter subsided, an avid fan of John the Revelator said, "I endorse 144,000% what he just said, and I didn't sign the moratorium." Fred Storteboom, no banner-waving crusader, observed: "They are using the non-signers list. I am a conservative. It is time for us to speak up as a collective conservative group."

A student raised his voice: "Tell the church!" Storteboom shot back: *"We will!"* And the way he said it suggested that the students' stockpile of paper reserves would soon go down.

How Many Signed?

On the evening news a reporter on Channel 5 asked Scharlemann: "Why did you not identify the students in the letter?" Scharlemann replied, "Because of the intimidation that goes on. It's fearful." Reporter: "Isn't it a Christian school? Aren't we talking about just ordinary student life?" Scharlemann: "It's harassment from peers. The pressure is great." The reporter, with evident relief in his voice, said, "Then it's *not physical intimidation.*"

About the same time, a group of eight students were gathered in Koburg dining hall discussing the letter sent out under Scharlemann's authorization. Some of them had signed the moratorium, others had not, and at least one of them was still attending classes. The consensus of the group was that even if the accusations were true, certainly 120 students did not maintain such a position. They felt that the minority student element of 120 was being used as a screen for the content of the letter, and they knew of no one who had failed to sign the moratorium who was in favor of the contents of the letter. After failing in attempts to set up an appointment for discussion of the matter with Scharlemann, the group settled for meeting him at the earliest possible time that day, namely, when he came out of class at 11:20 A.M.

Scharlemann told them that the letter gave the gist of concerns for minority students who were being approached by other students who were asking them whether they had signed the moratorium. He indicated that no one had signed the document, nor was there any intention to get signatures. On the other hand, said Scharlemann, he was in no position to convey confidential information on the formulation of the document, nor would he reveal the identity of the "signers." Just what he meant in Appendix 6 by the phrase "our names are on file" was never clarified. The number 120, roughly corresponding to the non-moratorium census, was, he said, "my estimate" of the number of students who would agree with it. Student Dave Reichert, he said, would receive a letter that would erase any misunderstanding. In concluding comment, one of the eight students estimated that perhaps six students might have assisted in the composition of the document. Another disagreed, "I have not talked to any student who claims to have signed it or had a part in its formulation or was in favor of it." His verdict coincided with colleague Robert Conrad's findings. Conrad had talked to a number of minority students but could not find one who had endorsed Scharlemann's alleged student letter.

Some of the mystery was dispelled after publication of the following explanation editorially attached to a later republication of a repudiation by a number of "conservative" students:

> After the "conservative" student document of 26 January 1974 (Appendix 6 of President Preus' *Message* to the Church) was released, other "conservative" students felt that their position had been misrepresented and they released the following letters; one is an open letter which summarizes their position and disavows any association with Appendix 6; the other is a personal letter from Seminarian Gary Phelps to President J. A. O. Preus and others, which answers each charge of Appendix 6 from his personal experience.

The "open letter" is here presented in its entirety:

> Concordia Seminary
> Saint Louis, Missouri
> February 1, 1974
>
> Dear Fellow Lutherans,
>   We the undersigned students of Concordia Seminary, Saint Louis did not vote for this moratorium. While we have taken differing positions among ourselves on the moratorium issue since it went into effect we have in common a "conservative" approach toward the Scriptures and the Lutheran Confessions.
>   We have openly stated our conservative postition to our fellow students and to faculty members both in the classroom and in other dis-

cussions. At no time were any of us harassed, bullied, or downgraded by our professors because we disagreed with them. Instead, they accepted us in love and dealt pastorally with us, and through their lives, teaching, and confession they have witnessed their faith to us.

Our fellow students also accepted us and were willing to discuss the issues in an open and honest manner. We were not forced to compromise our beliefs nor apologize for them. We believe this evangelical concern for us on the part of our peers can be seen in the passage of a resolution on January 21, right after the moratorium went into effect, that there be no "arm-twisting" done to make anyone comply with the moratorium, nor have we witnessed any such "arm-twisting."

We acknowledge that both the faculty and our fellow students are sinful people like ourselves, and therefore stand with us under God's wrath and in need of the forgiveness of sins through the atoning death of Jesus Christ on the cross. We also acknowledge that each of us, at any time, is capable of injuring a brother in Christ through unkind words and provoking attitudes, and our faculty is also capable of this, but it is our experience that they would be the first to admit such a tendency.

We the undersigned also assert that no one helped us make this statement. We were not coerced nor pressured into taking this stand except by our own dismay over the present crisis, by our concern that we all deal with each other in love, justice and integrity, and especially by our fear that the truth be lost through overstatement or misinformation, thereby closing the door forever on reconciliation between brother and brother.

cc: President J. A. O. Preus
    Dr. M. H. Scharlemann
    Jerry Miller
    (Signed)
    Fred Storteboom
    Charles P. Boerger
    Jose B. Fuliga
    Kim De Vries
    Vernon Kleinig
    Paul Rajashekar
    Thomas A. Duval
    Don Rosentreter
    Douglas A. Zike (with reservations)
    Jim Bryan
    Richard C. Noack
    Jerry A. Schulz
    Jim Pohlig
    James A. McDaniels
    David Jensen
    David C. Winningham (with reserve) [2]

Like the Pseudo-Isidorian Decretals, Preus' Appendix 6 had run into a bad case of peritonitis under the scrutiny of students' historical-criticism.[3]

Attorney Duesenberg, his mind swamped with a plethora of possible adjectives, defined Appendix 6 as "vicious," "repulsive," "unheard of," and "without precedent in the Church."

As could have been expected, Duesenberg's concern for maintenance of law and order was not applauded on all sides. Someone informed his chief employer in St. Louis that Deusenberg was using company stationery for personal business. Invited to discuss a question of "conflict of interest" and "use of company time," Duesenberg asked his front office to call in some of the offending stationery. Of course there was none, and Duesenberg said his only embarrassment was being an LC-MS Lutheran.

Trying to Save Jack's Soul

True to their promise, a committee of students went to work on "Project" Appendix 6 with a view also to "save Jack's soul."

On February 13, their collection of letters and exhibits, eight pages all told, went out to the congregations of the Synod. To demonstrate the maturity of judgment, the pastoral concern and ethical sensitivities of the participating students, including the most 'conservative,' I do not hesitate to quote at length from these documents. Ultimately history must record that the fortunes of Missouri cut many of the channels they did in 1974 and the years immediately following because of bureaucratic blundering and student resolution born in depths of conviction, which prompted one student on Outreach to tell a reporter of the *Eau Claire Leader-Telegram* (Tuesday, January 29, 1974) that accusation of professors without specific charges was a very serious matter: "We must abide by the provisions in the United States Constitution." In the same issue another replied, "There is no longer a doctrinal issue, but one of irresponsible use of power in the Church. In short, it has become a political issue."

In their covering paragraph for the documents the students wrote:

Brothers and sisters in Christ:
The enclosed materials were prepared prior to President Preus' February 13 letter to the pastors of our Synod. The pastoral tone of that letter is in marked contrast with his January 28 "Message to the

297

Church." We welcome the change in tone. We want nothing more than reconciliation. We share President Preus' concern that reconciliation happen. We feel that reconciliation can happen only after the truth is spoken in love. Out of love for our Church we want to speak the truth. We want The Lutheran Church-Missouri Synod to have the truth about Concordia Seminary which we feel "Appendix 6" distorts. May the truth we speak in the following pages lead to the reconciliation we all want.

Then under the date of February 13, 1974, they wrote:

Dear brothers and sisters in Christ:
    As seminarians, we write to you seeking your help. We would have preferred that it would not have been necessary to make this appeal to you, but we need your assistance in dealing pastorally with President Preus.

After citing the "sweeping accusations" made "against unnamed professors without documentation," the letter proceeded:

President Preus is the chief pastor in our synod. By allowing this letter to go to sixty thousand in our synod, President Preus has sinned against the Church and the Lord of the Church. He has encouraged rumor to be introduced from the pulpits where the forgiveness of sins should be preached.

The letter then went on to explain how Dr. Preus' letter had "clearly violated the words" of Jesus in Matthew 18, about first telling the brother his fault, then taking two or three witnesses, and finally telling "it to the church; and if he refuses to listen even to the church, let him be to you as a Gentile and a tax collector." (Matthew 18:17, Revised Standard Version)

After pointing out that President Preus had 1) refused to respond to requests for Preus' identification of the anonymous signers, "so that we might speak with them privately," 2) refused to respond to their expression of "deep sorrow over the slanderous accusations in 'Appendix Six, ' " and 3) had refused to respond to repeated pleas for a reply, the students informed the church that they went to speak with him in person. "But he said that he would not respond publicly at this time. (Summary D) Our concern has been to deal with President Preus in terms of St. Matthew 18, hoping all along that he would repent of this action."

The letter concluded with these sentences:

Now, as the words of St. Matthew clearly say, we must "tell it to the church." What President Preus has done by sending this unsigned letter is to further divide The Lutheran Church-Missouri Synod with suspicion. Even many of our "conservative" brothers on this campus who did not vote for the moratorium have soundly rejected the accusations in "Appendix Six" and the action of President Preus in allowing this letter to be sent to the whole church. You may read their response in the two attached letters (Letters E and F).

We ask you, for the sake of President Preus and our church, to hold President Preus accountable for his actions. Write him a personal letter. Discuss and act on this misdeed in your congregational meetings. Write your District President. Make your voice heard for the sake of our Lord's Church.

We are sent to gain the brother. Heeding our appeal is not to rebel against authority. It is to hear *the* Authority of the Church who would have us to be one, even as He and the Father are one (John 17: 21–23).

In Him,

The Moratorium Co-ordinating Committee, (Signed).
David G. Abrahamson, David M. Beckmann, Donald Duy, Boyd Faust,
Robert Heiliger, Michael Lohmann, Gerald Miller, Robert Rimbo,
Leon G. Rosenthal, George Schelter, Adolph A. Wachsmann,
James P. Wind.

We send this letter to you with the approval and commendation of the student body, as resolved February 13, 1974.

In addition to copies of the two unanswered letters, the students included a log of their attempts to reach Dr. Preus:

LOG C

February 4, 1974 4:00 P.M.	Spoke with President Preus' secretary. President Preus had sent no written response to our letters of Jan. 30 and 31. No date was set when we could expect a written response. He did intend to respond.
February 6, 1974 3:00 P.M.	Spoke with President Preus' secretary. President Preus had sent no written response to our letters of Jan. 30 and 31. No date was set when we could expect a written response. He did intend to respond.

299

February 11, 1974 11:30 A.M.	Spoke with President Preus' secretary. President Preus had sent no written response to our letters of Jan. 30 and 31. Secretary had not seen President Preus since Feb. 6. President Preus was out at this time. Asked for a time *when* he would respond. Secretary said to call back in the afternoon.
3:00 P.M.	Secretary of 11:30 conversation was out. President Preus' secretary would call back that afternoon.
4:55 P.M.	No return call from the secretary. Called back. No one in the office according to the night answering man.
February 12, 1974 11:15 A.M.	Talked with secretary who said President Preus was in a meeting but she would tell him of the call and she would call back after lunch regarding a meeting time.
1:40 P.M.	No reply from secretary. Called back and talked with another secretary than the 11:15 A.M. call. She informed us that there was a note regarding the 11:15 A.M. call. President Preus was out to lunch.

We arrived at 2:00 P.M. at 500 N. Broadway to set a meeting time. We were notified that President Preus had set an appointment for 5:00 P.M. of that same day, the 12th.

Then followed "Summary D" entitled

MEETING WITH PRESIDENT J. A. O. PREUS

Present were students Charles P. Boerger, Leon G. Rosenthal, and Adolph A. Wachsmann; President J.A.O. Preus, Rev. Dr. Edwin C. Weber, Dr. Milton Carpenter, Rev. Robert Sauer.

Purpose of meeting: To personally seek a response from President Preus regarding the Jan. 30 and 31 letters of the moratorium committee addressed to President Preus concerning "Appendix 6" of his "Message to the Church" dated January 28, 1974.

In this 2 hour meeting we began by expressing sorrow over the issuance of "Appendix 6." We felt that this document caused unjust division in our church and families. Likewise, we felt deep concern for the fact that this letter was allowed to be sent out without signatures and documentation. We also felt the letter was "slanderous" in its accusations. Therefore, we asked President Preus for a public apology and a statement to the church and seminary regarding "Appendix 6."

Dr. Preus expressed the fact that he was feeling a great deal of pressure from both "sides." He felt that he has been acting pastorally to hold down the various factions in the church, calling for talks and pursuing discussion rather than force to settle problems. He seemed to feel that he held the position to bring about unity and that a public apology or statement regarding "Appendix 6" at this time might in some way endanger his position as mediator.

Concerning "Appendix 6," he felt that the accusations against the "Faculty Majority" were true and could be documented. He admitted that he may have been wrong in sending the unsigned document to the church and that some advisors had given him the same opinion afterwards. He expressed the desire to be able to repent of all his sins at some point in the future. He recognized open letters as "political weapons" and asked that students not send out any type of public documents regarding this at this time, for he would consider this to be a political maneuver and could be detrimental to possibilities of reconciliation. To this we responded that this was precisely our objection to "Appendix 6."

While there was some attempt at listening to each other in this meeting, there also appeared to be a good deal of mistrust. It was suggested that we as students may have been judgmental in our action and for this they expressed their forgiveness to us. At this point we could see that President Preus was not going to make an explanation of his actions and public apology to the church and seminary community. Here the meeting was cordially ended.

From their summary one could understand the student's profound disappointment and sense of frustration. If even an endeavor to follow the Lord's outline of procedure in Matthew 18 was construed as being "judgmental," there could be no hope for reconciliation.

President Preus had already displayed unparalleled power over ministerial destinies. By following St. Matthew's prescription, three young men on the threshhold of their professional careers had taken a tremendous risk. In contrast to the anonymous "signers" of Appendix 6, who had challenged mere professors, these three men not only spoke words of power to the highest power in their church, but endorsed such concern for truth with their signatures:

Charles Boerger
Leon Rosenthal
Adolph Wachsmann

Looking back, they may well have recalled another politician who had asked for a delay in repentance (Acts 24:25).

Chapter 26

EXILED

On February 11, 1974, I wrote to a pastor in Florida:

Dear ———,
If I appear to write in haste, it is not because I value the less lightly your words of consolation and encouragement. But the time is very short and soon we shall be out of our quarters, unless there is a great change of heart.
Please support ELIM. I think the Lord is directing all of us through those channels. But all true Christians must now be mobilized. Fence-sitting is no longer possible for them. The question is not Jonah or Adam and Eve but justification through faith, and not by authoritative synodical fiat. Jesus Christ still is captain of the ship!

Peace,
(Signed)
Fred Danker

Seven days later, we met for the last time as faculty of Concordia Seminary at 801 De Mun Avenue.

After the opening devotion on the theme "Now Thank We All Our God," colleague Robert Smith read a document containing the following preamble: "You are herewith expected to respond to the resolution below, passed by the Board of Control on the evening of February 17, 1974. You will note that your affirmative reply by noon will be appreciated." It was signed, MARTIN H. SCHARLEMANN.

Addressed as it was to a faculty whose position had been officially declared intolerable in the church of God, this was a strange announcement. It was one more in a long series of data which suggested that false doctrine was not really the issue.

Smith went on to read the Document of Dismissal:

WHEREAS certain members of the faculty, administrative staff and the guest faculty, since on or about the 22d day of January, 1974, have failed and omitted to carry out their responsibilities and functions as employees under their contracts of employment, and

WHEREAS, although said members of the faculty, administrative staff and guest faculty whose names are set forth on the schedule attached hereto and made a part hereof, thereafter were requested by the Acting President to resume their said responsibilities and functions, said members of the faculty, the administrative staff and the guest faculty have failed and omitted to comply with such request, and

WHEREAS none of said members of the faculty, administrative staff or guest faculty, has a legal or other right, while continuing in the employment of Concordia Seminary, to not carry out the responsibilities and functions for which he was employed

NOW, THEREFORE, BE IT RESOLVED THAT:

The Board of Control directs the faculty, administrative staff and guest faculty to resume their respective responsibilities and functions as employees under their contracts of employment on February 19th, 1974, that on or before 12 noon February 18, 1974, they signify their assent and agreement in writing to Acting President Scharlemann to so resume their responsibilities and functions as aforesaid and those members of the faculty, administrative staff and guest faculty who fail to comply with the foregoing, having heretofore breached their respective contracts of employment, and they being in continuing breach of their contracts of employment have terminated their employment which results also in a termination of all of the rights and privileges of their respective positions with Concordia Seminary, including, but not limited to the following:

1. No salaries to be paid to said members of the faculty and the administrative staff for any period subsequent to the 18th day of January, 1974;
2. No payments be made to any such members of the faculty or of the administrative staff, who provides his own living quarters, for housing allowance or in lieu of rent, for any period subsequent to the 18th day of January, 1974;
3. No such member of the faculty who is housed in any of the seminary-owned homes shall be provided with such housing subsequent to February 28, 1974;
4. No payments shall be made to such members of the guest faculty for services heretofore rendered by them; and

303

5. All members of the faculty, administrative staff, and guest faculty whose names are set forth on the attached schedule shall remove their personal belongings from offices on the campus heretofore used by them and shall vacate such offices on or before February 28, 1974.

BE IT FURTHER RESOLVED, that these resolutions are without application to Dr. John H. Tietjen, to whom the contractual obligations of Concordia Seminary continue pursuant to by-law 6.79 (d) of the 1973 Handbook.

Waiting For Noon

At the words "without application to Dr. John H. Tietjen" there were jocular hissings and a wave of laughter, and a voice was heard, "The first shall be last." Colleague Gilbert Thiele shouted, "I move adoption."

Prof. Robert Bertram reported that the minority five on the Board of Control valiantly tried to resist passage of the document. With Dr. Edwin Weber, Preus' right-hand man, moving adoption and Mr. Fincke adding the second, passage was assured. In support of the hard-line action, Bertram reported, Scharlemann had said, "The way to handle rebellion is to crush it." A layman asked, "Is that the way you handle a rebellious son?" "It's legalistic!" "It's schismatic!" "You will fill the coffers of ELIM!" All such voices of the minority were to no avail. About 11:00 P.M. the document was passed by the majority members of the Board and Mr. Paul G. Nickel was "incoherent with grief," when he broke the news, said Bertram.

For a number of days the realization had been moving in on us that we might be compelled to teach our classes elsewhere as exiles from our campus, and it was necessary to think in terms of contingency plans, which in any form spelled "Seminary in Exile," or "Seminex." "Our friends on the Board of Control are now resigned to Seminex," Bertram told us in conclusion.

How we were to respond to the document was another matter. Our Faculty Advisory Committee (FAC) recommended "No Response," with the provision that no one was to construe this as precluding individual responses. Dr. Arthur C. Repp advised against class action, since the coach, Pete Pederson, was ill with pneumonia, Alfred Fuerbringer was awaiting surgery and Leonard Wuerffel was also unable to participate. Erwin Lueker finally moved that we give no answer, and on the passage of this motion Tietjen reminded the colleagues that the

304

motion did not preclude anyone from going to the Board and expressing his or her compliance.

Unusual communications became a part of this, which was to be the
strangest day. Each of us had received an envelope with a five dollar
bill and a cheering message from a lay couple. It read: "Thinking of
you. God has blessed us. We want to share with you." It was the most
wonderfully ridiculous Gospel reductionism I had ever experienced.
Such love and call to faith in the face of an uncertain future added six
zeros to the numeral. The Lord had not stopped multiplying bread!
Only the Holy Spirit could have invented such an original valentine,
when ELIM had only about $10,000 in its coffers.

About this time one of the colleagues said, "In 32 minutes I'm going
to be fired. What about medical and retirement benefits?" It was explained that pension plans would be paid through the end of March
and that medical insurance could be taken care of by putting in a plea
for "leave of absence, with good cause." Someone asked whether it
would be possible to conduct Seminex on the 801 DeMun quarters,
but counsel advised against what would certainly be interpreted as an
illegal action.

Three minutes before noon, Acting President Scharlemann strode in
and said, "I was just asked to convey to you Ed Weber's thanks for
your commitment to Article II of the Synod's Constitution as expressed at the Forum." This was in reference to a meeting held on the
weekend between representatives of the seminary community and
members of the Board of Control. Colleague Herbert Mayer asked,
"What does that mean, Dr. Scharlemann?" Scharlemann, having
completed his errand, replied: "I don't know. Excuse me for breaking
in." Dean Damm asked whether there was any legal implication in
Scharlemann's message. Bertram said that according to his and
Caemmerer's recollection, Ed Weber hadn't even held forth at the
Forum.

Answer To The Synod

High noon signalled that we were no longer employees of Concordia
Seminary. At exactly 12:01 our entire faculty majority, except for those
in sick bay and on sabbatical leave, rose and sang:

The Church's One Foundation Is Jesus Christ, her Lord;
She is His new creation By water and the Word.

305

From heaven He came and sought her To be His Holy bride;
With His own blood He bought her, And for her life He died.

Someone opened the windows to the quadrangle so that the assembled students could better hear our answer to the Synod.

Among our other guests that day were the Rev. Bertwin Frey, who had helped organize ELIM, Mr. Elwyn Ewald and the Rev. Samuel Roth.

"I've never been called Santa Claus before," said Roth in response to the introduction he had received. "I want to thank you again for the way in which you went about what you have done. . . . You are *heightening* your evangelical witness. Your answers to the reviling will show the students what your understanding of the Gospel is. We had a very good meeting over the weekend. And Seminex appears to be the best possible route to go. People on the spot pledged $500 minimum and others pledged to go out to the Districts. ELIM is behind this Seminex operation, not because we are sorry for you, but because this is the way to go."

Welcome From Elim

Elwyn Ewald took the floor and said, "Welcome aboard. Four months ago I made a decision. Today you made the same decision. You will accept by faith that God will take care of you and your families. You have drawn the conclusion that Dr. Preus and the Board of Control are teaching as gospel what cannot be tolerated in the Church of God. What is happening is *not* something that cannot be tolerated in the Church of God. . . . ELIM today has $10,000. You have therefore acted on faith. But there is a telephone campaign afoot to immediately make a quota of $150,000 in pledges. Loans to ELIM of $50,000 without collateral are anticipated."

Had he squinted a bit more into the very immediate future he could have seen $10,000 coming in cash and pledges from professors and their families at Concordia Teachers College, River Forest, Illinois. And theirs were only the first fruits from many supporting colleges and seminaries.

"The important thing is to speak of this entire matter in terms of the Gospel," continued Ewald. "With a bit of a heavy heart I heard some of you talking about staying here. Some of you were concerned about your offices. The decision you have made should free you to go overboard to carry out your tasks joyfully, having left all behind. Your decision is the decision that many others who want to be top theologians in the church will have to make. The Synod's District Presidents therefore must respond in the same way and assert that the theology approved at New Orleans is not to be tolerated in the Church of God." Then, with his eyes roving over the entire group, he asked, "Is there anyone who is in need today? We have $10,000 right now."

Tietjen's Changing Neighborhood

The Board's Action left us all with another bit of comic relief. On January 22 we had declared to the Board that we considered ourselves suspended with Dr. Tietjen. Now Tietjen wondered whether he should stay and permit the Board to go the whole route and turn his suspension into a dismissal, or tell the Board, "What you have done to them you can do to me." Colleague Ralph Klein brought the house down. "Is it true that you live in a changing neighborhood?" he asked Tietjen, who lived in one of the spacious houses on the seminary grounds. In a more serious vein, retiree Richard Caemmerer declared: "We have been fired. But John is standing in the middle of the fray, and he is still our leader in the middle of that fray."

The Synod's Checks Go To ELIM

On the same day, at our evening meeting, Tietjen announced his decision. "It is a unanimous household decision," he said. "I do not intend to take an action which would in effect be a resignation," for that, he declared, would be contrary to his whole approach in the proceedings. The Board of Control would not have such an easy way out of facing up to the theological and moral issues, he promised. "In any proceedings against you," he assured us, "I will be silent." "We have had a great deal of solidarity," he went on to say. "They have construed your self-suspension as resignation. At this point I identify with you. . . . I am making my checks available to ELIM, and we will live till May out of what savings we have."

The thought that the Synod would now be supporting ELIM was an interesting injection into our weary minds. Just about this time Bertram received a telephone call. As he left to answer it, there were shouts, "Deal! Deal!"

At this point Dean Damm reported that the students would meet in the morning at the gymnasium. Many of them, he said, would cast their lot in with Seminex. This was our first official announcement of our crossing of the Reed Sea, historical criticism notwithstanding. On Wednesday morning classes would begin at St. Louis University and at Eden Seminary.

Someone asked how synodical officialdom was reacting. Bertram reported that John Schuelke, Executive Secretary of the Board of Directors planned to call together the Board of Control and representatives of the Faculty Majority to continue the Forum begun on the preceding weekend, with a view to getting the faculty back into the classroom to educate students for the ministry. Feed-back on the Forum, they said, was good.

Colleague Repp knew too well the Synod's way of solving problems by interminable talking about them, and sized up the proposal: "The last time we dialogued with those people our paychecks were withheld. I don't know what they can do this time."

Bertram made a report on the quality of Vic Bryant's newsgathering service. Bryant was head of Preus' PR operation and had fed the media with the information that five members of the faculty, presumably of the faculty majority, were ready to return to class. As in the case of the alleged signers of Preus' infamous Appendix 6, not one faculty member was turned up. Pete Pederson, the athletic director, was the only one Bertram could remotely think of. Someone graciously suggested that Bryant might have confused his majorities and his minorities.

Since February 19 was right around the bend, colleague Smith reminded us that on that day a year ago we had all been commended by secret ballot of the Board of Control. But now, a year later when Dr. Scharlemann was asked by a reporter about the status of the faculty majority, he declared succinctly, "They are former faculty members."

Even Luther Called a Halt at Worms

At day's end some of us recalled letters we had received to the effect that we and the students should turn the other cheek. We also recalled that we had done that very thing when we accepted the invitation to our own lynching in the Fact-Finding investigation that led to Preus' Blue Book. Then there was colleague Arlis Ehlen, the non-renewal of whose contract was another slap in our faces. The welts showed again with Paul Goetting's non-reengagement. We had pleaded with the Board of Control to lift posthumously the cloud of heresy that rested over Dr. Arthur Carl Piepkorn's distinguished career; rebuff was all we had for our pains. Finally, the suspension of one of our Synod's really great theologians, Dr. John Tietjen. Those who wished to construe the faculty's decision of this day as self-justification or rebellious arrogance could do so. If they wished to say, "Why don't you permit yourselves to be ground to pulp?" that was their affair. The simple fact could not be denied. We had run out of cheeks and could only say, "Enough is enough!" Even Luther called a halt at Worms. As in July and October of 1973, we expected no pity nor congratulations. Only understanding, and especially awareness that if such things as we were experiencing could happen within a brotherhood, what must be the sense of helplessness of others for whom the sword drops: the poor, the disenfranchised, the hungry, the weak, minorities, Jews, Blacks, women, American Indians. All these have sat long at history's bargaining table. There is no word they know better than the promised "Tomorrow." Their bodies are dizzy from the turning. And they have no more cheeks to bleed.

On March 31, Dr. Scharlemann looked back on the events of this day and said, "All of this is so unnecessarily tragic . . . I just wish it was possible to roll back time by three months and perhaps work out a different decision than we did."

Preparing for the Crossing

"Score: with the Holy Spirit, 99. Opponents, 0," announced student body president Gerald Miller on Tuesday morning, February 19, 1974.

Dr. Richard Caemmerer had just finished a sermonette on Hebrews 11:8:

"Faith made Abraham obedient to God when He told him to leave for the place God had promised him." A buzz saw was whining away in a back room of the gymnasium, and Professor Mark Bangert twisted Galatians 4:24 a bit: "Which things are an allegory."

Then the students of Concordia Seminary moved into the business for which they had assembled—to hear answers to their questions and make a final decision about the continuation of seminary education. They had made the first move with their resolution of moratorium. Now the faculty, who had been fired, would continue educating students elsewhere. The only question was: How many? "After 12:00

noon yesterday," said Paul Lessmann, ministerial placement director, "I was most convinced that we *will* proceed with education." But in a demilitarized zone, he might have added.

Lessmann also assured the students that in line with an earlier resolution of the District Presidents, all currently qualified students would be placed. President Preus, he said, had offered an amendment to the District Presidents' Resolution to the effect that placement should be made according to synodical Handbook regulations. This was rejected on the ground that *"People* have divine calls. We are not ministers through handbook regulations." Despite ambiguities in the resolution, District President Arlen J. Bruns, Lessmann reported, had urged distribution of calls through the Seminary's regular experienced personnel.

"Things are extremely bright for the vicars (the third-year interns), but not so bright for the candidates." "But," said Lessmann, "District Presidents and we are making the point that "people count, not rules. . . . But believe me, we are optimistic. Believe me, placement *will* take place."

Someone asked whether it was true that Seminex would be an outreach of Lutheran School of Theology at Chicago, Illinois. Lessmann explained that graduates would receive a diploma indicating fully accredited status through that institution. The Chicago seminary, however, would not be involved in the ministerial certification procedure. The question of housing was on the mind of every student currently living in synodically owned quarters. Assurance was given that alternate housing could be provided.

"Public reaction," said Professor Bertram, "is enormous. Also from people who do not know us from Adam." This endorsement of New Orleans Resolution 3-09 loosened up the assembly. When Bertram went on to report that a Jewish realtor was so incensed at the repressive tactics and had offered his services, colleague Ralph Klein broke in: "Let's vote him a *Christus Vivit* award." (This was our Seminary's equivalent of the Congressional Medal of Honor.)

It was observed that the Chairman of the Board of Control, Ewald Otto, seemed to be in a "fairy-tale world" relative to the students and their thinking. Bertram said that Acting President Scharlemann might be able to tabulate around a hundred in favor of returning to classes on the grounds of Concordia Seminary.

Someone wanted to know where all the professors, who had received their eviction notices, would be moving? "How can we students be of help in moving them?" Bertram replied that there would be many groups involved, including students from the seminary, Lutheran High School faculty members and Roman Catholic sisters.

At this time Dean Damm outlined in detail the proposal for continuing education by reading a document entitled

CONCORDIA SEMINARY-IN-EXILE

Concordia Seminary-in-Exile ("Seminex") is the temporary name for a joint effort of the vast majority of the student body, faculty, and executive staff aimed at completing programs of theological education. Seminex means that the same students and faculty are getting back to the same synodically approved curriculum working out of the same Lutheran confessional commitment.

Seminex is not a new seminary, not a new institution; it is Concordia Seminary, but in exile. Seminex represents not a departure from synod but a commitment to the synod which has been rapidly departing from the best in its tradition. It is the only way we can see to complete theological education and simultaneously to call the synod back to its own evangelical fountainhead.

Seminex is an effort on the part of all of us—students, faculty and staff—to be true to our callings, loyal to our synod, faithful to our Lord. We are students, faculty and staff of the Lutheran Church-Missouri Synod, and we desire to continue serving within the Lutheran Church-Missouri Synod.

But why exile? Why can we not continue teaching and learning at 801 DeMun Avenue? The Board of Control meeting on February 17, by a 6–5 vote, issued an ultimatum to the faculty majority and executive staff:

1) that we return to our classes on February 19 and inform the Board of Control by noon of the 18th of our decision to conform to its demand,

or

2) that we would have our employment at the Seminary terminated immediately and that we would have to vacate offices and seminary-owned homes within 10 days.

We cannot return to our classes and pretend that we can have business as usual, even though we would like to. We wish we could remain in our offices and continue to teach in the classrooms at 801 DeMun.

What makes it impossible? The synodical administration and seminary Board of Control are silencing the Word of God, stifling the Biblical Gospel. That scriptural Gospel, which is the heart and focus of our synod's teaching and the wellspring of fraternal and evangelical actions and relationships, is under siege and is being crushed into silence.

Think what has recently happened to the teaching of the Gospel and to evangelical procedure. In the spring of 1970 President Preus

311

appointed a Fact Finding Committee to investigate the teaching at Concordia Seminary and later published to the entire synod his judgements about our teaching *(Report of the Synodical President,* 1 September 1972.) The Board of Control after many hours of personal interviews of individual faculty members voted by secret ballot, exactly one year ago today, on February 19, 1973, to "commend" each member of the faculty. Commending meant that no professor was guilty of false doctrine and that each did accept without reservation the Scriptures and the Lutheran Confessions.

Not satisfied with the conclusion reached by the Board of Control, President Preus sought to achieve his goals in new ways. He carefully orchestrated the New Orleans Convention (July 6–13, 1973), by stacking floor committees and controlling the entire convention process. The Convention gave him what he wanted: a new standard of orthodoxy (his own "A Statement of Scriptural and Confessional Principles"), a new Board of Control at Concordia Seminary and a specific resolution (3-09) condemning the doctrinal position of the faculty majority as "false doctrine ... not to be tolerated in the church of God."

New Orleans set in motion a reversal of our traditional evangelical procedures and of our heritage of Lutheran Confessional thinking. The turmoil of New Orleans with its deep polarization and its total disregard for the sizable minority has in the months since New Orleans been transplanted to our campus and other schools as well as to synodical boards and staffs, as the divisive and sectarian policies of New Orleans have been implemented.

At our school the Board of Control refused to renew the teaching contract of Paul Goetting; seven senior members of the faculty were suddenly made subject to a new retirement policy; and then on January 20 John H. Tietjen was suspended from his office as president. President Tietjen's case is unique in this whole series of actions because the Board of Control, in suspending him, publicly stated that it was acting on charges of false doctrine.

The Faculty Majority declared that John H. Tietjen teaches the same Lutheran doctrine (Article II of the Synodical Constitution) which it also teaches. Nearly the entire student body and the Faculty Majority and Executive Staff, in response to the suspension of John H. Tietjen and in recognition of the fact that the faculty is one with him in what it teaches, asked the Board of Control to do one of two things:

1) Clear President Tietjen and the rest of the faculty of the charges of false doctrine, or

2) Convict them all.

The Board of Control has in its February 17 action given its answer: it has fired the faculty majority and executive staff. In doing so, the Board of Control has evaded the doctrinal issue in which it claims to have so much interest. It turned a deaf ear to the appeal of students and faculty that it act with integrity and honesty. Instead, it used merely political and legal force to get rid of us, with no discussion of the central doctrinal issue.

President Preus has written much in recent days about forums and committees and discussions for achieving reconciliation. And yet it was Vice President Edwin C. Weber, President Preus' agent on the Board of Control, who introduced the motion to fire us if we would not capitulate.

We have been counseled by some of our friends in the church to begin Seminex classes at 801 DeMun. The action of the Board of Control makes that procedure impossible and indeed illegal. We have been fired and ordered to vacate these premises. If we want to teach, we must do so at another place.

Seminex is Concordia Seminary but not at 801 DeMun Avenue. A literal quiet, symbol of the silencing of the Scriptural Gospel, has descended upon these instructional facilities.

Seminex will conduct classes at other schools, in churches, and in student and faculty homes. Some homes are adequate for small seminar and discussion groups. Local congregations have offered to assist us with space. Most classes will meet, however, at St. Louis University and at Eden Seminary. Those schools have generously offered us classrooms with desks and blackboards and meeting rooms with special library facilities. By conducting most of our Concordia Seminary-in-Exile classes at St. Louis University and Eden Seminary buildings, we will be able to prevent scattering our community all around the city and avoid imposing the problems of commuting and scheduling that a dispersing of classes would entail. The generosity of St. Louis University and of Eden Seminary will enable us to maintain the integrity of the fellowship which God has granted us.

Seminex students will be placed as vicars and as pastoral candidates in congregations of the Lutheran Church-Missouri Synod. All of us are grateful to the Council of Presidents for their decision (February 8, 1974) to place all students. The students should not be penalized, the presidents said, on account of the present impasse. The faculty of Concordia Seminary-in-Exile will publish lists of students certified for vicarage and placement on the dates announced in the catalog. We trust that the church, which sent us these students, will find ways to place all vicars and candidates.

Seminex will continue or complete the programs of theological education in which students are enrolled and will see to it that all qualified students receive the proper theological degree (M.A.R., M. Div., S.T.M., Th.D) from an accredited theological school. We hope that the current crisis can be resolved before the end of May and graduation time, so that the degree may be issued by Concordia Seminary at 801 DeMun. Concordia Seminary-in-Exile does not itself have the authority to confer degrees, since it is not a separate institution. It is not as yet incorporated as a theological school and therefore is not accredited and cannot grant degrees. However, if the crisis continues beyond the date set for graduation, arrangements will be made to confer the appropriate degrees through an already accredited institution. The faculty of Concordia Seminary-in-Exile will bestow a diploma to every graduate attesting to the successful completion of theological education under a faculty committed to the doctrinal standards of Article II of the Constitution of the Lutheran Church-Missouri Synod. Furthermore, if the present impasse is not resolved, Seminex will be forced to continue programs of theological education into the Fall of 1974 and beyond.

Seminex is undertaken reluctantly but in the confidence that serious dialogue will result from our action, and in the hope that dialogue will achieve genuine reconciliation. Peace will return only after all parties in the present dispute, ourselves included, recognize that they have erred in misreading and misrepresenting one another, have hurt one another and diverted one another from the tasks for which they have been called, have failed to love one another and have become a stumbling block to faith and impeded the mission of the church, have been simply wrong in deeds and words. When that recognition is followed by repentance and mutual seeking of the divine grace, there will be joyous reconciliation. We pray for the coming of that day and pledge ourselves to renewed efforts to listen to our brothers and sisters and to examine our own conduct.

Underscoring the final paragraph, Dean Damm said, "I believe Seminex is the way to institute real dialogue."

There were further queries by students about academic programs, degrees and finances. Some thought it might be wise first to go home and wait things out and return to the seminary when the Synod returned to normalcy. Professor Erwin Lueker said, "I have no choice. I must go with Seminex." He said, the "wisest thing is to finish this quarter and the spring quarter. Great things are coming out of this. If you decide to go with us, I hope you will dream with us about some of the other things."

Richard Hoffmann, graduate student and pastor of St. Philip's congregation, St. Louis, said he represented a group whose grandparents were slaves. He then read a document drawn up by the members of St. Philips:

PREAMBLE:

We, the members of St. Philip's Lutheran Church, have witnessed the problems of the Lutheran Church-Missouri Synod become increasingly critical. Those church problems are spilling over into the Black

314

community demanding its vocal and active involvement. With one exception, Black clergymen are not present in the Saint Louis area. If they are to come and serve among us, any Black pastor will need to be assured of an informed and involved laity. We, Black lay persons of Saint Louis, find it necesssary to establish a mechanism to handle these problems. We affirm the Black Lutheran Caucus and solicit its support for our strategy to resolve the problems of the Saint Louis area, specifically, and the church at large, generally. We offer the following statement to make ourselves perfectly clear.

1. We reject and actively oppose, as American citizens, the unjust, unconstitutional, and immoral procedures of the President of the Synod, the Synod in convention, and the Board of Control of Concordia Seminary at Saint Louis and the lack of due process in the suspension of Dr. John H. Tietjen. As Black Lutherans, we have in our entire history experienced that same lack of justice, moral conviction, and lack of protection of civil and human rights.
2. We reject and actively oppose the refusal to renew the contract of Professor Paul Goetting, without reasons stated and without interview, when, as a sensitized member of the white community, he team-taught with the Rev. Albert Pero the course THE CHURCH IN THE CHANGING METROPOLIS, which was specifically designed to sensitize men in power to areas where conscienceless power confronts powerless conscience and to help men who affect us in their exercise of power to respond to the truth in their use of power as it affects our community.
3. We reject and actively oppose the Board of Control's action to remove that course from the curriculum when, at the District's urging, the new co-chairman of the District Board of Social Ministry and the Secretary of Evangelism used the course to sensitize these men to the needs and concerns of our community.
4. We reject and actively oppose the enforced retirement or placement on modified service faculty members who, in their 142 accumulated years of experience, have proved themselves sensitive to the needs of the Black community and actively responsive to them and to the needs of other cultures.
5. We reject and actively oppose the appointment of unsensitized and overt racists to positions in the church which will perpetuate in the educational and Synodical system the crippling effects of racism so evident to our own church in our own history and in the present efforts of our fieldworkers, the Seminary community, and our own efforts in the Saint Louis community.
   a. . . . .
   b. We resent and actively oppose the systematic release of not only a Board of Missions member who, as a Black clergyman, represented the sensitivity to express the needs and concerns of our community, but also the systematic release of sensitized members of the Mission staff and personnel.

    c. We reject and actively oppose the refusal of local Lutheran agencies and institutions to act forcefully and positively to express concerns brought to them consistently, particularly over the past two years.

    d. We reject and actively oppose the refusal of the Board of Control since 1970, when the needs of the Black students were first brought to their attention, to act decisively and responsibly to those continuing requests.

    e. We reject and actively oppose the gross mistreatment and misrepresentation of the Black fieldworker at our parish of whom we are properly proud in the light of his capabilities as a servant of Christ and as a representative among seminarians of our church community.

6. We reject and actively oppose the summary removal, as "theological fluff," of courses intent on development of pastoral skill, knowledge, and leadership as they apply to current issues in indigenous communities like our own.

7. We reject as iniquitous and pretentious the decisions of white boards and committees, predominantly insensible to our needs and priorities, without even the pretense of consultation with the community those decisions will affect.

8. We reject and actively oppose the Synod's schizophrenic public posture that funds are not available for the needs of minority groups while convention after convention of the Synod passed piously ineffective and innocuous resolutions regarding the need of minority groups.

9. We reject and actively oppose the demonic misuse of the democratic process to subvert, ignore, and ridicule minority issues that at their core are so entwined in the message of the Gospel that it is next to blasphemous for the church to remain immobile and emasculated.

We reject apriori any attempt to minimize or bypass these concerns as peripheral or insignificant in view of this church body's preconceived priorities.

We are compelled in the light of the church's continuing inability to hear and act to develop the mechanics that will permit this congregation to assist the Black community to do the following:

1. To call individuals and groups to account publicly for their public actions.

2. To provide a center for those whose priorities in the church are like our own.

3. To permit groups and individuals to bypass reluctant Boards, individuals, and committees.

4. To make sure that long-term struggles remain live issues.

5. To exert pressure here at the nerve center of the LC-MS and the Missouri District and the Seminary.

6. To do everything to insure that our priorities are "heard" by the Press and Media to discover all publicity channels.
7. To publicize "issues" within the community of St. Louis, and at large in the church.
8. To be the channel for needs of powerless or crippled congregations.
9. To coordinate power and potential of the Black Lutheran and Black community in general around our priorities.
10. To be an information center for Black Lutheran affairs.
11. To find friendly contacts in congregations, Boards, committees, etc.
12. To work for change in organizational structures to make them responsive to our priorities.
13. To provide the necessary perspective toward change.
14. To organize election of representatives to Synodical and District organizations and associations.
15. To express general needs of the Black community in St. Louis in Lutheran channels.
16. To discover at what level congregations, Boards, committees, etc., are responsive to our priorities.
17. To give young Black people a picture of vital Black Christian lay leadership so that there is hope and there are firm goals in the lives of young Black Lutheran Christians.
18. To support Black students in all of the Lutheran educational institutions of the St. Louis community in their quest for fair treatment and fulfillment of educational needs.

Now, two and a half hours later, at 10:55 A.M. Gerald Miller presented the following document known as

THE 'SEMINEX' RESOLUTION

Seminarian James Wind moved adoption. It read:

On January 21, 1974, students at Concordia Seminary declared a moratorium on all classes. We took this action in order to confront the crisis at our seminary and in our church. We declared to the Board of Control that the moratorium would remain in effect until either specific charges of false doctrine were brought against specific professors or those professors were exonerated. The Board of Control has done neither. Instead, the contracts of our teachers have been terminated.

We believe this response of the Board of Control to be both unchristian and immoral. For this reason, we find it impossible in good conscience to continue our education under the present seminary Board of Control.

Instead, we will continue to pursue our calling as students in preparation for ministry in the Lutheran Church-Missouri Synod under the terminated faculty. We believe they are innocent of any charges of false doctrine and, in fact, are faithful to the Holy Scriptures and the Lutheran Confessions.

We therefore resolve to resume our theological education in exile, trusting in the grace of our Lord Jesus Christ.

In the discussion that followed one student observed that President Preus would say "These kids followed the profs." In an earlier meeting of our faculty on February 14, seminarian David Abrahamson took up this canard and said, the student body is "generally favorable to Seminex and is ready to go. We are planning to gather on Tuesday (February 19) at 8:30 A.M.!" In the same meeting he had recited some of the students' sentiments:

"We would be damned if we did and damned if we didn't. I'd rather be damned for doing."

"Whatever action we take must not be viewed as divisive."

"A venture of faith."

"We have to make a decision sooner or later. Let's make it sooner."

"Let's put the burden on the church, where it belongs."

"Formation of Seminex would rule out compromise but not reconciliation."

"If we don't do it next week, we'll lose much of the momentum."

"If the Board thinks they're off the hook, they'll be sitting on it for a change."

Concluding his run-down of student opinion, Abrahamson said to this effect, "The students are not of the opinion that they are being led around by the faculty."

Uppermost in the minds of the students now gathered on February 19 was the question whether the resolution should be sent out to the entire church, so that the students' action might not be misunderstood. An amendment to that effect was passed with a few nays.

Someone then moved to close debate. Only a handful opposed voting the previous question. At 11:10 A.M. the resolution passed with approximately three in opposition and nine abstaining.

Graveyard of Missouri

We then proceeded out of the gymnasium. Two-foot-long wooden crosses, painted white, with names in black on the cross piece, con-

318

trasted here and there against the winter garb. Leading the procession was Charles Muse, with cross and banner. Joyfully the marching congregation sang "The Church's One Foundation." As we approached the quadrangle, we saw that it had turned into Flanders Field and Arlington Cemetery. Each of us on the faculty and staff saw his or her name speared into the ground. "A Mighty Fortress Is Our God" burst the air as we proceeded through the great arch of Luther Tower and down the steps to gather around and in front of the statue of Martin Luther. Then facing the Gothic fortress that remained behind us we heard these words read:

> "To subvert a man in his cause, the Lord does not approve."
>
> Lamentations 3:36

The Synod in Convention at New Orleans had questioned belief in the reality of the Exodus at Concordia Seminary. Acting President Scharlemann, who was watching the proceedings intermittently from his presidential office window might well have picked up the following words, whose spiritual power had opened up the Reed Sea in front of all pursuing tanks:

> By faith Moses, when he was born, was hidden three months by his parents, because they saw he was an exceptional child; and they were not afraid of the king's order. By faith Moses, when he had grown up, refused to be identified as a son of Pharaoh's daughter. He chose rather to suffer with the people of God, than to enjoy the fleeting pleasures of sin. He considered enduring of reproach in behalf of the Messiah greater wealth than the treasures in Egypt; for he had his eye on the reward. By faith he left Egypt, unafraid of the king's anger. He appeared to see the One who is unseen, so persevering was he. Through faith he kept the passover, and poured blood on the doorposts to keep the destroyer of the firstborn from laying a hand on his people. (Hebrews 11:23–28)

Two huge black panels then moved into place and closed the arch. Slashed downward across both of them were the letters

Next came the hammer blows. Fluttering in the wind was a small piece of paper on which were written the destinies of more than five hundred men and women.

To the ringing of Luther Tower's bells, whose sound the Acting President could not silence, the march continued to DeMun Avenue, the street that marked the boundary of Concordia Seminary's oak-treed facade. There Gerald Miller presented his peers to John H. Tietjen, who in turn presented to the students the adjunct faculty. He then read from Hebrews 13:13–14:

> Let us go forth therefore unto him without the camp, bearing his reproach. For here have we no continuing city, but we seek one to come.

"As we look back at that mighty fortress, we know these words are true," he said. "We will let God lead us where He wills. He will take care of you."

In his welcome to us, Dean Walter Brueggemann of Eden Seminary said: "Our hearts are very full of fear and anxiety for you, but with pride for your witness." With Jeremiah 29:10–14 as his text, Brueggemann assured us, "God will not renege on his promises. He will sustain and cherish you until he brings you back to your land. The Kingdoms of this world belong to our God. Hallelujah!"

At the announcement, "Classes begin on Wednesday at 8:00 A.M." the students clapped.

Dean Damm said: "We face East! There the new awaits us."

Seminex

According to schedule, the winter quarter for seminary education resumed on Wednesday, February 20, at St. Louis University and Eden Seminary. Removed from earshot of Luther Tower, we now could hear Saxon bells ringing in the belfry of the university church. They had been sold by the early Missouri Synod immigrants to Roman Catholics in St. Louis.

Since the founding of our Synod, we had put under heavy attack, along with modernists and liberals, "the Catholics" and "the Reformed." Now it was Catholics and Reformed people who honored their commitments to the academic Consortium of which they were a part by welcoming Lutherans, whose own church had not honored the decision of one of its own official boards prior to the New Orleans

Convention in 1973. The Administrations of both St. Louis University and Eden Seminary might have excused themselves from "interference in another church's affairs." But that was not their moral style.

No longer an accepted part of the Missouri Brotherhood, the exiles formed a community, where women also knew that their talents for ministry would not be threatened by theological fiat.

Professors and administrators at St. Louis University doubled up in offices and freed quarters for the executive staff of *Concordia Seminary, Now in Exile,* known the world over as *Seminex.* Professor Lucille Hager and her staff set up library facilities with reserve shelves in the Divinity School's Commons, a large room which served also as a community hall for sociability and negotiation of almost all Seminex business. Here Dr. Caemmerer posted his name-plate on a wall and held office hours. The sign read: *Enter without knocking.*

Skills and organization learned during the moratorium helped to move the operation into high gear. Since quick communication was of primary importance, one of the first installations by the Seminex carpenters, headed by Kevin Hormann, was a complex of pigeon holes. The only disaster was an attempt to transport an organ across the Reed Sea. The homemade instrument was much too loud for the small chapel, and no one received complaints from God after the liturgiologists substituted a lowly piano.

It was no easy matter to find housing. A number of professors and staff members who had received notice to vacate their seminary-owned homes within a ten-day period were pressed to find financing on such short notice for the purchase of different living quarters, but we discovered that Dr. Tietjen's words about God's promise to provide were very real and true. Second Presbyterian Church offered some large apartments for rent. We learned that some of the finest and most spacious housing was to be found in depressed areas of the city, and at generously low prices.

To move the contents of more than forty offices taxed the ingenuity and strength of students who volunteered for the task. But most annoying to them was the insensitivity behind the order to vacate within ten days. My own family was simply unable immediately to find a residence adequate to meet our varied needs, and closing procedures took time. Two of the students who helped us move were indignant that the acting administration which evicted us had, by legal phrasing, made it necessary first to move my library and office effects from the Seminary itself to our seminary-owned home, and again from there to our newly acquired residence. With four professors and less than a hundred students rattling around in a huge seminary there was simply no need for such haste. It not only gave Christianity a bad name, but from a purely secular point of view was bad PR for the Preus-Otten Brotherhood.

Pastoral Preus

Already in early February there had been rumblings to the effect that Acting President Scharlemann would remain in office only long enough to preside over the necessary dirty work. Projection of a seminary's image required something more than a "crush-rebellion" style of leadership during a holocaust. Therefore Scharlemann was soon to be initiated into the deeper mysteries of the Missouri Synod's collective ego. President "Jack" required imbalance in order to achieve his objective of authoritative control. Once in charge, however, he aimed to enshrine in his person the party of moderation. On his right would be the "crazies" and on his left the "extremists." Playing off one group against the other as he swam in the mainstream was the name of his political brokerage game.

To all appearances Scharlemann, therefore, had outlived his usefulness. His own decisive type of administrative mentality would find it difficult to cope with Preus' I-like-to-keep-my-options-open line. On February 20, Scharlemann said on CBS Channel 4, 6 o'clock news, that the Seminex students had been "led by all kinds of promises that they will have jobs in the church. This is not possible according to the rules of the church." He did not know Preus very well. Jack was actually a very "pastoral" president. The only catch was that "pastoral" in many contexts of Preusian usage meant that rules had to be bent when political priorities demanded it. Preus also knew the value of gaining extra political mileage out of an underling's necessarily unsavory performance in behalf of the over-all game plan by repudiating it as over-zealousness in the face of howls by moderates, whose good will had to be maintained. For example, on the same broadcast, just fifteen minutes earlier, Preus said that the faculty had "walked out" and that the Board of Control was "equally radical." Yet, it was his own first vice-president on the same Board who moved to *fire* the faculty, and Scharlemann was the Executive officer of the Board. Continually exposed to such rapid action on the political stock-exchange board, even the healthiest mentality can break. Whatever the precise diagnosis, the fact is that President Preus' brother Robert moved into

322

the Acting Presidency of Concordia Seminary at 801 DeMun Avenue, not long after the exile had taken place.[1] As he put it, "Dr. Scharlemann was a tired man." Thus Scharlemann, himself an instrument of the Preus-Otten purge, learned that there are limitations to survival in Missouri's administrative Brotherhood.

Chapter 27

DEATH AND RESURRECTION

Armageddon was more than one battle. Nor did it end with the suspension of Dr. John Tietjen and the founding of Seminex. Peace feelers, diplomatic missions, forays, and counter-defenses on many fronts kept Missouri in the headlines. To record and analyze even the most important developments that ultimately led up to the founding of the new church known as *The Association of Evangelical Lutheran Churches* will require another volume or two.

On the other hand, to defer commemoration of many who joined in the battle for what they considered truth and justice would suggest a callous disregard of their contributions and at the same time actually distort history by leaving the focus on a relatively few individuals and groups.

Therefore it is necessary quickly to traverse the broader range of the battlefields, to read the headstones there and hear the voices crying, in some cases, out of the very depths of ultimate concern. Nor can one with good reason object that the following Roll of Honor is read out of *Missouri In Perspective*. Where else but in ELIM's publication can one find such an extensive chronological death toll? As for objectivity, the fact is that ELIM's casualty list includes not only men and women who openly protested some of the Missouri Synod's actions and resolutions, but many who tried only to be kind and merciful, and moderate in their judgments. Some never uttered a word of criticism about their Synod. Some simply wearied in the struggle. Among them are clergy, nonclergy, professionals of varying expertise, self-styled laity, highly educated and less highly educated. But those who still insist, "we want to hear the other side," let them hear it now and then make their way through the cemetery.

324

The Other Side

The people whose names and words you are about to read are *rebels and insurgents.* They encourage *false doctrine.* Most of them are either themselves *Bible doubters* or give comfort to those who are. Some believe that *the book of Jonah is a parable.* Some think that *Isaiah was written by more than one author.* Some *questioned decisions of their Synod.* They *did not obey the Fourth Commandment.* They did not *condemn false teaching nor false teachers.* Some may not have been guilty, but they were *misled by others.* Many of them *gave money to ELIM.* Some *refused to be certified for ministry* by the faculty of Concordia Seminary, St. Louis, Missouri. Some *disobeyed the Bylaws of the Synod.* Many did not follow *proper procedures* in their dissent. Some *encourage prayer with non-Lutherans.* Etc., etc.

Roll of Honor

Even before the suspension of Dr. John Tietjen, three professors at one of the Missouri Synod's teacher training institutions, Concordia College, River Forest, Illinois, felt the Synod's axe. Despite endorsements by their department chairmen and the academic dean of the institution,

✝ John Groh
✝ Robert Friebus
✝ Robert Hausman

were notified by mail of their termination, without a statement of cause. Although the action was taken in November, 1973, no announcement concerning these professors was made until the students had departed for the Christmas holidays.[1]

About the same time a choir director in Cincinnati was cut off from the Sacrament of the Lord's Supper because he wished to give members of his congregation opportunity to discuss the consequences of the New Orleans convention. For this insistence on the right to think

✝ Paul H. Smith

was also dismissed from the congregation.[2]

Within less than a month of the founding of Seminex,

✝ Seminarians

325

from approximately one-third of the Missouri Synod's districts lost scholarship aid totalling about $98,000.[3]

Constitutionally guaranteed rights of congregational autonomy fell under a ruling of the Missouri Synod's Commission on Constitutional Matters on March 23, 1974. According to the ruling, congregations calling pastors from Seminex's graduating class were liable to "forfeit their membership in the Synod." Four of the five-member commission were appointees of President J. A. O. Preus.[4]

For exercising his right to question synodical administrative policy a highly respected educator,

✠ Stephen A. Schmidt

was replaced as head of the Education Department at Concordia College, River Forest.[5]

Despite appeals from sister churches in Papua N.G. and India, the Missouri Synod's Board of Missions refused to consider the reappointment or reinstatement of

✠ James Mayer

as Area Secretary for South Asia.[6] And on April 10

✠ William H. Kohn

resigned in protest against the same Board's "legalistic, isolationist, and separatist" actions.[7]

Weary of the "stacked decks, suppressed information and the raw use of power," on April 19, 1974,

✠ William F. Bulle
  ✠ Marion Kretzschmar
    ✠ Walter H. Meyer
      ✠ James W. Mayer

resigned from their positions as mission staff executives. On April 29

✠ William F. Reinking

added his body to the pile.[8]

I had to do "what my conscience told me to do," said the Executive Director of the Missouri Synod's Foundation,

✠ Victor O. Mennicke

As of April 15, he ceased raising funds for the Synod.[9]

On May 10–11 ELIM set up a new Lutheran agency for world missions, with James Mayer as coordinator and three other staff members, Marion Kretzschmar, Walter Meyer, and Paul Strege. They protested the policies of the Synod's Board for Missions as "unethical" and "sectarian," and assured other Christian groups that they were committed to work "complementarily, not competitively, with established denominational structures. . . . Our business is mission, not politics."[10]

In a meeting on May 23–24, ELIM's Red Cross division moved $40,000 to the aid of Seminex's

✠ Ministerial Candidates

who were under heavy fire of "legalism and the misuse of power."[11]

At issue in July was the question of a "restrictions on academic freedom" clause in the contract

✠ Raymond Fontaine

was offered at Concordia College, River Forest.[12]

The casualties at River Forest mounted so fast there was a mass burial in the July 15th issue of *Missouri in Perspective:*

✠ David Stein

was replaced as dean by Richard Korthals, an editorial member of *Affirm,* and "author of some of the most regrettable prose I have ever read," according to the college's necrologist, Dr. Stephen Schmidt. Other victims were

✠ Robert Hopmann
  ✠ Roger Gard
    ✠ William Wendling
      ✠ Carl Halter
        ✠ Max Heinz

"And that's only the beginning. New Orleans plays on," wrote Schmidt. "A new Board for Higher Education adopts a resolution limiting academic freedom, limitations which can be changed biannually at any synodical convention. . . . The resolution can only be called sinful and unChristian."[13]

"Pastor Fired; Another Forced to Resign." So ran the headline. Lahoma, Oklahoma had the distinction of seeing a Missouri Synod brotherhood oust

✠ David Hodgson

327

for protesting the mounting casualties in the Synod.[14] And two congregations located in Pettibone and Woodworth, North Dakota, cracked the liberty bell for their pastor.

✠ William E. Roten

Under Waldo Werning's capable napalming of the Synod's mission program

✠ William T. Seeber
✠ Phyllis Kersten
✠ Reuben J. Schmidt

asked for their headstones in a meeting of the Board of Missions, August 22–24.[15]

To lift the spirits in Missouri's field hospitals the following letter was released:

To: Voters' Assembly, First Lutheran Church, Ephesus
FROM: President, Lutheran Church—Mediterranean Synod

We, at headquarters, have recently become aware that your congregation is being served by one Mr. Paul Uvtarsus who is not a graduate of one of our recognized seminaries. We wish to inform you that the service of this man violates the LC-MS bylaws and may jeopardize your congregation's standing in the Synod.

Because he lacks the proper certification from a recognized faculty, you should be aware that he could well be teaching *false doctrine.*

Worse yet, we understand that he has even gone so far as to send out others to preach without so much as notifying our headquarters. Surely, these workers should be apprised that they must be considered ineligible for the pension fund, unless this situation is remedied in accordance with the bylaws.

Allow us to share a few other considerations with you in the interest of positive public relations:

We have learned of Mr. Uvtarsus' "over-the-wall-in-a-basket" incident in Damascus, which surely does nothing to enhance the image of the Synod, as it is mere showmanship for the benefit of the media.

Similarly, his quarrel with a fellowservant, the Rev. Barnabas, has caused great difficulties for our office of Public Relations.

His statement in a recent letter, "God forbid that I should glory in anything save the cross of Christ," clearly sounds like blatant Gospel Reductionism, which has been specifically rejected by the entire Mediterranean Synod in convention. Surely you would desire to have all his correspondence submitted to our board for doctrinal review in the future.

We also have serious reservations about his letters which meddle in the affairs of other churches, especially in Corinth. We would urge you to prevent him from such meddling and leave such affairs in the hands of proper authorities, who would use more tact.

Similarly his tolerance of so-called "charismatics," his supposed "thorn in the flesh," his all-night sermons, and his opposition to such time-honoured Synod traditions as circumcision all raise serious doubts about his fitness for service in our Synod. We urge you, therefore, to send him back to headquarters for an interview with us, so that responsible synodical officials can determine whether he is fit to serve you.[16]

The bombs kept dropping,[17] and five more faculty and staff called retreat from the field of combat at River Forest:

✠ James Kracht
✠ Edwin H. Homeier
✠ Randall Schnack
✠ Norman Liston
✠ William Bein

Yet there was no word of protest to report from the North Central Accrediting Agency.

It was no news to professors of Seminex, but it came as a surprise to

✠ Richard C. Eyer

when a few members in his congregation began to bring misquotations of sermons and catechetical material to synodical officials.[18]

From under the rubble at River Forest

✠ Stephen A. Schmidt

upheld what he called "the old standard of an open, free, vital academic community of diversity and trust. I prefer that one standard," he wrote, "to the double standards and doubletalk of the present hypocrisy, which uses the rhetoric of purity to mask the practice of purge."[19]

Despite the fact that

✠ John H. Tietjen

had informed Concordia Seminary's Board of Control of a previous commitment, the Board in his absence voted 6–5 to dismiss him. Once again the two witnesses, Harlan Harnapp and Leonard Buelow were present, this time for the *coup de grâce.*[20]

A veteran of other wars in the Missouri Synod, Concordia Seminary's retired professor

✠ Paul Bretscher

was denied one of his last wishes, namely to have his long-time friend and colleague, Dr. Richard Caemmerer, preach at the traditional memorial service for seminary professors. Acting President Ralph Bohlmann also maintained a traditional position, namely that the synod is not to be declared in the wrong. He therefore made the "pastoral" decision not to invite a man to preach who had "spoken a harsh word of judgment" against his institution.[21]

Smelling of the aroma of ELIM,

✠ Richard Osing

came under attack at Trinity Lutheran Church, Cedar Rapids, Iowa.[22]

After 21 years of service,

✠ Erich F. Brauer

was shot out of his executive position in the South Wisconsin District of the Missouri Synod.[23]

The new library at Concordia Seminary was named after his father, but

✠ Alfred A. O. Fuerbringer

who preceded Tietjen as president of the institution, was refused entrance under a set of restrictive regulations warmly defended by Dr. Ralph Bohlmann, the Acting President at 801 DeMun Avenue.[24] His experience was not unique. When I walked into the library, I was greeted with a mixture of horror and consternation by Head Librarian Larry Bielenberg who exclaimed to me, "You can't come in here, Dr. Danker." But he did permit me to remove my research papers and files relating to my work on a revision of a Greek-English lexicon.

Like soldiers on the front at Christmas, students at Seminex attempted to call a cease-fire and turned the other cheek by inviting the students and faculty at the 801 DeMun campus to use the library facilities of Concordia Seminary-in-Exile and to gather with them to celebrate the Holy Eucharist. Acting President Ralph Bohlmann followed the time-honored synodical custom of keeping the question warm on the back burner.[25]

✠ Melba Ann Krato

had served as a member of Concordia Seminary's Guild, a women's organization. Thinking of herself as a kind of Red Cross volunteer who had always helped "the boys," she had reached out also to Concordia Seminary's Exiles. Bohlmann inquired about the propriety of such action, and someone else asked her if she would similarly "support a Catholic." After the Guild's November Board meeting she was still stunned. "I have never seen such hate in the eyes of coworkers in the church before. It was unbelievable."[26]

More sisters were to find the brotherhood too constricted.

✠ Karen Grummer

submitted her resignation as teacher at the elementary school of the same congregation that had forced Richard Osing's resignation.[27]

In Burlington, Wisconsin,

✠ Two Women Elders

would find themselves under a doctrinal gun loaded with 1 Timothy 2:12: "I do not allow women to teach or to have authority over men; they must be quiet." A clergyman who was close to the case said in response to his District's administrative pressure: "To forbid full participation of women in the life of the congregation just because they are women seems to be culturally archaic; that is, it comes out of a past cultural mind set."[28]

Horrified by the casualty rate, 91 deaconesses and deaconess interns and 41 deaconess students at Valparaiso University had earlier joined the rescue squads.[29] Like the women at the tomb of Jesus Christ, they came. Addressing themselves to the Board of Control, Concordia Seminary, in care of Board Chairman Ewald J. Otto, they wrote:

> We, the undersigned, can no longer remain silent in the present Synodical crisis; we are called by our Lord Jesus Christ to give our witness to the church.
>
> We represent a variety of theological positions—some of us are conservative and some are moderate; some of us are members of ELIM and some of us consider ELIM divisive; but together we proclaim our unity in the midst of our diversity, together we proclaim that there is room for all of us in the church, and together we are of the conviction that the church is Christ-connected forgiven sinners who love each other in Christ, and who deal openly and honestly with each other.
>
> The Board of Control, Concordia Seminary, St. Louis, has convicted John Tietjen of "holding, defending, allowing, and fostering

331

false doctrine contrary to Article II." However, throughout the long process which has finally resulted in this conviction, the Board of Control has failed to specifically define the content and substance of that false doctrine. We must therefore painfully protest, to the Board of Control and to the church, against the process which has reached its culmination in the conviction of John Tietjen. We feel that a brother in the faith has been dealt with dishonestly and unlovingly.

We do not all agree on every theological issue with John Tietjen, but we are convinced that the handling of his conviction was carried out in an unchristian and unloving manner. We call to the church to join with us in assuming responsibility to halt this unlovingness, to cry out loudly and firmly for an atmosphere of trust, openness, and honesty, to petition the Board of Control, Concordia Seminary, St. Louis, either to demonstrate that John Tietjen is guilty of the false doctrine of which he is convicted, or, if this is impossible, to retract the conviction and publicly confirm John Tietjen innocent.

In the midst of our own diversity, we together hurt for John Tietjen, his family, our own congregations, and the entire church.

May God have mercy on us all!

The following deaconesses and deaconess interns signed the letter:

✠ Jamie Alden
✠ Marlene Anderson
✠ Karen Bakewicz
✠ Grace Jewett Baranski
✠ Jan Barnes
✠ Shirley Barnes
✠ Carolyn Becker
✠ Bonnie Belasic
✠ Kathie Bickel
✠ Catherine Bleuge
✠ Kathy Borgman
✠ Lois Braham
✠ Rachel Kriefall Brandt
✠ Sally Brandt
✠ Eileen Browne
✠ Patricia Bumby
✠ Verne Campbell
✠ Carol Dolberg
✠ Lynn Dorlon
✠ Cathy Dornon
✠ Edie Eickemeyer
✠ Betty Epie

✠ Norma Everist
✠ Sue Eyer
✠ Diane Fenske
✠ Hertha Fisher
✠ Mary Flohr
✠ Jan Fowler
✠ Louise Fox
✠ Ilene Gilmour
✠ Diane Greve
✠ Lorie Gruenbeck
✠ Anita Grunow
✠ Helen Haidle
✠ Sandy Harms
✠ Betty Havey
✠ Sue Heise
✠ Elaine Warinsky Herr
✠ Barbara Hinchey
✠ Judith Hoshek
✠ Edie Hovey
✠ Jan Janzow
✠ Kathy Jurgemeyer
✠ Vanette Kashmer

✠ Brenda Kasten
✠ Maralyn Kettner
✠ Barbara Kloehn
✠ Jan Krueger
✠ Donna Kummerick
✠ Burnette Kunz
✠ Winifred Lehenbauer
✠ Jeanne Lowe
✠ Karen Ludwig
✠ Eunice McKinney
✠ Lois Meier
✠ Diane Melang
✠ Sally Jane Meyer
✠ Evelyn Middlestadt
✠ Deborah Nebel
✠ Sheryl Olson
✠ Jan Orluske
✠ Kathy Peters
✠ Pam Peters
✠ Carol J. Petersen
✠ Eileen Peterson
✠ Diane Philipp
✠ Phyllis Pleuss
✠ Vivian Pohlman

✠ Dorothy Prybylski
✠ Jeanette Rebeck
✠ Diane Remer
✠ Jeanne Rowan
✠ Gwen Sayler
✠ Linda Schaefer
✠ Carol Schewe
✠ Evonne Schewe
✠ Karna Secker
✠ Jan Siemers
✠ Jocelyn Sproule
✠ Jan Tindall
✠ Judee Tomlinson
✠ Audrey Vanderbles
✠ Claire Visser
✠ Ruth Waetzig
✠ Ruth Walker
✠ Diane Warner
✠ Sue Wendorf
✠ Dianna Werlinger
✠ Susan Wild
✠ Louise Williams
✠ Joan Wolf

Also adding their signatures were the following deaconess students:

✠ Candy Batzelle
✠ Dorothy Boettcher
✠ Karen Burgess
✠ Marilyn Bischoff
✠ Cynthia Brown
✠ Kathy Bykonen
✠ Kathleen Delventhel
✠ Diana Dicharof
✠ Mary Doversberger
✠ Eva Fanslau
✠ Faith Feltz
✠ Ruth Fisker
✠ Sally Franz
✠ Ann Marie Gabriel
✠ Dawn Gerike

✠ Tracy Gennrich
✠ Barbara Giebel
✠ JoEllen Giffin
✠ Ruth Hanusa
✠ Denise Hegemann
✠ Jane Hinze
✠ Martha Kaempfe
✠ Donna King
✠ Cathy Krueger
✠ Ann Kuck
✠ Melissa Kyle
✠ Debra Lampson
✠ Suzanne Larson
✠ Debbie Lucht
✠ Lindy Luster

✠ Linda Morath
✠ Patti Muehrer
✠ Ann Marie Nuechterlein
✠ Judy Robinson
✠ Jean Sawyer
✠ Jill Schmidt

✠ Verna Schroeder
✠ Dawn Tyson
✠ Jan Voges
✠ Joanne Wehrmeister
✠ Linda Wuerdemann

But no one bleeding on the field heard from the Synod's male division, the Chaplains Corps.

Hong Kong, India, and New Guinea had already felt the impact of Missouri's war, but now Canadians became involved. The Ontario District Department of Missions informed a campus mission at Toronto,

✠ The University Lutheran Chapel

that a review of the ministry there was underway. That was synodicalese for "You had better wind up your affairs."[30]

Right-wingers were not satisfied to see exiles suspended, fired and subject to other synodical harrassment. Having hit them once they tried again on the rebound. For daring to come to the aid of the Seminex "rebels," by awarding academic degrees in May, 1974, the

✠ Lutheran School of Theology at Chicago

was subjected to the harassment of an investigation by the State of Illinois. Mr. Harold Olsen, chairman of the Board of Concordia Seminary, Springfield, Illinois, had instigated the proceedings with support from Robert Preus and other Board members. But he ended up without a case, and the attempt to invalidate the degrees of about 140 Seminex graduates was a dismal failure. By contrast, at its meeting in June, 1974, the American Association of Theological Schools had commended Eden Seminary, St. Louis Divinity School, and Lutheran School of Theology at Chicago for assisting the exiled students and faculty.[31]

There was no further room in the brotherhood for

✠ Joan M. Avey

Associate Dean of Students at what remained of one of the Missouri Synod's showpiece colleges.

In response to complaints about her non-reappointment and those of

✠ James Mahler

and

✠ Charles Dietz

President Zimmermann of Concordia College, River Forest, scarcely endeared himself to 500 students by telling them, "Some of us were making budgets when, you know, you were eating lollipops."[32]

Unable to hit him directly, parishioners of Salem Lutheran Church, Black Jack, Missouri, blew the boat out from under their senior pastor,

✠ Paul R. Heckmann

by abolishing the office of head pastor.

✠ David A. Peters

assistant to Heckmann, answered this unusual treatment of a divine call by tendering his resignation.[33]

In a kind of mass vaccination against the virus of heresy the Board of Concordia Theological Seminary, Springfield, Illinois, refused to retain

✠ William Wickenkamp

and a denial of tenure assured in the bylaws led to the resignation of

✠ Victor Bohlmann

Because he had tried to look out for the good names of fellow Christians in St. Louis,

✠ John T. Diefenthaler

also had to leave the Springfield brotherhood. He was accompanied by

✠ James Weis

who found his future at the seminary "sharply restricted."[34]

After the major gutting of his school,

✠ Lorman Petersen

once academic dean at Concordia Theological Seminary, decided that his school had "lost its ability to serve the whole church." His colleague

✠ Kenneth Ballas

was about as liberal theologically as William F. Buckley politically, but even he found it hard to breathe the oppressive atmosphere.[35]

Almost the last to hit the dust at the Springfield campus were

✠ Charismatics

some of whose gifts, despite First Corinthians 12, were not welcome in the brotherhood.[36]

After piling up a Guiness record of 12 years under indictment for teaching, among other equally heretical items, that the book of Isaiah was probably written by two different authors,

✠ Ralph Gehrke

one of the tattered platoon of good teachers left at Concordia Teacher's College, River Forest, joined the faculty of Pacific Lutheran University in the summer of 1975.[37]

A member of Redeemer Lutheran Church, St. Thomas, Ontario, Canada, described official pressure on his congregation as "blackmail." Along with his pastor

✠ Douglas Schweyer

he hoped to develop a new parish life. The Rev. Albin Stanfel, leader of the synodical brotherhood in the Ontario area, could be certain of synodical committee appointments in the future.[38]

Unable to engage in long-term planning in a today-you-see-it-to-morrow-you-don't church,

✠ Lorenz Grumm

found that the Missouri Synod had no room for his talents as stewardship executive.[39]

With all the answers known in advance, it was a foregone conclusion that the Synod's Board of Parish Education would cut down on staff. Concordia Pubishing House could not peddle books in an omniscient church, and its financial picture was as uncertain as that of the Missouri Synod in general[40] Hence there was little space left for

✠ Frederick W. Meyer	✠ Robert J. Hoyer
✠ Mary Brummer	✠ Mervin Marquardt
✠ Jack Muhlenbruch	✠ Barbara Kraemer
✠ John Schroeder	✠ Nancy Warner

The fate of at least some of the more than one hundred

✠ Concordia Publishing House Employees

whose jobs were generally phased out during the summer of 1975, could surely be traced to the fact that many of the Synod's best literary heads had for some time been rolling out of the brotherhood.[41]

About the same time Ralph Bohlmann refused to recognize the competence of the American Association of University Professors (AAUP) to judge whether the academic freedom of

✠ Arlis Ehlen

who had been dismissed in 1972 from his post in the Old Testament Department, had been infringed.[42]

In a flash of truce, Dr. John H. Tietjen was cleared of false doctrine during the summer of 1975 by the Rev. Oscar Gerken, conservative first vice-president of the Missouri District of the Lutheran Church-Missouri Synod.[43] It was the first official tacit admission that the students were right in demanding proof of false doctrine at Concordia Seminary before they called off their moratorium. Over forty faculty members and staff had said that they and Tietjen were in agreement on doctrine. On April 8, 1974, Professor Richard Caemmerer wrote in *Missouri in Perspective:* "... The Lutheran Church-Missouri Synod is in the grip of a vast swindle as it is being propagandized to believe that men are trying to take its Bible away or that falling dominoes are soon to rob it of the meaning of man's sin and God's Savior."[44] Caemmerer had never been a false prophet. He was considered to be so orthodox that out of six retirees, he was one of the three who was retained by Preus' group at retirement age.

On January 25, 1974, he had received this notification from Concordia Seminary:

> Dear Dr. Caemmerer:
> It is my pleasure to inform you that in its regular meeting of January 20–21, 1974, the Board of Control resolved to ask you to continue at full service as a professor of Concordia Seminary.
> My hope is that you will receive this notice in the awareness that the Board and I deeply appreciate what you have done for the benefit of many hundreds of persons with whom you have come in contact over the years of your service. Our hope is that you can continue in the years to come to devote yourself to the kind of creative activity which we have come to know as the hallmark of your devotion.
>
> Cordially,
> (signed)
> MARTIN H. SCHARLEMANN
> Acting President

Scharlemann's letter had completely ignored the issues in Caemmerer's protest on July 24, 1973 and his identification with the condemned theology of Dr. Tietjen. Therefore Caemmerer asked to be retired. Instead, he received his eviction notice on February 18, 1974.

Anyone with common sense knew by now that the real issue in the Missouri Synod was not Jonah, Adam and Eve, and other points of interpretation, but rather the use of power. Did Jesus Christ intend authority in the church to be used to get as many people out as possible, or to use the many and varied gifts of people to bring people in closer to God?

Yet bodies kept falling, and the bishops in the church took no collective action. Many ministers refused to engage their congregations in the struggle for truth and justice. "It will only weaken their faith to know what's going on in the church." Their net reward was to see the church they claimed to love fall into higher heaps of rubble.

Because they stood up for basic Jewish principles of dealing justly with one's neighbor, as defined in the prophetic writings of the Old Testament and repeated in the New Testament,

✠ Ronald Bruggeman

and

✠ Charleen Bruggeman

came under heavy fire in the same congregation that had ousted its head pastor by abolishing his office. As Caesars demanded renunciation of the name of Jesus Christ, so the Bruggemans were ordered to denounce the cause and theology of those who were united in protest against the oppressive policies of the Missouri Synod.[45]

With a single vote of 601 to 473 at the Brotherhood Convention in Anaheim, California, July, 1975,

✠ MEMBERS OF ELIM

felt the fire-bomb impact of the words "schismatic" and "offensive" to the Synod.[46] At this meeting, Vice-President Edwin C. Weber, who had conveniently used his conscience to attack Tietjen and his faculty now denied it to the Synod's bishops in the application of Bylaws.[47]

A further heavy weapon fashioned at Anaheim arranged for the demolition of the academic quality, as students over the years had come to know it, of the Synod's

✠ Senior College

at Fort Wayne, Indiana. The remaining faculty at Springfield was to be moved to the Fort Wayne campus, but most of Fort Wayne's faculty members, like the Jews under Nebuchadnezzar, were to be dispersed.[48]

Even the name

✠ Concordia Seminary in Exile

was threatened with legal action at Anaheim.

Five days after the convention's adjournment in Anaheim,

✠ Edward E. Busch

minister at Hope Lutheran Church, Glendora, California, was rolled out of his brotherhood.[49]

The town of Chickasha has the honor of securing notoriety in church history for Oklahoma through the action of First Lutheran Church, which rolled its two ministers

✠ Gerald Mansholt

and

✠ Stanley Padgett

out of the brotherhood.[50]

Professor John Klotz of Concordia Seminary "801" had the questionable theological distinction of interfering with a divine call in Anna, Illinois, and

✠ James Nickols

became the victim of a rescinded pastorate.[51]

Acting as though they, instead of Dr. Tietjen, had been under the gun, the two witnesses, Leonard Buelow and Harlan Harnapp, in late summer of 1975 were pondering their right to appeal their loss of the heresy charge against Tietjen.

After only one year at the front lines,

✠ Roger Harms

felt the impact of Anaheim's convention all the way in Barnes, Kansas.[52]

Reinstated six weeks after an enforced leave of absence,

✠ Theodore L. Scheidt

finally found his pastorate at Redeemer Lutheran Church, Lancaster, Ohio, unbearable.[53]

Almost himself the last pocket of resistance to purgation theology at the Springfield Seminary,

✠ Milton Sernett

left for Syracuse University in New York with two and a half pages of advice for President Preus, under date of August 22, 1975.[54]

More resignations from the Missouri Synod's Board of Parish Education came in Fall of 1975. The services of

✠ Evan J. Temple
  ✠ Daniel R. Burow
    ✠ Paul Pallmeyer

no longer were wanted nor available in the brotherhood.[55]

Fearing contamination from the virus of moderation, Redeemer Lutheran Church in Marshalltown, Iowa, voted against continuing

✠ Paul Discher

on their payroll, September 16, 1975. He was not even a member of ELIM, but the membership felt that he might have an Elimitic germ called "tendencies."[56]

Despite his willingness to accept certification from the 801 De Mun Seminary,

✠ Kenneth R. Storck

found that he was not out of the antiseptic tank even eight months after his initial interview. Yet no specific theological aberration was specified.[57]

By a vote of 111–56 on October 5, 1975,

Grace Lutheran Church
✠
Oklahoma City, Oklahoma

became the first "moderate" congregation to leave the brotherhood of the Lutheran Church-Missouri Synod.[58]

On October 20, 1975, Trinity Lutheran Church, Wheatland, Wyoming, could boast the termination of [59]

✠ Marvin L. Sackschewsky

With so many bodies moving out, President Preus was now finding more room for himself in the middle.[60] In keeping with the image he aimed to project, that of adherence to high standards of fairness, Preus did not hesitate to clobber his own supporters in order to appear the very spirit of fairness to those on his left. On October 24, 1975 he told a gathering at Concordia College, St. Paul, Minnesota, that their board (controlled by his own supporters) had acted too hastily in accepting the resignation of President Harvey Stegemoeller. The students and faculty, apparently unschooled in politics, were charmed and burst into an ovation. But there was no population explosion in the brotherhood.[61]

After announcement of his and his wife's membership in ELIM

✠ Frederick C. Watson

pastor at Messiah Lutheran Church, Evansville, Indiana, found his congregation in such a turmoil that he offered his resignation. He had graduated in 1974 from Concordia Seminary "801." [62]

An expert in development of educational materials and accomplished Old Testament scholar,

✠ Harold Rast

gave up his post as editorial director of the Synod's parish education program to become a staff officer for ELIM's task force on higher education. "Day by day," he said, "I have become progressively and painfully aware that the Missouri Synod is a dying organization."[63]

At Farmersville, Illinois, a locksmith from Springfield, Illinois, who may never have memorized the "Office of the Keys" was drawn into the fray. The minority conservative group contended it had the right to the keys of Zion Lutheran Church which had fallen into control of the majority. ELIM did not even figure in the contest. It all started when

✠ Jack Coale

an intern, or vicar, on assignment from Concordia Theological Seminary, Springfield, was asked to perform a wedding.[64]

Several years earlier

✠ Omar Stuenkel

had left the editorial staff of the Missouri Synod's official periodical, *The Lutheran Witness.* On November 7, 1975, also

✠ Eldon Weisheit

maintained his journalistic integrity by resigning from the *Witness* staff.[65]

341

Many ministers continued to refuse to "take sides" in the battle out of fear that their congregations might become polarized. At the same time they might have asked themselves whether a stance on the side of silence in the face of a theology of purgation and power was appropriate in a synod where membership called for responsible resistance to encroachment on the supremacy of the Bible as the only rule and norm of faith and practice. Other ministers answered this question with a resounding "No." In concert with the full and unadulterated confessional exposition of the Word of God, they challenged what they considered to be erosion of the doctrinal base of the Synod and espoused the cause of ELIM.

To those who had already paid their price because they refused to be people of price

✠ John M. Hilpert

who resigned his pastorate on November 23, 1975, added his spirit and body. "It was the simplest and fastest way to remove him," said a member of Our Saviour's Lutheran Church, Hillsboro, Illinois. Support for ELIM "was the only thing we could prove." Six months later Hilpert was directing service centers for refugees displaced by the Synod's war on non-approved dissent.[66]

In order that his congregation might become more aware of the problem it faced as a member of the Missouri Synod,

✠ William Traugott

resigned his pastorate in Loveland, Colorado. The majority in the congregation had earlier voted their confidence in him.[67]

Since

✠ Melvin M. Kieschnick

could not stop the Synod's movement toward fill-in-the-correct-blanks theology, one of the most "conflict-avoidance" executives in the Synod resigned in early 1976 from his position as Executive Secretary of the Board for Parish Education and head of the Synod's Division of Parish Services. "I deeply regret," he said, "that political manipulations, broken promises, and unproven accusations have created a climate in which it is extremely difficult to work with effectiveness and joy." He was afraid it would "get worse before it ever gets better."[68]

Layman

✠ E. D. Bolenbaugh

discovered that Kieschnick was right. This gentleman had raised funds for ELIM's various attempts to carry out the programs in which the Synod was felt to be remiss and was removed from his congregation's membership list. A member for 30 years, he had even agreed to step down from his ELIM post.[69]

Freedom to "air" the Gospel was denied on March 19, 1976 to

✠ William Bakewicz

Congregations participating in a weekly religious broadcast voted 9–8 to deny the program's airwaves to the Seminex graduate.[70]

A number of District Presidents, among them Charles Mueller and Arnold Kuntz, appeared to have cast themselves in the role of Gallio, a Roman governor who made a virtue out of comparative non-involvement (Acts 18:12–16). But an official in the Southeastern District of the Missouri Synod decided in early 1976 that events demanded a more definite stance. When he resigned from his post as vice-president of the District

✠ Paul T. Dannenfeldt

said, "I am one voice, at least, which could not support President Mueller's 'middle-of-the-road' course on synodical issues."[71]

Even President Preus seemed at last to recognize that coming on like gang-busters was not making his Synod a world-beater in Christian witness. Speaking as though he had just completed a script for the The Godfather, Part 3, he said: "This business of blasting each other and bombing each other and playing games with each other and politicking with each other, simply will not work." Participants in the meeting of the Missouri Synod's California and Nevada District, October 31–November 1, 1975, further heard him say: "Now I've tried it, I've been guilty—many in the room have—and I've learned it through the school of bitter experience."[72]

Eight of Missouri's bishops also felt that the carnage ought to stop. They met in Chicago, October 28–29, 1975, to affirm the right of synodical congregations to call and ordain Seminex graduates.[73] Preus was unwilling, however, to encourage coexistence and in April, 1976, he appeared to have lost all recollection of his call for a cease-fire and court-martialed four out of the eight. Despite the Synod's constitutional status as "advisory" to congregations, also in the matter of ordination to the ministry, Presidents

✠ Herman Frincke, Eastern District
✠ Harold Hecht, English District

343

✠ Rudolph Ressmeyer, Atlantic District
✠ Robert Riedel, New England District

were informed that their offices were now vacant because of their alleged violation of Anaheim Convention Resolution 5-02A.[74]

Shortly after the dismissal of the four bishops, President Preus appointed replacements. In accordance with his customary practice of personally driving the equivalent of a Red Cross Truck onto the battlefield after lighting a fuse, he wrote to the four districts involved: "We have had enough emotion and politics. Now let us have more sober thinking, proper application of Scripture and sensible action."[75] This diction suggested to symbolic vision a sandwich composed of an ignited bomb held in place by two oversize pieces of Wonder Bread. It also displayed careful avoidance of explicit description of the various strains of corporate insanity with which the Synod might have been afflicted. The faculties of both seminaries, Springfield, Illinois and St. Louis "801," were impressed with their Leader and affirmed their support of Preus in a joint meeting after the ouster.

As Moderates had learned from repeated experience, Preus' rhetoric did not stop escalation of body counts. College and university professors who had survived radical encounter in the Sixties must have found the challenge to their administrations during that period mild in comparison with the traumatic possibilities for Missouri's institutional self-clout in the Seventies. In a May 7 letter, Professors

✠ Victor Krause
and
✠ Walter Wangerin

added their resignations to 29 other departures from Concordia Teachers College, River Forest. Professor Stephen Schmidt, who seemed to be made of asbestos, had made his last stand and joined Krause and Wangerin in the following appraisal of the Missouri brotherhood: "We believe that a constant effort to be right and legal, rather than truly evangelical and pastoral clogs the Holy Spirit's channel of grace to the equipping of men and women for the educational ministries of the church." Dr. Leslie Zeddies, a professor of music at the college, noted their "battle-fatigue scars." In a letter to the May 14 *Spectator* he wrote the following epitaph: "To some these men are viewed as troublemakers and dissenters, raising embarrassing questions and refusing to comply. Another view, my own, is that each is a courageous, skilled and dedicated churchman, educator, and beloved colleague."[76]

As she watched her church's amazing ability to disintegrate and self-destruct before her very eyes,

✠ Sharon Soderling Kudenholdt

wrote: "Much of the travesty of the present situation seems to lie in the tremendous waste of human potential—professors, teachers, pastors, many of whom have served faithfully for more than a quarter of a century."[77]

Still more reports of casualties kept coming in. Scarcely a state in the Union was without representation on the Roll of Honor.

✠ Gerald D. Buss

44-year old pastor with seven children and graduate of the Seminary in Springfield, Illinois, resigned on April 19, 1976, from two congregations in Wisconsin.[78]

An administrative assistant to President Preus must not have heard Preus' confession of sins at the end of October, 1975. He helped cement polarity in Hutchinson, Kansas, and on April 25

✠ William A. Kaeppel

resigned from Christ Lutheran Church.[79]

"I personally finally realized that the Lutheran Church-Missouri Synod was hopelessly corrupt," said

✠ Robert G. Zimmermann

when he decided that selling real estate would give him greater opportunities for ministering to people than to serve as a minister in the Missouri Synod.[80]

Under the Rev. Merlin Meyer's activist pressure, the president of Concordia College, Bronxville, New York,

✠ Robert Schnabel

resigned and accepted a call to a non-Missouri Synod college in Iowa.[81]

To screen ministerial candidates who had graduated from Seminex, the Missouri Synod had set up a Colloquy Board composed of a synodical official and the presidents of the Synod's two seminaries. Out of a total of 176 Seminex graduates, eight had gone through the colloquy process. One of them was

✠ Daniel Comsia

who discovered that entry into the brotherhood was not possible without some institutional laundering of his conscience. He refused to pay the fee.[82]

By a vote of 296–75, the Missouri Synod's

✠ English District

voted separation from the Missouri Synod in a convention held June 17–20, 1976 on the grounds of Concordia College, River Forest, Illinois. The quality of churchmanship displayed at the convention by those who were moving out of the brotherhood was in marked contrast to the descriptions of power plays given by many pastors who had been forced out of their congregations. In order to effect a smooth transition, almost all leading officers of the district resigned. Following his resignation, Pastor Hecht was elected president of an interim organization known as the English Synod of the Evangelical Lutheran Church.[83]

The Missouri District's only Black pastor discovered that there was no discrimination in the use of purgatives. By a 186–151 majority, his district's convention voted to pull the economic rug out from under

✠ Sterling Belcher

But when they cut the subsidy, they also threatened the work Belcher was doing with scores of young people. He had been offering constructive alternatives in St. Louis' environment of crime and drug addiction. Therefore, when the District cut off Belcher,

✠ The Young Eternal Souls

heard the District saying that there was no room for them in Missouri's brotherhood.[84]

In what prophets from Old Testament times in related circumstances called "overkill," the St. Louis Seminary "801" Board resolved to initiate legal proceedings against

✠ Concordia Seminary in Exile (Seminex)

for use of the name "Concordia Seminary." The legal fact remained that the "801" school had been incorporated under the name "Concordia College." By contrast, at the time of his suspension, which ultimately led to the formation of the exiles' Seminary, Dr. Tietjen, despite the urging of his attorneys, declined on the basis of 1 Corinthians 6 to bring suit against the "801" Board for "denial of his civil and ecclesiastical rights."[85]

346

After July 2, 1976, the Philippines were to be minus the services of

✠ Thomas Schindler

who submitted his resignation to the Missouri Synod's Board for Missions.[86]

Things had been rather quiet at the Missouri Synod's teacher training college in Seward, Nebraska. With most of River Forest shelled out, purgatives could be moved to that sector of Missouri's vast empire. Leaving the college was difficult, "but I needed to maintain some degrees of personal freedom," said

✠ Charles Dull

a professor who had carried no batons nor waved any flags. The Board of the College had itself taken no action.[87]

Entire congregations found the heat in Missouri unbearable and voted to apply for membership in the Lutheran refugee camp known as the

✠ Association of Evangelical Lutheran Churches (AELC)

The first congregations in the new association included:[88]
Prince of Peace, Tulsa, Oklahoma
Grace, Oklahoma City, Oklahoma
Redeemer, Oklahoma City, Oklahoma
Christ Our Savior, Chickasha, Oklahoma
St. Paul's, Wellston, Oklahoma
Mount Calvary, Cahokia, Illinois
Resurrection, Alton, Illinois
St. Paul's, Fairview Heights, Illinois
Luther Memorial, Richmond Heights, Missouri
Bethlehem, Oakland, California
Our Redeemer, Livingston, California
New Life, Scottsdale, Arizona
Grace, West Springfield, Maine
Clifton, Marblehead, Maine
St. Matthew's, Bergenfield, New Jersey
Trinity, Brooklyn, New York
Good Shepherd, Palos Heights, Illinois
Gloria Christi, Allen Park, Michigan
Ashburn, Chicago, Illinois
Grace, Hastings, Michigan
Our Savior, Brooklyn, New York

Resurrection, Yardley, Pennsylvania
Peace, Cedar Rapids, Iowa
Grace, Evanston, Illinois
Peace, Cyril, Oklahoma
Zion, Kingman, Kansas
Faith, St. John, Kansas
Bethlehem, Brooklyn, New York
Atonement, Atlanta, Georgia
Good Shepherd, Irving, Texas
Mount Olive, Dallas, Texas

In a ruling dated August 13, 1976, the Missouri Synod's Commission on Constitutional Matters declared that pastors, teachers, or congregations that join the AELC would automatically forfeit their membership in the Synod.[89] This was another of Missouri's many official threats. President Preus found them useful in retarding impulses of moderation through the hesitation and fear they stimulated. On the other hand, like secret reserve weapons, threats could be implemented as the situation might prompt. Moderates had, however, after bitter experiences, learned to *act* with initiative instead of becoming easy pickings in *reaction.* Many of them where not about to sit any longer under Preus' missiles of Damocles wondering whether and when a synodical bomb would detonate. Preus could now look for other playmates to carry on his games. Taking the Synod at its word, Moderates resolved to provide relief for those who were marked for rolling out of the brotherhood. At their third annual meeting, August 18–20, 1976, members of ELIM adopted a budget of $732,200 for the succeeding six months.

The ELIM Assembly also concluded that it was time to put an end to the notion of APARTHEID in BROTHERHOOD. After a vote had been taken on the question of admission of women to ministry in the church through ordination, it was overwhelmingly recognized that the refugees from Missouri were a FAMILY OF GOD and no longer members of a restricted ecclesiastical lodge.

"I am being evicted by an ecclesiastical dictum that neither allows for discussion of the issues nor consideration of the people involved," said

✠ Herman Neunaber

President of the Southern Illinois District of the Missouri Synod when he left his official post in the brotherhood on August 27, 1976.[90]

Only a day earlier, world-renowned organist

✠ Paul Manz

submitted his resignation to the Board of Control of Concordia College, St. Paul, Minnesota. "In every sense, you have initiated this resignation by your declared insistence to uphold the legalistic atmosphere that has encroached upon our Synod," he wrote to the Board. Others who resigned from the institution included

✠ Patricia Spaulding
✠ Beverly Ferguson
✠ Walter Merz
✠ Keith Rockwood

The President of the district in which the college was located told the press that no resignations were actually forced. He also said that the Board "would not necessarily have taken action" against Dr. Manz on the basis of an Anaheim convention directive which barred synodical employees from membership in ELIM.[91]

Those who still insisted that the way to solve problems was to work from within the system found in

✠ Robert J. Riedel

an experienced teacher. In connection with his resignation, on September 27, 1976, as President of the Missouri Synod's New England District, he said: "I had hoped that by working from within, Synod might yet reverse its plunge into heterodoxy and once again become the evangelical synod it was. But that hope is now gone."[92]

About a month later, October 22,

✠ Waldemar Meyer

joined the four other bishops who had already resigned from their administrative posts. The Lutheran Church-Missouri Synod "consistently fails to use the Gospel in its dealings with people," concluded the President of the Missouri Synod's Colorado District. Rather, it relies "on legal pronouncements, majority votes, and the use of coercive power instead of seeking to persuade only by the Gospel."[93]

As one looking out from the great cloud of witnesses, the first President of the Missouri Synod, C. F. W. Walther, could now have seen Missouri's world-wide Field of Armageddon littered from end to end with the bodies of the Synod's finest. Men and women, veterans and recruits, professionals of every level, laypeople and clergy, were there.

In some sections he could have seen almost entire faculties strewn, which had been brought together over the years with administrative wisdom, but whose hundreds of years of total experience counted little to the brotherhood. In shocked dismay he could have seen entire congregations who were denied their right to reject unwanted advice, and whose only crime was to practice the hospitality of the Third Epistle of John. He could have seen sister churches in Hong Kong, India, the Philippines, Papua N.G. and other areas of the world awakening to the realization that a brotherhood had no room for sisters. He could have seen Blacks, Women and members of other Minorities, who knew that the prejudice against ELIM was but a symptom of the strangling Apartheid that was creeping like sands of the Sahara over the oases of civilization.

But as he continued to watch, Walther could have seen the vast expanse of the Battlefield heaving with breath drawn from the future. For the only viable alternative to death is resurrection. Once drilled into uniformity, the newly pulsating bodies began to display their diversity without looking behind them. The gloom of the pyramidal structure was gone. They were independent. Yet they looked for a way together. The sword that had cut them out of the brotherhood had driven them into membership in a CHURCH, not an exclusive Lodge or Brotherhood.

On December 3–4, 1976, many of the congregations and individuals who had felt the pain of the Missouri Synod's policy of exclusion and hard-line control linked arms at the founding convention of THE ASSOCIATION OF EVANGELICAL LUTHERAN CHURCHES. It was a unique event. For those who formed the new church did not do so in a spirit of separatism or schism, but precisely in order to break down barriers that divide Christians from one another. The group declared full fellowship with the 3.1 million member Lutheran Church in America and the 2.5 million member American Lutheran Church. Speaking of "sisters" as well as "brothers," the founding convention resolved to continue fellowship and cooperation with the Lutheran Church-Missouri Synod. Membership in the Lutheran Council in the U.S.A. and in the Lutheran World Federation also received endorsement.

What Walther had dreamed about, what the Missouri Synod had debated for over a century, all this and much more began to assume reality in December, 1976. By electing Dr. William Kohn as President of the AELC, members of the new church proclaimed their vision of outreach to the world. These erstwhile Missourians felt free now to pray with other Christians. In a memorable address Dr. Albert Pero,

Black theologian from the Lutheran School of Theology at Chicago, urged the new church to "be a FAMILY rich in diversity, a COALITION of all those of both minority and majority, black, white, yellow and brown, who commit themselves to exposing untruths, proclaiming the truth and acting out that truth."[94]

Chapter 28

CONCLUSION

"Who was right?" This is the question invariably addressed to history. The way the question is answered usually reveals partisan identity. The question is, however, not too helpful, for two or more parties in a conflict are scarcely ever exclusively right or wrong.

From the preceding analysis of the debacle in the Lutheran Church-Missouri Synod, it is apparent that neither practitioners of historical-critical methodology nor Herman Otten, liberalism nor conservativism, President Tietjen nor President Preus, majority nor minority faculty members at Concordia Seminary, were the heroes or villains in the conflict finally played out at Armageddon.

The evidence points rather to a chronic degenerative process characterized by a deep-seated conviction of the Missouri Synod that it was completely right. Any actions undertaken in concert with that conviction were therefore also right and it was willing to perpetuate its institutional identity at any cost.

Claims to have its doctrinal positions rooted in the Bible were especially persuasive to those who sought a strong base for faith, or a resource for authoritative pronouncement. Uniformity in the transmission of the traditional positions helped cement the certainty and strengthened authority. Combined with the societal-economic factors that were peculiar to the Synod's development out of an immigrant community, the approach to doctrinal security took on the aspect of an impregnable fortress. Rightness took shape in terms of synodical cohesion, and the cohesion determined what was right.

To maintain itself in the right, the Synod combatted with special vehemence two major enemies, historical criticism and unionism. The first had to do with what were considered illegitimate modes of biblical interpretation; the second with illegitimate modes of relating to other

352

Christians. As its chief offensive weapon the Synod emphasized inerrancy. This was the ultimate mystical line of defence that ringed the Synod. Inerrant words in chapter and verse of the Bible confirmed the authority of tradition. Once this understanding was ingrained, no matter what the Synod said or did, it would be right, for its words and deeds partook of the inerrant character of the Bible. Inerrancy in a book thus bred institutional inerrancy.

Accompanying this emphasis on inerrancy was a mode of interpretation which always came up with the answers found in the dogmatic tradition of the church. Also, there was a heavy emphasis on literal statements in the Bible. If the Second Epistle of Peter, it was argued, contains the statement that it was written by Peter, it is a *doctrine* that Peter wrote it. If Jesus refers to Jonah as being in the belly of a big fish for three days and three nights, that must be taken as proof that the prophet Jonah had actually been in a big fish. According to the Synod's official traditional view it is therefore not permissible to say that the story in the Old Testament is a parable which Jesus used to make a point, or that the point is valid regardless of what happened in real life to Jonah.

Since historical criticism questioned the correctness of such and many other hallowed interpretations, and since it denied that the Scriptures could be approached as a book that would come up with answers tailor-made to contemporary ways of thinking, it posed a formidable threat to a church which found security in inerrancy.

Like historical criticism, the efforts of the progressive mission staff, which worked in close liaison with members of other Christian communities, were a threat to synodical rightness. For a basic feature in the rightness syndrome was not only the obligation to make sure that joint worship was undertaken only when there was doctrinal agreement but also to *attack* those who differed. Ecumenical activity discouraged such hostility. Thus *inerrancy* and *anti-ecumenism* were the spikes that held the Synod together as an infallible unit. Historical criticism and ecumenism threatened this infallibility-cohesion syndrome. Hence practitioners of historical criticism or ecumenism both were called 'liberals.' 'Liberals' tended to take trips away from the frontier. 'Conservatives,' who held the line for the Synod's time-honored positions, were praised for maintaining the stockade.

Actually, the terms 'liberal' and 'conservative' were for a long time not so mutually exclusive, and their application, without some proviso, to members of the Missouri Synod prior to the Seventies merely contributes to historical confusion. Most members of the Synod did in fact

353

cooperate in maintaining the stockade, but some made more forays out of it than did others. Among those who preferred to stay within were clergy and laypeople who, with Otten's help, beat Missouri's drum without significant change of beat.

To all appearances, then, the Missouri Synod that came into the Seventies was still the most right church in Christendom, but some felt themselves very much right and others far less right.

Both Dr. Jacob A. O. Preus and Dr. John Tietjen entered into office approximately at the same time in 1969, and both were committed to the preservation of the Synod as the most right church in Christendom. From Tietjen's angle, it was most right because it was officially most Lutheran, that is, essentially gospel-oriented. Preus was also committed to its preservation as the most right organization in Christendom, but he saw it as basically law-oriented. Tietjen's image of the Synod, as developments demonstrated, was more that of an ideal than a concrete reality. He thought primarily in terms of Article II of the Synod's Constitution, but divorced from the Synod's layers of tradition. He received support from a very small minority who were able to evaluate their organization known as the Missouri Synod in terms of fidelity to its task as part of the total Christian Church. Preus' view of the Synod was more pragmatic. He knew where the people were, and most of them were not where the Gospel was. Gospel and Law were, therefore, on a collision course. Basically it was a question of primacy, and we, as faculty, began too late to grasp the hard realities.

During the Fifties and Sixties, the faculty had undergone a large turnover in personnel. Fresh methodological expertise was behind most of the doctorates. Biblical and Lutheran emphases were strong. There were no doctrinal aberrations in the Lutheran sense of the term. But the seminary and its products had indeed moved farther and farther away in their mode of expression from where the mainstream laity and older clergy were.

Herman Otten capitalized on the differences that surfaced between Synodical tradition and interpretation and the words and practices sponsored by faculty members and clergymen. While such a cleavage was developing, the administration of the Synod, including District Presidents and the faculties of the Synod's two seminaries, engaged in 'theological' discussions.

These discussions were not too fruitful, for the impression gained ground that there were differences in *doctrine* within the Synod, and that the differences necessarily emanated from those who deviated

354

from the Synodical line. That the *Synod* itself might be guilty of maintaining a false view of the relation between the Gospel and the Law was never really diagnosed. Preus, however, knew the Synod's soft spot, namely that the mainstream of the Synod was law-oriented, not gospel-oriented.

Second, it was a mistake to enter into theological discussion without clarifying for the Synod the difference between doctrine and theology. Had the clarification been made through administrative channels the Synod's members would have learned that doctrine is a fixed *datum,* and that theology is the *way one talks* about doctrine or explains what it means. Having learned this one distinction, the Synod would have found it more difficult to pillory diversity in theology by making it tantamount to heresy.

What should rather have been discussed was the question of the basic problem of the Synod—the need to be right. Was the seminary's obligation really to affirm tradition, or to help the church discover what the Biblical resources were for carrying out the church's mission in our time? If the latter, then it was time for the synodical administration, including especially the bishops of the church, to encourage their seminaries in discharging that responsibility.

We should have requested as a faculty that this discussion be carried on with the church as a whole, and that the official periodicals be open to popularizations of what was actually being taught at Concordia Seminary, with emphasis on the legitimacy of *diversity.* Had we said earlier, "Here we stand," the footing would have remained firmer at a later period.

At the same time we should have accompanied insistence on such points with a candid confession of sin to the world. We should have confessed to the churches of Christendom:

1. The immorality of our silence in the face of the shabby treatment accorded by us and our Synod to the Lutheran World Federation.
2. Our exploitation of the resources of other church groups in programs that were of interest to our Synod, while at the same time refusing to recognize and give thanks for the spiritual contributions they had to offer us.
3. Our arrogance in perpetuating the idea that our Synod was the purest doctrinal body on the face of the earth, whereas it was shot through with the disease of self-righteousness.

We should have confessed to the scholarly world:

1. That our seminary had too long aimed to benefit from scientific

discovery which lent credence to our faith-propositions, but had discouraged speculation on the frontiers of knowledge when it seemed to threaten our traditions.

2. That we helped our Synod skim the cream from scholarly publications, and yet permitted the world's scholars to be the victims of slanderous attacks that did not engage in serious scholarly rebuttal.

We should have confessed to our own church:

1. That we were guilty of patronizing it, in fear of being guilty of 'rocking the boat.'
2. That we were guilty of viewing time as a primary means of grace for solving the problems of our relationships to certain elements in the church.
3. That we were not spending enough effort to learn what the members of the church were thinking and how we might be of greater service to them.
4. That knowledge bred in us some unjustified impatience with clergymen who lacked the opportunity to be abreast of the learning that was at our disposal.
5. That we were guilty of insulting the laity by permitting them to be fed with pablum out of fear of continually upsetting the Synod's consensus.
6. That we shared the Synod's lust for infallible pronouncement. We should also have accompanied this particular confession with a plea that the church would absolve us of the necessity of that burden.

We did not do this. Dr. Preus thus came to a divided church and outflanked the Concordia Seminary faculty. Erroneously we thought that as the pastor goes, so goes the congregation. In the early stages of the war we thought primarily in terms of reaching the ministers. This was a basic error in judgment; Preus knew better. He knew that the primary allegiance of the members of the congregations would be to the Synod, not to the ministers. The ministers were intermediaries of authority, but the Synod was the bed-rock of authority, especially in the ethnic Midwest, and he as the President would be the court of final appeal. By addressing the fears and anxieties of the articulate people far to the right, he was able also to pick up those in the mainstream. Most of the pastors could be counted on not to 'disturb' their people, for most of them were of sound mind and viewed the 'taking of sides' as a posture of imbalance.

Thus Preus capitalized on both the unstable and the stable psyches of the Synod and won his war. He knew that the Synod would be willing to pay any price to preserve itself in the name of pure doctrine. The price included first-class faculties, the quality of its educational system, the broad goodwill generated by its publishing house, the integrity of its mission thrust throughout the world, commitments to sister churches, the good name of Lutheranism throughout the world, and the reputation of Christianity itself.

At the one moment when Preus seemed most vulnerable, when the tactics of the Synod's Mission Board conflicted with his own strategy in the elimination of Tietjen, the one group that could have detoured the Synod, namely the Council of District Presidents, failed to take a concerted stand. Thanks to them, Preus survived what loomed as a catastrophe for him. Thus even more than Preus and Otten, the District Presidents who did not identify with the few among them who recognized the crisis in the Synod must assume responsibility before the bar of history for the purge of Missouri. Through the congregations under their authority they *were* the Missouri Synod. Ultimately, neither Preus nor Otten destroyed the Synod. They were the chief instruments of its purging, but the Synod itself decreed its own catastrophe.

"Who was right?"

If purging an institution of all its rich diversity is the most creative possibility open to the mind;

if success is measured by the ability to destroy in a few years what has taken decades to erect;

if constriction of mind, insularity, and narrowness of purpose is the great goal of humanity;

if prejudice, with its vast progeny of bigotry, anti-semitism, racism, and sexism is the healing balm for civilization; and

if the Gospel is to add hate, suspicion, and deceit to the world instead of subtracting them,

then Preus and his supporters won the battle of Armageddon.

But it is just possible that these words, written by a young seminarian with eyes on the future, may challenge the verdict:

LISTEN MY PEOPLE

(Written by Dave M. Hartenberger)

They said, "You are young and needed in God's ministerium."
    I listened.
They said, "Enter the Synodical System."
    I entered.

357

NO ROOM IN THE BROTHERHOOD

They said, "God's Word and the Lutheran Confessions
    are the only norms."
    I nodded.
They said, "False doctrine is the culprit."
    I cringed.
They said, "God's Beloved Church is at stake."
    I assented.
They said, "Some will have to go."
    I waited.
They said, "You'll see friends and families lining up
    at opposite poles."
    I lined up.
They said, "We are now at war."
    I fought.
They said, "Some will be wounded."
    I bled.
They said, "Stand up and be counted."
    I stood.
They said, "Prepare to Pray."
    I prayed.
They said, "God has forsaken His Church."
    They lied.

NOTES

The following abbreviations appear frequently in the Notes. Others are used after first specification.

CN   *The Christian News,* edited by Herman Otten, New Haven, Missouri.
CP   *Convention Proceedings of the Lutheran Church-Missouri Synod* (with site and date of convention specified).
CWB   *Convention Workbook of the Lutheran Church-Missouri Synod* (with site of convention and date specified).
LW   *The Lutheran Witness.*
MIP   *Missouri in Perspective,* published by Evangelical Lutherans in Mission, St. Louis, Missouri.
LWR   *The Lutheran Witness Reporter.*

Chapter 1

1. *CN,* January 14, 1974, p. 8.
2. *CP,* New Orleans, Louisiana, July 6–13, 1973, p. 139.
3. *CN,* January 14, 1974, p. 6.

Chapter 2

1. G. Ernest Wright, *The Book of the Acts of God* (Doubleday: Garden City, New York, Anchor Books Edition, 1960).
2. Cf. Wright, pp. 13–18.
3. Eugene L. Rodgers, *A History of Christ Church Cathedral* (Christ Church Cathedral: St. Louis, Missouri), 1970, p. 8.
4. Walter O. Foerster, *Zion on the Mississippi: The Settlement of the Saxon Lutherans in Missouri 1839–1841* (Concordia Publishing House: St. Louis, Missouri, 1953), chapters 15 and 16. A forthcoming study of nineteenth century German Protestantism by John E. Groh explores the way in which Ger-

man Protestants functioned with what they considered "freedom, but always within authoritative structures." See also Groh's Dissertation (The University of Chicago, 1972): *Architects of the Kingdom: A History of Public Appeals to God's Kingdom in Nineteenth Century German Protestantism.*

5. Carl S. Meyer, *Log Cabin to Luther Tower: Concordia Seminary During One Hundred and Twenty-Five Years Toward a More Excellent Ministry 1839–1964* (Concordia Publishing House: St. Louis, Missouri, 1965), p. 191.

6. Meyer, p. 192.

7. *LW* 43 (1924), 482, quoted by Alan N. Graebner, *The Acculteration of An Immigration Lutheran Church: The Lutheran Church-Missouri Synod, 1917–1929* (Dissertation, Columbia University, 1965), p. 59.

8. Meyer, p. 181.

9. William Dallmann, *Why Do I Believe the Bible is God's Word?* (American Lutheran Publicity Board: Pittsburgh, 1910), p. 8.

10. F. W. C. Jesse. *Catechetical Preparations, Part I—The Decalog* (Concordia Publishing House: St. Louis, Missouri, 1919), p. 108 (1938 edition, p. 110). See also the detailed documentation by L. Richard Bradley, "The Curse of Canaan and the American Negro," *Concordia Theological Monthly* 42 (February, 1971), 100–110; "The Lutheran Church and Slavery," *Concordia Historical Institute Quarterly,* 44, no. 1 (February, 1971), 32–41 (C. F. W. Walther was of the "firm belief that negro slavery in the United States was a 'divine institution' and that those who did not agree were neither Lutheran nor Christian," p. 41).

11. Details in Jack Treon Robinson, *The Spirit of Triumphalism in the Lutheran Church—Missouri Synod: The Role of the "A Statement" of 1945 in the Missouri Synod.* (Dissertation, Vanderbilt University, 1972), pp. 126ff.

12. Paul L. Maier, *A Man Spoke, A World Listened: The Story of Walter A. Maier and the Lutheran Hour* (McGraw Hill: New York, 1963), p. 259.

13. *Speaking the Truth in Love: Essays Related to A Statement, Chicago Nineteen forty-five* (The Willow Press: Chicago, Illinois), pp. 77–80. Published in April, 1946, according to Robinson, p. 288.

14. Hartzell Spence, "The Man of the Lutheran Hour," *The Saturday Evening Post* 220 (June 19, 1948), 17, 88–94).

Chapter 3

1. Details in J. Robinson, *The Spirit of Triumphalism,* pp. 200ff. (See ch. 2, note 11.)

2. *Speaking the Truth in Love,* p. 11. (See ch. 2, note 13.)

3. Same, p. 12.

4. Same, p. 15.

5. Same, p. 17.

6. Same, p. 17.

7. Same, p. 18.

8. Same, p. 18.

9. Same, p. 18.

10. Same, pp. 18–19.

11. Same, p. 19.
12. Same, p. 19.
13. Same, pp. 19–20.
14. Same, p. 20.
15. C. S. Meyer, *Log Cabin to Luther Tower,* pp. 248–249. (See ch. 1, note 5.)
15a. Wallace H. MacLaughlin, "A Former U.L.C. Pastor Looks at the Agreement." No date (late Forties), p. 3. Much of the terminology recited by President Preus and other associates from 1969 on relative to purification of the Synod echoes the documents published at the end of the Forties. See, e.g., E. W. A. Koehler, "An Agreement," a four-page pamphlet (February 14, 1947), bearing the notation: "This paper was released at the request of a number of men from seven districts of Synod."

Likewise breathing hard on the Forty-Four was A. T. Kretzmann with his "The Biblical Principles of Church Fellowship: Prayer Fellowship" (no date, but about 1946), carrying the notation: "Price of this 4-page tract:—$1.00 per 100, postpaid. Order from: Rev. E. Wiedbusch, Elizabeth, Ill." R. G. Hoerber's 32-page investigation of Rom. 16:17, entitled, "A Grammatical Study of Romans 16,17" (no date, but before 1950) lacked the pastoral sensitivity expressed in the 18-page study, "Exegesis on Romans 16:17ff.," sent out by President J. W. Behnken (Oak Park, Ill., May 11, 1950), but without author's name. However, from the style I would conjecture that it is to be ascribed to Martin Franzmann, formerly professor at Concordia Seminary.

The hostility exhibited during President Jacob Preus' incumbency toward continuation of fellowship with the American Lutheran Church finds heated expression in the sixty-four page diatribe published by Theo. Dierks, S.T.D., "An Examination of the Proposed Doctrinal Affirmation." Dierks cited testimonials from P. E. Kretzmann, professor at Concordia Seminary from 1923–1946; M. F. Kretzmann, at the time Secretary of the Missouri Synod; E. T. Lams, former president of the Missouri Synod's Northern Ililnois District; W. Albrecht, at the time professor at Concordia Seminary, Springfield, Illinois; and two ministers Marcus Wagner and J. F. Boerger, Sr..

A classic critique of the Synod's position on relations with other Christians is Adolph A. Brux, *Christian Prayer-Fellowship and Unionism: An Investigation of Our Synodical Position With Respect to Prayer-Fellowship With Christians Of Other Denominations,* 1935, 101 pages.

16. Alfred Loisy, *My Duel with the Vatican: The Autobiography of a Catholic Modernist,* translated by Richard Wilson Boynton (E. P. Dutton: New York, 1924), p. 42.

17. "A Report to All Members of the Synod by the Praesidium of the Synod and Concordia Seminary, St. Louis, Mo." (November 29, 1961), p. 7.

18. Martin H. Scharlemann, "Roman Catholic Biblical Interpretation," *Festschrift to Honor F. Wilbur Gingrich: Lexicographer, Scholar, Teacher, and Committed Christian Layman,* edited by Eugene H. Barth and R. E. Cocroft (E. J. Brill: Leiden, 1972), pp. 209–222.

19. For a thorough discussion of the Church's responsibility in the modern world, see Hans Küng, *On Being a Christian,* translated by Edward Quinn (Doubleday: Garden City, New York, 1976).

Chapter 4

1. See Alan N. Graebner, *The Acculteration of an Immigration Lutheran Church,* pp. 104–105. (See ch.2, note 7.)

2 .*LW* 41 (1922), 129, cited by Alan Graebner, p. 131.

Chapter 5

1. The editor of *The Christian News* was fond of reminding President Preus of this impropriety.

2. *CN,* June 11, 1973, p. 9.

3. *LWR,* November 1, 1970, p. 2.

Chapter 6

1. Most of the details relative to my interview are documented in *Under Investigation,* Second edition [Clayton Publishing House: St. Louis, Missouri], 1971.

2. See the rebuke offered to self-righteous condemnation of the "Pharisees" as a class, *Jesus and the New Age According To St. Luke: A Commentary on the Third Gospel* (Clayton Publishing House: St. Louis, Missouri), pp. 68–69; also, the crimes of the leaders are not to be attributed to the entire ethnic group, p. 199. "Anti-Semitism," I pointed out, displays "its ugly head when especially the Christian reader of the gospel thinks that 'the Jews,' not he, are under the evangelist's scrutiny. Seven million Jews have known the pain of such evil application of the text," p. 228 (one instance of many). Lloyd Gaston failed to note these facts and also the point of my depth-structural analysis of Luke's own updating of the lessons of history (review, *Journal of Biblical Literature,* 94, no. 1, March 1975, 140–141). Other reviewers were more perceptive.

Chapter 7

1. *LWR,* November 1, 1970, p. 2.

2. My response was originally marked "Confidential," so as to preserve the Board's independence in the evaluation process.

Chapter 8

1. Cited by J. Robinson, *The Spirit of Triumphalism,* p. 141. (See ch. 2, note 11.)

2. "A Report to All Members of the Synod by the Praesidium of the Synod and Concordia Seminary, St. Louis, Mo.," November 29, 1961, p. 4.

Chapter 9

1. *CP,* Milwaukee, Wisconsin, July 9–16, 1971, p. 125.

2. Same, "President's Report," pp. 51–61.

3. Same, p. 165.
4. For the text, see end of Chapter 8.
5. Translation from *The New Life Testament,* translated by Gleason H. Ledyard. Special Edition for American Indian Mission, Inc., Custer, South Dakota. Copyright 1969, by Christian Literature Foundation.
6. See also the critiques by Walter E. Keller, "A Scrutiny of a Statement on Scripture," *The Cresset,* 35, no. 8 (June, 1972), 6–9; *The Cresset Reprints: A Review Essay of a Statement of Scriptural and Confessional Principles.* From *The Cresset,* May, 1973, and (Part II), October, 1973, co-operative effort of four professors in the Department of Theology, Valparaiso University: Walter E. Keller, Kenneth E. Korby, Robert C. Schultz, and David G. Truemper; and the 15-page formal statement of dissent addressed by Professor Arthur C. Repp to the Rev. Dr. Herman Scherer, President of the Missouri District of the Lutheran Church-Missouri Synod and to the Rev. Dr. Ralph A. Bohlmann, Executive Secretary, Commission on Theology and Church Relations (September 24, 1973).

Chapter 10

1. *CP,* Milwaukee, 1971, p. 122.
2. *Report of the Synodical President to the Lutheran Church-Missouri Synod: In compliance with Resolution 2–28 of the 49th Regular Convention of the Synod, held at Milwaukee, Wisconsin, July 9–16, 1971,* pp. 138–142. Hereafter abbreviated: Blue Book.
3. Blue Book, pp. 131–132.
4. Blue Book, pp. 2, 3.
5. Blue Book, p. 75.
6. Blue Book, p. 77.
7. Frederick W. Danker, *Jesus and the New Age,* pp. xviii–xix. Italics are ours. (See ch. 6, note 2.)
7a. Cf. Blue Book, p. 75.
8. See "Brother to Brother," November 20, 1970.
9. This evaluation was subsequently withdrawn from discussion, cf. *CP,* New Orleans, 1973, p. 38.
10. *Fact Finding or Fault Finding?: An Analysis of President J.A.O. Preus' Investigation of Concordia Seminary,* p. 2. Hereafter referred to as Tietjen Report.
11. Tietjen Report, p. 3.
12. Tietjen Report, p. 34.
13. Tietjen Report, p. 34.
14. Tietjen Report, p. 35.
15. Tietjen Report, p. 35.
16. The reference is to the publication of Frederick W. Danker, *Under Investigation.* (See ch. 6, note 1.)
17. Blue Book, p. 143.

Chapter 11

1. Martin Scharlemann, in *The Lutheran Scholar* 21, no. 3, (July, 1964), 26.

2. Quoted in Herman Otten, ed. *A Christian Handbook on Vital Issues: Christian News, 1963–1973* (Leader Publishing Co.: New Haven, Missouri, 1973), p. 791. Hereafter referred to as Hbk.

3. *CN,* July 2, 1973, p. 10.

4. *CN,* April 16, 1973, p. 4.

5. *Hbk,* pp. 526–533.

6. *Hbk,* pp. 693–712.

7. *Hbk,* p. 710.

8. *Hbk,* p. 710.

9. *Hbk,* p. 711.

10. *Hbk,* p. 303.

11. *Hbk,* pp. 621–624.

12. *Hbk,* pp. 608–611.

13. *Hbk.,* p. 613.

14. *Hbk,* pp. 614–615.

15. *LW,* 44 (1925), 341, cited by Alan N. Graebner, *The Acculteration of an Immigration Lutheran Church,* p. 128. (See ch. 2, note 7.)

16. *Hbk,* p. 616.

17. *Hbk,* p. 618.

18. *Hbk,* p. 633.

19. *Hbk,* p. 639.

20. *Hbk,* p. 598.

21. *Hbk,* p. 650.

22. *Hbk,* p. 658.

23. *Hbk,* p. 660.

24. *Hbk,* p. 669.

25. *Hbk,* p. 675.

26. *Hbk,* p. 691.

27. *Hbk,* p. 713.

28. *Hbk,* p. 720.

29. *Hbk,* p. 721.

30. *Hbk,* pp. 725, 740–748.

31. *Hbk,* p. 734.

32. *Hbk,* pp. 754–775.

33. *Hbk,* pp. 755.

34. *Hbk,* p. 774.

35. *Hbk,* pp. 774–784.

36. *Hbk,* p. 783.

37. *Hbk,* p. 791.

38. *Hbk,* p. 797.

39. *Hbk,* p. 799.

40. *Hbk,* p. 807.

41. *Hbk,* p. 810.

42. Harry Huth, "Synod's Doctrinal Resolutions," *Affirm,* 1, no. 1 (March, 1971), 5.

43. C.A. Swanson, "The Sem Inquiry," same, p. 8.

44. Dr. Robert Preus, "Suspend Fellowship," *Affirm* 1, no. 3 (May, 1971), pp 1,2,12.

45. "Missouri's Elites", *Affirm* 1, no. 4 (June A. 1971), 1. (The editorial is unsigned).

46. Rev. Raymond A. Mueller, "The Milwaukee Handbook," *Affirm* 1, no. 5 (June B, 1971), 16–18.

47. Dr. Robert Preus, "May the Lutheran Theologian Legitimately Use the Historical-Critical Method?" *Occasional Papers. Affirm* (Spring, 1973), p. 35.

48. Kurt Marquardt, "The Swing of the Pendulum: An Attempt to Understand the St. Louis 'Affirmations and Discussions," same, p. 16.

49. Martin Scharlemann, "Some Sobering Reflections on the Use Of The Historical-Critical Method," same, p. 5.

50. Martin Scharlemann, "Roman Catholic Biblical Interpretation," *Festschrift to Honor F. Wilbur Gingrich: Lexicographer, Scholar, Teacher, and Committed Christian Layman.* Edited by Eugene H. Barth and Ronald E. Cocroft (E.J. Brill: Leiden, 1972), p. 211, in reference to Vatican II.

51. Same, p. 213.

52. Same, p. 215.

53. Same, p. 217.

54. Martin Scharlemann, *Occasional Papers,* p. 6. (See above note 47.)

55. *Affirm* 3, no. 3 (June B, 1973).

56. Same, p. 1.

57. Same, p. 4.

Chapter 12

1. Martin H. Scharlemann, "Enrichment en Route: Congress on Theology", *The Lutheran Scholar,* 24, no. 4 (October, 1967), 31 (127).

2. Martin H. Scharlemann, "Biblical Interpretation Today (Continued)," *The Lutheran Scholar,* 25, no. 2 (April, 1968), 23 (55).

3. *CWB,* New Orleans, 1973, p. 61.

4. Same, p. 75.

5. Same, pp. 99–165.

6. Same, pp. 99–100.

7. Same, pp. 100–102.

8. Same, pp. 120–138.

9. Same, pp. 153–154.

10. *CP,* New Orleans, 1973, p. 56.

11. Andrew Schulze, *Race Against Time* (Lutheran Human Relations Association of America: Valparaiso, Indiana, 1972), p. 45.

12. *CP,* New Orleans, 1973, pp. 56–57.

13. Same, p. 62.

14. Same, p. 62.

15. Same, p. 63.
16. Same, p. 63.
17. Same, p. 64.
18. Same, pp. 163–165.
19. Same, p. 64.
20. Same, cf. p. 26; see *CP*, pp. 111–115 for the text.
21. Same, p. 31.
22. Same, p. 115.
23. Same, p. 31.
24. Same, p. 114.
25. Same, p. 128.
26. Same, pp. 140–142. In this report, CW refers to the *Convention Workbook;* CTM to *The Concordia Theological Monthly.*
27. *CP,* p. 206.
28. Same, p. 128.
29. *CN,* July 23, 1973, p. 1.
30. *Forum Letter,* 2, no. 7 (July, 1973), p. 4.
31. *CP,* p. 37.

Chapter 13

1. *CP,* 1973, p. 139. Vice-President Edwin C. Weber himself acknowledged the falsity of this charge. See chapter 26, p. 305
2. Alan Graebner, *The Acculeration of an Immigration Lutheran Church,* pp. 23–24. (See ch. 2, note 7.)
3. *CP,* New Orleans, 1973, p. 37.
4. Same, p. 37.
5. Same, p. 37.
6. *Forum Letter,* 2, no. 7 (July, 1973), p. 4.
7. Same, p. 4.
8. *CP,* New Orleans, 1973, p. 38.
9. Same, p. 38.
10. Same, p. 38.
11. *Forum Letter,* July, 1973, p. 4.
12. *CP,* New Orleans, 1973, p.139.
13. *Forum Letter,* July, 1973, p. 5.
14. The Resolution was worded:
    Whereas, The committee is mindful of the fact that less than a day remains for convention deliberation and that the matters contained in the above named overtures cannot be adequately dealt with on the floor of the convention, because of the press of other business and the time available; and
    Whereas, Adequate procedures are available in the *Handbook* of Synod to deal with the matter; therefore be it Resolved, That the matter of Dr. John H. Tietjen as president and professor of Concordia Seminary, Saint Louis, shall be dealt with in such manner as is permitted under applicable substantive and procedural provisions of the *Handbook* of the Synod. (*CP,* p. 140)

15. *CP,* 1973, p. 45.
16. *Forum Letter,* 2, no. 8 (August, 1973), p. 7.
17. Martin H. Scharlemann, in *The Lutheran Scholar,* 23, no. 3 (July, 1966), p. 14. In 1967 he said, "We live at a moment when it is desperately necessary to assemble theologians for the purpose of helping us all to discover where we are in history and what the future seems to hold. Lutherans in America have not been especially kind to theologians. Perhaps we have lived too closely to the frontier." *The Lutheran Scholar,* 24, no. 4 (October, 1967), p. 31 (127).

Chapter 14

1. Theodore Graebner, "The Burden of Infallibility: A Study in the History of Dogma," *Concordia Historical Quarterly,* 38 (1965), pp. 88–89. This paper was written in November, 1948, and circulated privately.
2. Same, p. 90.
3. Same, p. 92.
4. Same, pp. 92–94.
5. Same, p. 94.
6. *LW,* Sept. 16, 1973, p. 22.
7. *MIP,* October 22, 1973, p. 3.
8. *LW,* September 16, 1973, pp. 22–23.
9. *MIP,* October 22, 1973, pp. 4, 7.
10. *CP,* 1973, p. 139.
11. P. F. Koehneke, "The Evangelical Lutheran Church, The True Visible Church of God, " *The Abiding Word,* ed. by Theodore Laetsch, D.D., Concordia Theological Seminary, St. Louis, Mo. (Concordia Publishing House: St. Louis, Missouri, 1946), I, 300–301.
12. See the parenthetical note, *CP,* 1973, p. 139.

Chapter 15

1. *CN,* July 23, 1973, p. 4.
2. Same, p. 4.
3. *Handbook, The Lutheran Church-Missouri Synod,* 1973 Edition, Bylaw 6.79, p. 145.
4. "Evidence Presented by John H. Tietjen," no date, p. 3.
5. Handbook, The Lutheran Church-Missouri Synod, 1973, p. 145.
6. Same, pp. 145–146.
7. "Evidence," p. 3.
8. "Evidence," p. 4.
9. *MIP,* October 22, 1973, p. 1.

Chapter 16

1. "Evidence Presented by John H. Tietjen," p. 6.
2. *MIP,* December 3, 1973, p. 1.

3. *CN,* November 26, 1973, p. 2.

4. Since students were on off-campus intern duty (vicarage) during their third year of seminary education, no signatures were received from this class. The majority of them did in fact attend Seminex on their return to St. Louis.

Chapter 17

1. The result of the discontent came to expression in "A Report of the Commission on Theology and Church Relations of The Lutheran Church-Missouri Synod," September, 1974. It bears the title: "The Mission of the Christian Church in the World: A Review of the 1965 Mission Affirmations." The "Mission Affirmations" are printed as an Appendix.

2. *MIP,* January 28, 1974, p. 1.

3. Same, p. 3.

4. *MIP,* February 11, 1974, p. 7.

Chapter 18

1. For the text of "One Voice," see Chapter 16.

2. For details on Professor Paul Goetting, see Chapter 16.

Chapter 19

1. Martin H. Scharlemann, "Biblical Interpretation Today (continued)," *The Lutheran Scholar* 24, no. 2, (April, 1967), 15 (47).

2. Same, pp. 3–4 (35–36).

3. Martin H. Scharlemann, *Festschrift,* 1972, pp. 216–217. (See ch. 11, note 50.)

4. Same, p. 218.

5. Just as our faculty had emphasized the importance of Lutheran presuppositions in the use of historical-critical methodology, in order that it might not become an untheological pursuit, so Scharlemann observed that Roman Catholic presuppositions were operative within a "strong liturgical tradition and practice," *Festschrift,* p. 221.

6. This type of escape clause was long before questioned by none other than President John W. Behnken. Under date of April 30, 1946, he addressed the Missouri brotherhood relative to the "deplorations" of the Forty-Four, who had assured him that "no individual nor any specific group was meant, but that they referred merely to trends. We insisted," he wrote, "that trends certainly do not exist unless they can be based either on words or actions of individuals or groups." (p. 10)

The communication was sent from Dr. Behnken's office located in his very modest home at 533 S. Kenilworth Ave., Oak Park, Illinois. The fact that in less than a decade the Synod's offices mushroomed into a huge bureaucratic operation must be taken into consideration in evaluating the collision of tradition with gusts of change.

Like Behnken, Dr. E. W. A. Koehler, "An Analysis of 'A Statement,' " no date (about 1946), p. 3, challenged the Forty-Four, who had made general charges: "But we are told, 'We do not mean you and you.' Well, who, then, is meant? Does not the fact that such charges are made create a mutual suspicion among us? I may not find myself guilty of the sin charged in Point 2. Who is ?"

Chapter 22

1. *CP,* New Orleans, 1973,
2. January 24, 1974
   Dear Colleague,

   For the Board of Control I am asking that you resume your regular schedule of work on Monday morning, January 28. I am making this request that we can all transcend the problems of the moment in the interest of serving the students who have registered here to receive the service from you indicated by the seminary's catalog.

   If there ever was a time for all of us to show by our Christ-like example that we can live and work even under adverse circumstances, now is that time. And I am looking to you for such a witness, in keeping with the terms of our vocation as ministers and servants of the church.

   As I have tried to stress in my presentation to the student body, the Board of Control refused even to discuss what steps might be taken if the full class-schedule did not become effective again on Monday. The Board has assumed that all of us are mature and responsible persons and expects us to render the service asked of us.
   Sincerely,

   (Signed)

   MARTIN H. SCHARLEMANN
   Acting President
   MHS:hd
3. *CP,* New Orleans, 1973, p. 135.
4. Students discovered in the course of encounter with their critics that denials concerning statements could be expected even if there was only a slight rearrangement of words. It is important, therefore, to note that John C. Baur, in his column, "Something to Think About," *CN,* July 9, 1973, did not actually call Thomas a "garrulous black agitator." He did say that the letter, which he called "scurrilous," disclosed its writer as "black." A few lines later he wrote: "He is reported to be a swaggering agitator on the seminary campus and not at all the sort of student of whom we can hope that he will become a good shepherd of one of the Lord's flocks or a missionary to lost souls." Thomas' congregation was indignant over this attack on a very fine student (see the protest issued by St. Philip congregation, chapter 26. This is Thomas' letter, as reported in Baur's column:

"Dr.

"It does not surprise me that you could find a positive meaning in the Word

'Polarization', and especially as it affects our Church Body. After the brief visit which I had with you last winter concerning my article in the First Issue of the Seminar, I could only conclude that you just 'WILL' to not understand anything beyond your own experiences.

"At this point I am forced to Re-Affirm my statement made to you in our meeting. 'I certainly feel sorry for you.' Instead of praying to God for understanding and Love, you seem to be thanking God that you are not like other men; thanking Him for all your goodness. Instead of really seeing the greater implications of the Gospel of Jesus Christ, you draw from the Gospel a position of Superiority for yourself. Instead of trying to be an example of love, you seem to be overly concerned with giving people the terms for loving.

"Your understanding of the Term 'SOCIAL gospel' is an insult to your Theological training. Your lack of acceptance to the term 'Revolution' not only upsets the spirit of the early Americans, who were truly in revolt against England, but it defies good Pauline Theology. Besides that, you miss the serious message of Christ to men who would set themselves up in high places. It seems to me that this is why it is so easy for you, and others like you to hurl numerous abuses at different Ethnic groups in the name of Jesus Christ.

"Your line of reasoning my friend is a bit narrow. In fact it is Silly. I thank God daily that He has given me the power to 'turn-off' such 'Garbage' which you manage to sneak in as 'Pure Doctrine.' There is nothing pure about Racism. You insult the very dignity of every Black, Indian, and otherwise every oppressed person in the whole of the world. I am just sorry that there are a few foolish souls who would listen to such friendly Non-Sense.

"Oh yes, the Gospel of Jesus Christ does liberate me to live as a man. I do not have to wait until you or any other earthly authority gives me permission to understand the Gospel in a radical way. The Gospel is Radical. It talks about a Christ who was hailed King when a ruler sat on the chair. A Christ who had a Radical approach to healing the illness of men, of one who raised the dead and gave sight to the Blind. This Radical Gospel is what talks about a Christ who defied men who were inflicted with the sickness of being 'Pompus.' The Radical Gospel I speak of is the one which talks about a Christ who suffered and died on the Cross for my sins. A Christ who kept his Radical Promise and died all the way.

"The Gospel becomes Social as I see Jesus feeding five-thousand for both physical and spiritual needs. It is a Social as well as Political Gospel as I see Paul locked up for daring to tell the TRUTH. It is Radical, Social, Political and Great as I see Luther stand up to the 'Hard Noses' of his Day. And it is the same Gospel which Black people cling to today.

"The 'Galloping Moral disintegration of our Society' today is caused by people who speak without Words: Who engage in action without Helping; who speak out of knowledge without Wisdom. You will never know what it means to be poor today in America. You will continue to pass judgment Dr.   like it is your right, but we will continue to IGNORE You. It would really be great if you would just un-stop your Ears for a while my Friend.

"In Christ Jesus,

Chapter 23

1. For text of the letter, see beginning of chapter 20.
2. Initiative for the sending of this letter was taken by Bernhard A. Asen, Kenneth C. Haugk, Werner K. Boos and William H. Winkler.

Chapter 24

1. See also John C. Baur's evaluation, *CN,* February 4, 1974.

Chapter 25

1. See beginning of chapter 20.
2. The letter was carried in a Concordia Seminary student publication, *Seminar: A Forum for the Exchange of Scholarly Opinion and Creativity,* 1973, p. 28. See above for condensation of Phelps' letter.
3. President Preus had used another letter, alleged to have been signed by 30 students, in his Blue Book, pp. 131–132.

Chapter 26

1. *MIP,* April 22, 1974, p. 1.

Chapter 27

1. *MIP,* January 14, 1974, p. 1.
2. *MIP,* February 11, 1974, p. 2.
3. *MIP,* March 11, 1974, p. 3.
4. *MIP,* April 8, 1974, p. 1.
5. *MIP,* April 8, 1974, p. 7.
6. *MIP,* January 28, 1974, pp. 1,3.
7. *MIP,* April 22, 1974, p. 1.
8. *MIP,* May 6, 1974, p. 1.
9. *MIP,* May 6, 1974, p. 7.
10. *MIP,* May 20, 1974, p. 1.
11. *MIP,* June 3, 1974, p. 7.
12. *MIP,* July 29, 1974, p. 2.
13. *MIP,* July 15, 1974, p. 6.
14. *MIP,* August 12, 1974, p. 1.
15. *MIP,* September 9, 1974, pp. 1,5.
16. *MIP,* September 23, 1974, p. 2.
17. *MIP,* September 23, 1974, p. 3.
18. *MIP,* October 7, 1974, pp. 1,2.
19. *MIP,* October 7, 1974, p. 4.
20. *MIP,* October 21, 1974, pp. 1,5.
21. *MIP,* October, 21, 1974, p. 6.

22. *MIP,* November 18, 1974, p. 2.
23. *MIP,* December 2, 1974, p. 1.
24. *MIP,* December 2, 1974, p. 1.
25. *MIP,* December 2, 1974, p. 3.
26. *MIP,* December 2, 1974, p. 3.
27. *MIP,* December 16, 1974, p. 2.
28. *MIP,* February 10, 1975, p. 2.
29. *MIP,* November 4, 1974, p. 3.
30. *MIP,* December 16, 1974, pp. 2,5.
31. *MIP,* December 16, 1974, pp. 4,8.
32. *MIP,* January 27, 1975, p. 1.
33. *MIP,* January 27, 1975, pp. 1,2.
34. *MIP,* February 10, 1975, p. 2.
35. *MIP,* May 12, 1975, p. 3.
36. *MIP,* May 26, 1975, p. 1.
37. *MIP,* May 26, 1975, pp. 3,7.
38. *MIP,* April 28, 1975, pp. 6,7.
39. *MIP,* May 26, 1975, pp. 1,7.
40. *MIP,* April 14, 1975, p. 1.
41. *MIP,* June 9, 1975, p. 2.
42. *MIP,* June 23, 1975, pp. 1,7.
43. *MIP,* July 7, 1975, pp. 1,7.
44. *MIP,* April 8, 1974, p. 5.
45. *MIP,* July 7, 1975, pp. 1,8.
46. *MIP,* July 21, 1975, pp. 1,2.
47. *MIP,* July 21, 1975, p. 2.
48. *MIP,* August 18, 1975, p. 3.
49. *MIP,* August 4, 1975, pp. 1,2.
50. *MIP,* August 4, 1975, pp. 2,7.
51. *MIP,* August 4, 1975, pp. 2,8.
52. *MIP,* August 18, 1975, p. 2.
53. *MIP,* August 18, 1975, p. 2.
54. *MIP,* September 1, 1975, p. 1.
55. *MIP,* September 29, 1975, pp. 1,6.
56. *MIP,* September 29, 1975, p. 2.
57. *MIP,* September 29, 1975, p. 3.
58. *MIP,* October 13, 1975, p. 1.
59. *MIP,* November 10, 1975, p. 2.
60. *MIP,* September 15, 1975, p. 3.
61. *MIP,* November 10, 1975, p. 3.
62. *MIP,* October 27, 1975, p. 2.
63. *MIP,* October 27, 1975, pp. 3,4.
64. *MIP,* November 10, 1975, p. 5.
65. *MIP,* November 24, 1975, p. 3.
66. *MIP,* December 8, 1975, p. 3, and July 19, 1976, p. 8.
67. *MIP,* December 8, 1975, pp. 2,3.
68. *MIP,* February 2, 1976, pp. 1,8.

69. *MIP,* February 16, 1976, p. 3.
70. *MIP,* March 29, 1976, p. 8.
71. *MIP,* February 16, 1976, p. 2.
72. *MIP,* November 10, 1975, p. 7.
73. *MIP,* November 10, 1975, p. 3.
74. *MIP,* April 12, 1976, pp. 1,7.
75. *MIP,* April 26, 1976, p. 7.
76. *MIP,* May 24, 1976, p. 2.
77. *MIP,* May 24, 1976, p. 5.
78. *MIP,* June 7, 1976, p. 2.
79. *MIP,* June 7, 1976, p. 2.
80. *MIP,* June 7, 1976, p. 2.
81. *MIP,* April 12, 1976, p. 2.
82. *MIP,* April 26, 1976, p. 7.
83. *MIP,* July 15, 1976, p. 1.
84. *MIP,* July 5, 1976, pp. 2,4.
85. *MIP,* August 2, 1976, p. 2.
86. *MIP,* August 2, 1976, p. 8.
87. *MIP,* August 30, 1976, p. 2.
88. *MIP,* August 16, 1976, p. 1.
89. *MIP,* August 30, 1976, p. 1.
90. *MIP,* September 13, 1976, p. 1.
91. *MIP,* September 13, 1976, pp. 1,3.
92. *MIP,* October 18, 1976, p. 1.
93. *MIP,* November 8, 1976, p. 1.
94. *MIP,* December 20, 1976, p. 2, emphasis ours.

John Dornheim at Rumor control

Prof.
Martin H.
Scharlemann

Dr. William Kohn,
Mission Executive
and President
J. A. O. Preus

Moment of Decision, February 19, 1974

We hear you, Martin!

Toward the Quadrangle
of Concordia Seminary
February 19, 1974

March into Exile

Prof. Walter Brueggemann of Eden Seminary welcomes the Exiles

SEMINEX

CASEY JONES
SEMINEXS
STREAKER EXPRESS

Meeting the Press—Prof. Robert Bertram and President John H. Tietjen

Joy at Christ Church Cathedral, St. Louis

Welcome at St. Louis University

DIVINITY COMMONS
Rm 186 →

Free Coffee →

First Commencement of Seminex,
Gerald Miller at the Lectern

Another first! President
Tietjen congratulates Janith Otte

"Planning with the Church"

Prof. Ralph Klein invests Dr. Albert Pero

"Call Day." "Where is it?"

Photos by Steven M. Dietrich

Recruitment!